TRAVEL

AUSTRIA GUIDE

YOUR PASSPORT TO GREAT TRAVEL!

ABOUT THE AUTHOR

Angela Walker is a free-lance travel writer and journalist. She has lived in France, Belgium, and most recently Austria. Before moving to Europe, she worked as a reporter and editor for *The Associated Press* and *The Washington Post*.

HIT THE OPEN ROAD - WITH OPEN ROAD PUBLISHING!

Open Road Publishing now has guide books to exciting, fun destinations on four continents. As veteran travelers, our goal is to bring you the best travel guides available anywhere!

No small task, but here's what we offer:

• All Open Road travel guides are written by authors with a distinct, opinionated point of view – not some sterile committee or team of writers. Our authors are experts in the areas covered and are polished writers.

• Our guides are geared to people who want great vacations, great value, and great tips for both standard tourist sights *and* fun, unique alternatives.

• We're strong on the basics, but we also provide terrific choices for those looking to get off the beaten path and *experience* the country or city – not just *see* it or pass through it.

• We give you the best, but we also tell you about the worst and what to avoid. Nobody should waste their time and money on their hard-earned vacation because of bad or inadequate travel advice.

• Our guides assume nothing. We tell you everything you need to know to have the trip of a lifetime – presented in a fun, literate, no-nonsense style.

• And, above all, we welcome your input, ideas, and suggestions to help us put out the best travel guides possible.

AUSTRIA GUIDE

YOUR PASSPORT TO GREAT TRAVEL!

ANGELA WALKER

OPEN ROAD PUBLISHING

OPEN ROAD PUBLISHING

We offer travel guides to American and foreign locales. Our books tell it like it is, often with an opinionated edge, and our experienced authors always give you all the information you need to have the trip of a lifetime. Write for your free catalog of all our titles, including our golf and restaurant guides.

Catalog Department, Open Road Publishing
P.O. Box 20226, Columbus Circle Station, New York, NY 10023

Or you contact us by e-mail at:
Jopenroad@aol.com

1st Edition

ISBN 1-883323-32-0
Library of Congress Catalog Card No. 96-67034

Photos courtesy of the Austrian National Tourist Office, New York.
Maps by Rob Perry.

We have made every effort to be as accurate as possible, but we cannot assume responsibility for the services provided by any business listed in this guide; for any errors or omissions; or any loss, damage, or disruptions in your travel for any reason.

TABLE OF CONTENTS

1. INTRODUCTION

You're going to love Austria! Whether you're going on a family vacation, a skiing holiday, or a tour of Vienna, Austria has something for everyone. Austria is the ideal place to take the family, no matter what the season, with a wealth of hiking, biking, caving, and climbing available – and of course some of the best skiing in Europe. For those of you who'd rather sit back and enjoy the view, Austria has some of the most scenic countryside the world has to offer. The Alps cover about two-thirds of the country and its hundreds of crystal-clear lakes are ideal for swimming, sailing, and canoeing.

Step back in time by stopping off at one of Austria's several imperial cities. Experience the imposing grandeur of the medieval fortress crowning the city of Salzburg. Visit the lovely city of Innsbruck, rising out of the heart of the Alps, or soak up the elegance and sophistication of Vienna. Castles, monasteries, churches, and abbeys dot the pristine Austrian landscape, so no matter where you are, there is something of historical interest worth seeing.

Austria is a music lover's paradise, with festivals in cities throughout the country featuring the best in opera, jazz, classical, and folk music. The country has been home to some of the greatest composers music has ever known, including Mozart, Beethoven, and Haydn. Every night the Austrian hills really do come alive with the sound of music.

Austria has every type of accommodation to suit your particular needs, whether your taste runs to an ultra-sophisticated five-star hotel in downtown Vienna, spending the night in a hiker's mountain hut, or lending a hand down on the farm in the Alpine countryside. But what truly separates Austria is the friendliness of her people, who welcome strangers with a friendly greeting of *Gruss Gott*. Spend some time rubbing shoulders with the locals in one of the country's open-air beer gardens or linger over coffee and a slice of delicious Sachertorte at a Viennese cafe.

No matter where your vacation takes you, Austrian hospitality will make it a memorable one.

2. EXCITING AUSTRIA! - OVERVIEW

Whether you've decided to ski the sleek alpine slopes, sail along the blue Danube or visit the Hapsburg hallmarks, Austria has something that will interest any traveler.

VIENNA

Once the world music capital and the stronghold of the Hapsburg monarchy, visiting Vienna is like stepping back into the last century. No matter where you look, myriad architectural masterpieces meet your gaze, crowned by **St. Stephen's cathedral** in the heart of the old section. Most of the city's architectural treasures can be found inside **the Ring**, created by the emperor along the lines of the former city walls.

The legacy of the empire still remains. Vienna's most popular tourist attraction is the sumptuous **Schonbrunn**, the summer residence of Empress Maria Theresa. The **Belvedere Palace**, which now houses museums of medieval, Baroque and modern art works, is also worth a visit, as is the expansive **Hofburg Palace** with its collection of royal jewels, silver, and other royal knickknacks in the center of town. It's easy to imagine how the royals once lived in all their extravagant glory.

No visit to Vienna would be complete without experiencing some of the fabulous music composed by such greats as Beethoven, Mozart, and Strauss during their sojourns here. An evening watching the **Vienna's Boy's Choir** or the stallions of the **Spanish Riding School** is also memorable. Spend a few hours lingering over coffee and one of the sinful pastries, including the legendary Sachertorte, at a neighborhood coffee house, or have a beer in a local beer garden. And take a few hours just wandering the narrow streets, open boulevards, and extensive parks, where you'll get a real sense of life in this glorious capital city.

LOWER AUSTRIA

Lower Austria is right on Vienna's doorstep, but you'll feel as if you're entering a different world if you venture outside the city limits. The province encompasses the famed **Vienna Woods** and the **Danube River**, which flows down towards the capital.

Lower Austria is worth a trip to sample the rural flavor of the country and some of its warm, rural hospitality. The province is dotted with charming towns and villages of all sizes, most located along the banks of the Danube. Whether you decide to go to the small provincial capital of **St. Polten**, the wine center of **Krems** or **Wiener Neustadt**, conceived originally as a possible replacement to Vienna, you'll be charmed by the centuries-old town squares and their patrician buildings painted in candy-colored hues. Make sure to include a trip to **Melk**, the abbey considered one of the finest examples of Baroque architecture the world has ever known.

When you need to take a break, look for one of the telltale straw wreaths or pine branches marking the entrance of the neighborhood *Heuriger* (wine tavern). The proprietor will serve you wine bottled from his own vineyards and food prepared from farm fresh ingredients.

UPPER AUSTRIA & THE LAKE DISTRICT

Linz is the capital of **Upper Austria** and a major industrial center perched along the banks of the Danube. But the city has a charming old town to explore, including a 15th century castle, neo-Gothic cathedral, and one of the finest modern art collections in the country. The **Baroque Abbey of St. Florian**, where the composer Anton Bruckner played the organ, is a short detour away from the capital. A sinister reminder of Austria's past can be visited at the Nazi concentration camp at **Mauthausen**.

Many tourists take a trip to Upper Austria to visit the **Lake District**. A favorite of Emperor Franz Josef was **Bad Ischl**, who often visited his mistress at nearby St. Wolfgang. **Hallstatt** is one of the oldest and most picturesque towns in Austria and definitely worth a detour. No matter where you choose, the waters will be cool and inviting and the welcome warm.

SALZBURG

The Baroque city of **Salzburg** is one of Austria's great jewels, crowned by the imposing medieval fortress casting its mighty shadow over the old town. Once presided over by the archbishops, who made their fortune from the salt mined in the province, Salzburg is sprinkled with churches of all shapes and sizes and surrounded by mountain peaks.

Many visitors to Austria prefer Wolfgang Amadeus Mozart's hometown over any other. Most Americans are familiar with Salzburg even if they've never traveled here through the movie *The Sound of Music* starring Julie Andrews. The hills really do come alive with the sounds of music during the annual **summer festival**, which draws renowned artists and music connoisseurs from all over the world.

Venture out of the capital to see the splendor of the **Krimml Waterfalls** and hike the myriad mountains that dot the region. Salzburg also incorporates part of the Lake District, and the **Fuschl See** and **St. Gilgen** make convenient and beautiful daytrips. In cold weather, the province is transformed by snow, with sports enthusiasts strapping on their skis or skates to take advantage of this winter wonderland.

INNSBRUCK & THE TIROLIAN REGION

Innsbruck, Tirol's provincial capital, rises dramatically out of the mountains. Even in summer, the white-capped peaks provide an awesome backdrop to the medieval town. It's no wonder that Emperor Maximilian wanted to move Austria's capital here. Remnants of the city's former imperial glory, from the **Golden Roof** to **Maximilian's mausoleum**, are evident throughout Innsbruck's old town.

Today, Innsbruck and surrounding **Tirol** mean skiing. The province has served as host to the Olympic Games, and you can visit the former Olympic ski jump, bobsled run and skating arena. The region has some of the best ski runs in the world. Each year, thousands of tourists flock to **St. Anton's** in the west or **Kitzbuhel** in the east and all the other resorts in-between to challenge the slopes and then take in the after-hours fun in the resort towns below.

VORARLBERG

Located on the banks of **Lake Constance**, Vorarlberg's provincial capital **Bregenz** is within easy reach of neighboring Switzerland and Germany. The lake is swarming with sailboats and cruise ships during the summer months. Summer is also the time of the province's cultural festival set on a floating stage on the lake. Also worth a visit is the medieval city of **Feldkirch**. Or venture into the meadows and mountains in the surrounding countryside and in the **Bregenzerwald** from such cities as **Bezau**.

Many people don't first think of Vorarlberg for skiing, but the province also has the pristine *pistes* of neighboring Tirol. Author Ernest Hemingway once whiled away the winters in **Stuben**, and nearby **Lech** and **Zurs** have attracted royalty and other notables from around the world. You also won't have to dig as deeply into your pockets at the smaller resorts here.

CARINTHIA

Austria's southern most province, bordering neighboring Italy and Slovenia, is a land of castles and pristine scenery. You'll see the Italian influence throughout **Carinthia** in the arcaded courtyards and Renaissance architecture that permeate **Klagenfurt**, the provincial capital, **Villach**, and other town centers. One of Carinthia's most famous landmarks is the **Hochosterwitz Castle** made famous by Walt Disney in his animated classic *Snow White*.

The rest of the region is covered with mountains, including Austria's highest, the **Grossglockner**, and hundreds of lakes. During the summer months, Austrian vacationers descend on what is known as **The Carinthian Riviera** to soak up the rays in the country's sunniest province. Carinthia is also a swimming, fishing, biking, and hiking haven. During the winter months, the mountains are crisscrossed with skiers, snowboarders, and cross-country enthusiasts.

STYRIA

Styria's most famous export may be movie actor Arnold Schwarzenegger, who comes from the provincial capital of **Graz**, but the region is also known by wine connoisseurs for its exceptional vintages. Vineyards blanket a quarter of Styria, with forests covering another half – hence its reputation as the **Green Province**. Many vintners welcome visits where you can taste the best bottles of wine harvested from the nearby hillsides.

History buffs will enjoy the remarkably well-preserved medieval quarter of Graz. Styria is also home to the famous **Lippizaners stallions**. You can visit **Piber**, just outside of Graz, to see how the remarkable horses are raised. The western part of the province is part of the **Lake District** and the spa resort of **Bad Aussee** is definitely worth a trip.

BURGENLAND

Burgenland didn't even exist until after World War I. Made up of territory from Hungary, the province is still true to its Eastern European origins from the architecture to the cuisine. The provincial capital of **Eisenstadt** was once home to the Esterhazy princes, as well as musician Joseph Haydn. A music festival celebrating the works of the great composer is held in the Esterhazy palace every September.

Burgenland also is renowned for its vineyards. There are several wine roads you can travel with stops at the vineyards along the way where you can taste the different vintages. Burgenland is also home to the **Seewinkel National Park**, which incorporates more than a quarter of the province. The land surrounding the **Neudsiedler saltwater lake** is home to more than 300 plant and animal species and attracts sun worshipers during the summer months. If you're staying in Vienna, the attractions in Burgenland can be made in an easy day trip, and neighboring **Hungary** is just a quick hop across the border.

3. SUGGESTED ITINERARIES
FOR THE PERFECT AUSTRIAN VACATION!

Choosing an itinerary for your trip to Austria all depends on what you are interested in. The country provides a wealth of activities for every season, with different regions attracting tourists during different times of the year.

If you're heading to Austria for the **winter season**, you'll probably want to try your hand at skiing in Tirol, Vorarlberg, Carinthia or Salzburg provinces. Of course, you may prefer visiting some of the country's imperial cities which decorate themselves in high-style for the holidays.

As the weather warms, Austrians and foreigners alike flock to the myriad *Sees,* or lakes, in the Salzkammergut or head to the hills for hiking and biking. **Spring and summer** is also the time for many different cultural festivals around the country from opera to concerts to dance. It's also a good time to visit the castles, monasteries and other historical treasures sprinkled across the countryside. Many are only open from April through October.

If you're in the country during the **autumn**, make plans to visit Austria's many wine regions. You can travel up or down the blue Danube by boat, bike, train or car, stopping along the way at the tiny towns that border the famous river in Upper and Lower Austria. Take the time to get off the beaten track and partake of the hospitality at the neighborhood *Heuriger,* or wine tavern. Your host or hostess will serve the best of the wine they've produced themselves and often food made on the premises. Many offer simple but pleasant accommodations. Styria and Burgenland also have many vineyards to visit. The mild weather, delicious wine, and breathtaking scenery with the red and gold leaves of the vines dappled with the autumn light will take your breath away.

Here are some suggested itineraries to get you started on planning your journey:

VIENNA

Any trip to Austria should include the country's capital, **Vienna**. The imperial stronghold of the Hapsburg empire, Vienna still retains much of its 19th century charm, although some visitors are put off by the somewhat imperious attitude they encounter from shop keepers to waiters to opera ticket takers. But behind Vienna's gruff exterior lurks a heart of gold – you just need to be patient enough to discover it.

Day 1

Spend your first day taking in the sights inside the **Ring**, the old section of city where many of the principal monuments are located. Take a ride on the tram to get a feel for how the city is set up and then explore the old town, from **St. Stephen's Cathedral** to the **Hofburg palace**.

Day 2

The second day of your trip could be spent visiting **Schonbrunn** or the **Belvedere palaces**. Then spend the next day visiting some of the city's splendid museums. You need at least a week to get a real feel for the city, especially the architectural treasures that meet your gaze everywhere you look, but this quick glimpse will at least give you a sense of Vienna.

VIENNA EXCURSIONS

If you have at least a week, head into **Upper Austria**, **Burgenland**, or **Styria**. Lovely towns and villages are easily accessible from Vienna. The easy, rural charm and hospitality will win your heart. If you want to cover more ground, you can fly, drive, or take a train or bus to Salzburg and Innsbruck.

The old sections of the towns can easily be seen in a day or two, although you may end up wanting to spend even more time at both of them.

MOUNTAIN TOWNS & SKI VACATIONS

If **Salzburg** is your main destination, spend a couple of days exploring the old section on foot. Easy day excursions are possible to the lake resorts in the **Salzkammergut** with their clear, blue water surrounded by mountains. You're also just a hop, skip and a jump away from Munich and the rest of Germany, too. Innsbruck and **Linz** are also not too far away if you want to make day trips to these cities. In winter, skiing, ice skating, and other winter sports are possible in Salzburg and the surrounding area.

Serious skiers should head to **Innsbruck**. If you're staying for just a few days for your skiing vacation, make the Tirolean capital your base and explore the various resorts from there. The possibilities for longer skiing vacations in Austria are enormous from smaller, family-style resorts to posh, sophisticated vacation havens. There are several "ski circuses" that allow you to ski several different resorts using one lift ticket, which are available for the day or up to several weeks.

The provinces of **Tirol**, **Salzburg**, **Carinthia**, and **Vorarlberg** all cater to skiers and their families.

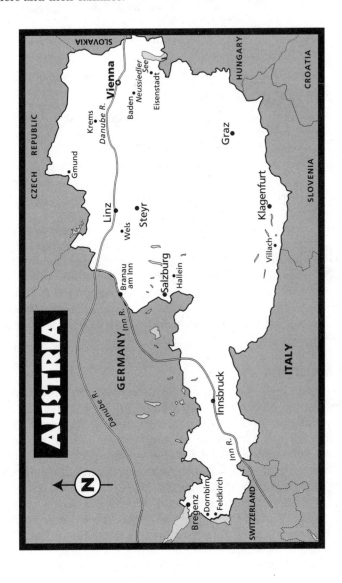

4. HISTORY

THE PREHISTORIC ERA

Located in the heart of Europe, Austria can trace its history back to prehistoric times. During the Palaeolithic era, the area around the Danube was settled between 80,000 and 10,000 B.C. The world-famous **Venus of Willendorf** and the **Tanzerin** artifacts were discovered in the Krems area and provide some of the earliest evidence of European cultures. The people living here during the Neolithic period were raising crops and livestock, and using metal tools.

In 1991, a mummified man from the Stone Age was discovered in the glacial ice of the Otzal Alps. He was an Indo-European **Illyrian**, who lived in what is now Austria during the early Iron Age between 800 and 400 B.C. The **Celts** settled in the **Hallstatt** region and mined the valuable commodities of salt and iron. The Celts had earlier migrated from western Europe and stayed in Austria to exploit the resources found in the area. Today, remains of the Celts are preserved in several local museum allowing modern-day tourists to trace their evolution.

ROMAN RULE

The Romans conquered the region and incorporated the area into their vast empire around the time of Christ. The Romans divided the region into the provinces of Rhaetia, Noricum, and Pannonia. The area was an important trading route and the Romans established the settlements of **Iuvavum**, now Salzburg, **Vindobona**, now Vienna, and **Brigantium**, now Bregenz. The biggest Roman town, with 20,000 inhabitants at the height of its power, was **Carnuntum**, east of Vienna.

As the Roman Empire declined, Germanic tribes moved into Austria devastating the country. In the sixth century, the Bavarians challenged the Slavs and Avars from the East for control of the region. Ultimately, the Bavarians triumphed and settled and farmed rural areas. As the former Roman settlement fell into disrepair, Christianity made important strides as the bishops gained power in Salzburg, Regensburg, and Passau.

THE HOLY ROMAN EMPIRE

The French king **Charlemagne**, after defeating the Avars, set up protectorates between the Enns, Raab, and Drau rivers to ensure that his kingdom remained intact. Austria was later attacked by the Magyars in the ninth century, who soundly defeated the Bavarian forces. Only in 995 did **Otto the Great** succeed in taking back the territory from the Magyars.

BABENBERG DYNASTY

The **Babenberg dynasty** ascended to power at the end of tenth century. Although there is speculation that the original Babenberg's held power in Melk, **Duke Heinrich II** chose Vienna in 1156 as his seat of power. The Babenbergs continued to extend their power and influence, moving north of the Danube and east and west of Vienna.

The Babenbergs methodically increased their territorial holdings. The family became one of the most powerful in the Holy Roman Empire when **Leopold III** married **Agnes**, the emperor's widow. The Babenbergs later received a piece of Bavaria from the emperor as a reward for their loyalty to him. **Leopold V** later inherited the Duchy of Styria, although he is probably more famous for the imprisonment of his English rival Richard the Lion-Hearted. Richard was released only after being forced to pay a hefty ransom, which Leopold used to fortify Vienna and Weiner Neustadt.

Tragedy destroyed the dynasty when in 1246 the childless Duke Friedrich II was killed in the **Battle of Leitha** against the Magyars. Various factions struggled for power of the region. Bohemian King Ottokar II Przemysl married the sister of the slain duke and rose to power after securing the local nobility's approval. But **Rudolph of Hapsburg** refused to acknowledge Ottokar, and would not to swear an oath of allegiance to the Holy Roman Empire. The two sides took up arms and Ottokar was killed in the **Battle of Durnkrut** in 1278. Rudolph took control, starting 600 years of **Hapsburg** rule in Austria and beyond.

HAPSBURG EMPIRE

The Hapsburgs met opposition to their rule initially. Subjects, in what is now Switzerland, rebelled against them, and the family lost those territories when they were defeated in the Battle of Morgarten. But the Hapsburgs maintained their hold on Austrian territory and acquired the **Earldom of Tirol** and parts of the **Windische Mark**.

Under **Rudolph IV**, known as the Founder, the **University of Vienna** was built and **St. Stephen's cathedral** was renovated into the gothic masterpiece tourists see today.

In 1483, **Albrecht V** was named King of Bohemia and Hungary and King of Germany. When he died without an heir a year later, the Tirolean Hapsburg **Friedrich** was named King of Germany and crowned emperor of the Holy Roman Empire only a few years later. Friedrich made a series of important alliances, laying the foundation for what was to become the **Hapsburg Empire**. His son was married to the Burgundian heiress Maria. Also through strategic marriages, his grandsons Ferdinand and Karl guaranteed the hereditary succession in Bohemia, Hungary, and Spain. The empire was so enormous it was decided to divide it into two parts: an **Austro-German empire** and a **Spanish-Dutch empire**. In 1526, Bohemia and Hungary were also absorbed into the empire following the death of the Jagellonian King Ludwig II.

But the Hapsburgs didn't have time to rest on their laurels as the Ottoman Empire began to encroach on their domain after the Turks took Constantinople in 1453. The Ottomans managed to fight their way to the fortified gates of Vienna before the Hapsburgs managed to turn them back in 1529 and 1683.

THE STORY OF THE CROISSANT

To commemorate the victory over the Turks, a Viennese baker created the **croissant**. *The fluffy pastry is in the shape of the crescent moon on the Turkish flag, so patriotic Viennese could symbolically eat their vanquished enemy.*

Following the victory over the Turks, Vienna, under the leadership of **Prince Eugene of Savoy**, underwent a Baroque building boom bonanza, molding the character of the city. But the future of the empire was again threatened in 1700, with no heir to inherit the Spanish part of the empire. The Hapsburgs lost that fight during the Spanish War of Secession, but did manage to hang on to their domination of The Netherlands and Italy. Emperor Karl VI later died without a male heir. But, under the **Pragmatic Sanction**, which allowed for female secession, Karl's daughter, **Maria Theresa**, was allowed to ascend the throne in 1740.

Maria Theresa faced threats from all sides, especially from the Prussian King Frederick II. She managed to hold on to all but the province of Silesia after fighting two wars during her 40-year reign. She bore 16 children, including the ill-fated **Marie Antoinette** who was later guillotined with her husband King Louis XVI during the French Revolution. Maria Theresa also started a series of land reforms, which was continued by her son **Joseph II**, who abolished serfdom and secularized monasteries and church property. The Hapsburg court also became a magnet for musicians, including **Joseph Haydn** and **Wolfgang Amadeus Mozart**, who played for Maria Theresa at Schonbrunn palace when he was only six years old.

The monarchy, however, was threatened by the ideology of the French Revolution, and the later emergence of **Napoleon**. The Corsican rampaged through Europe, and Austria suffered several significant defeats. Napoleon crowned himself emperor of France in 1804. Under pressure from France, **Emperor Franz II**, Maria Theresa's grandson, established the **Confederation of the Rhine**, which ultimately led to the disintegration of the Holy Roman Empire in 1806. Napoleon also took the emperor's daughter, Marie Louise, as his bride. She later bore him a son.

The old world order in Europe was restored after the **Congress of Vienna** in 1814, presided over by Austrian Chancellor **Clemens Metternich**. But only for a time; Metternich lost power in 1848 as a result of the middle class revolutions sweeping Europe. The liberals demanded an uncensored press and a written constitution. Under **Emperor Franz Joseph I**, a neo-absolutist monarchy was set up. Franz Joseph decided to maintain neutrality during the **Crimean War**, leading to Austria's isolation within Europe.

In 1859, Austria lost the battles of Magenta and Solferino, and was forced to give up Lombardy. Franz Joseph also acquiesced to local demands for the creation of a parliament. Austria was later expelled from the German Confederation, after the country's defeat at the **Battle of Koniggratz** in 1866. To the east, Austria brutally suppressed a rebellion in Hungary in 1848 with the help of the Russians. But a **dual monarchy** was formed in 1867, giving Hungary equal rights in a confederation.

Franz Joseph's 67-year reign was filled with personal turmoil. His son Rudolph murdered his mistress before turning the gun on himself. His wife, the Empress Elisabeth, renowned for her beauty, was assassinated by an Italian nationalist while on a trip abroad.

THE WORLD WARS

Europe maintained peace at the turn of the century through a series of complicated alliances. Austria was united with Germany and Italy in the **Triple Alliance**. But nationalist tensions were brewing. The working class was also demanding better conditions and higher wages. Austrian Archduke **Franz Ferdinand** was mowed down by an assassin's bullet in Sarajevo on June 28, 1914.

World War I began after Franz Joseph was persuaded to declare war on Serbia in retaliation for the archduke's death. He died two years before the war's end. In 1918, the **Central Powers** composed of Austria-Hungary, Germany, and Turkey were defeated, and the Hapsburg era came to a jarring close.

A day after Emperor Karl I renounced his throne, the delegates of the provisional national assembly proclaimed the state of the Republic of German Austria. However, the terms of the peace treaty ending the war prohibited the union with Germany. Austria lost its rights to South Tirol and the Sudetenland. But parts of western Hungary were added to the country, which today make up Burgenland.

The economy began to stabilize in the mid-twenties. But power struggles within the country became increasingly more violent. Opposing parties armed themselves and fierce street battles ensued. When several political assassinations occurred, and their accused murderers were acquitted, a demonstration was staged and subsequently crushed, leading to the deaths of more than 90 people.

The decades between the wars saw the rise of **Red Vienna**, a social-democratic movement. Innovative public housing, sports centers, and public baths were constructed during this period. The depression, however, left hundreds of thousands of Austrians unemployed. The worsening economic situation encouraged the rise of right-wing politicians who advocated establishing an authoritarian government modelled on Italian fascism.

Parliament was dissolved in 1933. The political turmoil that ensued ended in a civil war. A revolt by the Social Democrats in 1934 was defeated, but Federal Chancellor **Engelbert Dollfuss** was killed. Many of the Social Democrats were tried and sentenced to death. The new Federal Chancellor, **Kurt Schuschnigg**, attempted to maintain Austria's independence by aligning the country with Italy and Hungary.

German troops did not respect Austria's attempts at independence and invaded the country on March 12, 1938. But many Austrians were supporters of National Socialism and called for *anschluss*, or union, with Germany. In 1939, the name of Austria was abolished by their German occupiers. All able-bodied men were recruited into the German forces. The majority of Jews remaining in the country after emigration was severely curtailed in March 1938 were systematically rounded up and shipped to the Nazi death camps and killed.

When the war ended seven years later, Vienna was occupied by the victorious Allied forces. The city was divided into four sectors controlled by Americans, British, French, and Russians. The provisional government under **Karl Renner** declared an independent Austrian state on April 27, 1945.

POSTWAR AUSTRIA

Ten years later, on Oct. 26, 1955, the Austrian parliament passed the Federal Constitutional Law guaranteeing the permanent **neutrality** of Austria. The country also became a member of the United Nations that year. During the Cold War, Austria maintained its political and military neutrality, but for all intents and purposes the country was an integral part of Western Europe. Its open economy, democratic government, and cultural freedom made Austria much like any other European nation west of the Iron Curtain.

THE ECONOMY

The Austrian economy is based on a social market system. The post office, railroads, and the forestry commission are run by the government but most businesses are privately owned. A system of price subsidies are in place primarily serving the agricultural sector.

The gross domestic product was more than 1,900 billion schillings in 1991, the last year for which reliable figures are available. That amounts to about 245,100 schillings per citizen. In 1994, Austria became part of the **European Union**.

5. LAND & PEOPLE

LAND

Geography

Austria is a country of geographical contrasts, with the **Alps** rising out of the West to the **plains of the Danube** in the East. The country, which is 32,367 square miles, is landlocked, but has historically provided an important trading link between northern and southern Europe as well as the gateway between eastern and western Europe. Austria shares its borders with Germany, Italy, the Czech Republic, Hungary, Switzerland, Slovenia and Liechtenstein.

The country is comprised of nine provinces: Burgenland, Carinthia, Lower Austria, Salzburg, Styria, Tirol, Upper Austria, Vienna and Vorarlberg. The **Grossglockner Mountain** is the highest in Austria, rising up 12,465 feet, and the **Danube** is the longest river flowing 220 miles from Germany's Black Forest to the Black Sea. Austria has 88 large lakes and rivers and streams stretching more than 100,000 kilometers.

Flora & Fauna

Austria is also one of Europe's most heavily wooded countries, with 46 percent of its land covered by **forests**. Trees in the country's lower regions consist of beech and fir, giving way to mostly fir at higher altitudes.

Deer, hares, foxes, badgers, squirrels, pheasants and partridges flourish in much of the country. In the mountains, chamois, marmot, and ibex can be found. A variety of birds, including purple heron, live in the reed beds surrounding **Lake Neusiedl**, central Europe's only steppe lake.

There are several nature preserves, zoos with native animals, and botanical gardens for travelers interested in taking advantage of the abundance of natural wonders that Austria has to offer. Contact the Austrian tourist office for vacation package information.

PEOPLE

Austria is home to nearly 8 million people, and its ethnic diversity can be traced to its former heyday as the seat of the Hapsburg Empire. The majority of Austrians can trace their ethnic roots to German, Neo-Latin, and Slav peoples. The Magyars of Hungary are an exception, since they originated from the Ural-Altaic peoples.

The country is 98 percent German speaking. Under the Austrian State Treaty of Vienna enacted in 1955, the cultural integrity of two ethnic groups in Carinthia and Burgenland are guaranteed. A Slovak group lives in southern Carinthia and Croatians and Hungarians are in Burgenland. Vienna is also home to a significant number of Eastern Europeans.

Religion

Christianity first began to take hold in Austria at the end of the first millennium A.D. Today, a majority of Austrians, more than 80 percent of the population, are **Catholic**, and signs of their faith are apparent all over the nation, from cathedrals to monasteries to tiny shrines throughout the countryside. Almost 5 percent are Protestants and 5 percent belong to other religious denominations. The other 10 percent of Austrians say they don't belong to any religion.

Music

What description of Austria could be complete without including a part on the country's rich musical heritage. Vienna became a musical mecca to such classical composers as **Joseph Haydn**, **Wolfgang Amadeus Mozart**, and **Ludwig van Beethoven**.

As a child prodigy, **Mozart** was bounced on the knee of Empress Maria Theresa when he played for her at Schonbrunn Palace. The native of Salzburg was originally in the employ of the city's archbishop, but their personalities clashed and Mozart was summarily dismissed. He was later employed at the Viennese court where he composed his greatest operas including *Don Giovanni*, *The Marriage of Figaro*, and *The Magic Flute*.

Haydn worked as music director for Prince Esterhazy in Eisenstadt for several years. Both Beethoven's and Mozart's mentor, Haydn composed operas, symphonies, string quartets, ecclesiastical music and the oratories *Die Schopfung*, and *Die vier Jahreszeiten*.

Beethoven left Bonn for Vienna to study under the master Haydn. Like Mozart, he lived on the money he made from his compositions rather than on the subsidy of a patron. In 1805, his *Eroica* symphony was performed for the first time in Vienna. An unsuccessful premier of his opera *Fidelio* was held at the Theater der Wein. You can still visit the house where Beethoven composed part of his famous Ninth Symphony (see the

Vienna chapter), which today houses a popular *Heuriger*, or wine tavern, as well as his other residences around the capital.

Franz Schubert was a native of Vienna and a composer of romantic music, including a new genre which he invented called **The Leid**. His most famous Lieder cycles are *Die Schone Mullerin*, and *Die Winterreise*. Other composers of the 19th century included **Anton Bruckner**, who worked as an organist in St. Florian near Linz, and **Johannes Brahms**, who continued the romantic tradition in classical music. **Gustav Mahler** served as director of the Vienna Court Opera from 1897 to 1907 and helped to usher in the new age of modern symphonic music.

One of the most popular compositions to emerge out of the Austrian musical scene was the **waltz**, developed by **Joseph Lanner** and **Johann Strauss**. Strauss' sons, Joseph and Johann, took the waltz's popularity a step further than their father, developing symphonic pieces and operettas based on the musical form. The most famous of these is *Die Fledermaus*, which continues to be popular with today's audiences.

In the 20th century, Austria produced **Arnold Schonberg**, who created the modern classical music theory of "12 notes related only to one another." Alban Berg later used this 12-note theory in his unfinished opera *Lulu*.

Art & Architecture

Austria offers loads of varying architectural styles tracing the evolution of Europe. Pre-historic animal carvings have been found in the Hallstatt area as well as Celtic and Roman ruins in Magdalensberg in Carinthia, and the Roman settlements of the Carnuntum on the Danube and in Aguntum in East Tirol. An early Christian basilica also was discovered in what is now Carinthia.

The ecclesiastical art and architecture of the **Romanesque** period flourished in Austria, especially in the episcopal seats in Salzburg and Augustine, Benedictine, and Cistercian monasteries around the country in Melk, Gottweig, and Klosterneuburg. The best examples of Romanesque architecture can be found in the **Gurk** and **Seckau cathedrals** in Carinthia and Styria respectively. **Gothic** architecture became popular in Austria in the 13th to 15th centuries. The most obvious example, of course, is **St. Stephen's Cathedral** in Vienna. The **Minorite Church** and **St. Augustine's** in Vienna are also in the gothic style, comprised of a hall with naves of equal height.

The reign of Emperor Maximillan I heralded the age of **Renaissance** art and architecture in Austria, although several of the artists behind this movement were imported from Italy. These artists combined Italian influences with that of the local culture. Examples include the archbishop's residence and the cathedral in Salzburg and the mausoleum of Ferdinand

II in Graz. Austrian artists that rose to prominence included Wolf Huber, Max Reichlich, and Albrecht and Erhart Altdorfer.

No country epitomizes the **Baroque** style more than Austria, and it is for this art form that the country is justifiably most famous. The master of the Austrian Baroque style is **Bernhard Fischer von Erlach**, who blended the Italian Baroque style with a particularly Austrian sensibility. His masterpieces include the **Collegiate Church** in Salzburg and parts of the **Hofburg palace** and the **Karlskirche** in Vienna. Johann Lukas von Hildebrandt contributed equally to the rise of Baroque architecture in Austria. He designed the **Mirabell Palace** in Salzburg and the **Belvedere Palace** in Vienna. Jakob Prandtauer was another great Baroque master creating the world-renowned **Melk abbey** and the town of **St. Polten**. Notable Baroque sculptors include George Raphael Donner, who designed the fountain in the **Neuer Markt** in Vienna, Daniel Grann, Johann Michael Rottmayr and Balthasar Permoser. Austrian Baroque painters include Franz Anton Maulbertsch, Paul Troger and Johann Schmidt.

The **Neoclassical** period began at the turn of the 18th century and is exemplified in such Viennese buildings as the **Technical University** and the **Mint**. Sculptor Franz Anton Zauner designed the monument of Emperor Joseph II in front of the city's national library in this style. The period between the Congress of Vienna in 1814 and the revolutions of 1848 is called the **Biedermeier style**. Important artists include Georg Ferdinand Waldmuller, Freidrich Gauermann, and Rudolf von Alt.

But the period is probably best known for the furniture produced, reflecting the growing prosperity of a rising middle class. Under Emperor Franz Joseph I, the Viennese Ringstrasse was built on the site of the city's medieval fortifications. Architects were commissioned to design buildings bordering the wide boulevard of the Ring. Heinrich von Ferstel built the **Votive Church**, Theophil Hansen the **Parliament**, Friedrich von Schmidt the **Rathaus**, or town hall, Carl von Hasenauer the **Burgtheater** and Eduard van der Null and August Siccard von Siccardsburg the **State Opera House**.

The **Jugendstil** period started in 1897. Some artists led by **Gustav Klimt** and **Otto Wagner** of the "Kunstlerhaus" broke away to form the "Vienna Succession." Klimt was the forerunner of what later became to be known as **Viennese Expressionism**, emphasizing color, psychological themes, and structure, making ornaments and lines means of expression. Otto Wagner joined the Secession in 1899, breaking with his traditional architectural background. Wagner was one of the first modern architects favoring the use of glass and steel as building materials and forsaking extraneous ornamentation. His masterpieces include the **Post Office Savings Bank** and the **Steinhof Church**. His student, Joseph Hoffman, designed the Palais Stoclet in Brussels.

Adolf Loos attacked the architecture of Vienna's Ring, but he also found fault with the Secessionists, preferring pure functionalism over ornamentation. He designed the "house without eyebrows" across from the imperial palace at the Michaeler Platz, which in turn was criticized for its total lack of adornment.

Egon Schiele created daringly erotic works of arts depicting lovers in clinging embraces and stark portraits of prostitutes. The paintings shocked conventional critics. But like his architectural and musical peers, Schiele's legacy continues today in art galleries around the world.

6. PLANNING YOUR TRIP

BEFORE YOU GO

ACCOMMODATIONS

Austria offers an incredible range of accommodations for tourists from hotel rooms in converted castles and abbeys to *Zimmers* in private homes to alpine huts where hikers can spend the night in the mountains. If you are planning a tour of Austria's imperial cities than your best bet would be to stay in a city hotel or, if you prefer less costly accommodations, than choose a *pension*, which is often a more charming and intimate lodging experience.

Many resorts have chalets or hotels within a stone's throw of the slopes, whether you're interested in skiing or hiking. Many establishments have their own recreation facilities from swimming pools to discos to game rooms. Resort prices fluctuate widely depending on the season. Make sure to check in advance to confirm the price of your room.

Most hotels have their own restaurants, which are often of excellent quality. Some hotels include meals in their room price. Also, if you are partial to showers, make sure to ask in advance if your hotel room is so equipped. Many Austrian accommodations come with baths with hand-held shower heads.

If you are concentrating your vacation in a particular region, you may want to spend part of your time in a hotel and part of it in a *Zimmer*, or a room in a private residence. *Zimmers* allow you to get a glimpse of how real Austrians live, especially if you've decided to get off the beaten track. Be careful though, since most *Zimmers* usually close down early for the night. If you are planning to stay at a private residence, and know that you are going to arrive late, make sure that you inform your host or hostess in advance.

Many regions also offer the possibility of staying at a local farm. This is a nice choice of lodging if you are travelling with children who can pitch in and get a first-hand glimpse of how farm animals are raised. Produce and local milk and meat products also end up on the farmer's table so your tastebuds are in for a treat, too. Zimmers and farm accommodations are often family-style establishments. If you are looking for the height of elegance or want to pampered and coddled, this may not be the best option for you.

Reservations

Advance reservations at hotels, inns and Zimmers are recommended. Don't expect to be able to find a room without a reservation during high season. Making a deposit on your room is a good idea to insure that your reservation is secure.

CURRENT EXCHANGE RATES

The current exchange rate as of press time is roughly
10 schillings *per dollar.*

CAMPING & TRAILERS

You don't need any special custom documents if you're planning to bring a trailer into Austria. Make sure you check your planned route in advance; some Austrian passes prohibit trailers. If you are a member of an international camping association, you may be eligible for reduced prices at campsites. Children also pay discounted prices. Visitors can sleep outside authorized camping sites in their vehicles, but local restrictions may apply so check first with the local tourist office. A list of camping sites in Austria can be obtained through national tourist offices, automobile clubs, and camping clubs.

• **Camping and Caravaning Club Austria**, *Mariahilfer Strasse 180, A-1150 Vienna. Tel. 89-121 or 89-222*

• **Osterreichischer Camping Club**, *Schubertring 1-3, A-1010 Vienna. Tel. 71-199 or 71-1272*

CAR RENTALS

If you do decide to rent a car, try reserving through a major American agency in the U.S. The difference in rates is staggering, so you'll be sure to get the most from your vacation dollars if you book in advance. But if you do decide to rent in Austria, all the major agencies are represented in larger cities.

Obviously, smaller towns and villages often do not have car rental facilities, so plan to make arrangements in urban areas, where you'll probably also have to drop off your car.

CLIMATE

Austria has a moderate climate, but it can be very cold in winter and hot in summer so pack accordingly. The autumn and spring seasons are cool and can be rainy.

Austria can be divided into three climatic regions. In the east, the provinces have hot summers and less rainfall than the rest of the country. There's no surprise that the weather in the Alps is characterized by lots of rain or snow with short summers and long, cold winters. The rest of the country is somewhere in between, with more precipitation than in the east but with a more temperate climate.

CUSTOMS

Visitors from overseas are allowed to bring in two liters of wine, one liter of hard liquor and two cartons of cigarettes, 50 cigars or 250 grams of tobacco. Gifts valued at more than 2,500 schillings (about $250) or firearms can not be brought into Austria legally.

HOLIDAYS

Austria practically shuts down on Sundays, so you should plan your travel plans accordingly. On public holidays, most businesses close and many public services, like buses, have limited schedules or cancel their service. Austria observes many Catholic religious holidays, which change from year to year. Check with your travel agent or with the national tourist office for the dates of specific holidays when planning your trip.

Holidays include January 1 and 6, Good Friday, Easter Monday, May 1, Ascension Day, Whitmonday, Corpus Christi, August 15, October 26, November 1 and December 8, 25, and 26.

PACKING

If you're traveling to Austria for a ski vacation during the winter months, then be sure to bring along lots of layers, a heavy coat, and a good pairs of boots. Since spring and fall can be cool, be sure to bring along some sweaters, sensible walking shoes, and a rain coat. The summer months can be hot and muggy, but the temperature often drops as the evening cools, so don't neglect to bring along some sweaters or a light coat.

The Austrian sun shines intensely even during the winter months, so it makes sense to bring along some sunscreen, a pair of sunglasses, and a hat or cap. And bring an umbrella. Austria is notorious for its brief but often violent storms, so you don't want to get caught unprepared in a downpour. And if you're planning to do some hiking, biking, or other outdoor recreational activity, be sure to pack some insect repellant.

VISAS & PASSPORTS

North Americans traveling to Austria can enter the country with just a valid passport. No visa is required for visits up to 90 days. During each calendar year, you can stay in Austria without a visa for as long as six months, but you must leave the country for at least a week after the first three months have elapsed.

If you are staying in the country for longer than three days, you must register with the local police department. If you are staying at a hotel, they will automatically take care of this for you when you register. But if you are staying with friends or have arranged private accommodations, then you must register yourself.

GETTING TO & AROUND AUSTRIA

GETTING THERE
Airlines

Most major carriers fly to Austria, including **Austrian Airlines, Lauda Air**, and **Tyrolean Airways**. The airports in Vienna, Graz, Innsbruck, Klagenfurt, Linz and Salzburg have international service. **Tyrolean Airways** and **Rheintalflug** offer domestic flights within Austria.

For **Austrian Airlines** toll-free reservations in the US, *call 800-843-0002.*

By Air to Vienna

Austrian airports, including those in Vienna, Graz, Innsbruck, Klagenfurt, Linz and Salzburg, are serviced by major international carriers.

Vienna-Schwechat Airport is about a 20-minute drive from the city center. Taxis charge a 12 schilling fee for each piece of baggage. An airport surcharge of about 110 schillings will also be included. Non-stop bus service is available for 60 schillings. Buses leave from the **City Air Terminal**, Wien Mitte, Landstrasse, between 5 a.m. and 11 p.m. and from the airport to the City Air Terminal between 6 a.m. and midnight. For **airport information**, *you can call 711-10-23-31 or 22-32 around the clock.*

If you're connecting to a train after arriving on a flight into Vienna, buses run between the airport to the **Sudbahnhof** and **Westbahnhof train stations** between 6:40 a.m. and 10:40 p.m.

If you're flying into another major airport in Austria, consult the regional chapter in this book for more information.

By Air to Salzburg

The **Salzburg Airport** is located *at Innsbrucker Bundesstrasse 95. Tel. 662-80-550 or 662-85-2091; fax 662-80-5529; telex 633133.* For **Salzburg Airport Services**, *call 662-8055-251*; for **charter flight information**, *call 662-851-212; fax 662-851-215.* For **Austrian flight information schedules**, *call 662-8529-00.* The airport is open from 7 a.m. to 10 p.m.

Taxis take about 20 minutes to reach downtown, or you can catch bus number 77, which will take you to the old town. If you're flying into Munich International Airport, you can take a train to Salzburg. But a better bet may be to reserve a seat with the Salzburger Mietwagen. The service takes you from the airport directly to your hotel in Salzburg. Be aware, though, that you may be in for a wait at the airport, because there may be other passengers that will be riding with you. For information, contact the **Salzburger Mietwagen Service**, *Ignaz Harrer Strasse 79A, A-5020 Salzburg. Tel. 662-8161-0; fax 662-436324.* One way fare costs 440 schillings; roundtrip fare costs 730 schillings.

By Bus

Some 2,000 bus operators are also doing business in the country, including 190 international carriers. For more information, call Central Bus Information, *431-71101 outside of Austria or 222-71101 in Austria.*

By Train

There is also train service to major Austrian cities from cities around Europe if you're coming from a neighboring country. The Austrian Federal Railways operate trains on 5,800 kilometers of track. Trains run between major cities in Austria every hour or two. Reserving a seat will cost 30 schillings extra. Several discounted passes are available to tourists, including a cross-country rail pass, regional passes, senior citizen and group tickets and reduced return tickets for distances of up to 70 kilometers. Children under 6 travel free if they sit on a parent's lap. Kids six to 15 are entitled to half price tickets.

You can also transport your car on special trains. The service is available for rides between Vienna and Villach, Vienna and Salzburg, Vienna and Bischofscofen, Vienna and Innsbruck, Vienna and Feldkirch, Vienna and Lienz, Linz and Feldkirch, Graz and Feldkirch and Villach and Feldkirch. For more information on train service, call *43-1-1717 outside of Austria or 222-17-17 in Austria.*

GETTING AROUND AUSTRIA

Public transportation in Austria is very extensive. Most cities have comprehensive subway, streetcar, and bus networks making it easy to get around without renting a car. Even the smallest villages are accessible by bus or train.

LOCAL TOURIST INFORMATION

Once you've decided what parts of Austria you plan to visit, you can contact regional offices for more specific information about your planned destination such as the best ski resorts, language classes and festivals in the area. Be sure to request that the information be sent in English.

The **telephone country code** for Austria is 43. The zero before the city code only needs to be dialed if calling from inside the country.

- **Burgenland Tourismus**, *Schloss EsterhazyA-7000 Eisenstadt. Tel. (02682) 633 84; Fax: (02682) 633 84 20*
- **Carinthia Tourismus**, *Sjdkjsplatz 1A-9220 Velden. Tel. (04274) 52100; Fax: (04274) 52100-50*
- **Lower Austria Tourismus**, *Tourismusabteilung Hoher Markt 3A-1014 Vienna. Tel. (0222) 53 110 6110; Fax: (0222) 53 110 6330 or 6060*
- **Salzburgerland Tourismus**, *Alpenstrasse 96, Postfach 8A-5033 Salzburg. Tel. (0662) 620 506-0; Fax: (0662) 623070*
- **Styria Tourismus**, *St. Peter Hauptstrasse 243A-8042 Graz. Tel. (0316) 40 30 13-0; Fax: (0316) 403013-10*
- **Tirol Tourismus**, *Bozner Platz 6A-6010 Innsbruck. Tel. (0512) 53 20 59; Fax: (0512) 57 03 68 or 53 20 150*
- **Upper Austria Tourismus**, *Schillerstrasse 50A-4010 Linz. Tel. (0732) 60 02 21-0; Fax: (0732) 60 02 20*
- **Voralburg Tourismus**, *Romerstrasse 7/1 Postfach 302A-6901 Bregenz. Tel. (05574) 42 525 0; Fax: (05574) 42 525 5*
- **Vienna Tourismus**, *Obere Augartenstrasse 40A-1025 Vienna. Tel. (0222) 211 144; Fax: (0222) 21 68 492*

TOUR GUIDES

Guides are available to explain the sights to you in all major Austrian cities. Information can be obtained from regional tourist offices or through your travel agent.

YOUTH HOSTELS & ZIMMERS

Youth hostels can be found all over Austria. It is advisable to make reservations in advance if possible. For more information contact Osterreichischer Jugendherbergsring, *Schottenring 28, A-1010, Vienna. From outside Austria, call 431-5335-353 or in Austria 222-5335-353.*

If a hostel is booked, you might want to consider staying in a private *Zimmer* (rooms for rent in private houses), which cost slightly more than hostels, but you'll have your own room. Breakfast is usually included.

Check with the local tourist office for a list of available *Zimmers*. They can usually book them for you as well.

TOURIST OFFICES IN NORTH AMERICA

Austrian National Tourist Offices are an invaluable resource to consult when planning your trip to Austria. A mountain of brochures, maps, hotels and other practical information in English is available, just write, telephone or fax your request to the office closest to you.

In the United States
- **Chicago** – *500 North Michigan Avenue, Chicago, Ill. 60611. Tel. (312) 644-8029; Fax: (312) 644-6526*
- **Houston** – *1300 Post Oak Boulevard, Suite 960, Houston, TX 77056. Tel. (713) 850-9999; Fax: (713) 850-7857*
- **New York** – *500 Fifth Ave., New York, NY 10110. Tel. (212) 575-7723; Fax: (212) 730-4568*
- **Los Angeles** – *P.O. Box 491938, Los Angeles, CA 90049-8938. Tel. (310) 477-3332; Fax: (310) 477-5141*

In Canada
- **Montreal** – *Suite 1410, 1010 Sherbrooke Street West, Montreal, Quebec H3A 2R7. Tel. (514) 849-3708; Fax: (514) 849-9577*
- **Toronto** – *Suite 3, 3302 Bloor Street East, Toronto, Ontario M4W 1A8. Tel. (416) 967-3381; Fax: (416) 967-4101*

7. BASIC INFORMATION

DRIVING

If you're driving your own car into Austria, you won't need any customs documents when crossing the border. A valid American drivers' license and car registration is all you need. All drivers must be insured. Check with one of several automobile clubs located in Austria if you're unsure whether your insurance is valid. Children under the age of 12 are not allowed to sit next to the driver. They need to sit in the backseat and wear a seatbelt, along with all other passengers.

If you're traveling by motorcycle, you and your passenger must wear helmets. During the winter, you must have snow tires, which are necessary from Nov. 15 to the first Monday after Easter. During really snowy conditions, chains are required. Chains can be rented from the two Austrian automobile clubs, **OAMTC** or **ARBO**. Check a local phonebook for the branch nearest you. You can drive up to 62 mph an hour on trunk roads and 81 mph on the autobahn. For cars with trailers, the speed limit is 50 mph and 62 mph.

Don't drink and drive. The blood alcohol limit is 0.8 percent and is punishable by fines between 8,000 and 50,000 schillings. Your driver's license can also be confiscated.

EMERGENCY NUMBERS

Make sure you have these telephone numbers close at hand, since you never know when you may have an emergency. No area code is needed when dialing these numbers.

- *Ambulance: 144*
- *Fire: 122*
- *Police: 133*
- *Automobile Club emergency breakdown numbers:*
  OAMTC – 120; ARBO – 123

ECO-TOURISM

If you're interested in eco-tourism in Europe, you've chosen the right destination. As a country that depends substantially on tourist dollars, Austria has taken extraordinary measures to protect the country's natural resources and scenic beauty which visitors are flocking to see.

Austria has an extensive forest conservation program. Nationwide measures have been implemented to prevent high impact use of the country's forests by mountain delicate eco-systems.

ELECTRICITY

Austria uses 220/230 volts AC, singlephase at 50 cycles per second. So if you are planning to use American appliances, which use 110 volts, make sure to bring along a converter and a plug adapter.

HEALTH NEEDS

Medication is available at **Apotheken**, or pharmacies. If you need medication during off-hours, check any pharmacy window. The nearest pharmacy, open evenings, weekends and holidays, will be posted.

If you need a doctor during off-hours, you can check with the local police station, which will have names and addresses for you. All mountain resorts also have a special mountain rescue service.

MONEY & BANKING

The Austrian monetary unit is the **schilling**. One hundred **groschen** are equal to one schilling. Bills are in denominations of 5,000, 1,000, 500, 100, 50 and 20 schillings. There are also 20, 10, 5 and 1 schilling coins and 50 and 10 groschen coins.

Money can be exchanged at banks, post offices, and exchange kiosks. American Express checks are the most widely accepted traveler's checks. You can bring an unlimited amount of cash into and out of Austria.

The current rate of exchange is about 10 schillings to one US dollar.

Credit Cards

Don't assume that you can charge your hotel room or restaurant bill to your credit card, especially in smaller towns and villages. Many places don't accept credit cards, so plan to bring along extra traveler's checks or cash so that you don't find yourself coming up short. Credit cards that are accepted include American Express, Diners Club, Mastercard, and Visa.

MUSICAL ENTERTAINMENT

The Austrian opera and theater season is held from September to June. Some Viennese theaters continue their seasons during July and

August. The official concert season runs from October to June, but there are also several festivals and concerts featured during the off-season. Check with local tourist offices for details on performances.

LANGUAGE

German is the official language in Austria, but since English is a required course in the school system pretty much everyone speaks the language so you should have no problem communicating. Older Austrians and people in small villages may not speak English, however. If you run into that rare exception, you'd be amazed at how most people are patient and friendly and will try to help you find your way.

MEDIA

Don't expect to be seeing any movies during your trip unless you speak fluent German. Most American films are dubbed. However, if you are staying in Vienna several theaters show movies in their original versions or with German subtitles. Check a local newspaper to find out what version is being run. Newspapers in English are readily available at most kiosks, including the *International Herald Tribune*, *USA Today* and the European version of the *Wall Street Journal*.

Buying books in English is usually not a problem if you need something to read for your trip. Most large book stores in cities around the country have a selection of classics and best sellers available.

Although you won't be able to see any English language television unless your hotel has cable, you can turn into **Blue Danube Radio** at 103.8 on your FM dial. The station features a variety of English music from country to jazz to rock. News in English, German and French is broadcast throughout the day. Austrian Radio broadcasts news in English and French from 8:00 a.m. to 8:15 a.m.

PETS

You can bring your dog or cat into Austria as long as you can produce a valid vaccination certificate, including verification of rabies shots, with a certified translation of the documents in German. The vaccinations must be performed at least 30 days before entering the country, but not longer than a year before your arrival.

You may be surprised at how many hotels, pensions and *Zimmers*, or private rooms, will accept your pet during your stay in Austria. Check in advance when booking your hotel. Some hoteliers charge a supplement for pets.

POSTAL SERVICE

Post offices are generally open Monday to Friday from 8 a.m. to noon and from 2 p.m. to 6 p.m. Train station and main post offices are often open around the clock including Saturdays, Sundays and public holidays. Money also can be exchanged at all Austrian post offices.

Sending a postcard to the folks back home will cost 8.5 schillings. Stamps for letters are based on weight and start at 13 schillings when mailing to America.

RESTAURANT HOURS

In general, lunch is served between noon and 2 p.m. Dinner starts from 6 p.m. until usually 10 or ll p.m. A service charge of 10 to 15 percent is added to your bill automatically. However, if you are pleased with the service, it is customary to tip your waiter or waitress up to 10 percent of the bill.

SHOPPING

Most stores in Austria are open Monday through Friday from 8 a.m. until 6 p.m. Many close at lunchtime so don't try to do your shopping midday. Stores, groceries and markets are usually open until noon or 1 p.m. on Saturday. On the first Saturday of every month, many establishments stay open until 5 p.m. Stores are traditionally open the four Saturdays before Christmas until 6 p.m. Don't expect to pick up provisions on Sunday since it is nearly impossible to find anything open.

You can get reimbursed for the Value Added Tax (VAT) for items costing over 1,000 schillings. Be sure to inform the store's management when making your purchase. You will receive a form to be stamped at the airport before you check your luggage. Refunds can be collected at one of the banks in the airport.

If you're planning to leave Austria via train, make sure to ask the ticket office if a customs official will be on your train.If not, customs offices are located in all major railway stations. You can receive an exit certificate and, if you want, your purchases can be sent as part of your registered luggage.

SPAS

If you want to visit Austria for some rest and relaxation, not to mention pampering and preservation, visit one of the countries many spas and health resorts. Spas and health resorts are licensed and subject to periodic scientific checks. *For more information, contact Osterreichischer Heilbaderund Kurorteverband, Josefsplatz 6, A-1010 Vienna. If calling internationally, dial 43-1-512-1904. In Austria outside of Vienna, call 0-222-512-1904.*

TABAK-TRAFIK

Even if you're not a smoker, you'll want to keep track of where the nearest tobacconist is. Not only will you find cigarettes and newspapers, but you can also buy bus, streetcar, and U-Bahn tickets and stamps.

TELEPHONE

Making a phone call can be a real headache. Overseas fees and even local calls can be extremely costly. Avoid calling from your hotel where hefty surcharges are practically assured. You will still be charged local calling fees even if you use an American calling card. In Europe, the cost is eight schillings per minute, Monday through Friday from 8 a.m. to 6 p.m and six schillings per minute at all other times. If you need to make several calls, your best bet is to buy a local calling card from the post office, a news kiosk, or a tabak-trafik.

Post offices often have call boxes where you can make a phone call and then pay after you're finished. That way, you won't find yourself searching your pockets for schillings as your time is about to run out. To really save money, ask the postal clerk for the number in the call box. Then you can have the person you are calling ring you back.

Don't be alarmed that the number of digits for phone numbers seems to vary from four on up. Austria is updating its phone system so the number of digits fluctuate. When calling from one jurisdiction in Austria to another, you'll need to dial a zero first and then the three-digit area code for the region. When calling Vienna from within Austria, you must first dial 0222, but when dialing internationally, the city code is 1.

Faxing is also a good way to bypass the outrageous phone rates. Fax machines are available at the post office and the fees are reasonable even to overseas numbers. The **country code** for Australia is 0061, Canada and the U.S. is 001, and Britain is 0044.

PHONE HELP

Need help reaching out and touching someone? Here is a list of numbers to get you the information you need:
- *Directory assistance inside Austria: 1611*
- *Directory assistance for Europe: 1613*
- *Directory assistance for overseas: 1614*
- *Operator-assisted calls: 09*
- *Telegrams: 190*

TIME

Austria uses central European time. So if you're planning to call back home to the States, Austria is six hours ahead of Eastern Time (New York),

7 hours ahead of Central Time (Chicago), eight hours ahead of Mountain Time (Denver) and 9 hours ahead of Pacific Time (Los Angeles).

Daylight savings time in Austria begins the last Sunday in March and continues through September.

TIPPING

It is customary to tip up to 10 percent of your bill if you are happy with the service rendered at cafes, restaurants, hotels, taxis and hairdressers.

PUBLIC TRANSPORTATION

Public transportation in Austria is very extensive and punctual. Most cities have comprehensive streetcar and bus networks making it easy to get around without a car. If you do decide to rent a car, try reserving through an American agency in the U.S. The difference in rates is staggering, so you'll be sure to get the most from your vacation dollars if you book in advance.

But if you do decide to rent in Austria, all the major agencies are represented in larger cities. Smaller towns and villages will probably not have car rental facilities so plan to make arrangements in major urban areas. You will also have to drop off the car in larger cities.

WEIGHTS & MEASURES

Austria, like most of the world, uses the metric system. So instead of miles you'll be traveling in kilometers. In the grocery store, food is weighed in grams and kilos. Drinks and gasoline are sold by the liter. And altitude is measured in meters, not yards.

8. SPORTS & RECREATION

BIKING

Austria has miles and miles of **biking trails**. The country goes out of its way to make trails and roads accessible to bicyclists. Cities and villages alike have well-marked biking paths. Those trails that are shared with pedestrians are also marked.

If you want to get out of the city to do some biking in the great outdoors, the **Austrian Federal Railways** allows bikers to rent their wheels at stations throughout the country. Children's bikes are also available for rental. You can return your bicycle to any participating train station. Rail tickets are also reduced for cyclists, and special cars are especially adapted for bicycles. You can even ship your bike ahead to be picked up at the train station, which is nearest your destination. For bike reservations, *call 222-58-00-33-449;* for train information, *call 1717.*

CASINOS

If you want to try your luck, gambling establishments can be found around the country. Games include Roulette, Baccarat, American Roulette, Wheel of Fortune, Sic Bo, Poker and Blackjack. Many casinos also have slot machines.

Casinos operate all year round in Baden, Bregenz, Graz, Innsbruck, Linz, Riezlern/Kleinwalsertal, Salzburg, Seefeld in Tirol, Velden am Worther See and Vienna. During the summer and winter seasons, you can also gamble in Badgastein and Kitzbuhel. Casinos open in the 3 p.m. to 7 p.m. range. There is no cover charge except at the Velden and Graz casinos, where guests pay 210 schillings and receive 250 schillings in chips.

CAVING

Many people come to Austria for climbing the majestic peaks scattered across the country, but you may not realize that it's also possible to explore the mountains' innards. **Caving** is a very popular sport in the country and growing. Many local tourist offices can give you information on local caving clubs and guides who can lead you on a tour of the caves open to the public. Equipment rental is also possible at some locations.

You may be surprised by the underground world that you encounter from seething waterfalls to stalagmites and stalactites that have built up over thousands of years. For general information on caving, contact the **Verband Osterreichischer Hohlenforscher**, *A-1020 Vienna* or the **Landesverein Fur Hohlenkunde** in Salzburg, *Schloss Hellbrun, Objekt 9, A-5020 Salzburg*.

HIKING

Serious interest in hiking in Austria started in the 1860s, when exploring nature came into vogue as an organized form of recreation. Alpine societies were founded, maps outlining trails were published for the first time, and hiking and climbing equipment were developed.

Most mountain villages, no matter how small, have hiking programs based at the local tourist office. Guided day hikes, from two to seven hours, are often offered several days a week. Hikers will be charged a fee to pay for the guides. **Innsbruck** offers a free hiking program to visitors staying three nights or more in the city or in neighboring **Igls**. The season runs from June to September. Hiking equipment, including boots and backpacks, are available on loan.

Camping out is discouraged in Austria, where alpine weather is subject to change at a moment's notice. Instead, a system of **huts** has developed allowing hikers and climbers to stay and eat overnight so you won't have to lug around heavy backpacks and supplies. These are huts in name only. Most have full-service lodging facilities with restaurants or other food options available. The huts are usually about a four to five-hour hike apart so you can plan where to eat and sleep ahead of time. Since hikers don't have to carry their own supplies, the impact of people on the fragile alpine ecosystem is minimized.

Huts are required to house everyone there at nightfall. Private rooms are available on a first-come, first-serve basis. Bunks are also available at cheaper prices. Rooms cost about 250 schillings per person per night (about $25). A bunk will cost about 175 schillings. Breakfast is also available for an additional fee.

There are also self-service huts available to hiking association members and their guests. Only shelter is provided here. Reservations must be made in advance, and the hut's key must be picked up beforehand.

Hiker Etiquette

Some rules of Austrian hiker etiquette you should be aware of: You should take your hiking books off at the door and store them on available racks. Slippers or socks are worn inside the hut. This is often true, as well,

ALPINE CLUBS

For more information on hiking in Austria you can contact one of the organizations below. You also may want to consider becoming a member, depending on the amount of hiking you plan to do. You pay an initiation and an annual membership fee. As a member, you'll be charged abut 60 percent less for "hut" stays, earn a 25 percent reduction on train and bus rides in some mountain regions, have access to accident, liability, and rescue insurance and have access to maps and hiking guides. The Austrian National Tourist Office has applications available in English.

• Verband Alpiner Vereine Oesterreichs, Baeckerstrasse 16, A-1010 Vienna. Tel. 431-512-5488.

• Oesterreichischer Alpenklub, Getreidemarkt 3, A-1060 Vienna. Tel. 431-581-3858.

• Oesterreichischer Alpenverein, Wilhelm-Greil Strasse 15, A-6020 Innsbruck. Tel. 43-512-59-547.

• Oesterreichischer Touristenklub, Backerstrasse 16, A-1010 Vienna. Tel. 431-512-3844.

• Touristenverein "Die Naturfreunde," Viktoriagasse 6, A-1150. Tel. 431-892-3534.

• Oesterreichischer Touristenverein, Laudongasse 16, A-1080. Tel. 431-40-143-265.

• Europaeische Volkssport-Gemeinschaft Oesterreich, Koppstrasse 56, A-1160 Vienna. Tel. 431-492-3264.

when visiting an Austrian's home. Cooking, smoking and radios are not allowed in the bedrooms or in the bunk area. Lights out and complete quiet are required after 10 p.m.

U.S. Hiking Tour Operatiors

Hiking trips in Austria can be booked in advance through several U.S. travel agencies. Most of these trips include accommodations, two meals each day, and guided hikes of varying difficulties.

Try one of the following:

• **Adventure Sport Holidays**, *Tel. 800-628-9655; fax 413-562-3621.*
• **Alphorn Tours, Inc.**, *Tel. 800-ALPHORN; fax 215-794-7199.*
• **Guides For All Seasons**, *Tel. 800-457-4574; fax 916-994-3475.*
• **Mountain Travel Sobek**, *Tel. 800-227-2384; 510-525-7710.*
• **Swiss Hike**, *Tel. 360-754-0978; fax 360-754-4959.*
• **Wanderweg Holidays**, *Tel. 800-270-ALPS; fax 609-321-1040.*

SKIING

In 1897, Matthias Zdarsky wrote the world's first skiing manual and invented the first real ski binding. Eight years later, he organized the first shalom race in skiing history on the **Muckenkogel** in Lower Austria. **St. Anton am Arlberg** was the site of the first ski school and Austria continues to be a leader in the development and teaching of skiing techniques.

When World War II ended, Austria had only six ski lifts, but that number has surged to more than 3,500 lifts today. You can even ski here in the height of summer at eight glacier resorts. No matter what kind of runs you like to ski, you'll have your choice in Austria from steep slopes to moguls to glaciers. Several of the resorts offer overlapping tickets so you can ski all day without ever skiing down the same run.

You'll want to take a look at the extensive listings in the *Sports & Recreation* section of the Salzburg and Innsbruck & Tirol chapters, and to a lesser extent in the Vorarlberg, Lake District, and other destination chapters of this guide.

For cross-country skiers, Austria has 10,000 miles of cross country trails. Other winter sporting opportunities include swingbo, monoski, paraski, hang-gliding, snow-rafting, ski touring, skibobbing, tobagganning and ice skating.

For more information on skiing in Austria, contact the **Austrian Ski Federation**, *Olympiastrasse 10, A-6020 Innsbruck. Tel. 512-335010; fax 512-361998.*

American Tour Operators

Many American tour operators offer ski packages in Austria, including the following:
- **Adventures on Skis**, *815 North Road, Route 202, Westfield, MA 01085; Tel. 413-568-2855; 1-800-628-9655; fax 413-562-3621*
- **Adventure Tours**, *5949 Sherry Lane, #1900, Dallas, TX 75225, Tel. 214-360-5000; 1-800-999-9046; fax: 214-368-3457*
- **Ski Connections**, *15946 Wellington Way, Truckee, CA 96161; Tel. 916-582-1888; 1-800-SKI-1888; fax: 916-582-4893*
- **Value Holidays**, *10224 North Port Washington Road, Mequon, WI 53092, Tel. 414-241-6373; 1-800-558-6850; or 414-241-6379*
- **Wanderweg Holidays**, *519 Kings Croft, Cherry Hill, NY 08304; Tel. 609-321-1040; 1-800-270-ALPS; fax 609-321-1040*

9. TAKING THE KIDS

Parents traveling with their children to Austria are in for a pleasant surprise. Not only are children, from toddlers to teenagers, welcome, but there are several incentives to taking the kiddies along for the trip.

The Austrian countryside offers lots of choices for ideal family vacations. Many local farmers offer lodgings to families, and you can actually pitch in by feeding the animals or helping with the harvest. Check with regional tourist offices for details.

Babysitting is readily available for parents who may want a night out on their own. Many hotels have in-house facilities or can make arrangements to take care of the kids during the day or evening. If the hotel you're in doesn't offer this service, check with the local tourist office or university, which often can make babysitting arrangements for you.

There are many recreational activities you can participate in as a family. Skis and bike rentals are available for children, and hiking maps detail which trails are appropriate for children and the elderly. Skiing and mountaineering schools are plentiful throughout the country for Mom, Dad, and the kids. Take a cable car up one of the majestic Alpine peaks. Or head down under to one of the many salt mines or ice caves, which offer tours to amuse the whole family.

Culturally, Austria has many museums, concerts and castles that will keep even the most finicky child entertained. The country has a cornucopia of medieval fortresses, Renaissance castles, and Baroque palaces where children can pretend to step back in time. Many castles have exhibitions, concerts, or falconry displays to entertain the entire family, too.

Below is just a sampling of the fun possible for the kids. Each regional chapter will give you more detail about schedules, locations, and fees.

VIENNA

Most European capitals wouldn't be considered the ideal place to start a family vacation, but Vienna has something to offer everyone. One of the city's most famous landmarks is the giant ferris wheel at the **Prater amusement park**, where you can ride a carousel or be turned upside-down on one of several roller coasters.

The world-famous **Spanish Riding School** at the Hofburg will impress both children and their parents. **Schonbrunn castle** is a fairytale palace with an extensive coach collection, gardens, and showrooms. Or visit the **Donaupark** flower show gardens bordering the Danube.

LOWER AUSTRIA

The **Raabs Castle**, located 110 kilometers northwest of Vienna, houses a **Fairy Tales Museum**. Parents will also enjoy several rooms restored in the castle, which are open to the public.

LINZ

Outside of Vienna, you can take a boat ride down the Danube to **Linz**. Here, you and your children can ride Europe's steepest **mountain train**. The children's **grotto railroad** also features dwarf and fairy-tale scenes.

If you're in Linz during the Christmas season, you and your children will love the **Schlossmuseum**, housed in one of the oldest Austrian castles with a magnificent view of the city below. During the weeks before Christmas, the castle museum features an extravagant display of creches open to visitors. Each creche has dozens of figures in native costume on display and is a real treat for children young and old.

THE LAKE DISTRICT

A great day trip with children is the **Dachstein Caves**. There are more than 13,000 cubic meters of ice in the caves, which form dramatic peaks and gorges that you can explore on guided tours. There is a fascinating museum that gives you an idea of the challenges and strange life forms facing past cave explorers.

The Lake District is also famous for its **salt mines**. Children and their parents alike can race down the slides the miners used to access the caves, cruise across underground lakes, or ride the rails down to the mines. Two of the better known salt mines are those in **Bad Ischl**, and those in **Hallstat**.

SALZBURG

In **Salzburg**, make sure you visit the **Toy Museum** and pay a visit to the fortress overlooking the city with its torture chamber that will inspire thrills and chills. This Baroque city also is an ideal place to introduce children to opera at the **Marionette Theater**, which features full-length operas by Mozart and Rossini, acted out by the puppets. Parents won't be bored either. In the **Mirabell Gardens**, visit the dwarf garden with statues of the former court curiosities.

Not far from Salzburg, the **Wildpark Ferleiten** makes a nice detour. There are alpine animals, from deer to bears to birds of prey. Paths take you through the park to the various animals on display. There is also a children's playground with bumper cars, a kiddie train, and a carousel.

INNSBRUCK & TIROL

No visit to **Innsbruck** would be complete without a trip to the **Alpine Zoo** with many rare species native to the region. In the **Hofkirche**, the larger-than-life bronze sculptures of kings and queens surrounding Emperor Maximilian's tomb is a dazzling site. The tourist office in Innsbruck also publishes a guide on hotels in the province catering to children and their families. The guide clearly marks which hotels have facilities for babies, where pets are welcome and what kind of recreational facilities are available.

Elsewhere in Tirol, for the athletically-minded family in good shape, there's the **Family Bicycle Marathon**, a 25 to 50 kilometer race. To be eligible, at least one parent and one child between six and 14-years old must register for the race which starts on the **Mieminger Plateau**. Less strenuous but still good exercise is the **Alpinschule Innsbruck**, which offers 40 different hiking routes mapped out for you in the Stubai Alps, Tux Alps, Karwendel Mountains, and the Mieminger Mountain Chain. The hikes take between three and five hours. Hiking experience is not necessary. The hikes are appropriate for children over eight years old and for adults of all ages.

VORARLBERG PROVINCE

Each summer, Austria's western most province, **Vorarlberg**, hosts approximately 200 events during its **Children's Wonderland** program in city's around the region. Highlights include the **Giant Chocolate Festival** in Bludenz and the **Festival of Children's and Young People's Drama** in Brandnertal in July. Other activities include adventure hikes, hobby afternoons, and Indian villages.

Vorarlberg also has a **Family Club** program, with 32 participating hotels and restaurants and seven resorts. Family Club hotels will always be able to provide a cot for a child to sleep on, facilities for preparing baby food, a playground, game room, and babysitting facilities. Discounts for children and families are available as well as special programs for children like a "ski kindergarten."

10. FOOD & DRINK

If you're a fan of stick-to-your-ribs food than Austria is the place for you. This a real meat and potatoes kind of country with meals tending to be on the heavy side. Dieters should leave their good intentions at home to really enjoy the best of what the country has to offer in cuisine. During the glory days of the Hapsburg Empire, the Austrians borrowed heavily from the countries over which they ruled. The country's most famous dish, *Wiener Schnitzel*, actually originated in Milan. Goulash was just one of the dishes imported from Hungary.

What is called Austrian cooking is actually a melange of influences from Europe that have been adapted for local palates. But one of Vienna's most famous dishes, *Tafelspitz*, or boiled beef served with apple-horserad-ish, chive sauce and potatoes, was developed by city chefs for the emperor. Breakfast always include *semmel*, a white-bread roll. Butter and jam come with it. Cheese and ham or other cold cuts are also often served. Eggs are usually soft or hard boiled, although you can usually order your eggs fried or scrambled as well. Coffee or tea and juice are served too.

Lunch and dinner usually start with a soup or salad course, followed by a main dish and then dessert. Soups are often clear broth with an addition of noodles, vegetables or dumplings. Although you can usually order a green salad, the typical Austrian versions tend to be dressed with mayonnaise-based sauces. Pickled vegetables are also often served as a salad course.

Entrees usually include meat and a starch, although often no green vegetable, so ask before ordering. Chicken is usually roasted, although you can sometimes order it fried. Beef or pork can be stewed, roasted or fried, as in the case of *Schnitzel*, and is generally accompanied by potatoes, either boiled or fried. Rice or noodles are usually also offered. Being a predominantly Catholic country, fish or vegetarian dishes are generally served on Fridays.

WHICH WINE WITH WHICH DISH?

*If you're not sure which Austrian wine to order with what you're eating, the following list may help you make head or tails of the selections. If you're ordering **fish**, a bottle of Gruner Veltliner, Welschriesling, Rheinriesling, Weisser Burgunder or Neuburger should compliment your meal. With **veal and pork**, Gruner Veltliner and Welschriesling are good choices. **Beef and game** need stronger wines to compliment their flavors so try a bottle of St. Laurent or Weisser Burgunder.*

*Rheinrieslings, Muller-Thurgau, Traminer and Blauer Portugieser are good choices with **poultry**. To accompany **cheese**, Gruner Veltlin, Weisser Burgunder, Welschriesling and Blaufrankisch are solid selections. **Desserts** merit sweeter varieties including Traminer, Muskat-Ottonel and Muller-Thurgau.*

Save room for dessert, which is generally superb. Probably the most famous is the *Sachertorte*, a heavenly combination of chocolate cake and apricot filling covered with a layer of chocolate. But don't stop there. Austria has a wealth of cakes, strudels, and pastries to tempt the palate. Make sure to order coffee with your choice of sweet. Coffee is practically another art form in Austria, especially in Vienna. In coffee houses around the country, you can order everything from espresso to cappachino to a *melange*, a mixture of coffee and whipped cream. All are delicious. The country is also justifiably known for its beer and wine.

Several beers, including *Steigl*, are brewed in Austria. Make sure to spend at least one evening of your stay in a local beer hall or beer garden where you'll get a chance to get to know the locals, who are especially friendly after a beer or two. Seating is usually at benches and picnic-style tables so you'll literally be rubbing elbows with your neighbors.

Austria also has a reputation for excellent wines which grow in the Danube valley and in the southern and eastern provinces. If you're vacationing in Austria during the fall, take a drive along the Danube stopping at one of the local **Heurigen**, or wine taverns. Vintners sell and serve their new wines during the different stages of fermentation. Several Heurigen can also be found in Vienna in former wine villages now absorbed by the capital. (See the Vienna chapter for more details.)

AUSTRIAN CUISINE TERMS

If you're not familiar with the German language, wading through an Austrian menu can seem incomprehensible. Here are some common dishes that should help make your selections a little easier.

Soups

Fleischstruddelsuppe – broth with ground meat
Fritattensuppe – broth with sliced pancakes
Griessnockerlsuppe – broth with flour dumplings
Leberknodelsuppe – broth with liver dumplings
Markknodelsuppe – broth with bone marrow dumplings
Nudelsuppe – broth with noodles
Knoblauchsuppe – garlic soup
Bauernsuppe – cabbage and sausage soup
Erbensuppe – split pea soup

Beef

Beinfleisch – boiled beef ribs
Rindsbraten – braised beef
Rindsguasch – beef goulash
Rindsroulade – rolled steaks
Tafelspitz – boiled rump roast
Zweibelrostbraten – beef cutlet with onions

Veal

Gefullet Kalbsbrust – stuffed veal roast
Gerostete Leber – sauteed calf's liver
Kalbsleber gebacken – calf's liver baked in bread crumbs
Kalbsvogerl mit Rahm – veal knuckles cooked in sour cream
Naturschnitzel – sauteed veal scallop
Nierenbraten – roast loin of veal

Pork

Bauernschmaus – sauerkraut with various types of pork
Krautfleish – pork roast with sauerkraut
Krenfleisch – pork roast with horse radish
Schweinsschnitzel – scallop of pork

Poultry

Backhuhn – fried chicken
Brathuhn – roast chicken
Gebratene Ente – roast duck
Gans – goose
Truthahn – turkey

Game

Hasenrucken – saddle of hare
Hirschrucken – saddle of deer

Hirschragout – deer stew
Hirschschulter – shoulder of deer
Rehragout – venison stew
Rehrucken gebraten – saddle of roast venison

Fish
Fogosch – perch
Forelle – trout
Karpfen – carp
Hecht – pike
Saibling – local fish

Desserts
Buchteln – vanilla cream filled dumplings
Germknodel – sour-dough dumplings
Marmeladepalatschinken – pancakes with jam
Marillenknodel – apricot dumplings
Mohnnudeln – poppy seed dumpling dessert
Mohr im Hemd – chocolate pudding with whipped cream
Profesen – fritters stuffed with jam
Salzburger Nockerl – souffle
Topfenknodel – cream cheese dumplings
Zwetschkenknodel – plum dumplings

Drinks
Mineralwasser – mineral water
Rotwein – red wine
Weisswein – white wine
Gluhwein – mulled wine
helles Bier – light beer
dunkles Bier – dark beer
Kaffee – coffee
Tee mit Zitrone/Milch – Tea with lemon/milk
Saft – juice

Miscellaneous
Brot – bread
Eiern – eggs
Geback – pastry
Zucker – sugar
Gruner Salat – green salad

11. AUSTRIA'S BEST HOTELS

The right hotel can make or break your vacation. In general, accommodations in Austria are first-rate. But there are several extraordinary hotels around the country that will make your stay even more memorable. Most, too, have gourmet restaurants where you can indulge your penchant for fine dining.

In Anif
ROMANTIK HOTEL SCHLOSSWIRT
A-5081 Anif. Tel. 6246-72175; fax 6246-72175-80.
Doubles start at 1,300 schillings.
All credit cards accepted.

This is an exceptionally charming hotel on the banks of the pond fronting Anif's famous **Water Castle**. Some of the accommodations look out to the nearby castle, so make sure to request "a room with a view." The "Castle Inn" once belonged to the archbishops of Salzburg, and records indicate it started operating as an inn in 1607. In 1843, Count Alois von Arco-Stepperg, who owned the Water Castle, acquired the inn. Accommodations are also available in a 15th century annex.

The restaurant, decorated with blue and white tablecloths, manages to combine elegance and coziness at the same time. The menu features lamb, roast duckling and the ubiquitous *Wiener Schnitzel*.

In Bregenz
DEURING SCHLOSSLE
Ehre-Guta Platz 4, A-6900 Bregenz. Tel. 5574-47800;
fax 5574-4780080. Double rooms start at 900 schillings per person.
Visa, American Express and Diners Card accepted.

The castle hotel of **Deuring Schlossle** looms above the city on a hillside overlooking Bregenz's medieval old town. This first-class hotel is known for lavishing attention on its clients. Rooms are filled with rustic folk art and furniture. The smallest details are not overlooked even to the dried flowers hanging in the old stone alcoves.

The hotel also has an impressive restaurant with a lovely terrace for dining. The menu changes daily depending on seasonal ingredients. Heino Hubler is the chef, and the renown of his cooking has gourmets flocking to the restaurant from miles around. The dining room is elegantly decorated with Oriental rugs and white linens. A mini-golf course is also free for guests to use.

> *In Durnstein*
> ## HOTEL SCHLOSS DURNSTEIN
> *A-3601 Durnstein. Tel. 2711-212; fax 2711-351.*
> *Doubles start at 980 schillings per person.*
> *All credit cards accepted.*

Local legend says that the Brothers Grimm drew inspiration from this castle, which now houses the elegant **Hotel Schloss Durnstein**. The Baroque castle, overlooking the waters of the blue Danube, was built in 1630 by the Starhemberg princes.

Today, the hotel is beautifully decorated with Renaissance and 17th century furniture. Rooms have inlaid wood floors, high ceilings and chandeliers. The Hotel Schloss Durnstein also has a patio swimming pool surrounded by a rose covered wall. Fitness facilities and a sauna are also available to guests. The restaurant in the castle has a wide variety of fish dishes from which to choose, including trout with saffron and perch fillet. The wine list has a good selection of vintages from the Wachau region.

> *In Graz*
> ## SCHLOSSBERG HOTEL
> *Kaiser Franz Josef Kai 30, A-8010 Graz. Tel. 316-8070-0;*
> *fax 316-8070-160. Doubles start at 2,000 schillings, including breakfast.*
> *All credit cards accepted.*

Located at the foot of the Schlossberg, the elegantly appointed **Schlossberg Hotel** is filled with antique country furniture. The building dates from the 15th century and wonderfully combines a mixture of old world charm with modern amenities.

The hotel has a rooftop garden with a swimming pool, sauna, solarium, and fitness studio. Private guest parking is available. There is no restaurant in the hotel, but you're within easy walking distance of downtown Graz and the myriad restaurants located there, but far enough away not to be bothered by the crowds.

In Innsbruck
GOLDENER ADLER HOTEL-RESTAURANT
Altstadt, A-6020 Innsbruck. Tel. 512-586334; fax 512-584409.
Doubles start at 730 schillings per person. All credit cards accepted.

The **Goldener Adler Hotel** has a rich history since its founding in 1390. Emperor Charles V was reported to have eaten here in 1552. Emperor Joseph II later stayed here after visiting his sister Marie Antoinette in Paris.

The hotel continues this tradition of superior service today, with a helpful and charming staff. Rooms are elegantly furnished with regional pieces or more modern furniture depending on your preference.

The hotel also has an excellent restaurant featuring Tirolean specialties. Dishes include venison with cranberries, pork fillet with mushrooms and spinach dumplings. Tirolean and Austrian wines are also showcased on the menu.

In Klagenfurt
HOTEL PALAIS PORCIA
Neuer Platz 13, A-9020 Klagenfurt. Tel. 463-511590;
fax 463-511590-30. Doubles start at 675 schillings per person.
All credit cards accepted.

If you're a fan of Baroque opulence then the **Hotel Palais Porcia** is the place for you to stay. If elegant simplicity is more your style, stay away. The hotel combines a hodgepodge of styles from throughout the centuries from French chateaus to the Biedermeier period. You can choose a canopied bed in red plush in a recreation of the high Baroque style, or a room in icy blue satin mimicking Versailles. None of the hotel's 35-rooms are alike.

Guests are served a champagne breakfast in a replica of Versailles' Hall of Mirrors. Dozens of hand carved masks from Tuscany decorate the Renaissance Bar.

In Lake Fuschl
HOTEL SCHLOSS FUSCHL
A-5322 Hof Bei Salzburg. Tel. 6229-2253-0; fax 6229-2253531.
Rooms start at 1,300 schillings per person. All credit cards accepted.

The **Hotel Schloss Fuschl** is tops for its elegance, attentive staff and attention to detail. The hotel, which was built in 1450, was once a hunting lodge and summer residence for the Salzburg archbishops. Although literally just on the other side of the lake from Fuschl, the hotel has a secluded atmosphere. You'll feel like you're staying in your own private lake resort.

There's a real old world charm here, mixing antiques with the comfort of modern amenities. Rooms are beautifully decorated with oriental carpets, rich fabrics, and fresh flowers. There's a beauty farm is you're in the mood to be pampered. That striving for perfection is also apparent in the hotel's restaurant, which features a selection of local fish dishes.

In Salzburg
HOTEL SCHLOSS MONCHSTEIN
Monchsberg Park 26, A-5020 Salzburg. Tel. 662-84-85-55-0; fax 662-84-85-59. Doubles start at 2,900 schillings. All credit cards accepted.

The five-star **Hotel Schloss Monchstein** is located in a former castle, built in 1358, right at the top of the Monchsberg. Originally the castle was used for guests of the archbishop. In 1948, the castle was made into a hotel. The staff here is discreet and accommodating. Rooms are elegant, and the garden is expansive and ideal for an evening stroll.

The ivy covered castle's chapel is now available for christenings or weddings. If you decide to celebrate your special event here, a plaque commemorating the day can be added to the hotel's growing collection. The hotel also features the first-class **Paris-Lodron Restaurant** with a variety of authentic Austrian dishes and international favorites. Selections include prawns with ginger garlic butter with wild rice risoto, grilled tenderloin with truffle sauce and roast lamb.

In Vienna
HOTEL BRISTOL
Karntner Ring 1, A-1010 Vienna. Tel. 222-51-516-0; fax 222-51-516-550. Doubles start at 5,100 schillings. All credit cards accepted.

Across the street from the famous State Opera House on the ring, the **Hotel Bristol** was founded in 1894 by Karl Wolf, a brewery owner from Pilsenetz. The guest list reads like a Who's Who listing with such names as the Duke of Windsor, Enrico Caruso and Arthur Rubenstein. The personal touches in the hotel's 146 luxurious rooms and suites make you feel as if you're staying in someone's elegantly furnished private residence rather than a hotel.

Rooms are filled with antiques, original works of art and sumptuous fabrics selected from the Baroque, Regency and Biedermeier periods. Everything is perfectly coordinated with exquisite details such as hand-blown crystal chandeliers, ceiling stenciling and thick carpeting.

The Bristol's restaurant **The Korso** is one of Austria's finest. Covered with dark wood panelling and Baroque marble columns and hung with crystal and brass chandeliers, the dining room provides a sophisticated backdrop to any meal. Chef Reinhard Gerer has been awarded a Michelin star and three toques from Gault-Millau for his innovative menus and deft, light hand preparing classic favorites. For more informal dining, you can select the **Sirk Rotisserie** or the **Cafe**. Or have a drink in the **Bristol Bar**, the oldest cocktail bar in Vienna.

For business travelers, the hotel offers the Bristol Executive Center, with faxes, lap top computers, worldwide reservation system and Dow Jones news so you won't feel as if you've ventured too far from the office.

In Vienna
HOTEL IMPERIAL
Karntner Ring 16, A-1010 Vienna. Tel. 222-501-10-0;
fax 222-50-110-410. Doubles begin at 5,100 schillings.
All credit cards accepted.

If you want to be treated like royalty and visiting heads of state, then the **Imperial Hotel** is the right selection for you. Originally the hotel, near the State Opera House on the ring, served as the Wurttemberg Palace and was inaugurated as a hotel by Emperor Franz Joseph in 1873. This is a favorite hotel for many Austrians, and in 1994 the Hotel Imperial was awarded the World's Best Hotel by readers of *Conde Nast Traveler*.

All 128 rooms and 32 suites have been carefully restored to preserve their 19th century elegance. Most of the furnishings are antiques from hand carved bed frames to matching armories. Many walls are covered with intricate brocade as they would have been a century ago. The service is impeccable and your slightest whim will be taken care of in no time flat.

The **Restaurant Imperial** serves traditional Austrian specialties descended from the monarchy and lighter international cuisine in a dining room covered in dark wood panelling and overseen by a portrait of the Empress Elisabeth. The **Cafe Imperial** is a perfect spot for either a light dinner or a cup of coffee and a slice of the hotel's renowned *Imperial Torte*. Even if you choose not to stay at the hotel, the cafe is worth a visit.

In Vienna
HOTEL IM PALAIS SCHWARZENBERG
Schwarzenbergplatz 9, A-1030 Vienna. Tel. 222-798-4515;
fax 222-798-4714. Doubles start at 3,300 schillings per person.
All credit cards accepted.

The **Hotel Im Palais Schwarzenberg** was formerly the summer residence of the Schwarzenberg princes, and you'll feel like a member of royalty yourself during your stay here. The Baroque castle, created by the famous architects Lukas von Hildebrandt and Fischer von Erlach, was built in the 17th century and has a 18-acre park where visitors can stroll the day away. You'll forget you're in the heart of Vienna while staying in any of the hotel's 38 rooms or suites.

The elegance is continued in the interior where a grand staircase leads to the round, gilt lounge under the castle's marble dome. Hotel rooms are furnished with period antiques, old portraits and walls covered with silky satin. The bathrooms, though, are large and modern.

The Schwarzenberg's restaurant, overlooking the lush private grounds, features French and Austrian specialties including goulash in cream sauce and lobster timbale. An extensive selection of wines from the neighboring province of Burgenland are also showcased. Or you can relax in front of a roaring fire in the Kaminzimmer or the Palais Bar where you can eat a light lunch and snacks.

The Tennis Club Schwarzenberg has five clay courts open from May through October. There's also a private croquet course and a two-mile jogging track.

12. VIENNA

INTRODUCTION

Vienna (Wien) maintains the regal grandeur from when it was formerly the seat of the Hapsburg's sprawling empire. Austria's capital is the country's smallest province, but its most populous. The region only covers an area of 160 square miles, and is home to more than 1.6 million people – almost one-fifth of Austria's population.

The Romans called Vienna *Vindobona* 2,000 years ago when the city served as an important imperial stronghold. Centuries later, the Turks coveted the city's strategic location and laid siege to Vienna in 1529 and 1683. Vienna reached the zenith of its power in the late 19th century when the Hapsburg Empire included more than 50 million subjects in central Europe. Vienna today still retains much of its imperial glory from the Hapsburgs, who ruled for 640 years. Baroque castles, churches, and buildings from past centuries are scattered throughout the city.

But unfortunately you may also encounter a certain imperious attitude on the part of the Viennese. There is a certain brusque rudeness and rigidity that can drive visitors crazy. Just consider it part of the experience of sight-seeing in Vienna. You will be dazzled by the beauty of the architecture. **St. Stephen's Cathedral** looms above the skyline, marking the heart of the city's old section. The **Hofburg Imperial Palace** is nearby, as are the training grounds of the world famous **Lipizzaner stallions**. And don't miss the pageantry of the **Spanish Riding School**.

Opera houses and concert halls still resonate with music created at the height of the empire. Vienna is the city of music and no visit would be complete without at least one night hearing the **Vienna Boy's Choir** or a concert by one of its famed composers. Stroll along **the ring**, Vienna's famous boulevard created after the city's former fortification's were razed for its construction. Here you'll see classic buildings from the **Museum of Fine Arts** to the **Parliament** building to the neo-Gothic **Rathaus**, or city hall. Experience the lavish lifestyle of the Hapsburgs by visiting the **Belvedere Palace** and its formal gardens. And, of course, you must visit the city's most famous sight of all, **Schonbrunn Palace**, the Hapsburg's summer home. The bright yellow palace has 1,441 rooms, although only 45 are on public display. Then plan a visit to the ornate gardens and the palace zoo, which dates back to 1752, making it the oldest in Europe.

And when you've had your fill of former imperial glories, head over to the **Prater amusement park**, where you can ride the century-old giant ferris wheel and gaze over the entire city from a height of more than 200 feet.

ORIENTATION

Monuments, museums, and other sights of historical interest are designated with white signs bearing a gold eagle, the national crest of Austria. The signs also have red and white flags that mark the sights. You can figure out which district, or *Bezirk*, you're in by looking at the street signs. The number of the district is printed before the street name, so *5 Hamburgerstrasse* means that you are in the fifth district. Addresses are also printed this way, so the number preceding the street name is the number of the district.

If you are staying in Vienna for at least a weekend, you might want to invest in a **Vienna Card**. For 180 schillings, the card enables you to take all Viennese public transportation and offers reductions at selected museums, shops, cafes, restaurant and *Heurigen* taverns. You can buy the card at many hotels, tourist information offices, and Vienna Transport offices. You can also order the card from overseas with your credit card by calling *431-798-44-00-28*.

The tourist office also sponsors walking tours of the city and private tours can be arranged. The tours cost 108 schillings per person, excluding admission fees. Tickets for children cost 60 schillings. Children under 14 must be accompanied by an adult. Tours include "Imperial Palace and Its Emperors," "Architecture at the Turn of the Century," and "1,000 Years of Jewish Tradition in Vienna."

When dialing Vienna from abroad, the **country code** is *43* and the **city code** is *1*. From inside the country, however, Vienna's area code is *0222*.

Safety

Vienna is much less dangerous than most major cities around the world. But like any major metropolis, Vienna does have its share of minor crimes. Tourists should especially be aware of pickpockets around Stephansplatz near the cathedral, Karlsplatz, and Schwedensplatz. There tend to be quite a few drifters hanging around these areas and in the U-Bahn stations. They may approach you for money, but they are rarely aggressive. Keep an eye on your purse and wallets in these areas. Don't make yourself an easy target by being conspicuous with your money and taking out large wads of cash to pay for something.

But that said, Vienna is much safer than most American cities and you shouldn't be worried about taking public transportation in the evenings. If anything should happen, many major U-Bahn stations have police stations that can assist you.

ARRIVALS & DEPARTURES

By Air

Vienna-Schwechat Airport is 12 miles, or about a 20 minute drive, from the city center. Taxis charge a 12 schilling fee for each piece of baggage. An airport surcharge of about 110 schillings will also be included. See *Getting Around Town* below if you need to call a cab.

Non-stop bus service is available for 60 schillings. Buses leave from the City Air Terminal, *Wien Mitte, Landstrasse*, between 5 a.m. and 11 p.m. and from the airport to the City Air Terminal between 6 a.m. and midnight. Buses also run between the airport to the Sudbahnhof and Westbahnhof train stations between 6:40 a.m. and 10:40 p.m.

To reach Schwechat Airport information, *you can call 711-10-23-31 or 22-32 around the clock.*

By Train

There are several train stations serving the city, including the West Train Station (Westbahnhof) and the South Train Station (Sudbahnhof). You can purchase a ticket or get train schedules at any location, but check your ticket to confirm from which station you're leaving. All are accessible by U-Bahn or streetcar. For train information 24-hours a day, *call 17-17.*

By Car

If you're coming from Salzburg, the A1 east will take you directly into Vienna. From Graz, simply head north along the A2.

VIENNA TRANSPORT TIPS

There are several telephone numbers you can call for **transportation information** *in Vienna. So whether you're going by train, plane, or bus, here is a list to help you set up your schedule.*

Rail timetables *are available by calling 17-17 24-hours a day.* **Bus timetables** *are available by telephoning 711-01 from 7 a.m. to 7 p.m.* **Ship timetables** *are available by calling 1537. Schwechat Airport information is available at 711-10-22-31 or 32 24-hours a day.*

GETTING AROUND TOWN

By Bike

Vienna is a biker's dream of a capital city. There are miles and miles of bicycle trails, most separate from pedestrian paths. You'll have little problem getting around town, and drivers, in general, are more respectful of cyclists here than in other major cities. Many hotels have places to check your bike. Ask about facilities when you're making reservations.

If you're interested in sight seeing on two wheels, call **Vienna Bike** *at 319-1258.*

By Boat

If you'd like to see Vienna from the blue Danube, boat excursions are available from April to October by the **Danube Steamship Company**. For more information or reservations, *call 727-50-451.*

By Car

If you don't have to drive in downtown Vienna, by all means avoid it. The Viennese drivers are not known for their patience and you may find yourself greeted by annoyed honking as you try to negotiate the city's old streets. Matters are complicated by the fact that many streets are one way or pedestrian-only thoroughfares, so you may find yourself lost in no time. Parking is also a nightmare. So save the car for excursions outside of the city if you can. If you must venture into the city center, parking is available in limited parking zones. **Parking vouchers**, for up to an hour and a half, can be purchased at banks, newsstands, or tabaks.

If you plan to rent a car, try to make arrangements before your trip, since you'll save substantially on rates. Here are the international car rental offices in Vienna.

• **Avis,** *1010 Opernring 3-5. Tel. 587-62-41; fax 587-49-00; at the airport, 1100 Gudrunstrasse 179A. Tel. 601-87-0; fax 606-12-78 or 606-12-81.*
• **Budget**, *Hilton Hotel, on the Stadtpark. Tel. 71-46-565; fax 71-47-238; at the airport, 711-10-2711; fax 711-10-3728.*
• **Europcar**, *Richard Strauss Strasse 12. Tel. 505-42-00; fax 505-44-81; at the airport, Tel. 711-10-33-16; fax 711-10-37-16.*

If you have car trouble, call the **Automobile, Motorcycle, and Touring Association** for help around the clock *at 120* or the **Automobile, Motorcycle, and Bicycle Association** *at 123*.

By Horse-Drawn Carriage

Travel around the city as the Hapsburgs did in the last century via horse-drawn carriage, called *Fiaker* in German. The carriages, which get their name from the Church of St. Fiacre in Paris where hackney carriages once waited for clients, are available in front of the National Library near the Hofburg on Heldenplatz, next to St. Stephen's Cathedral, and on the Albertinaplatz.

Although once an integral part of the city's transportation, only about 40 carriages remain in service today. A 20 to 30-minute ride costs about 400 schillings. For 45 minutes to an hour, you'll pay about 800 schillings. Be sure to ask the price before setting off on your ride. If the history of the *Fiaker* interests you, there is a museum devoted to the subject. See *Seeing the Sights* below.

By Public Transportation

Part of the Viennese experience is taking a ride on a **tram** around the ring. Besides being imminently practical, freeing you from the hassle of driving, a ride on a streetcar will give you a good idea of how the city is oriented.

However, you may opt to take the **U-Bahn** subway system during rush hours since the trams are subject to the vagaries of Vienna's traffic. Otto Wagner, one of the founder's of Vienna's Art Nouveau movement, designed many of the stations used for the original **Stadtbahn**.

Several types of multi-use tickets are available. For 50 schillings, you can buy a ticket good for 24 hours on all trams, U-Bahns, and buses within the city. A 72 hour ticket is available for 115 schillings, and an 8 day ticket can be bought for 235 schillings. Other tickets include a 4-ride ticket for 60 schillings, a block of five tickets for 75 schillings, and a one week ticket for 125 schillings, for which you'll need a passport-size photo. Many U-Bahn stations have self-service photo machines where you can get your picture taken. Tickets can be bought at the Vienna Transport Authority's ticket sales offices in U-Bahn stations or tobacconists. Tickets can also be purchased for individual rides on the tram or bus from the driver, but they'll cost you slightly more.

Make sure you validate your ticket in the bus or tram or before entering a line on the U-Bahn. If you get caught with an unvalidated ticket, you'll be socked with a hefty fine. The city also operates **night buses** on several bus lines. Stops are marked with black signs with an "eye" to designate the night lines. Tickets cost 25 schillings. For **public transportation information**, *call 711-01*. The office is open from 7 a.m. to 7 p.m.

From May to October, you can also see the city in an **old-time streetcar**. For information or reservations, *call 587-3186*.

By Taxi

You can catch a cab around the ring and from specially marked taxi stands in the first district where most of the principal monuments are located. Taxi fares are metered. A 12 schilling surcharge will be added for rides between 11 p.m. and 6 a.m., on Sundays and public holidays, for cabs ordered by telephone and for individual pieces of luggage. Supplements are also added for rides to the airport. It's customary to tip drivers 10 percent of the total fare.

You can order a taxi by calling 1716, 31300, 40100, 60160 or 81400.

WHERE TO STAY

If you haven't already booked the accommodations for your stay, head over to the **Tourist Information Office**, *Karnter Strasse 38*. They will arrange a room for you daily between 9 a.m. and 7 p.m. If you're planning a longer stay or would prefer to stay in an apartment, the travel agency **Odyssee**,*8, Laudongasse 7, Tel.402-6061; fax 402-6061-11*, can help make a reservation for you at either a hotel or a sublet apartment.

The **Alda Travel Agency**,*1, Universitatsstrasse 11, Tel. 4021-6260; fax 408-3515*, can also arrange accommodations with families in private homes or apartments in the city. Otherwise, here is a list of hotels from the most luxurious and expensive to be found in Vienna to basic, bargain-basement accommodations.

In the listings below, the first number you'll see, in bold and preceding the name of the hotel, corresponds to the number on the hotel map we've provided for you. The number preceding the street name – immediately after the name of the hotel – is the district location, and the number after the street name is the street address. So Albatros, the first hotel reviewed below, is located in the 9th district on Liechtensteinstrasse, number 89.

1. ALBATROS, *9, Liechtensteinstrasse 89. Tel. 317-3508; fax 317-35-08-85. Doubles begin at 720 schillings per person, breakfast included. All credit cards accepted.*

The Albatros is close to the American Embassy and just a trolley ride away from the city center. The rooms here are comfortable and modern, although not as charming as some of the pensions inside the ring. But they are much more spacious, so you can spread out and not feel cramped. The restaurant at the hotel features the usual Austrian favorites. Guests can check their bicycles at facilities in the hotel.

2. AM STEPHANSPLATZ, *1, Stephansplatz 9. Tel. 534-05-0; fax 534-05-711. Doubles start at 860 schillings per person, breakfast included. All credit cards.*

You can't beat this hotel for location – right across the square from the cathedral. So if being in the heart of town is your main concern this hotel may be for you. Rooms are furnished in peachy pastels and silk flowers. The staff can be somewhat imperious, however. The hotel boasts a lovely cafe with cakes, coffees, and light meals available. Outdoor seating on the Domplatz is available during warm weather.

3. ANA GRAND HOTEL WIEN, *1, Karntner Ring 9. Tel. 515-80-0; fax 515-1313. Doubles start at 4,500 schillings. All credit cards accepted.*

The Ana Grand Hotel Wien is incredibly luxurious. Rooms are beautifully furnished in period furniture and rich fabrics. A business center, laundry, and hairdresser are among the special services available at this exceptional hotel. There is also a gourmet restaurant, **Le Ciel**. The restaurant, one of the best in Vienna, features Viennese dishes with a French touch. The **Unkai** restaurant specializes in Japanese cuisine from sushi to Sashimi. There are also two bars and a traditional Viennese cafe here.

4. AMBASSADOR, *1 Neuer Markt 5. Tel. 51-466; fax 515-1313. Doubles start at 1,575 schillings per person. All credit cards accepted.*

The dark wood panelling and plush, overstuffed furniture give you the impression that you're walking into an exclusive men's club from the last century. The slightly worn atmosphere wears well and adds to the overall elegance of this establishment rather than detracts. The staff is quite friendly, too. There are facilities to check your bike if you've brought it along on your trip.

5. ASTORIA, *1, Fuhrichgasse 1. Tel.51-577-0; fax 515-7782. Doubles start at 975 schillings per person, breakfast included. All credit cards accepted.*

Just off Vienna's most famous shopping street, Karntner Strasse, the Hotel Astoria is in the heart of the pedestrian quarter. Rooms are furnished in turn-of-the-century antiques and cool fabrics. The service is friendly and attentive also. The restaurants serves both classic Austrian dishes and international specialties.

6. AVIS, *8, Pfeilgasse 4. Tel. 407-74; fax 401-76-20. Doubles start at 440 schillings per person, including breakfast. All credit cards accepted.*

The Hotel Avis is one of several seasonal hotels operating during the summer months. During the rest of the year, "the hotels" serve as student housing facilities, so what you are basically getting is a dorm room. But you can't beat the price, and the young staff is incredibly friendly and helpful. The Hotel Avis is the most centrally located. Cooking facilities are available. And if you've brought along your bike, they have facilities to secure it during the evening.

7. EUROPA, *1 Neuer Markt 3. Tel. 51-59-40; fax 513-8138. Doubles start at 1,200 schillings per person, including breakfast. All credit cards accepted.*

The Hotel Europa is much more modern looking than most of the hotels you find inside the ring, with lots of chrome and glass. The staff is surprisingly down to earth, despite the crowds loitering in the lobby. The rooms are large and light streams through the large windows. If quiet is key, then request a room on the Neuer Markt rather than the bustling

Karntner Strasse. The hotel's restaurant, **Zum Donnerbrunner**, is first-rate with delicious variations on the usual Austrian classics. There's also a bar and typical Viennese cafe at guests' disposal.

Full

8. GRABEN HOTEL, *1, Dorotheergasse 3. Tel. 512-1531-0; fax 512-1531-20. Doubles start at 1,200 schillings. All credit cards accepted.*

The Graben Hotel is in the heart of the old town just off the pedestrian zone. The 46-room hotel is individually furnished with elegant simplicity. The staff is also accommodating and attentive. Austrian specialties are served in the **Restaurant Altenberg**. Or if you prefer the cuisine from Austria's southern neighbor, you can dine in the **Trattoria Santo Stefano**.

300 led

9. HOTEL AUSTRIA, *1, Am Fleischmarkt 20. Tel. 515-23; fax 515-23-506. Doubles start at 1,305 schillings, including breakfast. All credit cards accepted.*

The Hotel Austria is tucked away in an alley near the Schwedenplatz. The location ensures quiet, even though you're a five minute walk from the cathedral. Rooms are simply furnished and somewhat on the smallish side, but comfortable. A lounge is also available for guests' use.

10. HOTEL MAILBERGER HOF, *1, Annagasse 7. Tel. 512-0641-0; fax 512-0641-10. Doubles start at 1,800 schillings. All credit cards accepted.*

Housed in a building dating back to the 14th century, the Mailberger Hof hotel is situated on a quiet side street in the first district. The rooms are large, but look a bit tired. Apartments for guests staying at least a month are available. The hotel's restaurant serves traditional Viennese cuisines. The dining room is cozily furnished so you'll feel you haven't strayed too far from home.

11. HOTEL MERCURE, *1 Fleishmarkt 1a. Tel. 534-600; fax 534-60-232. Doubles start at 1,150 schillings per person, including breakfast. All credit cards accepted.*

The Hotel Mercure actually has two locations with an outside staircase leading to the second building. If you're going to stay here, ask for a room in the building at the top of the stairs, which overlooks a charming square near St. Rupert's, the oldest Church in Vienna. It's also more secluded than the other location just down the block. Regardless of which location you stay in, you'll be pleased with the level of service and the pleasant courtesy of the staff at both locations. The rooms are comfortable and well-appointed if a bit cold. Each features minibar, cable television, radio, and fax line. The hotel also has non-smoking floors.

12. HOTEL REGINA, *9, Rooseveltplatz 15. Tel. 404-46-0; fax 408-8392. Doubles start at 1,550 schillings, including breakfast. All credit cards accepted.*

The Hotel Regina is right behind the Votive Church in the university district. Rooms are simple but elegantly appointed. Apartments are also available. The staff, however, is a bit stand-offish. The hotel has two

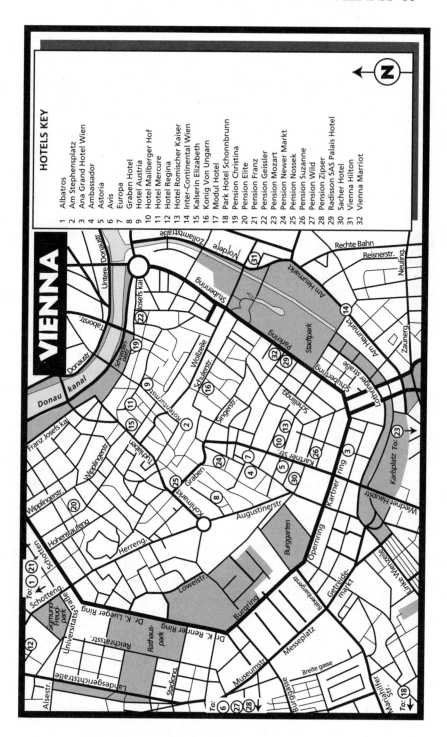

VIENNA

HOTELS KEY

1 Albatros
2 Am Stephensplatz
3 Ana Grand Hotel Wien
4 Ambassador
5 Astoria
6 Avis
7 Europa
8 Graben Hotel
9 Hotel Austria
10 Hotel Mailberger Hof
11 Hotel Mercure
12 Hotel Regina
13 Hotel Romischer Kaiser
14 Inter-Continental Wien
15 Kaiserin Elizabeth
16 Konig Von Ungarn
17 Modul Hotel
18 Park Hotel Schonnbrunn
19 Pension Christina
20 Pension Elite
21 Pension Franz
22 Pension Geissler
23 Pension Mozart
24 Pension Newer Markt
25 Pension Nossek
26 Pension Suzanne
27 Pension Wild
28 Pension Zipser
29 Radisson SAS Palais Hotel
30 Sacher Hotel
31 Vienna Hilton
32 Vienna Marriot

restaurants serving both international cuisine and Austrian favorites. Dishes include pork medallions in onion sauce and grilled lamb chops. Three daily menus are also featured.

13. HOTEL ROMISCHER KAISER, *1, Annagasse 16. Tel. 512-7751-0; fax 512-7751-13. Doubles start at 1,890 schillings. All credit cards accepted.*

A member of the Best Western hotel chain, this hotel was once a Baroque palace and was also used as an Imperial Engineering School during the time of Empress Maria Theresa. Rooms are furnished in a plush, overblown style in keeping with the Baroque theme. A parlor, furnished with lots of tapestry covered armchairs, is available as a guest lounge. The hotel is also within walking distance of the major sights inside the ring.

14. INTER-CONTINENTAL WIEN, *1, Johannesgasse 28. Tel. 711-22-0; fax 713-4489. Doubles start at 2,400 schillings per person. All credit cards accepted.*

The Inter-Continental Wien combines old world service with modern luxury. Period furniture and coordinated fabrics decorate the room. The hotel, overlooking the Stadtpark, also has non-smoking floors, an airline ticket office and 24-hour room service. As you would expect, the Inter-Continental houses the gourmet restaurant **Four Seasons**, which features a daily business lunch menu. Local favorites and international cuisine are offered. Viennese desserts and coffees are also available throughout the day. The hotel has a sauna, fitness room and solarium to pamper their guests.

15. KAISERIN ELISABETH, *1, Weihburggasse 3. Tel. 515-26; fax 515-267. Doubles begin at 950 schillings per person, breakfast included. All credit cards accepted.*

The Kaiserin Elisabeth is a hotel filled with old-world charm and style that surely would have pleased "Sisi" herself (Sisi is a nickname for Elisabeth). The hotel is richly furnished with colorful Oriental carpets and overstuffed armchairs. Staying here is like stepping back into the last century but with all the comforts and amenities of the 20th century. The service is helpful but unobtrusive. There is no restaurant, but breakfast and drinks are possible. Parking is available and you can keep your pet with you. The hotel has facilities for you to check your bike, too.

16. KONIG VON UNGARN, *1, Schulerstrasse 10. Tel. 515-84-0; fax 515-848. Doubles begin at 1,100 schillings per person, full continental breakfast included. Diners, Mastercard and Visa accepted.*

The Hotel Konig Von Ungarn is indeed fit for a king. Located in the shadow of St. Stephen's, you'll be right in the heart of the old town. The hotel is elegant from the plant-filled lobby to the cozy rooms, and was heartily recommended by several Viennese. Remodelling has not diminished its old-world character. The restaurant has both traditional Austrian cuisine and lighter selections. Parking and bicycling facilities are available.

17. MODUL HOTEL, *19, Peter Jordan Strasse 78. Tel. 47-660-0; fax 47-660-117. Doubles start at 950 schillings per person, including breakfast. All credit cards accepted.*

This place is the height of modernity. Rooms are large and light-filled, but a bit cookie-cutter like. But if comfort more than ambience is your priority, then this hotel may be just up your alley. A good choice for those who have no desire to travel back to the 19th century, but like their accommodations 20th century modern. The hotel has a good restaurant with both international and local dishes featured. Lighter items are also available. The hotel also offers supervision for children. Pets are welcome, too.

18. PARKHOTEL SCHONBRUNN, *13, Heitzinger Hauptstrasse 10. Tel. 878-04; fax 878-04-3220. Doubles start at 890 schillings per person. All credit cards accepted.*

Since you can't stay in Schonbrunn, the Parkhotel Schonbrunn is the next best thing. It's even the same shade of ocher. The hotel retains its turn of the century charm, but has lots of modern amenities from an indoor pool to exercise room to sauna. Ask for a room off the main street to avoid the noise. Austrian favorites are featured on the menu, although lighter fare is also a possibility. Linger over drinks in the hotel bar.

19. PENSION CHRISTINA, *1, Hafnersteig 7. Tel. 533-2961; fax 533-2961-11. Doubles start at 520 schillings per person, breakfast   included. Mastercard and Visa accepted.*

The Pension Christina is more serviceable than charming. Located near Schwedenplatz, this pension is centrally located and a real bargain. The rooms are a bit dreary though quite large: lots of brown, from the furniture to the fabrics, but a good value nonetheless.

20. PENSION ELITE, *1, Wipplingerstrasse 32. Tel. 533-2518-0; fax 535-5753. Doubles begin at 475 schillings per person, continental breakfast included. No credit cards accepted.*

The Pension Elite is one of the city's bargains, reasonably priced with a level of service unsurpassed at some of the more expensive establishments. The pension is furnished with lots of 19th century touches, from the tapestry covered chairs to the crystal chandeliers. Rooms are furnished individually, so you'll often find a hodgepodge of different pieces. Parking is available.

21. PENSION FRANZ, *9, Wahringer Strasse 12. Tel. 34-36-37; fax 34-36-37-23. Doubles begin at 595 schillings per person, breakfast included. All credit cards accepted.*

Dark wood panelling and antiques make this pension seem more like you're stepping into someone's private parlor rather than into a public pension. Rooms are comfortable but a bit on the smallish size. The staff is gracious and helpful. If individual style and a personal touch is high on your list, this pension will make your stay in Vienna a pleasant one.

22. PENSION GEISSLER, *1, Postgasse 14. Tel. 533-2803; fax 533-2635. Doubles begin at 475 schillings per person. All credit cards accepted.*

This pension is conveniently located near Schwedenplatz and the Danube. You won't find more of a bargain so centrally located. This area is a bit busy, so make sure to ask for a room off the street so you won't be bothered by the noise. Rooms are plain but comfortable. Don't expect the height of elegance, but you'll be pleasantly surprised by the personable service.

23. PENSION MOZART, *6, Theobaldgasse 15. Tel. 587-8505. Doubles start at 400 schillings per person. No credit cards.*

This is one the best bargains in Vienna, which is the main thing that recommends it. The rooms are clean, but sparsely furnished and somewhat dark. The entry way and breakfast area are also somewhat dank. But you can't beat its location near Karlsplatz, which means it's in walking distance to the major sights in the first district. If ambience is a major concern, cross this pension off your list. But if cost is your overriding consideration, then the Pension Mozart may be the place for you.

24. PENSION NEUER MARKT, *1, Seilergasse 9. Tel. 512-2316; fax 513-9105. Doubles start at 980 schillings, including breakfast. All credit cards accepted.*

The welcome at the Pension Neuer Markt is warm and cordial, like visiting a relative. The rooms are furnished in plain but serviceable pieces, nothing fancy but very comfortable. Ask for a room facing the famous fountain on the square. The central location makes it a real find. Breakfast includes fresh baked goods, whose savory aromas waft through the dining room. Hot meals can be ordered any time of the day as well.

25. PENSION NOSSEK, *1, Graben 17. Tel. 533-7041-0; fax 535-3646. Doubles start at 1050 schillings, including continental breakfast. No credit cards. Traveler's checks accepted.*

This small, family-run pension is in the heart of the old district, located between St. Stephen's cathedral, the shopping street Karntnerstrasse, and the Hofburg palace. This pension is tucked into a narrow courtyard off the square. Then, climb up to the second floor of the building to find the rooms. The accommodations are small, but cozy and the staff is very outgoing and helpful.

26. PENSION SUZANNE, *1, Walfischgasse 4. Tel. 513-2507; fax 513-2500. Doubles start at 495 schillings per person, full continental breakfast included. All credit cards accepted.*

The Pension Suzanne attracts a loyal following because of its proximity near the opera and its cozy charm. You can't beat the price either. This is an old-fashioned establishment with lots of attention to detail. Rooms are eclectically furnished with different 19th century pieces but very comfortable. Be sure to reserve ahead because the pension has a loyal following that returns year after year, and you may not be able to get a room otherwise.

27. PENSION WILD, *8, Lange Gasse 10. Tel. 406-5174; fax 402-2168. Doubles start at 315 schillings per person, including breakfast. No credit cards.*

This budget hotel is centrally located behind the Parliament within walking distance of most of Vienna's principal sights. But don't expect elegance at these prices. The rooms are clean but small. Cooking facilities are available, too, if you want to eat in for a change. A fitness room is open to guests.If you have a car, the reception can sell you a parking voucher for a fraction of the cost of a private lot.

28. PENSION ZIPSER, *8, Lange Gasse 49. Tel. 404-54-0; fax 408-5266-13. Doubles start at 470 schillings per person. No credit cards accepted.*

The Pension Zipser is housed in a delightful 19th century building. You'll find it behind the Rathaus, but you're still within easy walking distance to the sights inside the ring and public transportation. The staff goes out of their way to be helpful. The old-fashioned rooms are furnished with modern but bland pieces. However, they are quite comfortable, and you can't beat the price.

29. RADISSON SAS PALAIS HOTEL, *1, Parkring 16. Tel. 51-517-0; fax 51-22-216. Doubles start at 3,800 schillings. All credit cards accepted.*

Located on Vienna's ring, the 5-star Radisson hotel combines clean, modern lines with *fin-de-siecle* Austrian sophistication. Rooms are large and attractively furnished. A business service center allows you to set up shop with a fax, cordless phone, personal computer and even a secretary. Guests can unwind in the hotel's fitness room, sauna, or solarium. The hotel's restaurant **Le Siecle** is known for its fish flown in fresh daily. The **Palais Café** serves lighter fare. There is also the **Belami** bar where you can linger over drinks.

30. SACHER HOTEL, *1, Philharmonikerstrasse 4. Tel. 51-456; fax 5145-7810. Doubles start at 1,550 schillings per person. All credit cards accepted.*

The Hotel Sacher has become a veritable Austrian institution as much for its world-famous torte as for its high standard of luxury. Eduard Sacher, son of the Sachetorte's creator, opened the hotel in 1876. It was acquired by Hans Gurtler and his wife in1934.

Situated opposite the venerable State Opera House, the Sacher maintains the opulence of an earlier century when Austria was at the height of its influence and power. The hotel expertly combines the modern comforts of a 20th century hotel with the style and elegance of the 19th century. But the staff seems to have maintained too much of that 19th century imperious attitude. Of course you can enjoy a slice of

Sachetorte at the hotel's cafe, or have a drink in the intimate **Blue Bar**. The **Red Bar** features traditional Austrian cuisine by candlelight and music.

31. VIENNA HILTON, *3, Am Stadtpark. Tel. 717-00-0; fax 713-0691. Doubles start at 1,450 schillings per person. All credit cards accepted.*

The Hilton, just off the Stadtpark, has 600 rooms with cable television, air conditioning, telephone, and minibar. You won't forget the hotel atrium, with light streaming through the stained glass skylight. The Hilton seems more like its own private little village with shops, Budget car rental office, bike rental, hair dresser, health club and city airport shuttle service all on-sight. Parents can have one child stay free in their room.

The hotel is also home to the elegant **Arcadia Restaurant** with lamb dishes a particular specialty. **Mangostin Asia** features Asian dishes, the **Terminal Pub** serves Austrian food and the **Klimt Bar** has live music. The hotel caters to business people as well. Personal computers, secretarial services, fax machines, and other office amenities are available to guests.

32. VIENNA MARRIOTT, *1, Parking 12A. Tel. 51-518-0; fax 51-518-6736. Doubles start at 1,250 schillings per person. All credit cards accepted.*

The Vienna Marriott is situated just off the Stadt Park. And if you have business at the U.S. Consulate, the offices are housed here, too. The staff is friendly and outgoing. But the rooms are decorated with standard hotel furnishings that are somewhat lacking in the charm department.

A gourmet restaurant **Symphonika** is in the hotel with both Austrian and international cuisine featured. The **Parkring Restaurant** is more casual. Pastries, ice cream and coffee are highlighted in the **Garten Cafe**. Or have a cocktail in the **Cascade Bar** or the **Promenade Bar**. The hotel also has an indoor pool, fitness room, sauna, solarium and facilities to check your bicycle.

WHERE TO EAT

The Viennese are extremely proud of their cuisine. Culled from throughout the extensive empire under the Hapsburgs, Viennese food incorporates influences from abroad transforming foreign classics into new dishes all their own. The city's most famous dish *Weiner Schnitzel*, actually originated in Milan. Made traditionally with veal, you can now find less expensive versions using pork and turkey. Schnitzel is usually accompanied by french fries or potato salad.

Goulash, and the *paprika* that flavors many dishes, came from Hungary. Beef plays a primary role on Viennese menus, appearing in all different forms in consommes, soups with potatoes and vegetables or baked, roasted or boiled. Chicken, both roasted and fried, is also popular. In Vienna, you'll find restaurants from all over the world. And you can eat well and less expensively than in many other parts of the country. Make sure not to skip dessert, since the city's pastry shops deserve their decadent reputation. A variety of tempting cakes, pies, strudels, many served with a generous dollop of whipped cream, should be sampled.

Again, the first number listed in bold before the name of the restaurant corresponds to the number on the restaurant map provided. The number preceding the street name – immediately after the name of the restaurant – is the district location, and the number after the street name is the street address.

1. AUGUSTINERKELLER, *1, Augustinerstrasse 1. Tel. 533-1026; fax 319-9280. Moderate. Open daily 11 a.m. to midnight; Saturdays 11 a.m. to 1 a.m.*

If you can't make it out to one of the Heurigen on the outskirts of town, then this is the next best thing. Although locals may scoff at the somewhat touristy ambience, you'll enjoy the welcoming atmosphere. Schmaltzy accordion music and singing is also often played to complete the stereotypical image. A typical Heurigen buffet spread is available or you can order a la carte. The roast pork, served stabbed with a fork on wooden boards, is especially good.

2. DA MICHELE, *7, Kirchengasse 39. Tel. 523-8123. Inexpensive. Open Sunday through Friday, 11:30 a.m. to 2:30 p.m. and 6 p.m. to midnight. All credit cards accepted.*

Da Michele is a small, charming restaurant serving authentic Italian cuisine at very modest prices. The dining room is tiny but cozy, and the staff is friendly but unobtrusive. The pizzas are great with heaps of toppings and a crispy crust. The antipasto is good, too, although a bit too drenched in olive oil.

3. ESTERHAZY KELLER, *1, Haarhof 1. Open weekdays 11 a.m. to 10 p.m.; Saturdays and Sundays 4 p.m. to 10 p.m. All credit cards accepted.*

The Esterhazy Keller is a traditional tavern serving the standard classics such as Schnitzel and lighter fare like sandwiches and salads. This is more a place to get a quick bite or linger over a drink. During the summer months, there's pleasant outside seating in the alley-like street. This is a nice place to stop to catch your breath after a busy day sightseeing.

4. FIGLMULLER, *1 Wollzeile 5. Tel. 512-6177. Moderate. Open 11 a.m. to 10 p.m. All credit cards accepted.*

Locals say the Figlmuller serves the largest portions of Schnitzel in the city, and many Viennese insist it's the best in Austria. Don't be surprised if some of the meat ends up hanging off the plate. The atmosphere is festive and fun to accompany the generous portions.

5. GASTHAUS PFUDL, *1, Backerstrasse 22. Tel. 512-6705; fax 714-7797. Moderate. Open Monday through Saturday 9 a.m. to 2 a.m.; Sundays 9 a.m. to 3 p.m. All credit cards accepted.*

Decorated in dark woods and cheery green and white linens, the Gasthaus Pfudl has a welcoming atmosphere sure to please the most discerning customer. The restaurant feature a variety of classic Austrian dishes such as *Zweibelbraten*, or pot roast smothered in onions, and mushroom Schnitzel. There is also a modest selection of fish dishes.

6. GRIECHENBEISL, *1, Fleischmarkt 11. Tel. 533-1941. Moderate. Open 11 a.m. to 1 a.m. All credit cards accepted.*

The Griechenbeisl is Vienna's oldest restaurant and was first named "The Yellow Eagle" in 1500. It's changed hands through the centuries several times and has become a veritable institution. The menu features veal, goulash and the other standard dishes, but they tend to be over-priced for what you're getting. The staff also is somewhat brusque and unfriendly. Unless you want to have a "taste of history," you're better off going to one of the bistros in the nearby "Bermuda Triangle," the area in the first district off of Schwedenplatz.

7. HOSHIGAOKA SARYO, *1, Fuhrichgasse 10. Tel. 512-2720. Open noon to 2 p.m. and 6 p.m. to 10:30 p.m.; Sundays closed. All credit cards accepted.*

If you can't stand one more plate of Schnitzel and the thought of a plate of sushi gives you goosebumps, then head to Hoshigaoka Saryo. This is an exceptional Japanese restaurant. Everything from the crisp, clean lines of the decor to the impeccable service to the artful presentation of the dishes makes an evening here memorable.

8. ILONA STUBERL, *1, Braunerstrasse 2. Tel. 533-9029. Moderate. Open daily noon to 3 p.m. and 6 p.m. to 11 p.m. All credit cards accepted.*

If you have a yearning for authentic Hungarian cuisine, then you don't have too far to travel. Goulash is a specialty here and you can choose from pork, veal, or beef as well as other Hungarian specialties you probably won't be as familiar with. Everything is highly seasoned and lots of paprika is sprinkled over the dishes. The service is warm and friendly as well.

9. KITSCH & BITTER, *1, Ruprechtsplatz 1. Tel. 535-3039. Moderate. Open 6 p.m. to 2 a.m.; Friday and Saturday, 6 p.m. to 4 a.m. All credit cards accepted.*

In Vienna's "Bermuda Triangle," the Kitsch & Bitter is right across from St. Rupert's Church. The food is good but nothing exceptional. Stick to the basics here and you won't be disappointed. The restaurant attracts a young, hip crowd. Stay away later in the evening if you can't deal with smoke.

10. KUCHLDRAGONER, *1, Seitenstetteng 3. Tel. 533-8371. Moderate. Open 11 a.m. to 2 a.m.; Fridays and Saturdays 11 a.m. to 3 a.m. All credit cards accepted.*

Tucked behind St. Rupert's Church, you might miss the Kuchldragoner. That would be a pity, since the restaurant has a charm and intimacy all its own. The standard goulash and Cordon Bleu are featured on the menu with different daily specials added. The *Knodel* dishes, a cross between a noodle and a dumpling, are especially good. The restaurant also bakes its own bread.

11. LA CREPERIE, *Grunangergasse 10. Tel. 512-5687. Moderate. 11:30 a.m. to midnight. Visa and Mastercard accepted.*

You feel as if you'd stepped into a Parisian bistro walking through the doors of La Creperie with its lacy tablecloths, candles, and closely sandwiched tables. The restaurant offers a 320 schilling menu including coffee and aperitif. Or you can order separately such dishes as grilled lamb, mussels, and bouillabaisse.

12. MONGOLISH BARBECUE, *1, Fleischmarkt 4. Tel. 535-3176. Moderate. Open daily 11:30 a.m. to 2:30 p.m. and 5:30 p.m. to 12:30 a.m. American Express, Visa and Mastercard.*

The main attraction of this restaurant featuring Mongolian barbecue is the 220 schilling menu allowing you to eat your fill. Turkey, pork, beef and horse meat are all available for grilling. This is a restaurant for hefty appetites, more quantity than quality, but fun nonetheless.

13. PANDA, *7, Westbahnstrasse 35. Tel. 526-9488. Inexpensive. Open daily 11:30 a.m. to 11 p.m. No credit cards.*

This is one of several Chinese restaurants along the Westbahnstrasse. Most of them have only a few tables in a dark, kitschy dining rooms, and this one is no exception. But if the atmosphere doesn't throw you, you can eat large quantities of quite good Chinese food for only a few schillings. The Panda features a menu with cabbage salad, two eggrolls, hot and sour soup and about 10 choices of main dishes from plates of noodles to hot and spicy beef and chicken – for only 48 schillings.

✸ **14. RESTAURANT MARCHE**, *1, Ringstrassen Galerie. Tel. 512-5060. Inexpensive. Open daily 8 a.m. to 11 p.m.; Sundays and holidays 10 a.m. to 11 p.m. All credit cards accepted.*

If you want to grab a quick bite before the opera, then this is a good place to stop. Located in the nearby shopping arena on the basement level, the Restaurant Marche has individual booths where you can order a sandwich, an ice cream concoction at another, and grilled salmon at another – all for very reasonable prices. Don't expect gourmet dining here, but the service is friendly, fast, and efficient. This is a good place to bring children, because they're bound to find something they want to eat.

15. RESTAURANT STEIRERECK, *3, Rasumofskygasse 2, Ecke Weissgerberlande. Tel. 713-3168; fax 713-51-682. Expensive. Open noon to 2 p.m. and 7 p.m. to midnight. Visa and American Express cards accepted.*

One of the best restaurants in Vienna, if not the whole country, the Restaurant Steirereck is under the direction of Chef Helmut Osterreicher. Dishes include goose liver with oranges and venison with leeks and mushrooms. The restaurant also has a strong selection of cheeses and sweets to finish your dinner in style. The wine list is extensive with vintages from the Wachau, Bordeaux, Styria, and Piedmont.

16. ROCKY DOCKY'S WESTERN STEAK HOUSE, *16, Ruckertgasse 39. Tel. 450-3216. Moderate. Open Tuesday through Saturday 5 p.m. to 12:30 a.m.; closed Sundays and Mondays. All credit cards accepted.*

In the mood for a nice, thick, juicy American-style steak? Then head to Rocky Docky's Western Steak House. You'll feel like you just walked into a ranch house complete with steer heads and pelts. Steaks are grilled to order, or choose from the restaurant's chicken, pork, seafood, or turkey entrees. This is a fun place to bring children, too.

17. ROSA ELEPHANT, *1, Fleichmarkt 4. Tel. 533-7530. Moderate. 4 p.m. to 2 a.m.; Sundays 4 p.m. to midnight. Visa and Mastercard accepted.*

The Rosa Elephant is a hip place to dine for those in the know. Noodle dishes, pepper steak, and chicken smothered in tomato sauce are some of the items featured on the menu. Tables tend to fill up quickly so you may find yourself standing around. It also tends to get smoky and loud as the evening progresses. If you're looking for quiet intimacy, head elsewhere.

18. SCHONBRUNN PIZZERIA TRATTORIA, *5, Schonbrunnerstrasse 35. Tel. 586-4383. Inexpensive. Open daily 10 a.m. to 11 p.m. All credit cards accepted.*

This neighborhood hangout has ample portions and friendly service. Italian pizza and pasta dishes are the specialties, but don't overlook the Viennese selections. The huge Schnitzels are tasty and without the greasiness that can so often ruin this classic dish. The only drawback to this restaurant is the sappy American pop played a bit too loudly as background music. Otherwise, you're in for good food at bargain prices.

19. SILBERWIRT, *5, Schlossgasse 21. Tel. 544-4907. Moderate. Open noon to midnight. Visa and Diners accepted.*

The Silberwirt is everything a classic *Beisl*, or bistro, should be – nice atmosphere, good food, and pleasant service at reasonable prices. This restaurant is a bit outside the center but worth the trek to the Pilgramgasse U-Bahn. In summer, there is also a lovely guest garden to linger over drinks or dinner. Dinners include chicken smothered in mushrooms, fried eggplant, and spareribs. Specials change daily.

20. THAI KITCHEN, *5, Schonbrunner Strasse 23. Tel. 586-7885. Moderate. Open daily 6 p.m. to midnight; closed Monday. All credit cards accepted.*

If you're looking for a restaurant to tickle your tastebuds, the Thai Kitchen is it. The restaurant serves dishes deliciously seasoned with cilantro, lemongrass, and other Thai spices. The restaurant is cool and inviting with its bamboo screens and green and white linens. The service is exemplary, too.

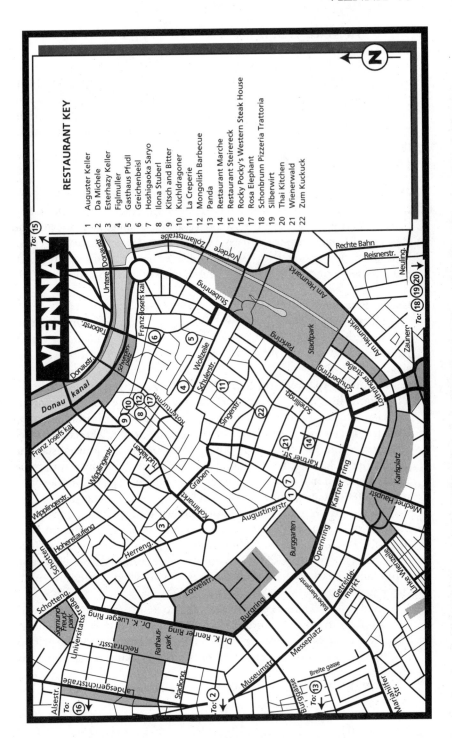

RESTAURANT KEY

1 Auguster Keller
2 Da Michele
3 Esterhazy Keller
4 Figlmuller
5 Gasthaus Pfudl
6 Greichenbeisl
7 Hoshigaoka Saryo
8 Ilona Stuberl
9 Kitsch and Bitter
10 Kuchldragoner
11 La Creperie
12 Mongolish Barbecue
13 Panda
14 Restaurant Marche
15 Restaurant Steirereck
16 Rocky Pocky's Western Steak House
17 Rosa Elephant
18 Schonbrunn Pizzeria Trattoria
19 Silberwirt
20 Thai Kitchen
21 Wienerwald
22 Zum Kuckuck

21. WIENERWALD, *1, Annagasse 3. Tel. 512-37-66. Inexpensive. Open daily 11 a.m. to 2 a.m. No credit cards accepted.*

Wienerwald is the McDonald's of Austria. The food is unexceptionable, but finicky children will love it. The chain, which has locations throughout Austria, specializes in grilled chicken, and is one of the country's few bargains. But you're still going to wind up paying more than you would for American fast food. This is a good place to get a late night bite to eat after an opera or concert.

22. ZUM KUCKUCK, *1, Himmelpfortgasse 15. Moderate. Open weekdays noon to 3 p.m. and 6 p.m. to midnight. All credit cards accepted.*

The Zum Kuckuck offers Austrian cooking at its best. The restaurant features a monthly menu which has included herring, veal knuckles, and bread pudding. A la carte offerings are also available, and not just the standard Schnitzel either. A tureen of game was one such savory selection. You won't go wrong with the wine list either. There's a small but impressive list of regional vintage. The dining room is small but intimate.

Coffee Houses

The coffee house is a veritable Viennese institution, as much a part of the city as St. Stephen's Cathedral or the Prater's giant ferris wheel. Coffee was actually introduced to Vienna by the Turks, who twice laid siege to the city.

According to local lore, Georg Kolschitzky received the coffee beans left behind by the retreating Turks as part of his reward for running messages through the enemy lines. The enterprising Kolschitzky then used the beans to launch Vienna's first coffee house. The city's coffee houses became an integral meeting place for artists, journalists, and philosophers at the turn of the century. The coffee house was transformed into a home away from home where many brilliant but destitute young intellectuals spent their days debating the dilemmas of the day.

No visit to Vienna would be complete without spending a couple of hours at one of the city's famous cafes. There are several different types of coffee houses. Look for **Cafe-Konditorei** if you're in the mood for a piece of pastry or a slice of cake to go with your coffee. **Cafe-Restaurants** offer light meals and other beverages if you want something more substantial.

Most cafes do not accept credit cards, so be prepared to pay cash. It is customary to tip by rounding out your bill to the next five shillings. Vienna's coffee houses are one of the city's best bargains: for the price of a cup of coffee, you can spend an entire day soaking up all the atmosphere.

BREZLG'WOLB, *Ledererhof 9. 533-8811. Open 11:30 a.m. to 1 a.m. with the kitchen staying open until midnight.*

This is more than a place to get a cup of coffee. The cafe offers visitors a chance to look at the artwork displayed, peruse the latest in literature, and listen to a concert.

CAFE CENTRAL, *1, Herrengasse 14. Tel. 533-3763. Open daily 8 a.m. to 10 p.m.; closed Sundays.*

Cafe Central is probably Vienna's most famous cafe. At the turn of the century the cafe attracted writers, journalists, artists, and radicals who came to discuss the concerns of the day. Such famous figures as poets Arthur Schnitzler and Peter Altenberg, critic Karl Kraus, architect Adolf Loos and Russian revolutionary Leo Trotzky visited this coffee house through the years.

CAFE DEMEL, *1, Kohlmarkt 14. Tel. 535-1717 or 533-5516. Open from 10 a.m. to 6 p.m.*

The owners of the Demel cafe once went to court in a dispute with the Sacher Hotel over which establishment had really developed the celebrated torte. You can guess who won, since a slice of Sacher torte is now a must for many tourists – here as well as at the Cafe Sacher. The 19th century still prevails here with scarlet plush and lots of brass.

CAFE GRIENSTEIDL, *1, Michaelerplatz 2. Open daily 8 a.m. to midnight.*

The Cafe Griensteidl served as a meeting place for Viennese writers during the end of the last century. Today, it's a good place to take a break after visiting the Hofburg.

CAFE HAWELKA, *1, Dorotheergasse 6. Open daily 8 a.m. to 2 a.m.; Sundays 4 p.m. to 2 a.m.*

The Cafe Hawelka has long attracted local artists, especially during the 1950s. You'll notice some original paintings from among the fantastic realists. These destitute young artists settled their debts to the cafe by paying with their canvases.

CAFE MAXIMILIAN, *9, Universitatsstrasse 2. Tel. 42-71-49. Open Monday through Friday 7 a.m. to midnight; Saturdays, Sundays and holidays 9 a.m. to midnight.*

The Cafe Maximilian attracts students from the nearby university. The cafe has a sunny terrace where you can enjoy the view of the nearby Votive Church across the park when the weather is fine.

CAFE MUSEUM, *1, Friedrichstrasse 6. Tel. 56-52-02. Open daily 7 a.m. to 11 p.m.*

The Cafe Museum was once known as the Nihilism Cafe. Built by Adolf Loos in 1899, the cafe was soon attracting artists, students, and some members of chic society. Serious chess players are also attracted by the atmosphere, and there is outside seating available when the weather is nice.

COFFEE TYPES

You may find yourself a bit daunted by all the coffee selections that you can choose from in the local coffee shops. Sometimes coffee is served with milk, with milk on the side, with whipped cream, or with a glass of water on the side, depending on where you order. If you have a preference, ask before ordering.

Here is a list of some of the most common types of coffee offered in coffee shops:

grossen Schwarzen – *large black coffee*
verlangert Kaffee – *weaker black coffee*
gekurzt Kaffee – *stronger black coffee*
vrauner Kaffee – *coffee with milk added*
Kaffee creme – *coffee with milk on the side*
Melange – *half coffee and half milk*
Mocca – *black coffee, like espresso*
schalegold Kaffee or **Braune** – *coffee with lots of milk added so that it is golden in color*
Kaffee mit schalgobers – *coffee with whipped cream*
Turkische – *strong black coffee brewed in a copper pot, often with sugar*
Einspanner – *mocca in a glass with whipped cream*
Wiener Eiskaffee – *strong, cold mocca with vanilla ice cream and whipped cream*
Masagran – *cold coffee served with ice and Maraschino*
Kapuziner – *small mocca with cream and grated chocolate*
Fiaker – *mocca with rum*

CAFE SACHER, *1, Philharmonikerstrasse 4. Tel. 51457/846. Open* noon to 3 p.m. and 6 p.m. to 11:30 p.m. All credit cards.

The Sacher is less known for its coffee than for its world famous Sacher Torte, a heavenly combination of chocolate and apricot. But you may be disappointed by the service, as surly staff members hustle customers. The management seems more interested in getting people in and out than allowing customers to linger over their coffee and cake. You're better off skipping this tourist trap and heading to one of the other cafes nearby. You'll wind up paying less and have a much more enjoyable experience overall.

CAFE SPERL, *4, Karolinengasse 13. Tel. 504-7334. Open 10:30 a.m. to midnight; Sunday and holidays 3 p.m. to 11 p.m.*

The Cafe Sperl is a personal favorite of mine, in operation since 1880. The cafe attracts a theatrical crowd due to its proximity to the Theater an der Wein. The Cafe Sperl is everything you'd expect from a traditional Austrian coffee house without the tourist hordes. You can also play billiards.

TIROLERHOF, *1, Fuhrichgasse 8. Tel. 512-7833. 7 a.m. to 9 p.m.; Sundays and holidays 9:30 a.m. to 8 p.m.*

The Tirolerhof boasts that it has fresh-made apple strudel. The strudel is excellent, but you'd have to have the patience of a saint to withstand the impossibly slow service and surly attitude of the waiters here.

Heurigen

No visit to Vienna or the surrounding region would be complete without a visit to the neighborhood **Heurigen**. As the grape vines along the Danube turn from green to red and gold in the fall, the locals head to the vineyards that dot the hillsides to savor the latest wine harvest.

The tradition started more than two centuries ago, when Emperor Joseph II in 1784 issued a proclamation allowing vintners in the suburbs of Vienna to sell food and wine on their premises. The Heurigen, or wine taverns, haven't changed much in the years since, although many are open year round these days. *Heurige* means "of this year" and refers to the new wine harvest, sort of like the Austrian version of beaujolais. And locals and tourists do their best to help drink as much of the new wine harvest as possible.

Vineyards first appeared in Austria in the third century A.D., when the Roman Emperor Probus initiated a campaign to encourage grape growing in the Roman provinces. The vines thrived in the region, and Austria's wine industry was born.

Today, dozens of tiny villages line the banks of the Danube as you head out of Vienna, seemingly unchanged by the centuries. You can locate the Heurigen by the telltale straw wreaths or pine boughs that mark the entrance and announce that new wine is ready for drinking. If you'd rather stay in the city, many Heurigen are only a local streetcar ride away to Grinzing, Heiligenstadt, and other former wine villages that were absorbed into the city limits as Vienna expanded over the years. You'll feel like you're stepping back in time a couple of centuries. Many of these neighborhoods still possess their village character.

Most Heurigen also feature a traditional **Schrammelmusik** band, which can be made up of an accordion, a bass, a fiddle, or even a zither with a singer crooning schmaltzy favorites. The songs are about love, wine and death, because, as a Viennese explained to me, "What else is there in life?"

Here is a selection of local Viennese Heurigen that you could try in the 19th district or venture out on your own. When you see the pine branch or wreath, you know you're in for a treat: great wine and lots of hearty food served buffet style.

ALTES PREKHAUS, *19, Cobenzlgasse 15, Grinzing. Tel. 32-23-93; fax 32-23-42-85. Moderate. Open 4 p.m. to midnight. All credit cards accepted.*

BEETHOVENHAUS, *19, Mayer am Pfarrplatz, Pfarrplatz 2, Heiligenstadt. Tel. 37-12-87 or 37-33-61; fax 37-47-14. Moderate. Open from 1 p.m. to midnight. All credit cards accepted.*

DAS KIRCHENSTOCKL, *19, Cobenzlgasse 3, Grinzing. Tel. 32-66-62; fax 440-3917. Moderate. Open 2 p.m. to midnight. All credit cards accepted.*

HEURIGER FUHRGASSL-HUBER, *19, Neustift am Walde 68. Tel. 440-1405; fax 440-2730. Moderate. Open 1 p.m. to midnight. All credit cards accepted.*

HEURIGER HENGL-HASELBRUNNER, *19, Iglaseegasse 10, Grinzing. Tel. 32-33-30 or 32-50-30; fax 32-86-96. Moderate. Open 1 p.m. to midnight. All credit cards accepted.*

HEURIGER REINPRECHT, *19, Cobenzlgasse 22, Grinzing. Tel. 32-14-71 or 32-13-89; fax 32-57-13/22. Moderate. Open from 3 p.m. to 11 p.m. All credit cards accepted.*

HEURIGER WOLFF, *19, Rathstrasse 46, Neustift am Walde. Tel. 440-2335. Moderate. Open 1 p.m. to midnight. All credit cards accepted.*

HEURIGER ZIMMERMANN, *19, Mitterwurzergasse 20, Neustift am Walde. Tel. 440-1207. Moderate. 3 p.m. to 11 p.m. All credit cards accepted.*

SCHUBEL-AUER WEINBAU, *19, Kahlenberger Strasse 22, Heiligenstadt. Tel. 37-22-22 or 37-47-67. Moderate. Open 2 p.m. to 11 p.m.; closed Sundays. All credit cards accepted.*

SEEING THE SIGHTS

Depending on the length of your visit, Vienna's highlights can be seen over a weekend or savored over several weeks. If you're only in this imperial city for a couple of days, you might want to confine you sight-seeing to *Inside the Ring* (see below), where the most famous monuments and museums are located. Try also to take in the **Belvedere** and **Schonbrunn palaces** to get a taste of what it was like to live as an emperor or empress.

If you're traveling with children or are a child at heart, the **Prater** park with its giant ferris wheel is a must-see attraction. For those who are staying for longer, take the time to get a feel for the city. No matter where you look, you'll be dazzled by the wealth of architectural styles on display throughout the city. Vienna has myriad churches, parks, smaller museums and neighborhoods to explore, too.

To make your sight-seeing easier inside the ring, the number in parentheses following the name of the sight corresponds to the numbers on the sight-seeing map on the next page.

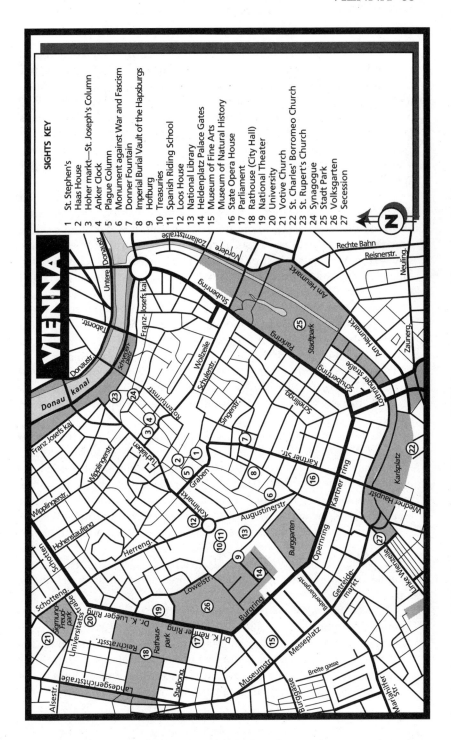

VIENNA

SIGHTS KEY

1 St. Stephen's
2 Haas House
3 Hoher markt—St. Joseph's Column
4 Anker Clock
5 Plague Column
6 Monument against War and Fascism
7 Donner Fountain
8 Imperial Burial Vault of the Hapsburgs
9 Hofburg
10 Treasuries
11 Spanish Riding School
12 Loos House
13 National Library
14 Heldenplatz Palace Gates
15 Museum of Fine Arts
16 Museum of Natural History
17 State Opera House
18 Parliament
19 Rathouse (City Hall)
20 University
21 Votive Church
22 St. Charles' Borromeo Church
23 St. Rupert's Church
24 Synagogue
25 Stadt Park
26 Volksgarten
27 Secession

Inside the Ring

The *Ringstrasse* was created when Emperor Franz Joseph ordered the demolition in 1857 of the city's fortifications, which encircled the old part of Vienna, to create a magnificent, wide boulevard. The 187-foot wide, 2.5 mile long boulevard was lined with trees and had room for a road, pedestrian walkway, and riding path. He then commissioned the most famous architects of the day to design the monumental buildings that surround the Ring. The stunning architecture, including the State Opera, Vienna University, City Hall, Parliament and the Museums of Fine Arts and Natural History, define the city's character.

Most of the major sights of the city are located in the old quarter and are easily accessible by foot. Start your visit in the center of the old city at **St. Stephen's Square (1)**, where the ancient gothic **St. Stephen's Cathedral**, with its colorful tiled roof picturing the Austrian imperial eagle, soars over the ancient part of the city. The cathedral, which is 352 feet long, 128 feet high in the nave with a 448 foot south tower, was built between the 12th and 16th centuries.

The Romanesque Giant Gate and the Towers of the Heathens were completed under the Bohemian King Ottocar II, who reigned between the Babenberg and Hapsburg dynasties. Duke Rudolf IV, credited as the church's founder, had St. Stephen's remodeled in the Gothic style. He laid the cornerstone of the nave in 1359. The South Tower was completed in 1433. The North Tower, however, was topped with a Renaissance spire in 1579 after the Gothic style went out of favor. Baroque elements were added during the 18th century.

The cathedral was seriously damaged during World War II when the Germans bombarded the city as they were fleeing eastward, but was later restored to its present glory. Be sure to get a glimpse of the Wiener Neustadt Gothic Altarpiece from 1447; the red marble sepulcher containing the remains of Emperor Frederick III completed in 1513 by Niclas Gerhaert van Leyden; the *Madonna of the Servant* dating from 1320; and the pulpit from 1514 with a "signature" relief of sculpture by Anton Pilgram.

Guided tours of the *Dom*, as it is called in German, are available Monday through Saturday at 10:30 a.m. and 3 p.m.; Sunday and holidays 3 p.m.

The **Cathedral Museum,** *1, Stephansplatz 6, Tel. 515-52-560*, is open Tuesday, Wednesday, Friday and Saturday from 10 a.m. to 4 p.m.; Thursday 10 a.m. to 6 p.m.; Sunday and holidays, 10 a.m. to 1 p.m. The cathedral's catacombs contain the remains of several of the Hapsburgs, including Duke Rudolf and Viennese bishops. Also housed here are 56 urns containing the intestinal remains of the Hapsburgs dating from 1650 through the 19th century. The catacombs can only be seen in a guided tour, Monday through Saturday at 10 a.m., 11 a.m., 11:30 a.m., 2 p.m., 2:30 p.m., 3:30 p.m., 4 p.m. and 4:30 p.m.; Sunday and holidays 2 p.m. to 4:30 p.m. on the half hour.

The **North Tower** contains Austria's largest bell, called affectionately "The Boomer Bell" by the Viennese. The original bell was cast from the guns left behind by the fleeing Turks after the siege of 1683, but it was destroyed during World War II. A new bell was cast and put in the North Tower in 1952. The bell is rung on New Year's Eve and other momentous events. You can visit the North Tower from April to September from 9 a.m. to 6 p.m.; October to March, 8 a.m. to 5 p.m. The South Tower is open daily 9 a.m. to 5:30 p.m.

St. Virgil's Chapel was uncovered when the U-Bahn was being built under the cathedral during the 1970s. The Gothic chapel is open daily, except Monday, from 9 a.m. to 12:15 p.m. and 1 p.m. to 4:30 p.m. Free admission Friday before noon.

Across the square from the cathedral is the post-modern **Haas House (2)** designed by Hans Hollein in 1990. The glass and steel modern building has attracted both admiration and derision, depending to whom you speak. The curved facade is on the site where the Roman garrison once stood when Vienna was called *Vindobona*.

A slight detour will take you to the **Hoher Markt**, where you'll see **St. Joseph's Column (3)**. This column was erected after the future Emperor Joseph I was safely delivered from the fighting during the War of the Spanish Succession. His father, Emperor Leopold I, had promised to construct the column if his son came back to the city alive. J.B. Fisher von Erlach designed a wooden column, but his son replaced it with a stone fountain depicting the marriage of the Holy Family. The Hoher Markt has a significant place in the city's history. Roman ruins underneath the square are open to visitors. In medieval Vienna, the executioner's scaffold, the pillory, and the law court were headquartered here.

Also on the Hoher Markt is the **Anker Clock (4)**, an Art Nouveau clock designed by painter Franz von Matsch in 1911. At noon, there's a daily parade of larger-than-life figures, including Roman Emperor Marcus Aurelius and composer Joseph Haydn, that move past the Viennese coat of arms accompanied by music. During Advent, Christmas carols are played daily at 5 p.m. and 6 p.m. To get here by subway, take the U-Bahn to Stephansplatz or Schwedenplatz.

Head back towards the cathedral square to the **Plague Column (5)**, *1, Graben*. The column was erected by Emperor Leopold I after Vienna was delivered from the plague. Historians estimate that as many as 150,000 people may have died from the scourge. L.O. Burnacini oversaw the column's creation and completion in 1693.

Continue your walking tour to **Albertinaplatz** where you can see a moving **Monument against War and Fascism (6)**, *1, Augustinerstrasse*, memorializing those Austrians killed by the Nazis during World War II. Hundreds of people died here during an air raid in the final weeks of the war, after seeking shelter in the building's basement. Their bodies were never recovered. Alfred Hrdlicka was commissioned by the city of Vienna to design the monument in 1983. The *Gates of Violence* sculpture represent the harsh Nazi occupation. The bronze sculpture is of a Jew forced to scrub the streets under the Nazi regime. A marble sculpture, *Orpheus Entering Hades*, symbolizes the war's destruction. Finally, a pillar bears an excerpt from the Declaration of Independence re-establishing the Republic of Austria in 1945.

The nearby **Donner Fountain (7)** *,1, Neuer Markt*, is located in what once was Vienna's Flour Market. The fountain depicts Providence surrounded by allegorical figures representing the Traun, Enns, Ybbs and March rivers which feed into the Danube. Empress Maria Theresa found the Donner's sculptures lewd and immoral and wanted them removed from the marketplace. The figures, today, on display are actually copies of the originals, which you can see at the Belvedere.

In the Neuer Markt you can also visit the **Imperial Burial Vault of the Hapsburgs (8)**. The double casket of Maria Theresa and her husband Emperor Francis I, designed by sculptor B. F. Moll, is particularly noteworthy because of its extravagance. In contrast, her son, Emperor Joseph II, chose a simple coffin. The last member of the family to be buried here was Empress Zita, the wife of the last emperor Charles I. She was entombed here with full regal honors in 1989 despite the dissolution of the monarchy after World War I. The imperial vault, *Tel. 512-6853*, is open daily 9:30 a.m. to 4 p.m.

The hearts of the Hapsburgs used to be kept in a special vault until 1878 in the **Church of the Augustiners**. The Heart Vault of the Hapsburgs in the Church of the Augustinian Friars, *1 Ausgustinerstrasse 3, Tel. 533-7099*, is open daily, except Sunday, from 10 a.m. to 5 p.m. and by prior arrangement. The U-Bahn is Karlsplatz or Oper.

From the imperial vault, continue your tour with a visit to the **Hofburg (9)**, *1 Michaelerplatz, Tel. 587-5554*, the royal palace of the Hapsburgs until 1918. You can visit several of the state rooms in the imperial apartments at the Hofburg. The original palace, known affectionately as just *die Burg* or "the Palace" by the Viennese, dates back to the 13th century, of which only the Swiss Courtyard remains today. Over the years, the Hofburg was enlarged and altered to the imposing 2,600 rooms it comprises today. The Hapsburgs were apparently against accepting hand-me-downs, since it was understood that no monarch could live in his predecessor's quarters and additions were routinely built.

The rooms open to the public are the former reception rooms and private living quarters of Emperor Francis Joseph I and Empress Elizabeth. On display are the famous portraits by court painter Franz Xaver Winterhalter of the empress, affectionately known as "Sisi." Her gymnastics equipment is also exhibited. The exercise room caused a minor scandal at the rigid court. The dining room is also set for a formal dinner with all the china, silver, and bric-a-brac that entails.

The Hofburg also contains a dazzling collection of Court Silver and Tableware, or *Silberkammer*. There were actually different servants in the Hapsburg court responsible for the silver and porcelain, kitchen wares, table linens and wine cellar. You'll understand why when you see extravagant items amassed by the royal family. The collection contains such treasures as a porcelain service given by Marie Antoinette and Louis XVI to the Empress Maria Theresa and a dessert service from British Queen Victoria given to Emperor Francis Joseph. The collection is housed *at 1 Hofburg, Tel. 533-1044*, open daily from 9 a.m. to 5 p.m. U-Bahn Stephansplatz.

The rest of the Hofburg houses the office of the Austrian president, the chapel where the Vienna's Boys Choir sings mass, and the hall in which the Spanish Riding School performs. The **Chapel of the Imperial Palace** at the Hofburg is open March through June and mid-September through December, Tuesdays and Thursdays 1:30 p.m. to 3:30 p.m.; Fridays 1:30 p.m. to 3 p.m. Admission to the royal apartments is 70 schillings for adults and 35 schillings for children; admission for the imperial jewel and silver collection is 60 schillings for adults and 30 schillings for children. The Hofburg is open daily from 9 a.m. to 5 p.m. Admission reductions are available with the Vienna Card. Take the U-Bahn to Stephansplatz.

The **Secular and Ecclesiastical Treasuries (10)** collection, *Tel. 533-7931,* is also on display at the Hofburg. The collection contains such rare pieces as the crown of the Holy Roman Empire from 962 worn by the Hapsburgs until 1806 and other royal jewels. A 400-year-old Austrian Imperial Crown, commissioned by Rudolf II when he resided in Prague, is also on display. When Emperor Franz founded the Austrian Empire in 1804, the crown became a symbol of the new state. The display is open daily, except Tuesday, 10 a.m. to 6 p.m.; Thursday 10 a.m. to 9 p.m. Tram D, J, 1 or 2 Burgring.

The Hofburg is also home to the world-famous **Spanish Riding School (11)**, *1, Josefsplatz 1.* J.E. Fischer von Erlach designed the Baroque structure so that the imperial horses could be exercised during the winter months. The school gets its name from the horses Emperor Maximilian II imported from Spain in 1562. (See *Nightlife & Entertainment* section for information on performances.)

Across from the Hofburg is the **Loos House (12)**, *1, Michaelerplatz 3*. The story goes that the building was so hated by the emperor after its completion in 1910 that he ordered curtains drawn on that side of the palace so that he would not have to lay eyes on it. "The house without eyebrows" as it was criticized was compared to the gridwork of a storm sewer. Loos believed that ornamentation was a "crime" in opposition to the ostentatious ornamentation favored by Baroque supporters. In the center of the square, you can see excavations uncovered by the city, including Roman ruins and part of the wall, which used to surround the imperial "Garden of Eden."

Walk through the tunnel underneath the Hofburg to reach the **National Library (13)**, *1, Josefsplatz*. The library was built by Joseph Emmanuel Fisher von Erlach after a plan by his father. The library's grand hall contains stupendous frescoes by Daniel Gran and can be visited by the public.

Head towards the **Heldenplatz Palace Gates (14)** on your way out of the library. This was once the location of the city walls and an open meadow. The open area was maintained to thwart approaching enemies who might try to invade the city. There was no cover, so they could be easily fired upon and Vienna adequately defended. Napoleon ordered that the old fortifications be razed when he occupied Vienna in 1809. What you see today was actually completed in 1824. The gates memorialize Austria's "Unknown Soldiers" from World War I. The two equestrian statues were created by Anton Fernkorn. One is of Archduke Charles who defeated Napoleon in the Battle of Aspern, and the other depicts Prince Eugene of Savoy, who defeated the Turks in the 18th century. It was also here that Hitler announced the annexation of Austria on March 15, 1938.

You are now on the ring and can cross over to the **Museums of Fine Arts and Natural History (15)**, *1, Burgring 5 and 7*, which are mirror images of each other designed by Gottfried Semper and Karl von Hasenauer. The museums were built to house the impressive collections amassed by the Hapsburgs. A huge statue of Empress Maria Theresa presides over the gardens dividing the two museums. The empress is surrounded by her advisors and was created by Kaspar Zumbusch.

The **Fine Arts Museum** contains one of the most impressive art collections in the world, including the most comprehensive array of paintings by Bruegel. The Hapsburgs also collected other masterpieces by such artists as Durer, Titian, Rubens, and Raphael. There are fine pieces from the classical world, too, including the cult chamber of Egyptian Prince Kaninisut and ancient Greek sculptures.

The collection in the **Museum of Natural History** was started by Empress Maria Theresa's husband, Francis Stephen of Lorraine. Objects on display include a collection with thousands of insects, meteorites, and fossils. There is also a special children's hall where youngsters can see and touch objects on display.

To your right facing the ring, is the **State Opera House (16)**, *1, Opernring 2*. August von Siccardsburg and Eduard van der Null designed the building completed in 1869. But the opera house was not well received, and van der Null committed suicide because of the criticism. The opera house was restored after it was bombed during World War II. Guided tours of the opera house are available upon request. Admission is 50 schillings for adults and 30 schillings for children. But better still, see a performance at this historic, intimate theater. If tickets are sold out for a performance, you might want to try standing room places.

The **Vienna State Opera** is one of the best in the world. The **Vienna Philharmonic Orchestra** has been led by such great musicians as Gustav Mahler and Richard Strauss. (See *Nightlife & Entertainment* section for information on performances.)

Following the path of the ring back past the museums are several noteworthy buildings. First is the **Parliament (17)**, *1, Dr. Karl Renner-Ring 3, Tel. 40-110-2211*, Tram D, J, 1 or 2 Stadiongasse/Parliament. The Greek Revival building was designed by Theophil Hansen and was completed in 1883. The Athena Fountain, which dominates the square in front of the parliament, was created by Karl Kundmann. The elected National Council and the Federal Council, delegated by the provinces, both serve here. Guided tours of the parliament are available Monday through Friday at 11 a.m. and 3 p.m. To the right of the building, is a memorial dedicated to Dr. Karl Renner, Austria's president from 1945 to 1950.

Next to the parliament is the **Rathaus (18)**, *1, Friedrich-Schmidt Platz, Tel. 403-8989*. The city hall was designed by Friedrich von Schmidt, who also built the Cologne Cathedral in Germany. The neo-Gothic style Rathaus building was completed in 1883, and looks much more like a church than a city hall, except for the armored sculptures that decorate the structure. The tower, topped by the Knight of City Hall, rises 321 feet over the Vienna skyline. Guided tours of the Rathaus are available Monday through Friday at 1 p.m. Group tours should be arranged at least one month in advance. Concerts are held in the arcaded courtyard during the summer months.

Across the street is the **National Theater (19)**, *1, Dr. Karl Lueger Ring*. The theater was designed by Gottfried Semper and Karl von Hasenauer and completed in 1888. The building was badly damaged during World War II and restored to its present splendor. Continuing along the ring is the **University (20)**, *1, Dr. Karl Leuger Ring*, the third oldest university in Central Europe after those in Prague and Cracow. The university was founded by Duke Rudolf IV in 1365. The present-day Italian Renaissance-style building was constructed between 1873 and 1884. Sigmund Freud attended the university and later taught here.

The gothic-style spires of the **Votive Church (21)**, 9, Rooseveltplatz, can be seen from the University. The church was commissioned by Emperor Maximilian of Mexico for his brother Emperor Francis Joseph, after he was saved from an assassination attempt. The church was designed by Heinrich von Ferstel and completed in 1879. Count Niklas Salm, who put down the first Turkish siege in 1529, is buried in the Baptismal Chapel.

Belvedere Palace

Prince Eugene of Savoy had the **Belvedere Palace** built as a summer residence outside of the walls of Vienna. Johann Lukas von Hildebrandt was commissioned to design the Baroque palace. After Eugene's death, the palace was taken over by the Hapsburgs. Archduke Francis Ferdinand, whose assassination in Sarajevo in 1914 sparked World War I, lived at the Belvedere at the beginning of the century.

Today, the palace buildings house art dating from the medieval era through the 20th century. The Upper Belvedere was used by Prince Eugene for ceremonies and gala events. Paintings from the 19th and 20th century are displayed from such artists as Schiele and Klimt. Prince Eugene lived in the Lower Belvedere from 1714 to 1716. The building is home to the **Baroque Museum**. The nearby **Orangerie** today showcases the **Museum of Medieval Austrian Art**.

Admission to the palace galleries is 60 schillings for adults; 30 schillings for children. The extensive gardens are open free to the public. You can reach the Belvedere by taking the D tram on the Ring.

Prater

The **Prater's** giant ferris wheel, or **Reisenrad**, is one of Vienna's most recognizable landmarks, appearing in countless films and postcards. The Reisenrad, rising 209 feet into the air and weighing more than 430 metric tons, was designed in 1896 by the English engineer Walter Basset. He designed wheels for London, Paris, and Blackpool, but these other specimens were dismantled and their parts sold. Vienna's Reisenrad survived, however, but most of it was destroyed in World War II. The landmark was rebuilt, and its 15 cabins have been in operation since 1947.

The Risenrad, *2 Prater, 26-2130*, is open May through September from 9 a.m. to midnight and during the rest of the year from 10 a.m. to 6 p.m. Fare reductions with the Vienna Card.

The rest of the amusement park is surprisingly large with thrill rides, haunted houses, carnival games and lots of highly caloric, festival food.

The park is sure to appeal to children, but adults may find the whole thing a bit kitschy. The park extends outward with ponds and woodland, a nice place to take a leisurely stroll or have a picnic. Another good place to eat is the **Pleasure Pavilion**, *Hauptallee*. The pavilion was remodelled in 1782 and was formerly used as a stop during imperial hunting trips. Today, you can take a break yourself at the cafe-restaurant on the sight.

Schonbrunn

Even if you only have a limited amount of time in Vienna, make sure you include a visit to Maria Theresa's summer palace, **Schonbrunn**, *13, Schonbrunner Schloss Strasse, 811-13-238*. This is an especially good place to visit if you are traveling with children with its coach collection, butterfly house, ornate gardens and the oldest zoo in Europe.

The enormous Schonbrunn, which means "beautiful spring," has 1,441 rooms to get lost in. Local lore has it that Emperor Matthias was the first to call the original family mansion by that name after discovering the spring while hunting. But the marauding Hungarians, led by Stephen Boczkay, ravaged the estate. Matthias had another hunting lodge built, but that one was destroyed in 1683 by the Turks after their invasion of Vienna. The Baroque master J.B. Fischer von Erlach designed the next replacement, which was built between 1695 and 1711 for Emperor Leopold I. The architect's original plan called for the palace to be built on the hillside where the Gloirette is now located. The location of the palace and the Gloirette were switched, because the change would prove less costly.

But in 1711, Emperor Karl VI ordered work on the palace stopped. Empress Maria Theresa came to the palace's rescue in 1740, ordering that the palace not only undergo repairs but be vastly enlarged for her 16 children and the rest of the royal household. Under the direction of Architect Nicolaus Pacassi, the work was completed with several changes made to the existing palace, including the **Great** and **Small galleries**. The palace is painted in the famous Maria Theresa yellow.

Maria Theresa was an avid collector of Eastern art and valuable porcelains, enamel work, and other Oriental pieces that are prominent in the **Lacque Room** and the **Round** and **Oval galleries**. Huge paintings by Johann Wenzel Bergl decorate several rooms of the palace. The **Room of Millions** is one of the most incredible examples of Rococo, decorated wall to wall with Indian and Persian miniatures. And in the **Hall of Mirrors**, 6-year-old Wolfgang Amadeus Mozart once gave a concert for the Empress. Room after room will dazzle you with the wealth and extravagance of the Hapsburgs. The grandeur of Schonbrunn apparently appealed to Napoleon, who set up shop here during his occupation of

Vienna in 1805 and 1809. His son, Napoleon II, along with the Archduchess Maria Louise of Austria, died at the palace in 1832 at the age of 21. Control of Schonbrunn was transferred to the state after Emperor Karl I abdicated in 1918 following the end of World War I.

The palace's **gala rooms** are open from April to October daily from 8:30 a.m. to 5 p.m.; November through March daily from 8:30 a.m. to 4:30 p.m. The Berglzimmer is open Saturday, Sunday, and holidays 9 a.m. to 4 p.m. Discounts are available to the palace and the other attractions with the Vienna Card. The **Butterfly House**, *at the Sonnenuhrhaus, Tel. 877-50-87-0), is open* daily May through September, 10 a.m. to 4:30 p.m.; October to April daily 10 a.m. to 3 p.m.

The **Gloirette** was built to memorialize the victory over Frederick II of Prussia in 1757. The pavilion is open from May through October from 9 a.m. to 5 p.m. The **Imperial Coach Collection**, *Tel. 877-3244*, contains coaches, carriages, sleighs, and riding equipment used by the imperial dynasty from 1690 to 1917. The highlight of the collection is certainly the Imperial Coach drawn by eight horses during imperial parades. The display is open to the public from April to October daily, 9 a.m. to 6 p.m.; November to March daily, except Monday, 10 a.m. to 4 p.m. The **Palmery**, *Tel. 877-50-87-0*, is open from May to September daily from 9:30 a.m. to 5:30 p.m.; October to April daily from 9:30 a.m. to 4:30 p.m. The palace park is open daily from 6 a.m. until dusk, and is a great place for a picnic during warm weather.

The **palace zoo**, *Tel. 877-9294-0*, was commissioned by Emperor Francis I to educate and entertain the court. The old buildings today are used to house older animals. Others are housed in modern enclosures that mimic their natural habitats. The **Imperial Breakfast Pavilion**, dating from 1759, can also be found here. The zoo is open to the public from November to January from 9 a.m. to 4:30 p.m.; February and October daily from 9 a.m. to 5 p.m.; March daily 9 a.m. to 5:30 p.m.; April daily 9 a.m. to 6 p.m.; May through September daily 9 a.m. to 6:30 p.m. A **marionette theater** performs during the summer months at the palace. For information or reservations, *call 817-3247; fax 817-32-47-4*.

You can take the U-Bahn to Schonbrunn on the U-4 line.

ARCHITECTURAL LANDMARKS

Vienna is a gold mine for architecture buffs. There are many beautiful buildings outside the Ring which are worth a look, including the following (arranged by district):

1st District

The **Ferstel Palace**, *1, Herrengasse 17*, was built by Heinrich Ferstel, the architect who designed the Votive Church. The Italian style "palace" was originally built for the National Bank of Austria and was the home of the Austrian stock exchange until 1877. The 12-stone statues on the facade represent the different parts of the Austro-Hungarian empire. In the center shopping arcade, you'll see a fountain of the *Danube Nymph* created by Anton Fernkorn.

The **Federal Chancellor's Office**, *1, Ballhausplatz 2*, holds a significant place in the history of the country. The building was originally designed by J.L. von Hildebrandt in 1717. Prince Metternich held many of the meetings of the Congress of Vienna (1814-1815) in the office rooms, and the ultimatum to Serbia, which led to World War I, was penned here. After World War II, the building became the seat of the Federal Chancellor's Office and the Foreign Ministry.

The **Secession**, *1, Friedrichstrasse 12, Tel. 587-5307,* got its name from the movement which started at the turn of the century by artists wishing to rid themselves of the establishment of the 19th century. Their motto was *to each age, its art. To art, its freedom.* The building, erected by Joseph Olbrich in 1897, was immediately derided by the Viennese, who nicknamed it the "Golden Cabbage." In the basement of the building is the famous Beethoven frieze by Gustav Klimt. Special exhibitions by contemporary artists are also on display. Open Tuesday through Friday 10 a.m. to 6 p.m.; Saturday, Sunday and holidays 10 a.m. to 4 p.m.

The **Ministry of Finance**, *1, Himmelpfortgasse 8*, was once the winter palace of Prince Eugene of Savoy. The palace was built by the Baroque genius J.B. Fischer von Erlach in 1698. J.L. von Hildebrandt was in charge of later renovations.

The **Old University**, *1, Dr. Ignaz Seipel Platz*, was originally founded in 1365. The Jesuits had the building renovated during the Counter-Reformation. The former theater contains a ceiling painting from the 18th century.

The **Post Office Savings Bank**, *1, Georg Coch Platz 2*, was designed by modern architectural pioneer Otto Wagner. The marble and aluminum building was completed in 1912.

The **Ronacher Theater**, *1, Seilerstatte 9*, was constructed by Ferdinand Fellner in 1872. But Vienna's municipal theater burned down a little more than a decade later. Fellner's son was commissioned to rebuild the theater used for musicals, operettas, comedies, and other performances. The theater was again restored following extensive damage during World War II.

3rd District

The **Radverleih City/Hundertwasserhaus**, *3, Kegelgasse 43, Tel. 713-93-95*, is a municipal housing project designed by painter Friedensreich Hundertwasser. The 50-apartment, multicolored building is free-form, emphasizing natural materials, terraces, and gardens planted in the structure. It's open daily from April through October, from 9 a.m. to 9 p.m.

Nearby is the **Kunst Haus Wien**, *3, Untere Weissgerberstrasse 13, Tel. 712-0491*. Hundertwasser bought this former factory and transformed it with different colored glass, metals, bricks, and multi-colored ceramic tiles. The space now holds a permanent collection chronicling the artist's work, temporary contemporary art exhibition space, a cafe and museum shop.

Guided tours are available upon request. The Kunst Haus Wien is open daily 10 a.m. to 7 p.m. Admission is 70 schillings for adults; 40 schillings for children. Admission reductions with the Vienna Card.

5th District

The **Margarenten Housing Project**, *5, Margaretenplatz 1*, was designed by Ferdinand Fellner and Hermann Helmer, the architect of the Volkestheatre. The project, completed in 1885, relies on a variety of architectural styles with neo-Renaissance facades, Alpine touches, and neo-Gothic turrets.

6th District

Viennese mayor Helmut Zilk asked painter Arik Brauer to design and decorate a public housing complex. The **Arik Brauer House**, *6, Gumpendorfer Strasse 134-136*, was the result with its large tile paintings. Architect Peter Pelikan helped design the 33 apartments finished in 1993.

The **Majolica House**, *6, Linke Wienzeile 40*, has been reproduced on myriad postcards. Art Nouveau architect Otto Wagner designed the residential building decorated with flowers composed of peach, green, and blue tiles. He also designed the adjacent building with gold medallions by Kolo Moser.

13th District

The **Werkbund Housing Project**, *13, Veitingergasse*, was designed by famous architects for the International Werbund Exposition in 1930. Single family residences, row houses, and other housing was designed by such famous designers as Austrian architect Adolf Loos, American architect Richard Neutra, and French architect Andre Lurcat.

19th District

The **Karl Marx Housing Project**, *19, Heiligenstadter Strasse 82-92*, was designed by Karl Ehn. The 1,600-unit complex is a symbol of the Social Democratic movement which dominated Vienna from 1919 to 1934. The housing complex, with its community facilities and interior courtyards, was a center of Social Democratic resistance during the civil unrest of 1934. The housing project was bombarded by the army to break the resistance.

22nd District

The **Vienna International Center**, *22, Wagramer Strasser*, houses several different international organizations, including the United Nations and the International Atomic Energy Agency. The four office tower is called "UNO city" by the Viennese. The UN pays 1 schilling a year to rent their office space.

CHURCHES & RELIGIOUS MONUMENTS

There are dozens of churches in Vienna, and many of them are architectural masterpieces in their own right. Here is a list of some of the most famous, again arranged by district.

1st District

The **Chapel of the Savior**, *1, Salvatorgasse 5*, was originally founded in the 13th century for use by the Old City Hall. The church's Renaissance facade was added in 1520.

The Gothic **Church Am Hof**, *1, Am Hof*, was finished in 1403, but was renovated in the Baroque style following a fire. The Baroque facade was added in 1662. Emperor Francis II renounced his position as Holy Roman Emperor of the German Nation in the church square here in 1806.

The **Church of the Augustinian Friars**, *1, Augustinerstrasse 7*, was built after Duke Frederick the Handsome founded a monastery of Augustinian friars in 1327. The church used to be the parish church of the Imperial Palace and the Hapsburg Court. It was here that the young Marie Antoinette married Louis XVI of France. The hearts and tombs of the Hapsburgs are housed here. Admission to the burial vault is 30 schillings.

The **Church of the Knights Hospitalers**, *1, Karntner Strasse 37*, seems like an anomaly located amid all the stores on Vienna's most famous shopping street. The Gothic church is believed to have been built in the 14th century. The facade, however, is Baroque and was added in 1808.

The **Church of the Scots** was founded by Babenberg ruler Heinrich Jasomirgott in 1155. The title "Scots" is actually an inaccurate translation of the Latin word "Scotti" but the name stuck. The church's present facade was added in the 19th century. The **museum** at the Abbey of the Scots, *1, Freyung 6, Tel. 534-98-600,* houses medieval paintings of Vienna. The museum is open Thursday through Saturday 10 a.m. to 5 p.m.; Sunday noon to 5 p.m. Admission reductions with the Vienna Card.

The **Church of the Teutonic Order** has Gothic roots from the 13th century but was transformed into the Baroque style like so many Austrian churches. Be sure to note the 16th-century Dutch winged altarpiece in the interior. You can also visit the **Treasury of the Order of Teutonic Knights**, *1, Singerstrasse 7, Tel. 512-1065.* The treasury contains such objects as a "Viper Tongue Credenza," to take the poison out of food, chalices, china and crystal. The display is open May through October, Mondays and Thursday through Sunday, 10 a.m. to noon; Wednesdays, Fridays and Saturdays 3 to 5 p.m. November through April, Mondays, Thursdays and Saturdays 10 a.m. to noon; Wednesday, Friday and Saturday 3 p.m. to 5 p.m.

The **Dominican Church**, *1, Postgasse 4*, was completed in 1634, replacing a previous building from the 13th century. If you're a fan of the Baroque, you must see the interior of the church with its lavish adornment. A part of the city's old fortifications can be found behind the church.

The **Franciscan Church**, *1, Franziskanerplatz*, was originally the site of a monastery built between 1383 and 1387. German Renaissance elements were added in 1603. Baroque painter J.G. Schmidt was among the painters who decorated the interior. The *Moses* Fountain in the square was designed by J.M. Fischer in 1798.

The **Jesuit Church**, *1, Dr. Ignaz Seipel Platz*, was completed in 1631 during the Thirty Years War and the Counter-Reformation. Be sure to note the ceiling painting, done by Andrea Pozzo, which is an optical illusion creating the impression that there is a dome on the church. The 10 a.m. service on Sunday features masses by Haydn, Mozart, and other great composers.

The Gothic **Minoritenkirche**, *1, Minoritenplatz*, was completed in the 14th century, although the church's tower was damaged during both Turkish sieges of the city. Ferdinand von Hohenberg had the church restored in 1784. In the interior, be sure to notice a mosaic replica of Da Vinci's *Last Supper*.

Our Lady's Column, *1, Am Hof*, was originally erected by Emperor Ferdinand II in 1646, but the column was replaced in 1667 by the present one. The emperor had vowed to construct the column if the city was delivered from the threat of Swedish forces.

The **Palace of the Archbishops**, *1, Rotenturmstrasse 2*, was believed to have been built by Giovanni Coccapani in 1630. The palace is still the residence of Vienna's archbishop. The museum of the diocese here

---

A SYNAGOGUE THAT SURVIVED

Before World War II, Vienna's Jewish community once numbered 170,000 people and the city had 94 synagogues and prayer rooms. After Hitler annexed Austria in 1938, most of the synagogues were destroyed during a night of terror on November 9. This Synagogue, 1, Seitenstettengasse 2-4, was probably saved owing to its location on a residential street.

Today, only about 7,000 Jews remain in Vienna. The others either emigrated or were killed in the Holocaust.

---

displays the first portrait north of the Alps: that of Duke Rudolf IV, who founded St. Stephen's Cathedral.

Vienna's first **Protestant Church**, *1, Dorotheergasse 18*, was originally built as a monastery in 1582. After Emperor Joseph II abolished monasteries in 1783 it was given to the Lutheran community for worship.

St. Ann's Church, *1, Annagasse 3B*, was originally constructed in the late Middle Ages, but was remodelled in 1629. Baroque painter Daniel Gran created the ceiling frescoes and the altar piece. The wood carving of Christ, his mother, and St. Ann is attributed to Veit Stoss or the Master of the Mauer Altarpiece.

The **Church of St. Mary's at the Stairs**, *1, Salvartorgasse*, was reconstructed in 1394. The building was restored after both Turkish sieges when it suffered substantial damage. The church gets its name because it used to be situated on a part of the Danube that touched the city's former fortifications.

St. Michael's Church, *1, Michaelerplatz*, was originally a Romanesque structure dating from the 13th century. The church was altered through the centuries. Its present appearance dates from 1792. Lorenzo Matielli designed the angels at the church's entrance. Catacombs, once used to bury the dead, are open to visitors.

Legend has it that the original **St. Peter's Church**, *1, Petersplatz*, was founded by Charlemagne in 792, commemorated in relief on the east facade. J.L. von Hildebrandt completed the church in its present form in 1733 following the design set forth by Gabriel Montani. The dome fresco was painted by Baroque artist J.M. Rottmayr.

St. Rupert's Church, *1, Ruprechtsplatz*, is Vienna's oldest, dating from about 740. The church's aisle and the lower level of the tower date from the 11th century. Modern stained-glass windows have been added, but rather from detracting from the ancient structure they enhance this beautiful church.

3rd District

The original **Church of St. Elizabeth's Convent**, *3, Landstrasser Hauptstrasse 4A*, was destroyed by a flood. Its much larger replacement was built in 1749 by F.A. Pilgram.

4th District

The **Church of St. Charles Borromeo**, *4, Karlsplatz*, is one of Vienna's most famous landmarks. Johann Bernhard Fischer von Erlach designed the Baroque church which was finished by his son Joseph Emmanuel in 1739. Emperor Charles VI had the church built after vowing he would build a great church if Vienna was delivered from an epidemic of plague in 1713. The dome of the church rises 236 feet high. The frescoes inside St. Charles were painted by J.M. Rottmayr in 1725. The altar depicting the assumption of the Virgin Mary was created by Sebastiano Ricci. A sculpture by Henry Moore was placed in the reflecting pool in front of the church in the 1970s.

6th District

The original church at the site of the **Mariahilf Church**, *6, Mariahilfer Strasse 55*, was destroyed by the Turks in 1683. The church which replaced it was probably built by Sebastiano Carlone in 1686. A monument to the composer Joseph Haydn stands in the church courtyard.

7th District

The **Abbey Church**, *7, Mariahilfer Strasse 24*, is also known as the Garrison Church because it was attended by soldiers from the nearby army barracks. The church was believed to originally have been built by J.E. Fischer von Erlach but was renovated in the 18th century.

The **Altlerchenfeld Parish Church**, *7, Lerchenfelder Strasse 111*, traces its roots back to the Romanesque period. The church was designed by Johann G. Muller. The frescoes inside the Parish Church of the Seven Sanctuaries were sketched by Joseph von Fuhrich.

8th District

The **Church of the Piarist Order**, *8, Jodok-Fink-Platz*, was designed by the Baroque master J.L. von Hildebrandt in 1716. The interior frescoes were painted by artist F.A. Maulbertsch. The column in front of the Church dedicated to the Virgin Mary was erected in 1713 during an outbreak of plague in that year.

14th District

Otto Wagner built the **Church am Steinhof**, *14, Baumgartner Hohe 1, Tel. 910-60-2391*, between 1904 and 1907 with its famous Art Nouveau copper-covered dome. Guided tours are scheduled Saturdays at 3 p.m. or by prior arrangement.

15th District

The **Church of Our Lady of Victory**, *15, Mariahilfer Gurtel*, was built in 1868 by Friedrich von Schmidt, the same architect who designed the Rathaus.

19th District

According to local legend, the **Church of St. Joseph**, *19, Josefsdorf*, was the site where mass was said before the Viennese victory over the Turks in 1683. A chapel in the church commemorates the historic event.

The site of **St. Leopold's Church**, *19, Leopoldsberg*, was once the location of the castle of the Dukes of Babenberg. Antonio Beduzzi designed the church constructed from 1718 to 1730. The church was restored after substantial damage incurred during World War II. A memorial across the square honors the more than 200,000 Austrians who died in Allied prisoner-of-war camps.

23rd District

The modern **Church of the Most Holy Trinity**, *23, Mauer*, corner of Georgsgasse and Rysergasse, was completed in 1976. About 4,000 tons of concrete was used for the church, designed by Austrian sculptor Fritz Wotruba. The walls are made up of 152 modular cubes arranged in irregular arrangements. Guided tours available upon request.

PARKS & GARDENS

Vienna has large parks and formal gardens sprinkled throughout the city. The parks are ideal for taking a break from sight-seeing or for an impromptu picnic. Here are some of the most famous by district:

1st District

The **Stadt Park**, *1, Parkring*, was the first park open to the Viennese public. Designed by Josef Selleny and Rudolf Siebeck, the Stadt Park (City Park) was inaugurated on August 21, 1862. Monuments to famous Austrians abound, including one of the most renowned in the city memorializing Johann Strauss Junior playing his violin as his muses swirl around him. At the **Kursalon** in the park, patrons can waltz away the afternoon from Easter to late October.

The **Volksgarten**, or Common Gardens, *1, Dr. Karl Renner Ring*, were put in place after Napoleon ordered the demolition of the Palace Bastion in 1809. Inside the park, you'll notice what looks like a Grecian temple.

The **Temple of Theseus** was built in 1823 after the Theseion in Athens. A memorial, by Hans Bitterlich and Friedrich Ohmann, to the Empress Elisabeth is also here.

The **Burggarten**, *1, Burgring*, was created when the Hofburg was expanded in 1820. The garden was off limits for all but the royal family and members of the Hapsburg court until 1918. A statue memorializing the composer Wolfgang Amadeus Mozart and several former emperors can be found in the park.

3rd District

You can enter the **Alpine Gardens**, *3, Landstrasse Gurtel 1, Tel. 798-3149*, from the grounds of the Belvedere Palace's park. The gardens, with a wide variety of well-marked native fauna, are open April through July, Monday through Friday 10 a.m. to 6 p.m.; Saturday, Sunday and holidays 9 a.m. to 6 p.m. The gardens are closed in cases of rain or high winds.

Medicinal plants were first planted at the **Botanical Gardens of the University of Vienna**, *3, Mechelgasse 2 or Landstrasser Gurtel 1, 79-794*, on the order of the Empress Maria Theresa on the suggestion of her personal physician. The gardens were donated to the university in 1757. The gardens are open from April through October, 9 a.m. to dusk. The gardens are closed in case of rain or strong winds. Guided tours are available during May and September, Wednesdays at 4:30 p.m.; June, July and August, second Wednesday of the month at 4:30 p.m.

10th District

The **Oberlaa Spa Park**, *10, Kurbadstrasse*, covers more than 250 acres with artificial ponds, playgrounds, restaurants, and a great view of the southern part of the city. The **Oprlaa Thermal Spring** reaches temperatures of 130 degrees. You can take an indoor or outdoor thermal bath in the sulphur enriched water.

13th District

The **Lainz Game Preserve**, *13, Hermesstrasse*, was created by the imperial court in 1557. Empress Maria Theresa had the park enclosed with a 15-mile wall in 1772. After World War I, the park, containing wild boars, elk, and deer, was opened to the public. An observation platform on the **Kaltbrundl Hill** affords a terrific view of the city and the surrounding Vienna Woods.

18th District

The **Turkenschanz Park**, *18, Hasenauerstrasse*, was named after the Turkish stronghold that was located here during the sieges of Vienna in 1529 and 1683. The English-style park was designed by Heinrich Ferstel and opened in 1888. The park has ponds, a petting zoo, and a fountain dedicated to the Turkish poet and freedom fighter Yunu Emre.

22nd District

The **Danube Park**, 22, *Wagramer Strasse,* was once a garbage dump. The 247-acre site was transformed for the Vienna International Horticultural Exposition in 1964. The Danube Tower is 827 feet and visitors can look out over the city on the observation platform. A revolving restaurant and cafe also offer spectacular views of the city.

MUSICAL MEMORIALS

Vienna was once the musical capital of the world, and musicians from all over Europe flocked to the city to make their fortune. There are still remnants of musicians from bygone days throughout Vienna, from Mozart to Beethoven to Schubert. Music lovers can see where their favorite composers and musicians lived, worked, and are buried.

Music lovers should also make a stop at the **Museum of Old Musical Instruments**, *Heldenplatz.* The museum has musical instruments through the centuries and many of the original instruments played by famous musicians who made Austria their home.

Beethoven lived all over Vienna, and several houses around the city bear testimony to the fact:

- **Beethoven Memorial Rooms**, *Pasqualati House, 1, Molker Bastei 8. Tel. 535-8905.* U-Bahn Schottentor. Beethoven lived here at different times between 1804 and 1815.
- **Beethoven House of the Heiligenstadt Testament**, *19, Probusgasse 6, Tel. 37-54-08.* Tram 37 Geweygasse. Beethoven wrote his *Heiligenstadt Testament* here in 1802, despairing over his increasing deafness.
- **Beethoven House of the Eroica**, *19, Doblinger Hauptstrasse 92. Tel. 369-1424.* Tram 37 Pokornygasse. Open daily 9 a.m. to 12:15 p.m. and 1 p.m. to 4:30 p.m. Closed Mondays. Fridays, free admission until noon. Beethoven worked on his Heroic Symphony (Symphony Number 3) here from 1803 to 1804. He originally dedicated the piece to Napoleon. but later changed his mind in his disappointment that the French leader was abandoning the ideals of the revolution.
- **Beethoven House** at *3, Ungargasse 5*, where the composer created his Ninth Symphony in 1823.
- **Beethoven House** at *8, Trautsongasse 2*, where the Creed of the Missa Solemnis was composed in 1820.

Other houses the great composer lived in include the house *at 19, Kahlenberger Strasse 26*, in the summer of 1817 and 1824; *at 19, Pfarrplatz*

2, briefly during 1817; and *at 19, Grinzinger Strasse 64*, in 1808. When he found out that the playwright Franz Grillparzer's mother liked to listen to him play the piano, Beethoven decided to forgo playing until the family moved away.

Countess Anna Maria Erdody, one of Beethoven's patronesses, hosted the composer several times at her country estate. Today, the **memorial**, *21, Jenewingasse 17*, features concerts by the composer. Beethoven died at the house which stood at *9, Schwarspainierstrasse 15*, in 1827. The house on the site today is from a later period, though.

And if you're truly a fan there's the **Beethoven Monument**, *1, Beethovenplatz*, created by Kaspar Zumbusch in 1880 in honor of the illustrious musician.

Other noteworthy sights in musical history around Vienna:

Cemetery of St. Mark, where Mozart is buried but unfortunately in an unmarked grave, *3, Leberstrasse 6-8*. A monument to the famous composer has since been erected. Open April and October, 7 a.m. to 5 p.m.; May and September 7 a.m. to 6 p.m.; June through August, 7 a.m. to 7 p.m.; November through March 7 a.m. until dusk. Tram 18, 71, 72 Landstrasser Hauptstrasse/Rennweg.

Central Cemetery, with memorials to Beethoven, Mozart, Schubert, Brahms, Gluck, Strauss and Schonberg, *11, Simmeringer Hauptstrasse 234*. *Tel. 719-01 or 760-41*. Open November to February, 8 a.m. to 5 p.m.; March, April, September and October, 7 a/m/ to 6 p.m.; May through August, 7 a.m. to 7 p.m. Tram 71 or 72.

Gluck Residence, *4, Wiedner Hauptstrasse, 32*. Composer Christoph Willibald Gluck lived and died in 1817 at this house.

Haydn's Residence, with the **Brahms' Memorial Room**, *6, Haydngasse 19*. *Tel. 596-1307*. Open daily, except Monday, 9 a.m. to 12:15 p.m. and 1 p.m. to 4:30 p.m. Admission free before noon on Fridays. U-Bahn Zieglergasse. The composer Joseph Haydn lived here from 1797 until his death in 1809.

The **Musikverein**, *1, Dumbastrasse 3*, is the home of the Vienna Philharmonic. The building was designed by Theophil Hansen and was completed in 1869.

Mozart Memorial, "Figaro House," *1, Domgasse 5*. *Tel. 513-6294*. Open daily, except Monday, 9 a.m. to 12:15 p.m. and 1 p.m. and 4:30 p.m. Admission is 15 schillings for adults; 5 schillings for children. U-Bahn Stephansplatz. Mozart composed his opera *The Marriage of Figaro* at this 17th century apartment when he lived here from 1784 to 1787.

Schubert's Birthplace, *9, Nussdorfer Strasse 54*. *Tel. 34-59-924*. Open daily, except Monday, 9 a.m. to 12:15 p.m. and 1 p.m. and 4:30 p.m. Tram 37 and 38 Canisiusgasse. Schubert was born here on January 31, 1797.

Schubert's Last Residence, *4, Kettenbruckengasse 6. Tel. 57-39-072.* Open daily, except Monday, 9 a.m. to 12:15 p.m. and 1 p.m. to 4:30 p.m. U-Bahn Kettenbruckengasse. Schubert died here on November 19, 1828. **Strauss' Residence**, *2 Praterstrasse 54. Tel. 24-01-21.* Open daily except Monday 9 a.m. to 12:15 p.m. and 1 p.m. to 4:30 p.m. U-Bahn Nestroyplatz. It was here that Strauss created his most famous composition, *The Blue Danube Waltz* in 1867. **Wagner's Residence**, *7, Doblergasse 4. Tel. 93-22-33 or 523-22-33.* Open Monday through Friday 9 a.m. to noon. From July to September visits upon request. Tram 46 Strozzigasse.

HIDDEN TREASURES

Vienna has a lot of smaller museums and historical sights that are among some of the city's hidden treasures. If you are in Vienna for a longer stay, you may want to pay a visit to some of these special sights.

Albertina Collection of Graphic Arts, *1, Augustinerstrasse 1. Tel. 534-83.* Opening hours 10 a.m. to 4 p.m. U-Bahn, tram, bus Karlsplatz/Oper. Admission 45 schillings for adults; children 20 schillings.

Aquarium, *6, Haus des Meers, Esterhazypark. Tel. 587-1417.* Open daily 9 a.m. to 6 p.m. U-Bahn Neubaugasse.

Archives of the Austrian Resistance, *Old City Hall, 1, Wipplingerstrasse 8, ground floor. Tel. 534-36-779.* Open Monday, Wednesday and Thursday 9 a.m. to 5 p.m. U-Bahn Stephansplatz or Schwedenplatz. The building served as Vienna's city hall until 1885. The sight was donated to the city council in 1316 after it was confiscated by the Hapsburgs. It's previous owner, Otto Haymo, had participated in a plot to overthrow the imperial rulers.

Bauernfeld Memorial Room, *19, Doblinger Hauptstrasse 96. Tel. 37-69-39.* Open Saturdays 3:30 p.m. to 6 p.m. and Sundays 10 a.m. to noon. Closed during July and August. Tram 37 Pokornygasse.

Circus and Clown Museum, *2, Karmelitergasse 9. 211-06-127 or Tel. 34-68-615.* The museum features costumes, photos and posters chronicling the history of Austrian circuses. Open Wednesday 5:30 p.m. to 7 p.m.; Saturday 2:30 p.m. to 5 p.m.; Sunday 10 a.m. to noon. Tram N or 21 Karmeliterplatz.

Clock Museum, *1, Schulhof 2. Tel. 533-2265.* Open daily except Monday 9 a.m. to 4:30 p.m. The museum has more than 3,000 clocks on display, including a wrought-iron tower clock that once graced St. Stephen's Cathedral. Free admission until noon on Fridays. Admission is 30 schillings for adults; 10 schillings for children. Reduced tickets with a Vienna Card. U-Bahn Stephansplatz.

Collection of Religious Folk Art, including an old monastic pharmacy, *1, Johannesgasse 8. Tel. 512-1337.* Open Wednesdays and Sundays, 9 a.m. to 1 p.m. U-Bahn Karlsplatz or Oper.

Doll and Toy Museum, *1, Schulhof 4, first floor. Tel. 535-6860.* Open daily, except Monday, 10 a.m. to 6 p.m. U-Bahn Stephansplatz or Herrengasse.

Electro-Pathological Museum, *15, Selzergasse 19. Tel. 92-72-72.* Open Tuesday through Friday, 8 a.m. to 9 a.m. and noon to 1 p.m. U-Bahn Johnstrasse.

Ephesus Museum, *1, Heldenplatz, New Palace.* Open 10 a.m. to 6 p.m. Admission 30 schillings. U-Bahn Volkestheatre. The museum houses a collection of artifacts unearthed in 1900 from Ephesus in Turkey.

Esperanto Museum, *1, Hofburg, Michaelertor. Tel. 535-5145.* Monday and Friday, 10 a.m. to 4 p.m. and Wednesday 10 a.m. to 6 p.m. Learn all about the official world language. U-Bahn Stephansplatz.

Ethnological Museum, *1, Neue Burg, Heldenplatz. Tel. 534-300.* Open daily, except Tuesday, 10 a.m. to 4 p.m. Tram D, J, 1, 2 Burgring. The museum contains collections from cultures around the world accumulated from as far back as the 16th century.

Fashion Collection of the Historical Museum of the City of Vienna, *12, Hetzendorfer Strasse 79. Tel. 802-1657.* Open daily, except Monday, 9 a.m. to 12:15 p.m. and 1 p.m. to 4:30 p.m. Tram 62 Schloss Hetzendorf. The building was originally built as a hunting lodge for Sigismund Count Thun in 1694.

Fiaker Museum, *17, Veronikagasse 12. Tel. 40-106-0.* Open the first Wednesday of each month from 10 a.m. to noon and by prior arrangement. U-Bahn Josefstadter Strasse.

Film Museum, *1, Augustinerstrasse 1. Tel. 533-70-54-0.* October through May, Monday through Saturday 6 p.m. and 8 p.m. Films shown include classics and avant-garde films. U-Bahn Karlsplatz and Oper.

Fire Fighting Museum, *1 Am Hof 7. Tel. 531-99.* Open Sundays and holidays from 9 a.m. to noon. The former civic armory was originally built in the 16th century and was used to store fire fighting equipment from 1685 onwards. The museum is open Monday through Friday by reservation. U-Bahn Herrengasse.

First Aid Museum, *15, Pillergasse 24/1. Tel. 89-145-8311.* Open Thursdays 4 p.m. to 8 p.m. U-Bahn Meidling Hauptstrasse.

Folklore Museum, *8, Laudongasse 15-19. Tel. 406-8905.* Open Tuesday through Friday 9 a.m. to 5 p.m.; Saturday 9 a.m. to noon; Sunday 9 a.m. to 1 p.m. Tram 5 or bus 13A Laudongasse. The museum details the customs, costumes and other folklore from across the country.

Freud's House, *9, Berggasse 19. Tel. 319-1596.* Items donated by Freud's daughter Anna include original furniture from his waiting room, objects from his collection of antiquities and first editions of his books. Open July through September 9 a.m. to 6 p.m.; October through June 9 a.m. to 4 p.m. Admission is 60 schillings for adults; 40 schillings for children.Admission reductions with the Vienna Card. Tram D Schlickgasse.

Fuchs Museum, *Otta Wagner Villa 1, 14, Huttelbergstrasse 26. Tel. 914-8575.* Open Monday through Friday 10 a.m. to 4 p.m. by reservation. Bus 148 or 152 Campingplatz Wien West 1.

Geymuller Museum, *18, Khevenhullerstrasse 2. Tel. 479-3139.* Open March through November, Tuesday, Wednesday, Friday, Saturday and Sunday 10 a.m. to 5 p.m. Guided tour Sundays at 3 p.m. This muesuem features the Sobek clock and watch collection. Bus 41A Khevenhullerstrasse.

Glass Museum, *1, Karntner Strasse 26. Tel. 512-0508.* Monday through Friday 9 a.m. to 6 p.m.; Saturday 9 a.m.to 1 p.m. Groups should reserve in advance. U-Bahn Karlsplatz and Oper.

Gold and Silversmith Museum, *7, Zieglergasse 22. Tel. 93-33-88 or 523-4096.* Wednesdays 3 p.m. to 6 p.m. and by prior arrangement.Closed during July and August. U-Bahn Zieglergasse.

Heimito Von Doderer Memorial Room, *Alsergrund District Museum, 9, Wahringer Strasse 43. Tel. 40-034-127.* Open Wednesday 9 a.m. to 11 a.m. and Sunday 10 a.m. to noon. Tram 5, 37, 38, 40, 41, 42 Wahringer Strasse/ Spitalgasse.

The **Hermes Villa**, *13, Lainzer Tiergarten. Tel. 804-1324,* was built by Emperor Franz Joseph for his wife "Sisi," who wanted to escape the imperial court. Unfortunately, the villa in the Vienna Woods was still not far enough away for the hapless royal. Today, the villa houses special exhibitions organized by the Historical Museum of the City of Vienna (see below). Open Wednesday through Sunday and holidays 9 a.m. to 4:30 p.m. Admission is 30 schillings for adults; 10 schillings for children. Admission reductions with the Vienna Card. Free admission Fridays before noon. Bus 60B Lainzer Tor.

Historical Museum of the City of Vienna, *4, Karlsplatz. Tel. 505-8747.* Open daily, except Monday, 9 a.m. to 4:30 p.m. Admission is 30 schillings for adults; 10 schillings for children. Admission reductions with the Vienna Card. U-Bahn Karlsplatz or Oper. The museum documents the history of the city from the first settlements on the Danube, through the 640 year reign of the Hapsburgs, to the 20th century.

Islamic Center, *21, Hubertusdamm 17. Tel. 30-13-89.* Open daily, except Friday, 9 a.m. to dusk. Guided tours can be reserved. Bus 20B Islamic Centre.

Jewish Museum of the City of Vienna, *1, Dorotheergasse 11. Tel. 535-0431.* Open daily except Saturday 10 a.m. to 6 p.m.; Thursday 10 a.m. to 9 p.m. Admission reductions with the "Vienna Card." U-Bahn

Stephansplatz. Housed in a building dating from the Middle Ages, the museum contains art, archives, and objects documenting the rich history of the Jewish population in Vienna.

Kunstforum, *1, Freyung 8. Tel. 711-91-5741.* Open daily 10 a.m. to 6 p.m.; Wednesday 10 a.m. to 9 p.m. Admission is 90 schillings for adults; 45 schillings for children. Admission reductions with the Vienna Card. U-Bahn Herrengasse.

Kunsthalle, *4, Karlsplatz. Tel. 587-9663.* Open daily 9 a.m. to 6 p.m.; Thursday 9 a.m. to 9 p.m. Admission is 45 schillings for adults; 30 schillings for children. U-Bahn Karlsplatz. The Kunsthalle features temporary contemporary art exhibitions.

Lehar-Schikaneder Mansion, *19, Hackhofergasse 18. Tel. 3718-213.* Visitors must reserve visit in advance. Tram D Nussdorf.

Memorial to the Victims in the Austrian Resistance Movement, *1, Salztorgasse 6. Tel. 534-36-775.* Open Monday 2 p.m. to 5 p.m.; Thursday and Friday 9 a.m. to noon and 2 p.m. to 5 p.m. Groups must reserve in advance. Tram 1 or 2 Salztorbrucke.

Museum of Applied Arts, *1, Stubenring 5. Tel. 711-360.* Open daily, except Monday, 10 a.m. to 6 p.m.; Thursday 10 a.m. to 9 p.m. U-Bahn Stubentor. The museum contains a fine collection of Viennese Art Nouveau. The building, designed by Heinrich von Ferstel, is the oldest museum of applied arts on the continent.

Museum of Crime and Law Enforcement, *2, Grosse Sperlgasse 24. Tel. 214-4678.* Open daily, except Monday, 10 a.m. to 5 p.m. Tram N or 21 Karmeliterplatz.

Museum of Globes at the National Library, *1, Josefplatz 1, third floor. Tel. 534-10-297.* Open Monday, Tuesday, Wednesday and Friday 11 a.m. to noon; Thursday 2 p.m. to 3 p.m. U-Bahn Karlsplatz or Herrengasse.

Museum of Heating Technology, *12, Langenfeldgasse 13-15. Tel. 85-29-503.* Open Tuesday 1 p.m. to 6 p.m. or by prior arrangement. U-Bahn Langenfeldgasse.

Museum of Horse Shoeing, Harnessing and Saddling, *3, Linke Bahngasse 11. Tel. 711-55-372.* Open Monday to Thursday 1:30 p.m. to 3:30 p.m. or by advance reservation. Tram O Ungargasse.

Museum of Horticulture, *10, Kurpark Laaer Berg. Tel. 68-11-70.* Open May through October, Wednesday to Friday 10 a.m. to 2:30 p.m. Tram 67 Laaer Berg Strasse.

Museum of Medical History, *9, Wahringer Strasse, 25/1. Tel. 403-2154.* Open Monday through Friday 9 a.m. to 3 p.m. Tram 37, 38, 40, 41 and 42 Schwarzspanierstrasse. You'll find life-size anatomical models purchased in 1785 by Emperor Joseph II to train Austria's military doctors.

Museum of Military History, *Arsenal, Building 18. Tel. 795-61-0.* Open daily, except Friday, 10 a.m. to 4 p.m. Admission is 40 schillings; 20

schillings for children. Exhibitions on military and naval history from 1600 to 1918. Tram 18 Ghegastrasse.

Museum of Modern Art Ludwig Foundation, *Liechtenstein Palace, 9, Furstengasse 1. Tel. 317-6900.* Open daily, except Monday, 10 a.m. to 6 p.m. Tram D Furstengasse.

Museum of the 20th Century, *3, Schweizer Garten. Tel. 799-6900.* Open daily, except Monday, from 10 a.m. to 6 p.m. Tram D, O or 18 Sudbahnhof. The museum, originally the Austrian pavilion at the Brussels World's Fair in 1958, houses special exhibitions of modern art.

Museum of Natural History, *1, Maria-Theresien Platz. Tel. 521-770.* Open daily, except Tuesday, 9 a.m. to 6 p.m. Admission is 30 schillings for adults; 15 schillings for children. Collections on mineralogy, petrography, zoology, anthropology, prehistory and precious stones. U-Bahn Volkstheatre.

Museum of Pathological Anatomy, *Old General Hospital, 9, Alser Strasse 4, Spitalgasse 2. Tel. 438-672.* Open Wednesday 3 p.m. to 6 p.m.; Thursday 8 a.m. to 11 a.m.; first Saturday of the month, 10 a.m. to 1 p.m. Tram 5, 43 or 44 Lange Gasse.

National Library, Grand Hall, *1, Josefsplatz 1. Tel. 534-10-397.* January through May, November and December, Monday through Saturday 10 a.m. to noon; June through October, Monday through Saturday 10 a.m. to 4 p.m. U-Bahn Karlsplatz.

National Theater, *1, Dr. Karl Lueger Ring 2. Tel. 514-44-2613.* Guided tours July and August, Monday through Saturday 1 p.m., 2 p.m. and 3 p.m.; September, October, April, May and June, Tuesday and Thursday 4 p.m.; Sunday 3 p.m.; November through March, tours made upon request. Tram D, 1 or 2 Rathausplatz.

Neiderhart Frescoes, *1, Tuchlauben 19. Tel. 535-9065.* Open daily, except Monday, 9 a.m. to 12:15 p.m. and 1 p.m. and 4:30 p.m. Free admission on Fridays before noon. U-Bahn Stephansplatz. The medieval ceremonial hall dating from approximately 1400 was discovered during the remodelling of an apartment. The oldest secular wall paintings in Vienna, the frescoes depict songs by Neidhart von Reuenthal.

Old Bakery, *8, Lange Gasse 34. Tel. 406-1101.* Open Tuesday through Sunday and holidays, 10 a.m. to midnight. Closed during August. Tram J Ledergasse.

Old Smithy, *1, Schonlaterngasse 9. Tel. 512-8329.* Open Monday through Friday, 10 a.m. to 3 p.m. and by appointment. U-Bahn Stephansplatz.

Planetarium, *2, Prater, Hauptallee, near the giant ferris wheel. Tel. 24-94-32.* Guided tours Sunday at 3 p.m. and 5 p.m. and upon request. August through mid-September closed. U-Bahn Praterstern.

Prater Museum, 2, *Prater, Hauptallee at the Planetarium. Tel. 24-94-32-77.* Tuesday through Friday, 9 a.m. to 12:15 p.m. and 1 p.m. to 4:30 p.m.; Saturday, Sunday and holidays 2 p.m. to 6:30 p.m. Admission free Fridays before noon. U-Bahn Praterstern.

Roman Ruins Am Hof, 1, *Am Hof 9. Tel. 505-87-47.* Saturday, Sunday, and holidays 11 a.m. to 1 p.m. U-Bahn Herrengasse.

Roman Ruins Underneath the Hoher Markt, 1, *Hoher Markt 3. Tel. 535-5606.* Open daily, except Monday, 9 a.m. to 12:15 p.m. and 1 p.m. to 4:30 p.m. Admission free Fridays before noon. U-Bahn Stephansplatz.

Soccer Museum, *in the Praterstadium, 2, Meiereistrasse 7. Tel. 727-18-0.* Open Monday and Friday 10 a.m. to 1 p.m.; Tuesday and Thursday 2 p.m. to 6 p.m. Groups should make reservations. Tram 21 Stadion.

Stadtbahn Court Pavilion Hietzing, *by Otto Wagner, 13, Schonnbrunner Schloss Strasse. Tel. 877-1571.* Open daily, except Monday, 9 a.m. to 12:15 p.m. and 1 p.m. to 4:30 p.m. Admission free Fridays before noon. U-Bahn Hietzing.

Stadtbahn Pavilions Karlsplatz, *by Otto Wagner, 1, Karlsplatz.* Open April through October daily, except Monday, 9 a.m. to 12:15 p.m. and 1 p.m. to 4:30 p.m. U-Bahn Karlsplatz or Oper.

State Museum of Lower Austria, 1, *Herrengasse 9. Tel. 531-10-3505.* Open Tuesday through Friday 9 a.m. to 5 p.m.; Saturday noon to 5 p.m.; Sunday 9:30 a.m. to 1 p.m. U-Bahn Herrengasse. The museum has exhibitions detailing the history of the province.

Stifter Museum, 1, *Molker Bastei 8. Tel. 535-8905.* Open daily, except Monday, 9 a.m. to 12:15 p.m. and 1 p.m. to 4:30 p.m. Admission free Friday before noon. U-Bahn Schottentor.

Streetcar Museum, 3, *Erdbergstrasse 109. Tel. 7909-44-903.* Open May through October, Saturday, Sunday and holidays from 9 a.m. to 4 p.m. U-Bahn Schlachthausgasse. Discounts available with the Vienna Card. Sightseeing tours with "old-timer" tram possible May through October, Saturday, Sunday and holidays. Tram departs from Karlsplatz at 11:30 a.m. and 1:30 p.m. Tickets available in the Karlsplatz U-Bahn station *(Tel. 7909-44-026).* The museum contains more than 80 historic streetcars.

Theater Museum, 1, *Lobkowitzplatz 2. Tel. 512-8800-0.* Open daily, except Monday, 10 a.m. to 5 p.m.; 1, Hanuschgasse 3, memorial rooms for Hugo Thimig, Josef Kainz, Max Reinhardt, Caspar Neher, Hermann Bahr, Fritz Wotruba and others, 1, Hanuschgasse 3. 512-2427. Open Tuesday through Friday, 10 a.m. to noon and 1 p.m. to 4 p.m.; Saturday and Sunday 1 to 4 p.m. Admission is 50 schillings for adults; 30 schillings for children. U-Bahn Karlsplatz or Stephansplatz.

Tobacco Museum, 7, *Mariahilfer Strasse 2. Tel. 526-1716.* Open Tuesday through Friday, 10 a.m. to 5 p.m.; Saturday, Sunday and holidays 10 a.m. to 2 p.m. U-Bahn Babenbergerstrasse.

Undertaker's Museum, *4, Goldeggasse 19. Tel. 501-95-227.* Open Monday through Friday, noon to 3 p.m. and by prior arrangement. Tram D Schloss Belvedere.

Urania Observatory, *1, Uraniastrasse 1. Tel. 24-94-32 or 712-61-91-15.* Guided tours when skies clear. Open Wednesday, Friday and Saturday at 8 p.m.; Sunday 11 a.m. Closed during August. Telescope observation, computer graphic Uraniastar. U-Bahn Schwedenplatz.

Viticultural Museum, *19, Doblinger Hauptstrasse 96. Tel. 37-69-39.* Open Saturday 3:30 p.m. to 6 p.m.; Sunday 10 a.m. to noon. Closed during July and August. Tram 37 Pokornygasse.

Wittgenstein Palais, *3, Parkgasse 18. Tel. 713-31-64.* Open Monday through Friday, 9 a.m. to 12:30 p.m. and 2 p.m. to 6 p.m. U-Bahn Rochusgasse.

NIGHTLIFE & ENTERTAINMENT

You never have to spend a quiet evening doing nothing in Vienna, unless you want to. Each night you can take your pick of a wide variety of concerts, operas, plays, and other performances.

If you can, try to catch a performance at the **Stadtoper** or **City Opera House**. If tickets are sold out, you might want to try purchasing standing room tickets, which will only set you back 20 or 30 schillings depending on where you stand. This is a lot better than it sounds, since there are several intermissions in most productions so you can rest your legs, and the standing room area is surprisingly comfortable with padded railings to lean on. The 30 schilling standing room tickets give you the best view in the house, too, after the orchestra seats. It can get pretty stuffy though, so make sure to dress in cool clothing. Standing room tickets are also available to the **Volksoper** and at other performances. These tickets are the major entertainment bargain in town.

Several festivals take place each year in Austria, beginning with the **Operetta Festival** in February. The **Haydn Festival** and the **Festival of Sacred Music** are both held in March. The **Vienna International Festival** starts in mid-May and continues through June. The **Summer of Music** begins in July and finishes up in August. Also in July are the **Spectaculum**, showcasing ancient music, and the **International Youth and Music Festival**. The **Schubert Days** in November and **Advent in Vienna** round out the season.

There are also several other concert series geared specifically for tourists. If you are a serious music lover, steer clear of the costumed hawkers who sell the tickets near St. Stephen's, the Opera House, and other tourist sights. You'll be disappointed by the selections of classical "classics." But if you're just interested in getting your feet wet where classical music is concerned, these concerts may be right for you. Many feature familiar pieces, and the concerts are usually short. Here are a few to choose from:

- **Vienna Walzer Orchestra**, featuring musicians from the Viennese academy of music and dancers for the city ballet company. Tickets start at 350 schillings. *For reservations, call 512-6263; fax 512-6265.*
- **Mozarthaus Concert**, costumed musicians play pieces for guitar and cello by Haydn, Mozart, Bach, Vivaldi and others in Mozart's former residence. Tickets start at 330 schillings. *For reservations, call 310-5710.*
- **Schonnbrunner Schlosskonserte**, Mozart and Johann Strauss classics played by a women's orchestra at Schonbrunn. Tickets start at 170 schillings. *For reservations, call 81-21-78; fax 811-13-268.*

The tourist office publishes a bulletin with all the performances for the month listed, from operas to concerts to plays to cabarets. The brochure has ticket prices, addresses and telephone numbers so you can plan your entertainment schedule accordingly. If you need tickets for concerts, musicals or theater performances, contact the **Vienna Ticket Service**, *Borsegasse 1, A-1010 Vienna. Tel. 534-1363; fax 534-1379.*

TICKET TIPS

Any trip to Vienna would not be complete without attending a performance at the **Opera House**, *the* **Volksoper**, *the* **Burgtheathre**, *or the* **Akademietheatre**. *If you plan ahead, your chances of getting a ticket to the performance you're interested in are a lot better.*

To order tickets by mail or fax, contact: **National Theatre Booking Offices**, *Hanuschgasse 3A-1010 Vienna, fax 514-44-2969. Tickets for the State Opera House or the Volksoper should be ordered at least three weeks in advance. Tickets for the Burgtheatre and the Akademietheatre should be booked at least ten days in advance. Tickets can be ordered by phone and charged to your credit card by calling 513-1-513. Tickets can be reserved up to a week before the performance. Standing room tickets must be purchased at the box office.*

To purchase tickets to other performances, contact the **Vienna Ticket Service**, *587-9843; fax 587-9844.*

Vienna Boy's Choir

The **Vienna Boy's Choir** has become an international institution and a symbol of the city. Every Friday during May, June, September, and October, the choir sings at the **Konzerthaus** at 3:30 p.m. Performances include a mixed program of waltz music, folk songs, and madrigals. Tickets cost 370 schillings or 420 schillings.

Tickets can be purchased through: **Reiseburo Mondial**, *4, Faulmanngasse 4, Tel. 588-04 extension 141; fax 587-1268.*

The choir also sings at Sunday mass, beginning at 9:15 a.m., and on holidays at the **Chapel of the Imperial Palace**, *1, Hofburg, Schweizerhof.* Tickets range from 60 schillings to 250 schillings.Standing room is free. Written orders for seats should be sent at least eight weeks in advance to the **Hofmusikkapelle**, *Hofburg A-1010 Vienna.* Do not send cash or checks.

Tickets should be picked up the Friday before the performance between 11 a.m. and noon or on Sunday between 8:30 a.m. and 9 a.m. Tickets for remaining seats are available Friday at 5 p.m. for the following Sunday. There is a two ticket limit per person.

BALL BONANZA

The ball season is as integral a part of Vienna as Sacher Torte or the Vienna Boy's Choir. If you're visiting the city between New Year's and Ash Wednesday, the start of the Easter season, then kick up your heels at one of the myriad balls available throughout the city. A date at the Hofburg dancing to waltzes by Strauss is a night dreams are made of.

But attending a ball doesn't come cheap. Expect to pay 800 to 1000 schillings per ticket; student tickets are also available. The tourist office has scheduling and ticket information. Reserve early if you want to guarantee getting a ticket. If you forgot your tails at home or left your ballgown behind, there are rental services available.

Here is a list of the most popular balls available:

__Bonbon Ball__, Konzerthaus. Tickets: Verband der Susswarenhandler Osterreichs, Klosterneuburger Strasse 30, A-1200 Vienna. Tel. 330-3121 or 330-7884.

__Coffee-House Ball__, Hofburg. Tickets: Club der Weiner Kaffeehausbestzer, Stubenring 8-10, A-1010 Vienna. Tel. 514-50-241.

__Flower Ball__, City Hall. Tickets: Am Heumarkt 2B, A-1030 Vienna. Tel. 71-116-97247.

__Industry and Technology Ball__, Musikverein. Tickets: Ballburo Industerie und Techniker Cercle, Reitschulgasse 2, A-1010 Vienna. Tel. 533-9061.

__Lawyers' Ball__, Hofburg. Tickets: Juristenverband, Juristizpalast, Postfach 35, A-1016 Vienna. Tel. 521-52-3882.

__Magician's Ball__, Vienna Hilton Hotel. Tickets: Rabenhof 22, A-1030 Vienna. Tel. 712-5452.

__Philharmonic Ball__, Musikverein. Tickets: Wiener Philharmoniker, Bosendorferstrasse 12, A-1010 Vienna. Tel. 505-6525.

__Physicians' Ball__, Hofburg. Tickets: Arztekammer, Weihburggasse 10-12 A-1010 Vienna. Tel. 515-01.

__Rudolfina-Redoute__, Hofburg. Tickets: KOSTV Rudolfina, Lenaugasse 3, A-1080 Vienna. 405-4811.

Spanish Riding School

Performances of the **Spanish Riding School**, *1 Hofburg, inner court-yard; U-Bahn Stephansplatz*, are held at 10:45 a.m. and 7 p.m. and last about an hour and a half. Tickets range from 220 schillings to 800 schillings. Standing room costs 170 schillings. Tickets should be reserved in writing as early as possible. Send your request to the **Spanische Reitschule**, *Hofburg, A-1010 Vienna*. Tickets can also be ordered through ticket and travel agencies, but agencies will add a hefty commission of at least 22 percent to the ticket price.

You can also watch the stallions being trained. These performances with music last about an hour and begin at 10 a.m. Tickets cost 220 schillings and can only be ordered through travel or ticket agencies. For 80 schillings for adults and 20 schillings for children, you can watch regular training sessions, Tuesday through Saturday from 10 a.m. to noon. Tickets are sold at the entrance to the inner courtyard of the Imperial Palace and no reservations are necessary. To purchase tickets, contact the **Vienna Ticket Service**, *Tel. 587-9843; fax 587-9844.*

English Language Theater

Of course, this being Vienna, most theater productions are in German. However, if you have a taste for a theater production in English, there are two theaters in the city serving your needs:
• **International Theater**, *9, Mullnergasse/Porzellangasse. Tel. 319-6272.*
• **Vienna's English Theatre**, *8, Josefsgasse 12. Tel. 402-1260.*

The **Serapionstheater** performs mime dramas at the *Odeon, 2, Taborstrasse 10. Tel. 214-5562.*

Movies

Vienna has several theaters showing films in their original version. That means you can catch your favorite flicks in English. Local papers will list the daily program schedules. There will be a code indicating which movies are in the original and which are dubbed into German.

Try the following:
• **Burg Kino**, *1, Opernring 19. 587-8406.*
• **Hadyn-Kino**, *6 Mariahilfer Strasse 57. 587-2262.*
• **Stadtkino**, *3, Schwarzenburger 7. 712-6276.*

Bars, Pubs, & Beerhalls

If you're looking for nightlife, head to the **Bermuda Triangle** in the first district off of Schwedenplatz where you can while the night away listening to music in smoke-filled bars. Other hotspots for after-hours fun include the neighborhood around the **Stubentor**, between the Naschmarkt and Spittleberg.

Here is a list to get your bar-hopping started. All are in the inexpensive to moderate price range.

AERA, *1, Gozagagasse 11. Tel. 533-5314.* Open daily 10 a.m. to 2 a.m. Aera features two menus, theatrical performances, and concerts.

AMERLINGBEISL, *7, Stiftgasse 8. Tel. 526-1660.* Open daily 9 a.m. to 2 a.m. Alternative music with a charming inner courtyard.

CAFE TERRASSINGER, *4, Rechte Wienzeile 27. Tel. 587-2236.* Open Sunday through Friday 4 p.m. to 2 a.m.; holidays 2 p.m. to 2 a.m. A wide spectrum of music is featured nightly at the Cafe Terrassinger.

CHELSEA, *8, Piaristengasse 1. Tel. 408-5196.* Open daily from 7 p.m. to 4 a.m.; Sundays 4 p.m. to 4 a.m. Independent and underground music is played at Chelsea on Sundays.

JAZZCLUB SIXTH, *6, Gumpendorferstrasse 9. Tel. 56-87-10.* Open Sunday through Thursday 9 p.m. to 2 a.m.; Fridays and Saturdays 9 p.m. to 4 a.m. Live jazz is played at the Jazzclub Sixth.

JAZZLAND, *1, Franz Josefs Kai 29. Tel. 533-25-75.* Open Tuesday through Saturday 7 p.m. to 2 a.m. Jazzland has live music performed between 9 p.m. and 1 a.m.

JAZZSPELUNKE, *6, Durergasse 3. Tel. 587-0126.* Open Monday through Friday from 6 p.m. to 2 a.m.; Saturdays and Sundays from 11 a.m. to 2 a.m. Great jazz and good food are the attractions at Jazzspelunke.

KAKTUS, *1, Seitenstettengasse 5. Tel. 533-1938.* Open Sunday through Thursday 6 p.m. to 2 a.m.; Fridays and Saturdays 6 p.m. to 4 a.m. Kaktus plays the latest music sweeping the charts and gets crowded in the wee hours.

KRAH KRAH, *1, Rabensteig 8. Tel. 533-8193.* Open daily 11 a.m. to 2 a.m.Krah Krah has more than 50 different brands of beer to order.

MA PITOM, *1, Seitenstettengasse 5. Tel. 535-4313.* Open Monday through Thursday 11:30 a.m. to 3 p.m. and 5:30 p.m. to 1 a.m.; Saturdays 11:30 a.m. to 3 p.m. and 5:30 to 2 a.m.; Sundays 5:30 p.m. to 1 a.m.Across from the lovely St. Rupert's Church, the bar and restaurant is decorated in a black and white motif. Outdoor seating is available in warm weather. Ma Pitom attracts a young, chic crowd.

MILES SMILES, *8, Lange Gasse 51. Tel. 428-4814.* Open Sunday through Thursdays 8 p.m. to 2 a.m.; Fridays and Saturdays 8 p.m. to 4 a.m. Miles Smiles offers jazz from post-1955.

ROTER ENGEL, *1, Rabensteig 5. Tel. 535-4105.* Open Monday through Wednesday 3 p.m. to 2 a.m.; Thursday through Saturday 3 p.m. to 4 a.m.; Sundays 5 p.m. to 2 a.m. Live music is played each day and customers can play billiards at the upstairs table.

SALZAMT, *1, Ruprechtsplatz 1. Tel. 533-5332.* Open daily 5 p.m. to 4 a.m. Seating is available outside St. Rupert's Church. Food is served from 6 p.m. to 1 a.m.

SANTO SPIRITO, *1, Kumpfgasse 7. Tel. 512-1631*. Opens daily at 6 p.m.; closing time varies. Santo Spirito features exclusively classical music.

SPEKTAKEL, *5, Hamburgerstrasse 14. Tel. 587-0623*. Open daily from 5 p.m. to 2 a.m.; during the summer, 7 p.m. to 2 a.m. Cabaret and theater performances are featured with the food here.

THELONIOUS MONK, *1, Sonnenfelgasse 13. Tel. 512-1631*. Open daily 8 p.m. to 4 a.m. Jazz is the attraction at Thelonious Monk.

TUNNEL, *8, Floriangasse 39. Tel. 42-34-65*. Open daily 9 a.m. to 2 a.m. Live music is played in the basement of this three-story establishment. The good, cheap food attracts a lot of students.

Dancing

If opera is not your thing and you can't bear to sit through one more classical concert, head to the dance floor at one of the following discos or dancehalls.

L.A. DISC CLUB, *1, Himmelpfortgasse 23. Tel. 513-8302*. Disco open Thursday through Saturday 9 p.m. to 4 a.m.; cafe open Wednesday through Sunday 8 p.m. to 4 a.m.; Friday and Saturday 8 p.m. to 5 a.m.; Karaoke show Thursday nights.

MOVE, *8, Daungasse 1. Tel. 43-32-78*. Open daily 9 p.m. to 4 a.m.; Friday and Saturday, 9 p.m. to 5 a.m. Ladies' night on Tuesday and Thursday; students' night on Monday and Wednesday.

NACHTWERK, *23, Dr. Gonda Gasse 9. Tel. 616-8880*. Thursday through Saturday 8 p.m. to 5 a.m. Midnight laser, light or dance show.

P1, *1, Rotgasse 9. Tel. 535-9995*. Sunday through Thursday 9 p.m. to 4 a.m.; Friday and Saturday 9 p.m. to 6 a.m.

U4, *12, Schonbrunner Strasse 222. Tel. 85-83-18*. Monday and Tuesday 11 p.m. to 4 a.m.; Wednesday through Sunday 11:00 p.m. to 5 a.m.

VOLKSGARTEN, *1, Burgring/Heldenplatz. Tel. 533-0518*. Open daily 8 p.m. to 5 a.m.

Gambling

The **casino** is housed in the **Esterhazy Palace**, *41 Kartner Strasse*, which dates from 1698. Available games include Roulette, Baccarat, American Roulette, Wheel of Fortune, Sic Bo, Poker, Blackjack and slots.

SHOPPING

Shops are open, in general, between 9 a.m. and 6 p.m. Monday through Friday and 9 a.m. to noon Saturday. If you're caught without provisions on the weekend, the stores in the Westbahnhof and Sudbahnhof train stations are open from 7 a.m. to 11 p.m. daily.

On the first Saturday of each month, shops stay open until 5 p.m. There are several pedestrian-only shopping streets in the first district leading from St. Stephen's Cathedral to the Imperial Palace, such as **Graben** and **Kohlmarkt**. Here you will find lots of designer togs where fashionable Viennese shop and pay hefty prices for the privilege. The most famous shopping street in Vienna is **Karntner Strasse**, where you can buy such typical Viennese items as Sacher Torte, Augarten china, Thonet furniture and Lobmeyr glass. Be sure to note the "Nail Studded Stump," *Stock-im-Eisen-Platz*. The story goes that each time a blacksmith left the city he hammered a nail into the stump for good life.

If you'd prefer to browse the local department stores, head to **Mariahilfer Strasse**, the city's largest shopping street. Mariahilfer Strasse, as well as **Landstrasser Hauptstrasse** and the **Favoritenstrasse**, are among the favorite shopping destinations for locals.

If you're looking for more serious shopping in antiques or artworks, **Artecent Vienna** can help organize your visit. A member of the business will arrange a shopping itinerary for you, arrange visits to art auctions and accompany you if you desire. No commission is charged. For more information, *call 504-8331 or 504-8582*.

Or stop by for a visit to the **Dorotheum**, *1, Dorotheergasse 17*, one of the most famous auction houses in the world – originally home to a chapel and convent built in 1360 in honor of St. Dorothy. But like many monasteries throughout the country, Emperor Joseph II had the convent abolished in 1782. Emperor Joseph I converted the building into a Pawn Shop and Inquiry Office. Today, visitors can browse through the collectibles in the neo-Baroque building before the items go on the block. Auction schedules are posted at the Dorotheum.

Vienna has several open air markets from which to choose. For fresh produce, meats, breads and delicacies, try the **Rochusmarkt** in the third district on Landstrasser, Hauptstrasser, and Salmgasse (U-Bahn Rochusgasse); the **Naschmarkt** in the fourth district at U-Bahn Kettenbruckerngasse; and the **Brunnenmarkt** in the 16th district at Brunnengasse (U-Bahn Josefstadter). The markets have a lot of food stands where you can eat a quick, inexpensive lunch or snack.

Every Saturday from 9 a.m. to 6 p.m. there is a giant flea market on the **Weinzeile**. (U-Bahn Kettenbruckergasse). For those who are interested in arts and crafts, there are three different open air markets. In the first district at the **Danube Canal Promenade** between Schwedenplatz and Schottenring, a craft market is held weekends from May to September.

The **Spittelberg** arts and crafts exhibition is in the seventh district every weekend from April to November and Sundays in December. In the **Heiligenkreuzer Hof** in the first district, there is an arts and crafts market on the first weekend of the month from April to November and weekends in December.

SPORTS & RECREATION

In addition to the listings below, the **Vienna Youth Information** office can give you local sporting information on where to rent equipment, where the municipal facilities are, and other sport related information. **Jugend-Info Wien**, *1, Bellariapassage. Tel. 526-4637.* Open Monday through Friday, noon to 7 p.m.; Saturdays 10 a.m. to 7 p.m.

Biking

If you don't have your own bike, but you'd like to take advantage of the extensive cycling trails in Vienna, there are several places where you can rent a bike for an hour or more. Make sure to take along a piece of identification, which the bike rental will retain during the rental period. Rates average about 40 schillings per hour.

- **Radverleih City/Salztorbrucke**, *1, Alstadtseitige Donaukanalpromenade by the Salztorbrucke. Tel. 535-34-22.* Open from April to October, daily 10 a.m. to 7 p.m.
- **Radverleih Hochschaubahn**, *2, Prater by the Hochschaubahn. Tel. 26-01-65.* March through October, Monday through Saturday 10 a.m. until dusk; Sundays and holidays 9:30 a.m. to dusk.
- **Radverleih City/Hilton Park Center**, *3, Landstrasser Hauptstrasse 2. Tel. 713-93-95.* Open daily 9 a.m. to 7 p.m.
- **Radsport Nussdorf**, *19, Donaupromenade by the DDSG-Anlegestelle. Tel. 37-45-98.* Open February through April and November, 9 a.m. to 6 p.m.; May through October 8 a.m. to 8 p.m.
- **Radverleih Floridsdorfer Brucke**, *21, Donauinsel by the Floridsdorfer bridge parking lot. Tel. 278-86-98.* Open daily 10 a.m. until dusk.
- **Radverleih Ostbahnbrucke**, *22, by the Schnellbahnstation Lobau. Tel. 22-81-75.* Open May through October, Monday through Friday from 10 a.m. until dusk; Saturday, Sunday and holidays 9 a.m. to dusk.
- **Schuh-Ski Radverleih**, *22, Donauinsel by the Reichs Bridge. Tel. 23-65-18.* April through October daily from 9 a.m. to 8 p.m.
- **Radverleih Steinspornbrucke**, *22, Raffineriestrasse by the Steinsporn Bridge.* Open May through October daily 9 a.m. to 7 p.m.
- **Freizeitzentrum Lobau-Weidiger**, *22, Raffineriestrasse. Tel. 28-05-065.* Open mid-April through October daily from 10 a.m. until dusk.

You can also rent bicycles at local train stations. Rentals cost 50 schillings per day with a train ticket or 90 schillings without. The bikes can be returned to any manned rail station in Austria.

• **Westbahnhof.** *Tel. 58-00-329-85.* Open daily 4 a.m. to midnight.
• **Bahnhof Wien Nord/Praternstern.** *Tel. 58-00348-17.* Open 6:30 a.m. to 6:30 p.m.
• **Sudbahnhof.** *Tel. 58-00-358-86.* Open daily 6 a.m. to 9 p.m.

Bicycle tours, in German, French, Italian and English, are also available. The tours, sponsored by Vienna Bike, last between two and three hours. The cost ranges from 800 schillings for between one and four people to 1,115 schillings for groups up to 20 people. Contact **Vienna-Bike**, *9, Wasagasse 28/2/25. Tel. and fax, 319-12-58.*

You can take your bicycle on the U-Bahn Monday through Friday from 9 a.m. to 3 p.m. and after 6:30 p.m.; Saturdays after 9 a.m.; Sundays and holidays all day. A bicycle symbol is on the door of the cars where bikes are allowed. A half price ticket must be purchased for the bicycle. No bikes are allowed on the U-6 line.

Swimming

If your hotel has no **swimming pool**, you can still go for a dip in a municipal pool. To find the location nearest you, *call 15-35.*

DAY TRIPS & EXCURSIONS

Danube Boat Tours

One romantic way to see the towns along the **Danube** is by boat. Visits can be arranged to Passau in Lower Bavaria, Linz, Melk, Krems, Vienna and Bratislava in the Slovak Republic.

For information on boat trips along the Danube offered from April through October, you can contact the **Danube Steamship Company** *at 727-50-451.*

The Vienna Woods

The famed **Vienna Woods** are remarkably accessible from the city. Take the 38 tram to the end of the line and then catch a local bus to the woods. The Tourist Information office can provide information to you with suggested hikes and tours of the area.

PRACTICAL INFORMATION

American Express Office

The local American Express office can take care of your money and reservation needs. **American Express**, *Kaerntnerstrasse 21-23, A-1015 Vienna. Tel. 515-400; fax 515-4070.* Open Monday to Friday 9 a.m. to 5:30 p.m.; Saturday 9 a.m. to noon.

Auto Club

The **Austrian Automobile and Touring Club/Travel Department,** *Schubertring 1-3, A-1010 Vienna. Tel. 711-990; fax 71199-1473,* is headquartered in Vienna. The club can answer your questions on touring the country by car.

Credit Cards

If your credit cards are lost or stolen, you can call the following numbers 24 hours a day to make a report.
- **American Express,** *Tel. 51-29-714*
- **Diners,** *Tel. 50-1-35*
- **Mastercard,** *Tel. 71-7-01-0*
- **Visa,** *Tel. 53-4-87-77*

Consulates

- **Australian Consulate,** *4, Mattiellistrasse 2-4. Tel. 512-85-80-164.* Open Monday through Friday from 9 a.m. to 1 p.m. and 2 p.m. to 5 p.m.
- **British Consulate,** *3, Jauresgasse 10. Tel. 714-61-17.* Open Monday through Friday 9:15 a.m. to noon and 2 p.m. to 4 p.m.
- **Canadian Consulate,** *1, Schubertring 12. Tel. 533-36-91.* Open Monday through Friday 8:30 a.m. to 12:30 p.m. and 1:30 p.m. to 3:30 p.m.
- **U.S. Consulate,** *1, Gartenbaupromenade 2. Tel. 313-39.* Monday through Friday 8:30 a.m. to noon and 1 p.m. to 5 p.m.

Dental Services

If you need a dentist on the weekend or after hours, *call 512-2078.*

English Language Book Stores

Most newsstands sell English language newspapers like the *International Herald Tribune* along with a wide selection of English and American magazines. Most stores have a selection of English books. Vienna even has its share of exclusively English language book stores, including:
- **American Discount,** *4, Rechte Wienzeile 5. Tel. 587-5772; fax 2236-47127; 7, Neubaugasse 39, Tel. 93-37-07; 15 Lugner City, Gablenzgasse 5-13.*
- **Big Ben,** *9, Porzellangasse 24. Tel. 319-6412.*
- **The British Book Shop,** *1, Weihburggasse 24-26. Tel. 512-1945 or 512-2682; fax 512-1026.*
- **Shakespeare & Company,** *1, Sterngasse 2. 535-5053; fax 535-50-53/16.*

Emergency Phone Numbers

- **Ambulance,** *144*
- **Police,** *133*
- **Fire Department,** *122*

Exchanging Money

Banks in Vienna are open Mondays, Tuesdays, Wednesdays and Fridays between 8 a.m. to 3 p.m. Thursdays, banks stay open until 5:30 p.m. Some banks are closed between 12:30 p.m. to 1 p.m. for lunch. At the **airport**, money can be changed at the exchange bureau at the arrivals and departures concourses. The arrivals' office is open daily 8:30 a.m. to 11:30 p.m. The departures' office is open Monday through Friday, 8 a.m. to 6 p.m.

You can also change money at the **City Air Terminal** if you are taking an airport bus to or from the airport. The office is open Monday through Saturday 9 a.m. to noon and 1 to 6:30 p.m. and Sunday 9 a.m. to 1 p.m.

You can change your dollars into schillings 24-hours a day at the **Central Post Office**, *1, Fleischmarkt*. Exchanges are also available at the Westbahnhof, from 7 a.m. to 10 p.m. and the Sudbahnhof, between 6:30 a.m. to 10 p.m. Several travel agencies in the city center also can change your money. **Automatic change machines** are located *at Schottenring 1, Operngasse 8, and on Swedenplatz.*

Guided Tours

Vienna Sightseeing Tours offers a variety of guided tours for those short of time. The tours tend to be expensive though, and somewhat perfunctory. You can do a much better job on your own. Tours include a visit to the Spanish Riding School, a tour of Vienna by night and visits of Memorials for Famous Composers. Tickets range in price from 220 schillings to 740 schillings for adults and 160 schillings to 480 schillings for children. **Vienna Sightseeing Tours**, *Stelzhammergasse 4/11, A-1031 Vienna. Tel. 712-46-83-0; fax 712-46-83-77.*

Tours are also available through the Vienna Guide Service. Fees for a half-day tour cost 1,115 schillings and whole day tours cost 2,230 schillings. **Vienna Guide Service**, *19, Sommerhaidenweg 124. Tel. 44-30-94-0; fax 44-28-25.*

Laundromats

You can do your laundry at the following locations:
- **Munzwascherei Karlberger**, *3, Schlachthausgasse 19. Tel. 78-81-91*. Open Monday though Friday 7:30 a.m. to 6:30 p.m.; Saturdays 7:30 a.m. to 1 p.m.
- **Munzwasherei Margentenstrasse**, *4, Margaretenstrasse 52. Tel. 587-0473.* Open Monday through Friday 7:30 a.m. to 6:30 p.m.; Saturday 8 a.m. to 11 a.m.
- **Schnellwascherei Haydn**, *6, Stumpergasse 1A. Tel. 564-8914.* Open Monday through Thursday 7 a.m. to 5:30 p.m.; Fridays 7 a.m. to 1 p.m.

Lost & Found

Lost Property Office, *9, Wasagasse 22. Tel. 314-44-9211 or 9217.* Open Monday through Friday, 8 a.m. to noon.

For property lost on Viennese **public transportation**, *call 7909-43-500.* For items lost on the **train**, *call the Westbahnhof at 58-00-32-996 or the Sudbahnhof 58-00-35-656.*

Medical Treatment

The following hospitals have outpatient departments that can help you in case you have a medical problem:

- **Allgemeines Krakenhaus**, *9, Wahringer Gurtel 18-20. Tel. 404-00-0.*
- **Lorenz Bohler Unfallkrankenhaus**, *20, Donaueschingenstrasse 13. Tel. 331-100.*
- **Hanusch-Krankenhaus**, *14, Heinrich Collin Strasse 30. Tel. 94-21-51-0.*
- **Krankenhaus Lainz**, *13, Wolkersbergenstrasse 1. Tel. 801-10-0.*

Pharmacies

Several pharmacies are open 24 hours a day in case of emergencies. The address of the nearest open pharmacy will be posted in the window of each closed shop. *For pharmacy assistance, call 15-50.*

Post Offices

Post offices are open in general Monday through Friday from 8 a.m. to noon and 2 p.m. to 6 p.m.; Saturdays from 8 a.m. to 10 a.m.

The **Main Post Office**, *1, Fleischmarkt 19*, and the post offices at the Westbahnhof, Sudbahnhof, and Franz Josefs Bahnhof are open 24 hours a day.

Psychiatric Hotline

The hotline *(Tel. 310-8780)* is available Monday through Friday from 8 p.m. to 8 a.m.; Saturdays, Sundays, and holidays around the clock.

Radio

Blue Danube Radio has radio programs in English from 6 a.m. to 7 p.m. News is also broadcast on the half hour in English, French, and German. You can find the station on 103.8 MHz and 92.9 MHz on your radio dial.

Rape Hotline

The hotline is available from 9 a.m. to noon and Tuesdays and Thursday from 6 p.m. to 9 p.m. *Tel. 93-22-22.*

Religious Services

Vienna has several church services in English.

- **Anglican-Episcopal Christ Church**, *3, Jauregasse 17-19. Tel. 713-1575.* Holy communion 8 a.m.; sung eucharist 10 a.m.; evening service first two Sundays of the month 6 p.m.; morning service third Sunday of the month 10 a.m.
- **Evangelical Grace Church**, *7, Kenyangasse 15. Tel. 479-7306.* Service 10:45 a.m. Sunday.
- **Evangelical International Chapel of Vienna**, *19, Kreilplatz 1. Tel. 37-76-14.* Children's service 9:30 a.m.; all ages 11 a.m. Nursery service available.
- **International Baptist Church**, *6, Mollardgasse 35. Tel. 804-9259.* Service 11:30 a.m.
- **International Church of Christ**, *3, Rennweg 1. Tel. 718-5968-0 or 214-7496; fax 718-5068-9.* Services 10:30 a.m. and 6:30 p.m.; Wednesdays 5 p.m.
- **Jewish Services** in English, German, and Hebrew are held at *2, Schuttelstrasse 19A, Door 3. Tel. 88-76-25.* Shabbat services every Friday at 7:00 p.m.
- **Roman Catholic Community** is located at *9, Rooseveltplatz 8. Tel. 408-505014 or 983-7379.* Mass 11 a.m.
- **United Methodist Church**, *15, Sechshauser Strasse 56. Tel. 893-6989.* Service 11:15 a.m.; nursery available.
- **Vienna Christian Center**, *7, Halbgasse 17. Tel. 318-7410.* Service 6 p.m.; nursery and underground parking available.
- **Vienna Community Church**, *1, Dorotheergasse 16. Tel. 505-5233.* Services 11:30 a.m.

Tipping

A service charge is added to your hotel and restaurant bill. However, if you are pleased with the service, it is customary to tip an additional 5 to 10 percent of the check. Taxi drivers and hair dressers also are generally tipped the same amount.

Weather

For the latest weather information, *call 15-66.*

13. LOWER AUSTRIA

INTRODUCTION

Lower Austria's English motto is "the culture vulture on Vienna's doorstep," and the region abounds with castles, monasteries, fortresses, and churches to sate the most fanatic history buffs. Lower Austria sprawls 7,400 square miles and has a population of 1.46 million citizens. The region is the country's breadbasket, with the highest percentage of cultivated land and its biggest wheat supplier.

Make sure the **Stift Melk**, one of the most spectacular monasteries in Europe and surely the most famous in Austria, is on your itinerary. The provincial capital is **St. Polten**, where you will see lovely Baroque pastel palaces lining the squares in the pedestrian quarter. If you like wine at all, or just want to see some very pretty countryside, visit the terraced vineyards and medieval villages in the **Wachau** (the wine-producing hillsides) of the **Weinviertel**, and then head to the lush verdure of the heralded **Vienna Woods**. Step back to the time of the Romans by visiting a temple dedicated to the goddess Diana and the famous **Pagan's Gate**.

The Imperial Court in Vienna used to retreat during the hot months to summer residences in Lower Austria. Today, the modern Viennese are following in the footsteps of their famous forbearers to take advantage of the region's more than 450 ponds, 18 golf courses, 1,900 tennis courts, and miles of hiking and biking trails along the Danube. If you really want to get back to the land, you can stay at one of the local farms that will let the whole family lend a hand harvesting and feeding the animals. If you prefer a more leisurely way to spend your time in LowerAustria, you can visit the sulphur thermal springs in **Baden**, which has been a favorite bathing spot since the time of the Romans.

Spoil yourself at one of the areas many spas and hot springs – any city with the word *Bad* (German for bath), in its name is a good bet for a pampered vacation stay. Check my *Where to Stay* section of this chapter as part of your sight-seeing itinerary. Many special hotels and restaurants are located in extraordinary locations and have their own historic attractions that are worth a detour. You'll be surprised at how reasonable a night at a castle can be for modern-day lords and ladies.

ORIENTATION

If you're staying in Vienna, **Niederosterreich**, or Lower Austria, is just a hop, skip, and a jump from the capital. A trip along the Danube and a visit to some of the charming towns that dot the landscape is definitely worth a day if not more. Even if you prefer to spend the night in Vienna, all of the towns in the province are in easy reach, so you won't feel pressured about getting back.

The region is also easily accessible by train. Or, if you're lucky enough to be in the area during late spring to early autumn, you can take a boat that will dock at points along the Danube.

LOWER AUSTRIA TOURIST INFORMATION

Before setting off on your exploration of Lower Austria, you might want to contact one of several information bureaus which can provide bike and hiking maps, book hotel rooms, and give you advice on how best to get the most out of your trip.

• Niederosterreich-Information, A-1010 Vienna, Heidenschuss 2. Tel. 53-33-114-34; Telex 115220.

• Information Autobahnraststation St. Polten, A-3385 Vollerndorf. Tel. 27-49-27-47; fax 27-49-27-21.

• Upper Austrian Danube Area Information, Landesfremdenverkehrsamt Oberosterreich, A-4020 Linz, Schillerstrasse 50. Tel. 732-6630-210.

ARRIVALS & DEPARTURES

By Air

The nearest airport is in Vienna, where you can either rent a car or take one of the frequent trains that run between Salzburg and Vienna and between Vienna and Graz.

By Boat

If you'd like to take a boat trip down the Danube, excursions are available from April to October by the **Danube Steamship Company**. For more information or reservations, *call 727-50-451*. For **ship timetables**, *call 1537*.

By Car

If you're the type of person who wants to get where you're going quickly and don't mind what the view is like along the way, then take the

Autobahn going east towards Salzburg. Get off at Melk and then make your way west towards Vienna, stopping at sights along the way.

For those of you who like a slower paced visit, take the scenic route along the Danube, where you can stop off at any of the small towns that strike your fancy. This is especially appropriate if you're yearning to sample the wines of the region, a highly recommended way to spend a day during your visit.

By Train

Train travel into the Wachau region is simple, although local trains make frequent stops along the way. For **train information**, *call 17-17*.

GETTING AROUND LOWER AUSTRIA

By Bus

Bus timetables are available by telephoning *711-01* from 7 a.m. to 7 p.m.

By Car

If you run into car problems, *call 120 or 123* for around-the-clock emergency assistance.

WHERE TO STAY

Selecting accommodations is almost as much fun as exploring Lower Austria. A number of former castles, fortresses, and monasteries have been transformed into world-class hotels allowing visitors to experience what it was like to live in an earlier age.

As mentioned below in our *Where to Eat* section, most of the better restaurants are attached to hotels, inns, and guesthouses, and they are reviewed as part of each hotel below. The few restaurants independent of hotels are reviewed separately in *Where to Eat*.

Baden bei Wien

GRAND HOTEL SAUERHOF, *Weilburgstrasse 11-13, A-2500 Baden bei Wien. Tel. 2252-41-2-51-0; fax 2252-48-0-47. Doubles start at 1,100 schillings per person. All credit cards accepted.*

Composers Ludwig van Beethoven, Carl Maria von Weber and Antonia Salieri are among the famous guests that have graced this elegant hotel. The hotel dates back to the 12th century, but today has every modern amenity available to pamper its guests. Behind the bright yellow facade, the Roman baths have been modernized to include the top spa and beauty accommodations while still maintaining the character of a turn-of-the-century bath house. Baden's casino is also housed here for gamblers. Visitors also can stroll the lush park grounds where the hotel is situated.

HOTEL SCHLOSS WEIKERSDORF, *Schloss Gasse 9-11, A-2500 Baden bei Wein. Tel. 2252-48301; fax 2252-48301-150. Doubles start at 575 schillings per person. All credit cards accepted.*

Surrounded by a beautiful garden, the Hotel Schloss Weikersdorf brings to life the atmosphere of Austria's imperial age. There is a modern emphasis on health, however, with indoor and outdoor tennis courts, a swimming pool, and sauna. The hotel restaurant features both traditional Austrian cuisine and dietetic fare. Or after all that exercise, relax in the hotel's comfortable bar.

PARKHOTEL BADEN, *Kaiser Franz Ring 5, A-2500 Baden bei Wien. Tel. 2252-44-3-86; 2252-80578. Doubles start at 700 schillings per person. All credit cards accepted.*

If you need a break and want to enjoy "taking the cure," the Parkhotel Baden will pamper you accordingly. Rooms are comfortably furnished and have balconies with views of the hotel's expansive garden. Fitness facilities include an exercise room, swimming, and sauna. The restaurant has both traditional cuisine and dietetic specialties available for the health conscious.

Drosendorf

SCHLOSS DROSENDORF, *A-2095 Drosendorf. Tel. 2915-3210; fax 2915-2263. Doubles start at 360 schillings per person. All credit cards accepted.*

The Gothic and Romanesque Drosendorf Castle was rebuilt after a fire at the end of the 17th century, incorporating many Baroque elements. But you don't have to be a member of the nobility to stay at the castle today.

The Schloss has 63 beds, and guests can stroll through the castle's lush grounds, relax in its sauna, or dine in the tavern. Biking facilities are available, and pets are welcome.

Durnstein

GASTHOF SANGER BLONDEL, *A-3601 Durnstein. Tel. 2711-253. Doubles start from 960 schillings per person. No credit cards accepted.*

The Gasthof Sanger Blondel is in the heart of the medieval town of Durnstein. The comfortable 34-bed guest house has a large garden shaded by chestnut trees. The hotel also has a garage, bicycle rentals, and zither concerts to entertain guests. Breakfast features home-made apricot jam and a specially made Muesli cereal. The restaurant serves traditional favorites but also has less caloric selections for the health conscious. The wine served is from the Schendl family's own vineyards.

HOTEL-RESTAURANT RICHARD LOWENHERZ, *Klarissinnenkloster, A-3601 Durnstein. Tel. 2711-222. Doubles start from 800 schillings per person. All credit cards accepted.*

The Hotel Richard Lowenherz is located in a former cloister near the Danube River. Remnants of the monastery still remain providing a romantic atmosphere for guests. The hotel is beautifully appointed with elegant furniture and Oriental rugs. Guests can take a dip in the pool during warmer weather. A highlight of the hotel is the restaurant where visitors can sample vintages from the estate. Dishes featuring fish and game, from the nearby river and countryside, are a specialty.

Friedersbach

HOTEL SCHWEIGHOFER, *Friedersbach 53, A-3533. Tel. 2826-7511; fax 2826-7511-54. Doubles start at 490 schillings per person. All credit cards accepted.*

This 4-star hotel in the Waldviertel has stylishly furnished rooms and apartments. Pamper yourself in the hotel's swimming pool, steam bath, solarium or sauna. The hotel's **Waldviertler Stuben** restaurant features both Austrian cooking and international cuisine. A good selection of regional wines are also on the menu.

Gloggnitz & Krems

BURGHOTEL KRANICHBERG, *A-2604 Gloggnitz. Tel. 2662-8242; fax 2662-8386. Doubles start at 450 schillings per person. No credit cards accepted.*

Located at the gateway to the Semmering pass, the Burghotel Kranichberg was once a monastery founded in 1094 by Bavarian Benedictine monks. Breathtaking mountain scenery surrounds the former monastery. The hotel combines the right touch of history with modern amenities. Health conscious guests can take advantage of the hotel's swimming pool, sauna, and fitness facilities. A restaurant and bar at the hotel serve Austrian food and wine.

GOURMET-HOTEL AM FORTHOF, *Donaulande 8, A-3500 Krems. Tel. 2732-83345; fax 2732-83345-40. Doubles start at 450 schillings per person. All credit cards accepted.*

Helga Figl runs this 20-room hotel filled with personal touches and feminine decor. The hotel has parking for guests. Biking, swimming, and sunning facilities are also available. A star attraction at the hotel is the restaurant, which specializes in regional dishes. Local vintages are also featured. Selections can also be made from a diet menu.

STEIGENBERGER AVANCE HOTEL KREMS, *Am Goldberg 2, A-3500 Krems. Tel. 2732-710-10; fax 2732-71010-50. Doubles start at 750 schillings per person. All credit cards accepted.*

Tucked in the rolling green hills and the surrounding vineyards, the huge hotel Krems is located in an idyllic spot. Rooms are comfortable and modern. Fitness activities include swimming, exercise, and biking for guests. The hotel also offers children's facilities, and pets are welcome. The hotel has a bar and restaurant serving standard Austrian dishes.

Krumbach

HOTEL SCHLOSS KRUMBACH, *Schloss 1, A-2851 Krumbach. Tel. 2647-2209-0; fax 2647-2209-88. Doubles start from 950 schillings per person. All credit cards accepted.*

Imagine spending the night in a dream castle on top of a hillside, and you'll have an idea of what a night at the Hotel Schloss Krumbach is like. The turreted castle is out of a storybook. But rooms are modern and cozy. Swimming, tennis, golf, biking, exercise facilities and a sauna are available for guests. Pets can stay too, and the hotel offers children's activities.

A star attraction of the hotel is its restaurant. Fresh produce is grown on the premises which goes into the restaurant's gourmet dishes. And you can have a drink before dinner at the hotel's bar.

Melk

HOTEL ZUR POST, *Linzerstrasse 1, A-3390 Melk. Tel. 2752-2345 or 4407; fax 2752-2345-50. Doubles start at 450 schillings per person. All credit cards accepted.*

Located on the "Main Street" of town, the Hotel Zur Post is in the shadow of the magnificent Stift Melk. The 27-room hotel has comfortable rooms and a warm welcome. Typical Austrian dishes are served at the hotel restaurant, and outdoor seating is available during the warmer months. Pets are welcome. Swimming and sauna facilities are also available to guests.

Modling

BABENBERHOF, *Babenbergergasse 6, A-2340 Modling. Tel. 2236-222-46 or 473-87; fax 2236-22-24-66. Doubles start from 600 schillings per person. All credit cards accepted.*

This 50-room hotel is in the center of the pedestrian section of the historic part of Modling, conveniently located near Vienna. Karl and Elfrieda Breyer will welcome you with open arms to this old-style guest house.

The Babenberhof also has a restaurant for guests with outside seating during warm weather. Traditional dishes are featured as well as local wines.

Muhldorf

BURG OBERRANNA, *A-3622 Muhldorf. Tel. 2713-8221; fax 2713-8366. Doubles start at 600 schillings per person. All credit cards accepted.*

This former castle, transformed into a luxury hotel, is perched above the town of Spitz. The castle's chapel dates back to the 12th century. Visitors will feel as if they have stepped back in time when knights and ladies populated the country. Rooms are furnished with antique furniture and rugs. Guests can pass the time in front of the fire in the manor-style lounge.

Specialties from the Wachau are served in the **Castle Tavern**, decorated with traditional hunting motifs. Wine from the region is also showcased here.

Rastenfeld

SCHLOSSRESTAURANT OTTENSTEIN, *A-3532 Rastenfeld. Tel. 2826-254. Moderate. Open April through October; the castle gallery is open free of charge during July and August. Closed Tuesdays. All credit cards accepted.*

Not a hotel, but if you're staying nearby, the 12th century Ottenstein Castle has a comfortable restaurant and romantic garden with traditional Austrian cuisine. Special events throughout the year include wine tastings, barbecues, medieval banquets and a cake and pastry week. The castle includes an architecturally important Romanesque chapel, and its Popes' Room has 241 portraits of the pontiffs through the ages.

Rosenau

SCHLOSS ROSENAU, *A-3924 Rosenau 1. Tel. 2822-8221 or 8226. Doubles start at 490 schillings per person. Open March 23 to November 3 daily 9 a.m. to 5 p.m. and by prior arrangement. All credit cards accepted.*

The Schloss Rosenau was built in 1590. The Renaissance structure was reconstructed as a Baroque castle in the 18th century under Count Leopold Schallenberg. Today, the castle holds the **Austrian Freemasons' Museum**, with the lodge rooms and temple on display as well as details on the origin and history of the movement. The hotel has a sauna and an indoor swimming pool to pamper guests, and the restaurant has a good selection of Austrian wines and cuisine.

Spitz an der Donau

HOTEL NEUE WELT, *Ottenschlager Strasse 30, A-3620 Spitz. Tel. 2713-2254; fax 2713-2875. Doubles start at 365 schillings per person. All credit cards accepted.*

This 36-room hotel is run by Ewald Stierschneider. Rooms in this modest guest house are comfortable and several have balconies. Swimming and biking facilities are available. The hotel has a restaurant with both dietetic and classic Austrian dishes on the menu.

HOTEL WACHAUERHOF, *Hauptstrasse 15, A-3620 Spitz. Tel. 2713-2303; fax 2713-2403. Doubles start at 400 schillings per person. Mastercard accepted.*

This flower-bedecked hotel has 54-beds. The Mistelbauer family runs the Hotel Wachauerhof with careful attention to details and lots of old world charm. Rooms are small but cozy. The hotel's restaurant features both classic cuisine and health conscious alternatives. Swimming and parking facilities are also available to guests.

St. Polten

HOTEL METROPOL, *Schillerplatz 1, A-3100 St. Polten. Tel. 2742-70700-0; fax 2742-707-00-133. Doubles start at 1,480 schillings, including breakfast. All credit cards accepted.*

The rooms at the Hotel Metropol are large and comfortable. The decor is standard hotel fare, however, and lacking somewhat in charm. But the hotel is modern, well-equipped and a nice place to relax after a hard day of sight-seeing. There's also a steam bath, a solarium, and sauna. The restaurant features traditional Austrian cuisine and international dishes.

STADTHOTEL HAUSERECK, *Schulgasse 2, A-3100 St. Polten. Tel. 2742-73336; fax 2742-78386. Doubles start from 440 schillings per person, including breakfast. All credit cards accepted.*

Located at the beginning of the city's pedestrian section, the 60-bed Stadhotel Hausereck has friendly service and comfortable rooms, all with radios, cable television and minibars. The Hauser family also runs the hotel's cafe-restaurant serving the usual Austrian specialties.

Weiner Neustadt

FREIZEIT TEMPEL, *Weiner Werksstrasse 109, A-2700 Weiner Neustadt. Tel. 2622-23595; fax 2622-23595-99. Doubles start at 690 schillings per person. All credit cards accepted.*

The Freizeit Tempel knows how to pamper a guest while keeping you healthy. The hotel has exercise classes, badminton, squash, and tennis courts and billiards for guests. The restaurant has gourmet choices for those who want to indulge and lighter courses for those watching their figures. Rooms are comfortable, but the standard hotel furniture lacks warmth.

HOTEL CORVINUS, *Ferdinand Porsche Ring, A-2700 Weiner Neustadt. Tel. 2622-24134; fax 2622-24139. Doubles start at 695 schillings per person. All credit cards accepted.*

The modern 68-room Hotel Corvinus has a courteous, efficient staff. Rooms are sparsely decorated, but comfortable in cool pastels. Guests can also take advantage of the hotel's pool, steambath, sauna, whirlpool, and solarium. The restaurant has both international dishes and regional favorites. Guests can lounge in the hotel garden during the summer months.

Zwettl

STIFT ZWETTL, *A-3910 Zwettl. Hotel Tel. 2822-3181 or 17; Restaurant Tel. 2822-3145. Open May 1 to October 31 daily; guided tours for 10 people or more 11 a.m, 2 p.m. and 3 p.m. Guided tours from November 1 to April 30 by prior arrangement.*

This Cistercian Monastery was founded by the Kuenrings in 1138 and showcases Romantic, Gothic, Renaissance and Baroque architecture. Today a restaurant on the site serves traditional Austrian cuisine and local wines. Guests will feel like they're stepping back in time to an earlier romantic age when lords and ladies ruled the environs.

WHERE TO EAT IN LOWER AUSTRIA

Local chefs have added nouvelle cuisine touches to traditional dishes, producing lighter fare with an emphasis on local produce and game. There are also Bohemian and Moravian influences in such dishes as *Skubanki*, pieces of baked potato rolled in poppy seeds, sugar and melted butter and *Liwanzen*, a sort of dumpling filled with prune puree. Poppy seeds also dot pastries and croissants in local bakeries.

If fish is a favorite, try the fresh **carp** which has been cultivated by convents and monasteries in the Waldviertel for centuries. Salted meats are also a specialty, including pickled pigs feet baked and served with cabbage. *Saumeisen* are a type of meatballs made from spiced, ground pork on a bed of sauerkraut.

Apricots are also grown along the banks of the Danube. During the spring, the trees are awash with blossoms, a truly lovely sight. Apricots flavor pastries, dumplings, and liquor produced here. Some of Austria's finest wines are grown in the Wachau, so be sure to sample a bottle or two during your stay. Look for the telltale straw wreaths hung outside the Heuriger, or wine tavern, to signal that local new wines are available for tasting. Ask the proprietor to recommend one or two and then sit back and enjoy. Hearty, country fare is usually available at very reasonable prices, so eat up and enjoy the bounty of the harvest.

As in many other parts of Austria, outside the big cities most of the good restaurants are attached to hotels, inns, and guesthouses, which are listed and reviewed above in *Wherre to Stay*. Below is a sampling of the better restaurants not attached to hotels:

Baden bei Wien

WEINBAU EDUARD UND WALTRAUD CEIDL, *Voslauer Strasse 15, A-2500 Baden. Tel. 2252-44493. Moderate. Open January, March, July, September and November 11 a.m to midnight. All credit cards accepted.*

The Ceidl family runs this wine cellar and restaurant. The wine list is overwhelming with choices ranging from Cabernet Sauvignon, Merlot, and Welschriesling. Guests can choose from a warm or cold buffet to go along with their vino.

Durnstein

RESTAURANT LOIBERNERHOF, *Unterloiben 7, A-3601 Durnstein. Tel. 2732-2890. Moderate. Closed Tuesdays. All credit cards accepted.*

The Restaurant Loibnerhof is situated along the banks of the Danube in a delightful vineyard. The restaurant dates back four hundred years and serves traditional, hearty Austrian fare. The wines are harvested from the Knoll family's own vineyards.

WEINGUT-HEURIGER BRUSTBAUER, *Oberloiben 2, A-3601 Durnstein. Tel. 2732-873-00. Open daily March through October, 10 a.m. to midnight. No credit cards accepted.*

If you're in the mood for a classic evening at a local wine tavern, head to the Brustbauer. You can sample the local vintages from thirty different varieties listening to schmaltzy Austrian folk tunes played by a traditional group. This *Heuriger*, which formerly served as a monastery, also has sandwiches and other light items to snack on while you're sipping your wine.

Krems

KREMSER STADTBEISEL, *Ledergrasse 3, A-3500 Krems. Tel. 2732-84280. Moderate. Open 6 p.m. to midnight. All credit cards accepted.*

Regina Peranek runs this friendly *Beisel*, or bistro, in the heart of Krems. You'll find the usual *Schnitzel* on the menu but also interesting variations on regional specialties. Wines from the Wachau are prominently featured on the menu.

TOROS RESTAURANT, *Schmid Gasse 13, A-3500 Krems. Tel. 2732-79651. Inexpensive. Open 11 a.m. to 11 p.m.; closed Sundays. No credit cards but traveler's checks accepted.*

The friendly service at Toros Restaurant sets it apart from other establishments. You'll feel like a long-lost relative by the welcome you'll receive. Turkish cuisine is the specialty here, with an emphasis on grilled meats. Well-seasoned dishes and heaping portions at extremely reasonable prices are the norm.

ZUM GOLDENEN HIRSCHEN, *Dreifaltigkeisplatz 1, A-3500 Krems. Tel. 2732-82044. Moderate. Open Monday through Saturday 8 a.m. to 10 p.m. Visa and Mastercard accepted.*

The Zum Goldenen Hirschen is a popular local hangout with a strong selection of regional wines and beer. Traditional selections like goulash and *Schnitzel* are on the menu, as well as more unusual dishes such as beef in cognac cream sauce. The one drawback is that the restaurant can get very smoky, but there is a large guest garden for dining in warmer weather.

HEURIGEN HISTORY

*The history of the **Heurigen**, or wine taverns, goes back through the centuries. Celtic settlers in the Wachau region originally cultivated wine vines, but it was the Roman occupiers who really turned the area into a grape grower's paradise. Some of these ancient presses are still used today. In the Middle Ages, the tradition of making wine was virtually lost. But the art was revived again during the Renaissance. Thirty-one monasteries began cultivating vines and making wine from the harvest.*

The tradition of the Heurigen wasn't begun until 1784, when Emperor Joseph II enacted a law allowing local vintners to sell their wine and food on their own premises tax-free. And thus a thriving institution was born.

St. Polten

DRUNTER UND DRUBER, *Kugelgasse 6, A-3100 St. Polten. Tel. 2742-55755. Moderate. Closed Sunday. All credit cards accepted.*

This beer *Beisel*, or bistro, features traditional cooking like you'd expect from grandma's kitchen. Spare ribs are a specialty. There's live music every Saturday.

GLASNOST, *Dr. Karl Renner Promenade 1A, A-3100 St. Polten. Tel. 2742-72949. Moderate. Open 7 p.m. to 4 a.m. All credit cards accepted.*

This restaurant and bar features live music. The joint is jumping, so if you're looking for a quiet evening out, look elsewhere. But if you want to paint the town red, Glasnost may be right up your alley.

PARZER AND REIBENWEIN PALAIS RESTAURANT, *Riemerplatz 1, A-3100 St. Polten. Tel. 2742-53017-30 or 31; 2742-53017-29. Moderate. Open Monday through Friday from 7 a.m. to 7 p.m.; Saturdays 7 a.m. to 3 p.m. Diners, Mastercard and Visa accepted.*

The elegantly appointed Palais Restaurant is located in the heart of St. Polten's old section. The restaurant features traditional Austrian specialties from *Schnitzel* to goulash as well as lighter fish and vegetable selections. The menu also has a strong wine list with many regional choices.

Wiener Neustadt

CASA DEL VINO, *Burggasse 3, A-2700 Wiener Neustadt. Tel. and fax: 2622-841-93. Moderate. Open Monday through Friday 11 a.m. to 7 p.m. All credit cards accepted.*

Located in the heart of Wiener Neustadt, this self-proclaimed "wine library" has bottles of the best wines from the Wachau to Styria. Call ahead for information on the wine tastings often sponsored by the Casa del Vino. Owner Jurgen A. Steinbrecher can give you tips on the best vintages.

SEEING THE SIGHTS

Altenburg

The **Benedictine Monastery**, *Altenburg 1, Tel. 2982-3451,* has more stucco work than any other in Austria, and in this Baroque oasis that's saying something. Manuscripts dating from the Middle Ages, reliquaries and ecclesiastical treasures in gold and silver are housed in the monastery. Exhibitions are on display in the Imperial Wing.

Altenburg is 90 kilometers northwest of Vienna. The monastery is open from Easter to November 1, daily from 9 a.m. to noon and 1 to 5 p.m. Visits during the rest of the year must be made by reservation.

Artstetten

The public can visit the **castle and tomb of Archduke Franz Ferdinand**, *Artstetten 1, Tel. 7413-8302,* whose assassination in Sarajevo led to World War I. Objects from his private life and from the Austro-Hungarian monarchy are on display, memorializing the last glory days of the empire.

Artstetten is 98 kilometers west of Vienna. Open from April 1 to November 2 daily from 9 a.m. to 5:30 p.m. During the rest of the year, tours for groups of 25 people or more can be made by prior arrangement.

Asparn

Asparn's **castle**, dating originally from 1717, contains a museum of early history. The park surrounding the castle has reconstructed buildings from the prehistoric age with displays showing how early man once lived.

Asparn is 53 kilometers west of Vienna. **Museum of Early History**, *A-2151 Asparn/Zaya. Tel. 2577-239.* Open from April through November 15, Tuesday through Sunday, 9 a.m. to 5 p.m.

Bad Deutsch Altenburg

Bad Deutsch Altenburg has a **museum** with exhibitions on how the Romans lived in Austria. Displays include topics such as Oriental culture, the emperor and the provinces, the emperor and the army and civil life.

Part of the town of Petronell can be visited with a reconstruction of the temple of Diana Nemesis and an ancient sewer system. Remains of a triumphal arch, amphitheater, palace and other Roman excavations are on view.

Altenburg is 46 kilometers east of Vienna. **Archaeological Museum Carnuntum**, *Badgasse 40-46, A-2405 Bad Deutsch-Altenburg. Tel. 2165-62480.* Open daily 10 a.m. to 5 p.m.; closed Mondays.

Baden bei Wien

Visitors have been flocking to **Baden bei Wien** since the Romans ruled to "seek the cure." The town, in the green hills of the Vienna Woods, is known for its medicinal springs and health resort and was favored by the Hapsburg imperial family from 1803 to 1834. Baden also is known for its casino housed in a spectacular 19th century building and worth a detour in its own right. The Biedermeier style dominates the architecture and gardens. No wonder that Mozart, Beethoven, Liszt and Josef and Johann Strauss all came here to relax.

Baden is 29 south of Vienna, and is also easily accessible by train. For more information, contact **Baden Tourist Information**, *Hauptplatz 2, A-2500 Baden. Tel. 2252-86800.*

Durnhof

Travelers can visit the former 12th century **farm houses** and Romanesque and Gothic **chapels** here belonging to the Cistercian Monastery of Zwettl. You'll also find the Museum of Medicine and Meteorology, which traces the development in these two sciences from ancient times to the modern era, including superstitions and local customs. Don't forget to take a look at the national garden of Lower Austria here.

Durnhof is 118 kilometers northwest of Vienna. **Cistercian Monastery**, *A-3910 Zwettl, Durnhof. Tel. 2822-3180.* Open April through November daily 10 a.m. to 6 p.m. Closed Mondays. Prior arrangements should be made for guided tours.

Durnstein

One of the loveliest towns along the Danube in the Wachau, **Durnstein** was first documented in 1347. Narrow, winding medieval streets are bordered by ancient, stone-hewn houses. Towering over the top of the town is the **Kuenringer castle**, where the English king Richard the Lion-Hearted was imprisoned between 1192 and 1193. The story goes that his faithful servant Blondel went from castle to castle singing his ballads. When the words of his song were returned, he knew he had found his king.

Unfortunately, the story has a less romantic ending. Richard was only released after paying a hefty ransom of 35,000 kilos of silver to Duke Leopold V. Today, you can climb the summit to get a better look at the crumbling remains. The top of the hill affords a spectacular view of the surrounding countryside crisscrossed with vines from the nearby vineyards. The **Monastery of Augustinian Canons** here was founded in 1410, but Baroque elements were added in 1710 when it was renovated by Provost Hieronymus Ubelacher. The monastery was dissolved by Emperor Joseph II in 1788. The Baroque church, the 12th century cloister, and the terrace are open to modern-day visitors. You can also climb the Baroque **tower** for a magnificent view of the town and the Danube flowing below.

Durnstein is 77 kilometers west of Vienna. **Stift Durnstein**, *A-3601 Durnstein/Wachau. Tel. 2711-375.* Open April 1 to October 31 daily from 9 a.m. to 6 p.m. Guided tours are given every hour on the hour.

Eckartsau

The Baroque **castle** in **Eckartsau** was built from 1722 to 1732 by the master architect J.E. Fischer von Erlach. The castle served as a hunting lodge for the Hapsburgs. In fact, Emperor Karl used the royal residence as his last domicile before going into exile in 1918.

Eckartsau is 38 kilometers east of Vienna. **Schloss Eckartsau**, *A-2305 Eckartsau. Tel. 2214-2240.* Open April through October, Saturday, Sundays and holidays from 11 a.m. to 1 p.m. by guided tour.

Furth

The **Benedictine Gottweig Monastery** in the Wachau region is on the Danube south of Krems. The Erentrudis chapel, crypt, and gatekeeper's lodge showcase the monastery's medieval beginnings from 1083. The monastery itself was built according to the design of the Baroque architect Lukas von Hildebrandt. Guided tours of the Imperial Wing are available. Dine at the monastery's terrace restaurant where many of the wines and food is produced at the abbey. Concerts are also held at monastery. Hiking is possible through the surrounding forests and vineyards.

Furth is 72 kilometers west of Vienna. **Stift Gottweig**, *A-3511 Furth. Tel. 2732-85581; Fax 2732-85581/266; Restaurant Tel. 2732-84663.* Guided tours available from April 1 to October 31 at 10 a.m., 11 a.m., 2 p.m. 3 p.m. and 4 p.m. or by reservation.

Gaming

Duke Albrecht II founded the **monastery** here in 1332. The Carthusians, or "white monks," lived here until 1782 when the monastery was dissolved on the orders of Emperor Joseph II. The building was transformed into the Baroque style in the 18th century. The Gothic hall, prelate hall, and library still exist.

Gaming is 130 kilometers southeast of Vienna. **Kartause Gaming**, *A-3292 Gaming. Tel. 7485-8466.* Open all year round.

Geras

The **monastery** here was founded in 1153 and architectural remnants of the period can be observed in parts of the Baroque basilica. A "new building" at the monastery was constructed in 1738, which now can be reserved for overnight stays. Courses are also held at the site throughout the year for aspiring artists. Don't miss the monastery's famous marble hall, with frescoes by the painter Troger.

Geras is 97 kilometers northwest of Vienna. **Stift Geras**, *A-2093 Geras. Tel. 2912-345; Fax 2912-349; Hotel Tel. 2912-3320.* Open May to October daily from 9 a.m. to noon and from 2 p.m. to 5 p.m. or by prior arrangement. Closed Mondays.

Gmund

This Renaissance castle with its Gothic wings served as the seat of the Streun family until 1636. The Baroque interior of **Schwarzenau** was commissioned by Count Pollheim and designed by the artist Giovanni Batista d'Allio. Relax after your tour at the castle coffee house.

Schwarzenau is 117 kilometers northwest of Vienna. **Schloss Schwarzenau**, *A-3900. Tel. 2849-2342.* Guided tours of the castle from April 27 to October 27, daily 9 a.m. to 6 p.m.

Grafenegg Castle

The Romanesque **Grafenegg castle** is the most important of its kind in modern-day Austria. Tourists today can dine in style at the castle's restaurant. Exhibitions and concerts are held from May 1 to October 26, as well as the "Grafenegger Advent" festival in December and the "Romantic Music Week" every two years.

Grafenegg is 61 kilometers northwest of Vienna. **Schlossverwaltung Grafenegg**, *A-3485 Haitzendorf. Tel. 2735-2205; administration, extension 22.* **Castle Tavern**, *Schlosstaverne Grafenegg, A-3485 Haitzendorf. Tel. 2735-758420.* Open Tuesdays and Thursdays from 1 p.m. to 5 p.m.; Saturdays, Sundays and public holidays from 10 a.m. to 5 p.m.

Greillenstein

The Renaissance **castle** here dates from 1588 and features a court-yard with arcades and a Baroque garden. You can visit a Renaissance bathing pool, the Hall of the Turks commemorating the Austrian-Turkish wars, and a collection of Baroque garden dwarves, kept at the royal court as curiosities. If you're feeling in a romantic mood, the castle can be rented for weddings.

Greillenstein is 96 kilometers northwest of Vienna. **Schloss Greillenstein**, *A-3592 Greillenstein. Tel. 2989-8321 or 8200*. The castle is open April 1 to October 31 daily from 9 a.m. to 5 p.m.; July 1 to August 31 daily from 9 a.m. to 6 p.m.; November 1 to March 31 by reservation only.

Hardegg

The 12th century Romanesque **fortress** here in the Thaya Valley is privately owned, but you can visit a museum honoring Emperor Maximilian of Mexico, with a collection of armor and weaponry belonging to Prince Khevenhuller-Metsch and exhibits on local history and culture. A chapel at the fortress is available for weddings.

Hardegg is 92 kilometers north of Vienna. **Burg Hardegg**, *A-2082 Hardegg 1. Tel. 2949-8225 or 2916-400; fax 2916-425*. Open daily 9 a.m. to 5 p.m.; July and August 9 a.m. to 6 p.m. During the winter, guided weekend tours are available to groups of 5 people or more, *call 2949-8202*.

Heidenreichstein

The **Heidenreichstein castle** is a storybook palace complete with a 13th century watchtower, ramparts, drawbridges, and moat. Parts of the castle are open to the public with historic furnishings and exhibitions on display.

Heidenreichstein is 135 kilometers northwest of Vienna. **Heidenreichstein Schloss**, *A-3860 Schremser Strasse 1. Tel. 2862-2268*. Open mid-April to mid-October. Guided tours only, for a minimum of five people, are conducted daily at 9 a.m., 10 a.m., 11 a.m., 2 p.m., 3 p.m. and 4 p.m. Closed Mondays.

Heiligenkreuz

The **Cistercian monastery** here was founded in 1133 and contains architectural styles through the ages including Gothic, Romantic, and Baroque elements. The monastery has a chapel built in the Romanesque and Gothic styles, cloister, Gothic windows, and a Trinity column in the courtyard.

Heiligenkreuz is 31 kilometers southwest from Vienna. **Stift Heiligenkreuz**, *A-2532 Heiligenkreuz. Tel. 2258-2282*. Open daily 9 a.m. to 11:30 a.m. and 1:30 p.m. to 4 p.m.

Heldenberg

The first written record of the Castle Wetzdorf here was in 1190. The castle was transformed into the Baroque style in 1726 and later neo-classical elements were added.

Heldenberg is 54 kilometers northwest of Vienna. **Schloss Wetzdorf**, *A-3704 Glaubendorf. Tel. 2956-2751.* Open May through October, Saturdays, Sundays and holidays. Tours are given at 11 a.m., 2 p.m., 4 p.m., 5 p.m. and by prior arrangement.

Klosterneuburg

The **Augustinian monastery** here was founded in 1144 by Margrave Leopold. The monastery was reconstructed in 1730 modelled after the Escorial. Be sure not to miss the enameled Verdun altar, hand-carved, wooden choir and oratory and the gothic column in the Abbey Square.

Klosterneuburg is 12 kilometers west of Vienna. **Stift Klosterneuburg**, *A-3400 Klosterneuburg. Tel. 2243-6210-2123.* Open year round; guided tours given on the hour.

Krems

The medieval town of **Krems** has a 1,000 year old history, and was once a trading center for wine, salt, and iron. Still surrounded by vineyards, the city today is a center of Wachau wine production.

The **Und Monastery** was first constructed in 1614 by the Capuchin monks who were given the land by Archbishop Marcus Siticus of Salzburg. The church of the monastery burnt down in 1656, but was rebuilt with money from the Countess Katharina Werdenberg. A well on the site became know for its curative powers and was attributed with healing everything from the plague to cattle diseases. When the monastery was ordered secularized in 1796, the monastery became a hospital for wounded soldiers.

Today, Und is still known for its healing water, but the modern elixir comes out of a wine bottle rather than a well. More than 100 Austrian wines are available for tasting or to take home to stock your own private wine cellar. Enjoy a good meal, listen to a concert, or visit one of the exhibitions on-site to complete your experience. **Weinkolleg Kloster Und**, *A-3504 Krems-Stein, Undstrasse 6. Tel. 2732-73074; Telex 7188.* Open daily 10 a.m. to 8 p.m. Arrangements for guided tours of the wine cellar and wine tasting with staff commentary should be made prior to visiting the monastery.

Other sights of historical interest in Krems include the restored and renovated Dominican monastery, the powder magazine dating from 1477, and the statue of the *Man without a Head* from the 16th century. The

Stein Gate, with its two rounded towers, was constructed in 1480 and connects Krems with its twin city of Stein. The parish **church of St. Veit** was one of the first Baroque buildings in Lower Austria. In the late Gothic Piarist Church, you'll find a high altarpiece by Kremser Schmidt.

Krems is 75 kilometers west of Vienna.

Langenlois

The **Schloss Gobelsburg** is the formal ancestral seat of the Kuenrings. The Cistercian monks of Zwettl have farmed the estate and harvested grapes for wine there since 1740. Today, the castle contains a branch of the **Austrian Museum of Folklore**. Rustic glassware and furniture are on exhibit. Summer visitors can enjoy wine tastings in the Baroque courtyard.

Langenlois is 70 kilometers northwest of Vienna. **Schloss Gobelsburg**, *A-3550 Langenlois. Tel. 2734-2422.* Open April 30 to October 26 daily from 10 a.m. to noon and 1 p.m. to 6 p.m.

Lilienfeld

Duke Leopold VI founded this **Cistercian monastery**, the largest medieval monastery in Austria, in 1202. Baroque elements were added later in the 18th century. A Romanesque and Gothic basilica and cloister from the 13th century are still in existence. Displays on the Babenberg dynasty are also on display.

Lilienfeld is 77 kilometers west of Vienna. **Stift Lilifeld**, *A-3180 Lilienfeld. Tel. 2762-52204.* Open year round, Monday through Saturday from 9 a.m. to noon and 2 p.m. to 4:30 p.m.; Sundays and holidays 2 p.m. to 4:30 p.m.

Luberegg

The castle here once served as the summer residence for Emperor Francis II. Luberegg is 88 kilometers west of Vienna. **Schloss Luberegg**, *A-3644 Emmersdorf. Tel. 2752-71755.* Open daily April through November from 9 a.m. to 5:30 p.m.

Mailberg

The **Castle Mailberg** was founded by the order of the Maltese Cross. The Gothic castle is home to a Maltese Cross museum, festival hall, and a bed and breakfast inn.

Mailberg is 63 kilometers north of Vienna. **Schloss Mailberg**, *A-2024 Mailberg. Tel. 2943-2251.* The museum is open May through September, Saturdays, Sundays and holidays 10 a.m. to noon and 2 p.m. to 5 p.m.

Marchegg

The medieval castle here was reconstructed during the 17th century. Today it houses a **hunting museum** detailing the history of the hunt in Lower Austria.

Marchegg is 44 kilometers east of Vienna. **Jagdmuseum**, *A-2293 Marchegg. Tel. 2285-224*. Open March 15 through November, Tuesday to Sunday 9 a.m. to noon and 1 p.m. to 5 p.m.

Maria Taferl

Maria Taferl, *The Sorrowful Mother of God*, pilgrimage church was completed in 1710. The Baroque church has a dome designed by Jacob Prandtauer and frescoes painted by Antonio Beduzzi. The high altar is located on the spot where a crucifix once stood that was said to heal true believers. The church site was also probably once used by the Celts as a place of worship. Maria Taferl is in a romantic wooded area 443 meters above the Danube on the edge of the Wachau. Visitors to the pilgrimage center, with more than 600 hotel beds, have a panoramic view of the foothills leading to the Alps.

Maria Taferl is 96 kilometers west of Vienna. **Fremdenverkehrsverein Maria Taferl**, *A-3672 Maria Taferl, Tel. 7413-415 or 7413-6355; fax 7413-6355-83*.

Mayerling

It was here at this former hunting lodge that the Crown Prince Rudolf, the only son of Emperor Franz Josef and heir to the throne, shot and killed his mistress before committing suicide in 1889. Today, the ill-fated residence serves as a **Carmelite convent**.

Mayerling is 35 kilometers southwest of Vienna. **Jagdschloss Mayerling**, *A-2534 Alland. Tel. 2258-2275*. Open daily 9 a.m. to 12:30 p.m. and 1:30 p.m. to 5 p.m.; Sundays and holidays 10 a.m. to 12:30 p.m. and 1:30 p.m. to 5 p.m.

Melk

The bright yellow **Benedictine monastery** looms majestically above the plains and is deservedly one of the most famous Baroque monuments in all of Austria. The monastery was built between 1702 and 1736, following the design of architect Jacob Prandtauer. The library's fresco was painted by Paul Troger and dates from 1732.

But the highlight of the monastery is surely the incredible gilt-covered cathedral with ornate frescoes painted by Johann Michael Rottmayr between 1716 and 1721. The imperial apartments, where Emperor Karl VI, Empress Maria Theresa, Pope Pius VI, and Napoleon once stayed, now house the monastery's museum. Be sure to make a stop on the terrace to catch a glimpse of the magnificent view of the Danube valley and the cathedral's exterior.

The history of the monastery dates back to 1089 when Margrave Leopold II gave the church, castle, and land to the Benedictine Abbot Sigibold. Today, present-day monks are still in residence and more than 700 students attend the monastery school.

Melk is 87 kilometers west of Vienna. **Benediktinerstift Melk,** *A-3390 Melk. Tel. 2752-2312-232; fax 2752-2312-249.* Open from May through September from 9 a.m. to 6 p.m.; Palm Sunday to April and the month of October, 9 a.m. to 5 p.m.; November to March 11 a.m. to 2 p.m. or by reservation. Guided tours in English are possible. Admission is 50 schillings for adults, and 25 schillings for students.

Modling

Just a stone's throw from Vienna, **Modling** was once first settled during the Stone Age. Members of Austria's Babenberg dynasty lived in the castle here. Nicknamed "the Austrian-Switzerland," the area also attracted the composers Franz Schubert and Beethoven. Other sights worth noting are the Romanesque charnel house dating back to the 13th century, the Ducal court, the 16th century city hall, the parish church and the many burgher houses scattered throughout the old town.

Modling is 30 kilometers south of Vienna. **Modling Tourist Information,** *A-2340 Modling. Tel. 2236-267-27.*

Niederweiden

The Earl of Starhemberg defended Vienna in 1683 against the Turks. He later had J.B. Fischer von Erlach design this magnificent Baroque **castle,** which contains a late Gothic parish church, a column dedicated to the Virgin Mary from the 18th century, and a 17th century pillory.

Niederweiden is 47 kilometers east of Vienna. **Schloss Niederweiden,** *A-2292 Engelhartstetten. Tel. 2214-2176 or 2803.* Open daily April to November from 10 a.m. to 6 p.m.

Poggstall

The **Rogendorf Castle** contains the **Lower Austrian Museum of Legal History**, which claims the only original torture chamber in the whole of the German-speaking world. The castle museum also has a fine collection of legal memorabilia.

Poggstall is 109 kilometers west of Vienna. **Museum fur Rechtsgeschichte,** *Schloss, A-3650 Poggstall. Tel. 2758-3310.* The castle is open April 1 to October 30 9 a.m. to 5 p.m. Closed Mondays.

Raabs

The **Raabs Castle** houses a **Fairy Tales Museum**, a perfect trip for the kids. Parents will enjoy several rooms restored in the castle, which are open to the public.

Raabs is 110 kilometers northwest of Vienna. **Schloss Raabs**, *Oberndorf 1, A-3820 Raabs. Tel. 2846-659*. Open May to October, Mondays through Thursdays 8 a.m. to noon and 1 p.m. to 4:30 p.m.; Fridays 8 a.m. to noon and 1 p.m. to 2 p.m.; Saturdays, Sundays and holidays 9 a.m. to noon and 1 p.m. to 5 p.m. Reservations should be made for visits from November to May and for guided tours.

Rappottenstein

The **Rappottenstein fortress** is situated high above the Little Kamp and was built between 1157 and 1176. The fortress boasts a Romanesque watchtower, a Gothic hall with a 15th century courtyard and kitchen and a Gothic chapel.

Rappottenstein is 124 kilometers west of Vienna. **Burg Rappottenstein**, *A-3911 Rappottenstein. Tel. 2828-250*. Visitors can only see the fortress on guided tours of the site: 10 a.m., 11 a.m., 2 p.m., 3 p.m., 4 p.m. and 5 p.m. Tours from May 1st to September 30 daily except Mondays; tours are held Saturday, Sundays and holidays on Easter and from April 15 to April 30 and October 1 to October 31.

Riegersburg

This Baroque country **castle** was the seat of the former governor of Lower Austria, Prince Khevenhuller-Metsch. The castle **museum** houses state rooms with 18th century furniture and the only antique kitchen with still-functioning appliances in Austria.

Riegersburg is 101 kilometers northwest of Vienna. **Schloss Riegersburg**, *A-2092 Riegersburg 1. Tel. 2916-201, 332 or 400; fax 2916-425*. Open April 1 to November 15 daily 9 a.m. to 5 p.m.; July and August 9 a.m. to 7 p.m.

Rohrau

Rohrau is the birthplace of the famous Haydn composers Joseph, in 1732, and Michael in 1737. Today "number 60" is the home of a **Haydn museum**.

Rohrau is 46 kilometers southeast of Vienna. **Haydn Geburtshaus**, *A-2471 Rohrau. Tel. 2164-2286*. Open Tuesday to Sunday from 10 a.m. to 5 p.m.

Rosenburg

In the 11th century, a fortress was built here and was expanded into a Renaissance **castle** in the 16th century. The castle boasts the largest intact **jousting** arena in Europe. **Falconers** entertain visitors with displays on the castle terrace. Period furnishings, paintings, and weapons are also on display.

Rosenburg is 84 kilometers northwest of Vienna. **Rosenburg Schloss**, *A-3573 Rosenburg. Tel. 2982-2911.* Open April 1 to November 15 daily 9 a.m. to 6 p.m.; guided tours daily from 9 a.m. to 5 p.m; falconry displays daily at 11 a.m. and 3 p.m. Guided tours for groups of 15 people or more are available by reservation from November 16 to March 31.

St. Polten

St. Polten was made the provincial capital of Lower Austria in 1986. Visitors can see the foundations from the Augustinian Canon monastery, dating from the eighth century. But most of the town is Baroque in appearance following the plans of Jacob Prandtauer. The Baroque pastel palaces of the former nobility and wealthy burghers line the squares in the pedestrian quarter.

St. Polten is 62 kilometers west of Vienna. **Magistrat der Landeshauptstadt St. Polten**, *Rathaus, A-3100 St. Polten. Tel. 2742-52531.*

Schallaburg

One of the most exquisite Renaissance castles north of the Alps, the Schloss now houses the **international exhibition center** of Lower Austria. The two-story arcades are from the 16th century and are decorated with terra cotta statues. The castle also has a Gothic chapel and lovely gardens.

Schallaburg is 84 kilometers west of Vienna. **Schloss Schallaburg**, *A-3382 Schallaburg. Tel. 2754-6317.* Open May 18 to October 27, Monday through Friday, 9 a.m. to 5 p.m. Guided tours by prior arrangement.

Schloss Hof

Prince Eugene of Savoy bought this 16th century **fortress** in 1725. He had the Hof Castle reconstructed in the Baroque style by Lukas von Hildebrandt. Empress Maria Theresa bought the castle in 1755.

The Hof Castle is 47 kilometers east of Vienna. **Schloss Hof**, *A-2294 Schlosshof. Tel. 2285-6580.* Open daily from March to November, 10 a.m. to 5 p.m.

Schneeberg Rack Railway

Take a ride on an old-fashioned steam railroad car along the rack railway built in 1897 as it climbs up the scenic **Hochschneeberg**. The trip to the top takes about an hour, as you pass through lush woods with a spectacular view of the surrounding mountains. The station is the highest in Austria – 1,795 meters above sea level.

The **Berghaus** at the top has a sauna, solarium, and home cooking, including yeast dumplings. Hiking is also possible in the vicinity. Admission is 250 schillings for a round trip ticket; 125 schillings for children and students. Tickets can be purchased at the Wien Sudbahnhof, Wien Meidling, Modling, Baden and Wiener Neustadt train stations. The **Puchberg am Schneeberg** station is about a one and a half hour drive from Vienna.

For more information, *call 2636-2225-0 or 3661; fax 2636-3262.*

Seitenstetten

The Benedictine monastery here was founded in 1112. Baroque elements were added by architect J. Munggenast. Frescoes by the artist P. Troger are in the marble hall, the library and in the chapel. A collection of his paintings are also on display.

Seitenstetten is 146 kilometers southwest of Vienna. **Stift Seitenstetten**, *A-3353 Seitenstetten. Tel. 7477-42300.* Open daily from Easter through November from 10 a.m. to 11:30 a.m. and 3 p.m. to 4:30 p.m.

Senftenberg

Senftenberg is a haven for those "seeking the cure." The health spas feature electrophysical and hydrotherapy. Swimming, bowling, saunas, tennis and solariums are also available. History buffs will want to visit the fortified church **Imbach**, the oldest Gothic church of its kind in German-speaking Europe. The organ in the church dates back to 1605. Fortress ruins towering above the town and old houses are also attractions.

Senftenberg is 72 kilometers northwest of Vienna. **Senftenberg Tourist Information**, *Tel. 2719-2319; fax 2719-8300.*

Spitz

The first recorded record of the town of **Spitz** dates back to 865, and homes from the Renaissance and the Baroque periods still exist. A beautiful late Gothic church remains as well. The town is surrounded by the terraced vineyards that produce excellent wine grapes. Hikers will enjoy the 50 kilometers of trails that crisscross the area. Fishing, biking, boating, swimming and tennis facilities are also available.

Spitz is 82 kilometers west of Vienna. **Spitz Tourist Information**, *A-3620 Spitz. Tel. 2713-2362 or 2248.*

Wachau Wine Road

A trip to Lower Austria is usually a day trip from Vienna or even Salzburg and Linz. Plan a bike ride, boat trip, or car travel along the banks of the Danube in the **Wachau** wine growing region. The towns are charming and will give you a real sense of what village life is like in rural Austria. Use the *Seeing the Sights* section above to map out the trip that best meets your needs. You'll be pleasantly surprised by the warm welcome as well, especially if you're coming from stuffy Vienna.

The history of the region stretches back to prehistoric times. It was here that the famous **Venus of Willendorf**, the first depiction of the female form in Western art, was found from the Palaeolithic era. The Romans later built settlements in the region. They were followed by the Huns and the Awar tribes. During the Middle Ages, the Knights of the Cross traveled through the river valley three times between 1096 and 1189 on their way to fight the infidels during the crusades.

VINO VARIETIES

*The mild climate of the Danube River Valley is ideal for producing quality wines. Long, warm autumn days enhance the growing period, but the cool fall nights helps prevent the decomposition of the acid in the fruit. Wines are full-bodied and fragrant. Once steep mountain slopes have been terraced through the years and are crisscrossed with vines, which form a green and purple quilt across the hillsides. **Rheinriesling** and **Gruner Velterliner** are grown along the rocky peaks. In the river valley, grapes producing bottles of **Neuburger** and **Muller-Thurgau** are grown.*

*Specialties of the region include the **Himmelsstiege**, from Durnstein, **Tausendeimerberg**, from Spitz or the **Sandgrube**, **Ried Klau**, or **Ried Achleiten**.*

Weiner Neustadt

What would become the city of **Weiner Neustadt** was founded by Leopold V in 1194. The Babenberg duke realized the strategic importance of the area and christened it *Nova Civitas* or new city. In the 15th century, the city became the official seat of the monarchy with Hapsburg emperor Frederick III setting up shop in the town.

The spectacular Romanesque **cathedral**, towering over the surrounding buildings, merits a visit with its lifesize wooden statues of the 12 apostles. The **main square** also has several historically significant buildings dating from the Middle Ages through the Renaissance. In the northwest corner of the town are the former fortifications and a tower built during the 13th century, where instruments of torture were stored when they weren't being used on some hapless prisoner. The **town wall** was financed by some of the money left over from the ransom paid for the release of the English king Richard the Lion-Hearted.

Wiener Neustadt is 45 kilometers south of Vienna. **Weiner Neustadt Tourist Information**, *Herzog-Leopold Strasse 17, A-2700 Wiener Neustadt. Tel. 2622-23531-368.*

Weitra

The Kuenrings originally built this **fortress** here. The Renaissance castle was enlarged in 1590 using plans by Pietro Ferrabosco. A fire damaged the castle, which was reconstructed in 1757. Visitors can view the fortress' arcaded courtyard, Baroque chapel, and 19th century theater.

Weitra is 142 kilometers northwest of Vienna. **Gasteinformation Weitra**, *Rathausplatz 1, A-3970 Weitra. Tel. 2856-2998.* Open daily May through October from 9 a.m. to 6 p.m.

Ysper Gorge

Located in the southern Waldviertel, the **Ysper Gorge** is the natural wonder of Lower Austria. Water tumbles over boulders dropping some 300 meters into the gorge and the valley below. You can hike up to the top of the gorge. A terraced trail has been built allowing for easy walking. The Ysper flows through its namesake valley past the towns of Pisching, Altenmarkt, and Ysper.

Ysper-Weitental Tourist Information, *Tel. 7412-52421; fax 7412-52421-5.*

NIGHTLIFE & ENTERTAINMENT

Many of the smaller towns in Lower Austria feature concerts during the summer months. As most performances and dates vary each summer, check with local tourist offices for details.

In **Melk**, you can attend the **Pentecost Concerts** *at the Melk Abbey.* There is also a theater festival at the abbey during July and August. The city of **Baden** hosts an **operetta festival** during the summer months. Or gamblers may prefer trying their luck at the local **Baden Casino**, *in the Kurpark,* which opens for business at 3 p.m. daily.

SHOPPING

There are several **markets** in the provincial capital of **St. Polten**, including one in the main square on Thursdays and Saturdays. On Herrenplatz, there is a small daily market. A bio-market at the Traisenpark shopping center, Dr. Adolf Scharf Strasse 3-9, is held Thursdays from 2 p.m. to 8 p.m. The provincial capital flea market takes place every

Saturday and Sunday from 8 a.m. to 3 p.m. in the Antik-Treff, St. Polten Unterradlberg. Another flea market is held at the corner of Austinstrasse and Ortweingasse the first Saturday of each month.

  Wine is the highlight of any trip to Lower Austria, so buy a bottle or even a case to commemorate your visit. After the harvest, vintners sell wine at the various stages of fermentation. *Most* is the wine that is still grape juice just beginning the fermentation process. *Sturm* is the next stage in the wine process. It tastes sweet like juice but packs quite a punch. The "new wine," Austria's version of the beaujolais nouveau, comes next.

SPORTS & RECREATION
Biking

The Danube River flows 230 kilometers through Lower Austria and bike and hiking trails run along its banks. The Austrian Railways has a special train service called **Rad-Tramper** just for hikers and bikers, with cars especially equipped with bicycle racks. It costs 40 schillings to transport your bike or if you purchase an **Umweltticket** for families and seniors, your ticket is half-price.

If you don't want to bother with the hassle of transporting your bicycle, men's, women's and children's rentals are available at the Greifenstein-Altenberg, Klosternburg-Weilding, Korneuburg, Krems-on-the-Danube, Melk, Pochlarn, Spitz on the Danube, Traismauer, Tulln and Ybbs-on-the-Danube train stations. You can return your rental bicycle at any of the above participating stations.

If you travel to the rental station by train, your bicycle will only cost you 45 schillings per day. After 3 p.m., your travel card will still be valid for the reduced rate the next day. Otherwise, the cost is 90 schillings. No deposit is required, but you must show some form of valid identification like a passport.

If you want to be sure of getting a bike, reserve ahead of time, especially on weekends. *Reservations can be made by calling 222-58-00-33-449.*

Golf
• **Golf Club St. Polten**, *Schloss Goldegg, A-3100 St. Polten. Tel. 2741-7360.* Eighteen-hole golf course.

Horseback Riding
• **Riding Club St. Polten-Wagram**, *Im Dorfl 3, A-3100 St. Polten. Tel.2742-251302*
• **Riding Club**, *Albrechtsberg Castle, A-3390 Melk. Tel. 2754-6170*

Swimming
• **Municipal Swimming Pool**, *Handel Mazetti Strasse, A-3100 St. Polten. Tel. 2742-72991.* Pool with 70-meter slide.

Tennis & Squash
• **Allround Tennis Center**, *Strattersdor, A-3100 St. Polten. Tel. 2742-253338.* Indoor and outdoor courts, with mini golf.
• **Leisure Park Megafun**, *Am Ratzersdorfer See, A-3100 St. Polten. Tel. 2742-251510.* Indoor and outdoor courts, squash, bowling, billiards and darts.
• **Squash and Fitness Center City Treff**, *Schulze Delitzsch Strasse 7, A-3100 St. Polten. Tel. 2742-7655-0*
• **Squash Center**, *An der Schutt 42, A-3500 Krems. Tel. 2732-8120 or 81250*

PRACTICAL INFORMATION
Credit Cards
If your credit cards are lost or stolen, you can call the following numbers 24 hours a day to make a report. The numbers are located in Vienna, so first dial area code *0222.*
• **American Express**, *Tel. 51-29-714*
• **Diners**, *Tel. 50-1-35*
• **Mastercard**, *Tel. 71-7-01-0*
• **Visa**, *Tel. 53-4-87-77*

Emergency Phone Numbers
• **Ambulance**, *Tel. 144*
• **Police**, *Tel. 133*
• **Fire Department**, *Tel. 122*

Exchanging Money
In general, local banks are open Monday to Friday, 8:30 a.m. to 12:30 p.m. and 2 p.m. to 4:30 p.m. Banks are closed Saturdays, Sundays, and public holidays.

Pharmacies
Pharmacies are typically open Monday to Friday from 8 a.m. to 12:30 p.m. and 2:30 to 6 p.m.; Saturdays 8 a.m. to noon. Some pharmacies are open during lunch, at night and on weekends and holidays.

Closed pharmacies post in their windows the name, address and number of the nearest open pharmacy in case of emergencies.

Post Offices

Most post offices are open Monday through Friday from 8 a.m. to noon and 2 p.m. to 6 p.m.; Saturdays from 8 a.m. to 10 a.m.

Tipping

A service charge is added to your hotel and restaurant bill. However, if you are pleased with the service, it is customary to tip an additional 5 to 10 percent of the check. Taxi drivers and hair dressers also are generally tipped the same amount.

Weather

For the latest weather information, *call 15-66.*

14. UPPER AUSTRIA

INTRODUCTION

Upper Austria has something for everyone. There are gentle rolling hills in the north, the **Danube Valley** running through the province's center, the **Alpine foothills** leading to the Alps, and the beautiful, world-renowned **Lake District**.

Linz is the main city in this region, and there's plenty to do in town and nearby. Another of Upper Austria's most famous attractions is **St. Florian**, just 15 kilometers from Linz. The huge Augustine monastery is definitely worth a detour for connoisseurs of Baroque art.

Bikers will love the easy rolling hillsides bordering the Danube. Many local hotels cater to bicyclists' needs and have facilities on-site for storage and repairs. The picture-perfect **Muhlviertel** beckons hikers with its tempting woods and foothills. The northern portion of the Muhlviertel is covered with forest and is renowned for its terrific hiking. The province's pretty northwestern corner is called the **Innviertel and the Hausruckwalk**. Upper Austria is 4,624 square miles wide and has 1.34 million inhabitants.

ORIENTATION

If you're staying in Salzburg, a quick detour into Upper Austria is an easy day trip. Or if you're biking, hiking, or drinking your way up the Danube, from Vienna or Lower Austria, you'll see more breathtaking scenery, charming villages, and historic buildings in this province.

LINZ

Located on the Danube, the provincial capital, **Linz**, is a major production center for iron, steel, and chemicals. But despite its industrial reputation, the city has a lovely old quarter to explore on foot. First mentioned in Roman archives in 410 A.D. under the Celtic name *Lentia*, Linz became a market town in 906 A.D.

ARRIVALS & DEPARTURES

By Air

The **Linz Airport** is located at *Postfach 11, A-4063 Horsching*. A taxi from the airport into central Linz will cost approximately 280 schillings.

By Car

Linz is 201 kilometers from Vienna, 129 kilometers from Salzburg, and 284 kilometers from Innsbruck. The A-1 Autobahn runs west to Salzburg and east to Vienna.

By Train

Linz is conveniently located on the rail lines running between Vienna and Salzburg, with trains scheduled each hour. The **train station** is located on *Bahnhofstrasse 3, Zugauskunft.*

For **train information**, *call 17-17.*

UPPER AUSTRIA TOURIST TIPS

If you are planning a trip to Linz or the surrounding province, you can get additional information about where to stay, eat, and visit through the local tourist office.

Linz Tourist Board, Urfahrmarkt 1, P.O. Box 117, A-4040 Linz. Tel. 732-7070-1777; fax 732-700494. Open November through April, Monday through Friday from 8 a.m. to 6 p.m.; Saturdays from 8 a.m. to 11:30 a.m. and 12:30 p.m. to 6 p.m.; Sundays and holidays, 9 a.m. to 11:30 a.m. and 12:30 p.m. to 6 p.m.; May through October, Monday through October 7 a.m. to 7 p.m.; Saturdays 9 a.m. to 7 p.m.; Sundays and holidays 10 a.m. to 7 p.m.

If you want to find out information about Linz through the internet, the address – get ready for this – is http://www.gup.uniLinz.ac.at:8001/CityOfLinz.

GETTING AROUND LINZ

By Car

If you plan ahead, you'll save a lot of money by renting your car at home. Here are the local car rental offices in Linz.

• **Avis**, *4020 Schillerstrasse 1, A-4040 Linz. Tel. 732-66-28-81; fax 732-60-55-70; at the airport, Tel. 66-28-81.*

• **Budget**, *Novotel Linz, Wankmullerhofstrasse 37, A-4040 Linz. Tel. 732-34-62-22; fax 732-34-62-23; at the airport, Tel. 72-700-293.*

• **Europcar**, *Wiener Strasse 91, A-4040 Linz. Tel. 732-60-00-91; fax 732-60-00-91-13; at the airport, Tel. 727-00-297.*

Free parking is available at the Urfahr Market below the Niberlungenbridge on the northern banks of the Danube. There is no time limit. A path leads from the parking area to the shopping district. Indoor and outside garages and paid parking zones are also available throughout the city. Hourly parking costs approximately 10 to 30 schillings per hour.

If you have car problems, you can call *120* or *123* for assistance. The local automobile clubs are **ARBO**, *Hafenstrasse 6, A-4040 Linz, Tel. 732-79-811* and **OAMTC**, *Wankmullerhofstrasse 58, A-4040 Linz, Tel. 732-33-330.*

By Public Transportation

Trams and buses are available to all parts of the city. A "maxi" day ticket is available for 35 schillings. Single tickets can be bought at machines at the stops, but you must have change. Multi-trip tickets can be bought at tobacco shops or at the **ECG customer center**, *Landstrasse 85.*

By Train

You can see the sights in Linz's old section by hopping aboard the **Linz City Express train**. The bright yellow train leaves daily on the hour between 10 a.m. and 6 p.m. from the Main Square. Tours last about half an hour.

GETTING OFF THE BEATEN TRACK

If you're interested in seeing more of Lower Austria, here are the tourist offices for the noted cities around the province. Don't forget to take a look at the **Lake District** *chapter for places to visit in the Salzkammergut.*

Braunau Am Inn Tourist Office, *Stadtplatz 9. Tel. 7722-2644; fax 7722-4395.*

Ferienregion Muhlviertel, *Blutenstrasse 8, A-4040 Linz. Tel. 732-23-5020; fax 732-712-400.*

Ferienregion Phyrn-Eisenwurzen, *Am Kirchenplatz 7-9, A-4560 Kirchdorf/Krems. Tel. 7582-2450; 7582-4907-20.*

Scharding Tourist Information Office, *Rathaus, A-4780 Scharding. Tel. 7712-4300 or 3154-28; fax 7712-4320.*

Wels Tourist Information, *Stadtplatz 5, A-4601 Wels. Tel. 7242-43-4-95; fax 7242-47-9-04.*

Werbegemeinschaft Donauregion, *Goethestrasse 27, A-4020 Linz. Tel. 732-60-18-08; fax 732-65-01-73.*

WHERE TO STAY

Many of the hotels featured here have fine restaurants where you can dine in style. So you have the option to eat in or venture out. The first hotels listed are in Linz, and remaining hotels are listed by town.

As mentioned below in our *Where to Eat* section, most of the better restaurants are attached to hotels, inns, and guesthouses, and they are reviewed as part of each hotel below. The few restaurants independent of hotels are reviewed separately in *Where to Eat*.

Linz

BEST WESTERN SITZ HOTEL, *Fiedlerstrasse 6, A-4040 Linz. Tel. 732-736-4410. Doubles start at 750 schillings per person, including breakfast. All credit cards accepted.*

This 108-bed hotel is centrally located near the new city hall. A member of the Best Western chain, the staff is courteous and attentive. The hotel is modern and luxurious with a sauna, solarium, and fitness center for guests. Clients can dine in the hotel's **Paladino** restaurant, get a light bite to eat in the **Bistro** or grab a drink in the lobby bar. Parking is available on the premises.

HOTEL DONAUTAL, *Obere Donaulande 105, A-4020 Linz. Tel. 732-795566; fax 732-795-566-7. Doubles start at 390 schillings per person. All credit cards accepted.*

This intimate 15 bed hotel is literally a stone's throw away from the banks of the Danube. Traditionally furnished, the hotel is just a 15 minute walk to Linz's main square. But you'll feel like you've discovered your own little idyll far away from the crowds. The hotel also has a good restaurant serving traditional Austrian cuisine in a romantic setting. A guest garden is available to guests, too.

HOTEL SCHILLERPARK, *Am Schillerplatz, A-4020 Linz. Tel. 732-695-0103; 732-695-09. Doubles start at 980 schillings per person, including breakfast. All credit cards accepted.*

The Hotel Schillerpark is Linz's only five-star hotel and the height of luxury for businessmen and tourists alike. The Schillerpark is also home to the city's casino for those who like to gamble. The 160 bed hotel boasts a gourmet restaurant which also caters to the special needs of dieters. You can even bring Fido along for the trip, and parking is available on the premises.

HOTEL WOLFINGER, *Hauptplatz 19, A-4020 Linz. Tel. 732-773-2910; fax 732-773-291-55. Rates for doubles begin at 450 schillings per person, including breakfast. All credit cards accepted.*

The family-run Hotel Wolfinger is located right on Linz's main square in the heart of the old town. Rooms are comfortable, but if peace and quiet is your objective, you may want to request a room off the square during the summer months. Parking is available for guests. The 90 bed hotel welcomes bikers traveling along the Danube and has facilities for bike storage on-site. Big appetites can fuel up at the generous breakfast buffet served daily.

LANDGRAF SUITES, *Haupstrasse 12, A-4020 Linz. Tel. 732-736-4410; fax 732-730-841. Doubles start at 750 schillings per person, including breakfast. All credit cards accepted.*

The neo-Gothic Landgraf Suites is located in the center of the city at the Nibelungenbridge. Suites range in size from 33 to 61 square meters and are equipped with kitchen facilities. If you prefer to be served, a restaurant is available to guests at the Best Western Spitz Hotel across the street. Parking is available at the hotel, and pets are accepted.

Bad Hall

SCHLOSS FEYREGG, *A-4540 Bad Hall. Tel. 7258-2591. Doubles start at 900 schillings per person. All credit cards accepted.*

The Feyregg Castle was converted by the Baroque architect Johann Michael Prunner and has been lovingly restored to all its former glory. The former summer residence of the Spital am Pyhrn abbey can trace its origins back to the early Middle Ages. Owner Ruth Maria Harmer runs this 11-room hotel. Rooms are beautifully furnished with antiques and rich fabrics. Guests will also enjoy wandering the Rococo gardens.

Branau am Inn

GASTEZIMMER AM THEATERPARK, *21 Linzer Strasse, A-5280 Braunau Am Inn. Tel. 7722-3471; fax 7722-3471-30. Doubles start at 640 schillings. No credit cards accepted.*

This traditional 19-room guest house is located in the city center and has a garden for guests in the courtyard of the hotel. Rooms have full bath, television, radio. The hotel also has a garage for easy customer parking.

HOTEL POST, *10 Stadtplatz, A-5280 Braunau Am Inn. Tel. 7722-3492 or 3415; fax 7722-3415-2. Doubles start at 660 schillings. No credit cards accepted.*

The Hotel Post is located right on the main square and has a sidewalk cafe overlooking the Stadtplatz, where you can sit and watch the world go by. The hotel also features a sauna, solarium, and breakfast buffet for guests.

SALZBURGER HOF, *Salzburger Strasse 55, A-5280 Braunau Am Inn. Tel. 7722-3154; fax 7722-3154-2. Doubles start at 500 schillings. All credits cards accepted.*

Located 10 minutes from the center of town, the Salzburger Hof offers basic rooms with full bath, telephone, and television for a reasonable price. The hotel also has a restaurant and a garden for guests who want to while away the afternoons.

Freistadt

GASTHOF DEIM, *Bohmergasse 8-10, A-4240 Freistadt. Tel. 7942-2258-0; fax 7942-2258-40. Doubles start at 430 schillings per person. All credit cards accepted.*

The Gasthof Deim is full of rustic charm with its stone hewn walls and wildflower decorations. Rooms are cozy and welcoming. Guests can relax in the sauna or sun themselves on the guest patio. The 31 room hotel also has a restaurant serving regional and national favorites. Light alternatives are also featured. A good selection of Austrian wines is on the menu as well.

HOTEL GOLDENER ADLER, *Saltgasse 1, A-4240 Freistadt. Tel. 7942-2112-0; fax 7942-2112-44. Doubles start at 390 schillings per person. All credit cards accepted.*

The bright yellow Hotel Goldener Adler is a welcome respite for weary travelers. The hotel staff is friendly and helpful. Guests can enjoy swimming, an exercise room, sauna, golf and fishing nearby. A down-home restaurant is on the premises featuring hardy Austrian dishes. Low calorie fare is also an option.

Scharding

FORSTINGERS WIRTHAUS, *Unterer Stadtplatz 3, A-4780 Scharding. Tel. 7712-2302 or 3298; fax 7712-23023. Doubles start at 605 schillings per person. All credit cards accepted.*

Willi and Margret Forstinger make sure their guests are well attended to at their 34 bed hotel located right on the city square in Scharding. Rooms are small but cozy. Pets are welcome and rates are discounted for children. The hotel also has a fine restaurant with low-calorie selections for the diet conscious.

HOTEL ZUR STIEGE, *Schlossgasse 2-6, A-4780 Scharding. Tel. 7712-3070; fax 7712-3070-84. Doubles start at 460 schillings per person. All credit cards accepted.*

You can't miss the bright lime green, flower-bedecked facade of the Hotel zur Stiege. The hotel is among Scharding's "Silver Row" of terraced houses. The service is also memorable at this three-star, 46 bed hotel. Rooms are comfortable and clean. The hotel has a cozy restaurant serving both classic Austrian fare and diet dishes for those seeking the cure.

KNEIPP & GESUNDHEITSZENTRUM DER BARHERZIGEN BRUDER, *Kurhausstrasse 6, A-4780 Scharding. Tel. 7712-3221; fax 7712-3221-400. Doubles start at 770 schillings per person. All credit cards accepted.*

This 116 bed hotel is ideal for guests seeking the cure. Surrounded by trees and lush grounds, the hotel offers a variety of health related services included a doctor on the premises. Exercise, swimming, cycling and saunas are all possible. The staff is accommodating but unobtrusive. Rooms are comfortable and tastefully furnished.

KURHOTEL GUGERBAUER, *Kurhausstrasse 4, A-4780 Scharding. Tel. 7712-3191; fax 7712-3191-50. Doubles start at 490 schillings per person. All credit cards accepted.*

Karl and Katharina Gugerbauer run this 50 bed hotel located on the banks of the Inn. The hotel is dedicated to rest and relaxation, and the hotel staff makes sure that all their guests' slightest needs are catered to. Swimming, exercise, a steam room and sauna are available for guests. A doctor is available for consultation for those seeking the cure. Diet menus are also available to diners at the hotel's restaurant.

Steyr

HOTEL MADER, *Stadtplatz 36, A-4400 Steyr. Tel. 7252-53229; 7252-53229-15. Doubles start 490 schillings per person. All credit cards accepted.*

This is a beautiful hotel right in the heart of the old town. The Hotel Mader is filled with interesting architectural elements, like beautiful columns and arches. You can dine in the courtyard when the weather is warm. Rooms are small but charming. Fishing, biking, golfing are all possible in the near vicinity.

ROMANTIK HOTEL, *Haratmullerstrasse 1-3, A-4400 Steyr. Tel. 7252-53410; fax 7252-4820255. Doubles start at 490 schillings per person. All credit cards accepted.*

Overlooking the river, this is a family-style establishment. The 50 room hotel is homey and inviting. Sports enthusiasts will like the fishing, golf, biking, and sauna available in the area. The hotel restaurant features both Austrian favorites and lighter selections. A bar is also in the hotel, and outdoor seating is possible when the weather is nice.

STADTHOTEL STYRIA, *Stadtplatz 40-42, A-4400 Steyr. Tel. 7252-51551-54; fax 7252-51551-51. Doubles start at 520 schillings per person. All credit cards accepted.*

Located in the heart of town, the Stadthotel Styria is run by Frau Ingrid Huemer. The old building is well maintained, although the rooms are somewhat small. The hotel has a certain old-world charm that discerning guests will enjoy. There is no restaurant on the premises, but breakfast is available. Guests can also order drinks at the bar. Visitors can attend to their beauty needs at a salon at the hotel. There is also a sauna to relax in.

Wels

HOTEL HAUSER, *Backergasse 7, A-4600 Wels. Tel. 7242-43495 or 235-708; fax 7242-47904. Doubles start at 525 schillings per person. All credit cards accepted.*

Edmund Hauser runs this 23 room, bright yellow hotel. Rooms are comfortably furnished and light-filled. A variety of sports activities are available including golf, biking, and working out. The hotel restaurant has a variety of regional delicacies, and outdoor seating is available during the summer months. A bar is also on the premises.

HOTEL ROSENBERGER, *Adlerstrasse 1, A-4600 Wels. Tel. 7242-622360; fax 7242-62236-60. Doubles start at 705 schillings per person. All credit cards accepted.*

Run by the Best Western hotel chain, the Hotel Rosenberger has 106 modern rooms. The staff is efficient and attentive. Guests can enjoy exercise, biking facilities, and a sauna. Pets are also welcome. Parking is available at the hotel, too. You can unwind in the hotel bar and afterwards enjoy a meal at the restaurant, where both Austrian specialties and international favorites are featured.

WHERE TO EAT

Upper Austria has given its own regional culinary twists to many national favorites. The *Linzer Schnitzel* adds a spicy, savory herb crust to veal, turkey, or pork fillets. Boiled beef, minced meat dumplings, and roast beef are also popular. The traditional liver soup is varied here by frying the liver first giving it a distinctive, earthy flavor. A sort of ravioli, made from potato rather than flour, is a delicacy to be tried here. They are served with bacon, ham, ground beef, or cabbage and usually topped with a cream sauce or cheese.

And of course, top off your meal with a slice of *Linzer Torte*. The region's most famous sweet has a almond pastry filled with red currant jam and decorated with a lattice crust – simply delicious. If your sweet tooth still is not satisfied, then try ginger bread slices coated with chocolate or *Kraphen*, doughnuts stuffed with cream or apple puree.

Upper Austria also is known for its **beer**. The *Stiftsbrauerei Schlagl* is the only monastery in Austria that contains a brewery. Or you could make a stop at the **Privatbraurerei Hofstetten**, the oldest private brewery in the country, or at the **Schlossbrauerei Weinberg**, a castle brewery near Freistadt.

As in many other parts of Austria, outside the big cities most of the good restaurants are attached to hotels, inns, and guesthouses, which are listed and reviewed above in W*herre to Stay*. Below is a sampling of the better restaurants not attached to hotels:

Linz

DONAUTAL, *Obere Donaulande 105, A-4020 Linz. Tel. 732-77-19-66. Moderate. Open Monday through Thursday and Sundays from 11:30 a.m. to midnight. All credit cards accepted.*

Located about ten minutes from the city center, the Donautal is a traditional Linz guest house on the banks of the Danube. No wonder that fish is featured prominently on the menu. The trout is especially good. If you're looking for a romantic evening for two, this is the place to go for good food, friendly service and a beautiful view of the river.

FISCHRESTAURANT BENETSEDER, *Industriezeile 76, A-4010 Linz. Tel. 732-66-79-96. Moderate. Open Monday through Friday, 9 a.m. to 6 p.m.; Saturdays 8 a.m. to 5 p.m. All credit cards accepted.*

If fish is what you favor than this restaurant is just what the doctor ordered. All different types of seafood are featured on the menu, including fresh selections from the nearby Lake District. The atmosphere is friendly and welcoming, too.

LINZER NUDELOPER, *Haupstrasse 56, A-4020 Linz. Tel. 732-23-95-80. Moderate. Open Monday through Saturday, 5 p.m. to 1 a.m. All credit cards accepted.*

Locals say that the Linzer Nudeloper has the best noodles in town. You can choose from a variety of different provincial dishes with a variety of sauces, from tomato to cream. Toppings include ham, mushrooms, and cheese. Stuffed noodles, either sweet or salty, can also be selected. And if you're not in the mood for pasta, the menu also has a variety of other Austrian specialties from which to choose.

SCHNITZEL GOURMET, *Landstrasse 11, A-4020 Linz. Tel. 732-77-23-77. Inexpensive. Open Monday through Friday 10 a.m. to 8 p.m.; Saturdays 10 a.m. to 2 p.m. No credit cards accepted.*

If you want a quick but satisfying bite to eat while you're sight-seeing in Linz, head to the Schnitzel Gourmet. A plate full of crispy schnitzel will set you back only 35 schillings. Schnitzel sandwiches cost only 29 schillings. Side orders of french fires, potato salad, and green salad are also available.

STEAK'S BAR & RESTAURANT, *Untere Donaulande 12, A-4020 Linz. Tel. 732-77-05-066. Moderate. Open daily 11 a.m. to midnight. All credit cards accepted.*

Feeling homesick for a nice, thick T-Bone? Then Steak's Bar & Restaurant is the place for you. The restaurant also features Tex-Mex specialties as well as other American classics. This is also a good place to take finicky children.

URSULINEHOF, *Landstrasse 31, A-4020 Linz. Tel. 732-77-46-86. Expensive. Open daily 9 a.m. to midnight. All credit cards accepted.*

As the name suggests, this restaurant is housed in what was once an Ursuline convent. The convent was sold to Upper Austria's government 20 years ago and turned into a cultural center. The restaurant's menu changes with the seasons due to the availability of ingredients. Traditional Austrian cuisine is served with flair and a light touch, which you'll find refreshing. The wine list has both regional and international selections.

ZUR LINDE, *Brucknerstrasse 28, A-4020 Linz. Tel. 732-66-98-59. Moderate. Open daily 10 a.m. to midnight. All credit cards accepted.*
This friendly guest house whips regional dishes just like mamma used to make. The restaurant is especially known for its *Schweinsbraten*, or roast pork. Finish off your meal with a piece of their excellent Topfrenstrudel, or strudel filled with sweet cheese – the Austrian version of cheese cake. You can relax over a beer in the guest garden during warm weather.

ZUM SCHWARZEN WALFISH, *Ottensheimerstrasse 102, A-4020 Linz. Tel. 732-23-98-05. Moderate. Open daily 11 a.m. to 11 p.m.; closed Sundays and Mondays. All credit cards accepted.*
Grilled meats are the specialty at this guest house on the banks of the famous Danube. If you're in the mood for something heavier, try one of the varieties of *Knodel*, or noodle dishes, served with ham, cheese and other toppings. Several salads are also featured on the menu, which can be something of a rarity here in Austria and a welcome relief to the vegetarians among you.

Branau Am Inn

AMADEI, *Salzburger Vorsyadt 13, A-5280 Braunau Am Inn. Tel. 7722-5266. Inexpensive. Open daily 9 a.m. to 11:30 p.m. No credit cards accepted.*
This outdoor cafe specializes in huge ice cream concoctions with such flavors as kiwi, amaretto, and marzipan. The milkshakes are especially good.

KAMMERWIRT, *Salzburger Strasse 29, A-5280 Braunau Am Inn. Tel. 7722-3284. Moderate. Open daily 10 a.m. to 2 p.m. and 5 p.m. to midnight. No credit cards accepted.*
This family style restaurant is built in a pseudo-medieval fortress along the old fortification walls bordering the Inn river. The dinner menu changes nightly but usually feature a homey selection of grilled meats, sausages, and traditional noodle dishes.

KNOLLMAYR, *Stadtplatz 5, A-5280 Braunau Am Inn. Tel. 7722-33401. Inexpensive. Open 8 a.m. to 6 p.m. Closed weekends. No credit cards accepted.*
If you want to take a break over coffee and cake, this cozy cafe is just the place for you. Comfortable banquettes, panelling and a personable, if harried, staff make this cafe a real find. They even have a non-smoking section.

SEEING THE SIGHTS IN LINZ

Start your tour of Linz in the **Hauptplatz** or main city square. Designed in the 13th century, the Hauptplatz at 13,000 meters squared was the largest in Austria at that time. If you wander off the square along the narrow, medieval alleys you'll discover some architectural treasures from ancient arches to original Roman fountains.

The **Old Town Hall**, or *Rathaus*, on the square was originally designed by Master Christoph and constructed in 1513. The octagonal corner turret with lunar clock and several vaulted rooms survived a later fire. Today's exterior dates from 1659 and was expanded when it was combined with neighboring buildings. Portraits of Emperor Frederick III, Anton Bruckner, Johannes Kepler and the mayors Hoffmandl and Prunner are painted on the walls.

Taking a detour down **Rathausgasse**, you'll find the house where **Johannes Kepler** lived from 1612 to 1626. Kepler wrote his *Tabulae Rudolphianae* at number 5 Rathausgasse. Going back to the Hauptplatz, you'll see the **Pillar of the Holy Trinity** dating from 1723 in the center of the square. The Baroque column, made of white marble from Salzburg, is 20 meters high and was executed by Sebastian Stumpfegger. The pillar was erected in thanks for the deliverance of the city from the threat of war in 1704, a fire in 1712, and the plague in 1713. The patron saints Sebastian, Florian, and Karl Borromaus are depicted around the pillar. At Hauptplatz 18, music by Austrian composers is played on the carillon bells at 11 a.m., 2 p.m., and 6 p.m.

Heading off the Hauptplatz is the **Klosterstrasse**, where you will find the **Minorite Church**. The double-naved church was originally a Minorite monastery dating from 1236. After the Reformation, the church was given back to the order in 1678. The church was rebuilt in 1751 by Johann Matthias Krinner in the single-naved Rococo style you see today. The ornate stucco work in the church is by Kaspar Modler and the high altar fresco is by Martin Schmidt. The neighboring monastery building now holds government offices. The Renaissance **Landhaus**, with its three inner arcaded courtyards, is now the seat of the Provincial Governor, the regional parliament, and the government. Stone mason Peter Guet created the *Fountain of the Planets* in 1582 picturing – you guessed it – the planets.

Wolfgang Amadeus Mozart stayed in the three-story Renaissance building farther down the street. It was here in the 16th century building that Mozart composed his Linz Symphony after being invited to the city in 1783 by the Count of Thun. If you make a right into the Altstadt heading into the old quarter, you'll run into the **Waaghaus**. The building was originally owned by the Scherffenberger family and bought by the city in 1524. Today the site has been converted into a large indoor market.

Down the street you'll see the **Kremsmunstererhaus**, where according to local lore Emperor Frederick III died in 1493. The building was taken over by the Kremsmunster monastery in 1507 and the building was remodelled in the Renaissance style in 1580 by Christoph Canevale. Max

Martin Spaz later added two turreted onion domes and an extra story to the site in 1616.

Make a left along the narrow **Hofberg street** which will take you up to the **Schlossmuseum**, *Tummelplatz 10, Tel. 77-44-19*, with a magnificent view of the city below. The first mention of the castle appeared in 799. It was completely rebuilt in 1477 by Emperor Frederick III. All that remains of the original structure are the castle walls and the west gate, with the imperial coat of arms still intact. Dutch architect Anton Muys in 1600 again remodelled the castle according to the wishes of Emperor Rudolph II. The castle was later used as a hospital during the wars with France and then served as a prison and a military barracks.

Today, the castle houses a **regional museum** with an excellent collection of medieval artworks as well as musical instruments, ancient arms, and folk crafts including the oldest marionette in central Europe. During the weeks before Christmas, the castle museum also has an extravagant display of creches open to visitors. Each creche has dozens of figures in native costume on display and is a real treat for children young and old.

Leaving the castle through the Westgate will take you to **St. Martin's Church**. Archaeologists have found the original Roman foundations. If you look carefully, you'll also notice many stones with Roman inscriptions and a Roman oven. The church also is the site of a former Carolinian imperial residential hall. The walls of the church still show the doorways and windows of the church from Gothic times. Follow the **Romerstrasse** along the castle walls to the **Herrenstrasse**, which will lead you to the **Bischofshof** and the **new cathedral**.

The bishop's seat was originally built in 1721 by Franz Michael Pruckmayr for the Kremsmunster monastery. The iron gateway at the entrance of the Bischofshof was created by Valentin Hoffman in 1227. The nearby Neo-Gothic cathedral was commissioned by Linz Bishop Franz Joseph Rudigier in 1855. The plans of the cathedral were designed by Vinzenz Statz, one of the Cologne cathedral architects. The cathedral's spire rises up 134 meters. A special ruling required that the spire not be higher than St. Stephen's in Vienna. The **Linz Window** details the history of the town.

On your way back to **Landstrasse**, the town's main shopping street, you'll pass several churches. The **Carmelite Church**, constructed in 1674 by J.M. Prunner among others, was modelled after St. Joseph's in Prague. The **Ursuline Church** was built by locals Johann Haslinger and J.M Krinner. The church eventually was converted into a cultural center after it vacated by the Ursuline nuns in 1968. The nearby **Seminary Church** was built between 1718 and 1725 by J.M Prunner.

Continue down the **Harrachstrasse** to the **Stadtmuseum Nordico**, *Bethlehemstrasse 7, Tel. 7070-3600*. The museum, which was a training center used by the Jesuits, today holds a collection of archaeological artifacts from the Carolinian times to the Biedermeier period chronicling Linz's history. Down the street is the Baroque **old cathedral**, where the composer Anton Bruckner once played the organ. Pietro Francesco Caroline designed the cathedral built between 1669 and 1678. **Anton Bruckner** served as the organist of the cathedral from 1856 to 1868. The nearby **Parish Church** was originally built in 1286 as a three-naved Romanesque Church but was converted to its current Baroque style in 1648. The right wall of the cancel contains the heart of Emperor Frederick III.

Across the river is the **New Gallery of the City of Linz**, *Blutenstrasse 15, Tel. 7070-3600*. The museum has one of the most important modern art collections in the country. In 1995, the museum had a large exhibition featuring the works of French artist Henri Matisse. If you have the time, take a detour to see the city's **Botanical Gardens**. Bus 27, which will drop you off right in front, leaves every 15 minutes from the Taubenmarkt. More than 8,000 plant species, including water lilies, cacti, and coffee trees are available for viewing year round.

NIGHTLIFE & ENTERTAINMENT

Linz is home to several festivals including, the **International Bruckner Festival** and the **Ars Electronica** avant-garde festival. Many church concerts also feature the music of Anton Bruckner who lived in Linz and St. Florian. Linz is also host to the **Festival of Minor Arts** in November and the **Dance Days** in March.

If you're traveling with children, a fun way to spend a few hours is on the **Postlingberg**, the steepest adhesion railway in the world. The railway was built in 1898 based on the designs of Franz Zola, father of French novelist Emile Zola. The Linz grotto train runs from Palm Sunday to November 1.

If you prefer the **pub** scene, several hotspots are available in the "Bermuda Triangle" in Linz's old town. There is also a **casino** in Linz at *Am Schillerpark, Rainerstrasse 2-4*. The casino is open from 3 p.m. to midnight. Players can try their hand at roulette, red dog, black jack, poker and baccarat.

SHOPPING

If you've come to Linz to shop, start off your expedition on **Landstrasse**, a pedestrian-only zone lined with shops for every taste. Many of the streets running perpendicular to Landstrasse have boutiques to browse. The streets around the **main square** and the **Urfahr** also have many shops. The local tourist office brags that Linz is especially known for its **women's shoes**.

Traditionalists may prefer the **annual market weeks**. Almost 200 years ago, the first market was held in the Urfahr parish on the Danube. Today the tradition continues during the first week of May and October with market stalls, entertainment, and food and drink attracting more than half a million visitors to Linz. During Thursday and Saturday evenings, fireworks are set off. If you're not in the area during this time, every Saturday from 7 a.m. to 2 p.m. a **flea market** is held in the main square. During the advent season before Christmas, Linz has a **Christmas market** with pastries, toys, and crafts from around Upper Austria. The market in the **Hauptplatz** and in the **Volksgarten** starts in mid-November. A living nativity scene is also on display.

Stores are generally open from 9 a.m. to 6 p.m. Monday through Friday and Saturdays from 9 a.m. to noon. Some establishments close for lunch, so be prepared for that eventuality. Stores usually remain open the first Saturday of the month until 5 p.m.

SPORTS & RECREATION
Biking & Hiking
The **Danube** flows through Upper Austria and affords a wonderful opportunity for biking and hiking along the river. Boat cruises are also possible. For more information, *call 71-00-08 or 663-77-077.*

Skiing, Sailing, & Swimming
Skiing is possible in the **Salzkammergut** section of the province. See Chapter 15, *The Lake District* for details on resort information. Sailing, swimming, and other fun in the sun is also available in the province's part of the Salzkammergut. Again, see Chapter 15 for details.

DAY TRIPS & EXCURSIONS FROM LINZ
Agrarium
Located in the middle of the Upper Austrian foothills, **Almegg** is home to the **Agrarium plant park**, with more than 70 different gardens on display. Gardens are organized by theme such as medicinal plants, a witch garden, and plants from the Bible. Austrian agricultural techniques are also on display. Children can participate in craft courses offered at the park.

Produce from the area may be purchased from local farmers at the **9-Schmankerl market**. Have a picnic with the freshly baked bread, cheese, bacon and cider bought here.

Agrarium, *Schloss Almegg 11, A-4654 Bad Wimsbach. Tel. 7245-25810; fax 7245-25810-22.* Guided tours are available in English, German, French and Italian. The park is open daily from May 1 to October 26, 9 a.m. to 6 p.m. Admission is 140 schillings for adults; 70 schillings for students; children under 6 free. Picnic basket rentals cost 50 schillings.

Braunau am Inn

Braunau on the River Inn has the rather dubious distinction of being the birthplace of Adolf Hitler, although you won't find this in any of the tourist office information. Several gable-roofed houses in the old part of the town date from the 14th and 15th century. **St. Stephen's cathedral**, built between 1439 and 1436, was originally constructed as a place of worship for artisans and guilds, and the chapels that line the sides of the cathedral are dedicated to individual trades. Be sure to take a look at the Renaissance epitaph to the alderman and member of the fire brigade, Hans Staininger, who was know as the man with the long beard. But the beard ended up costing him his life when he tripped over it while fighting a fire.

Walk back into the center of town to see the city gate topped by a tower with a high tent roof dating back to the founding of the town in 1260. The street running through the city gate will lead you to **Hitler's birthplace** on the Stadtplatz. The yellow house is not open to the public. Before the house, a simple stone marker, taken from the Mauthausen concentration camp in Austria, serves as a memorial to those who died in the Holocaust stating simply, *For peace, freedom, and democracy to remind us of the millions who died at the hands of fascism.*

Walking back through the city gate, you can head down to the river, which marks the frontier between Germany and Austria. Parts of the fortification walls that protected the city during the Gothic period are still in existence along the river banks.

Braunau am Inn can be reached by train from Salzburg and Linz. By car, take route 147 north of Salzburg. **Braunau am Inn Tourist Office**, *A-5280 Braunau am Inn. Tel. 7722-2644; fax 7722-4395.*

Freistadt

The medieval town of **Freistadt** is the ideal place to begin your visit of the **Muhlviertel** with its ancient fortifications, towers, and narrow lanes. A horse-drawn railroad used to take riders from the Salzkammmergut to Budweis in southern Germany. The ancient station near Rainbach will explain to modern visitors how traveling once was.

Friestadt is 60 kilometers from Linz, and 20 kilometers off the A8. **Freistadt Tourist Information**, *A-4240 Freistadt. Tel. 7942-2974; fax 7942-3207.*

Mauthausen

During World War II, 200,000 people were killed at the **Mauthausen concentration camp**. Today, a museum documents the suffering of the people who lived and died here. Some of the original barracks still stand. Memorials to the people who were worked to death in the camp are displayed outside the camp. The "Staircase of Death" leads to the quarry where Jews, Russians, Poles and other prisoners were literally worked to death. When they were too exhausted to continue, they were killed by the SS officers, who pushed them to their deaths. The memorial is open from February until mid-December from 8 a.m. to 6 p.m. Admission for adults is 15 schillings; 5 schillings for students.

By car, take the Autobahn A1 until you reach the Enns exit. Mauthausen is 16 miles east of Linz. You can also reach Mauthausen by taking a train to St. Valentin and then transferring from there. The station is 6 kilometers from the camp. The Bundesbus will take you to within 2 kilometers of the camp.

Mauthausen Tourist Information, *A-4310 Mauthausen. Tel. 7238-2269, 2243 or 3860.*

Oberndorf

Oberndorf is where *Silent Night, Holy Night* was composed. The song was first performed on Christmas eve in 1818. Although the original St. Nicolas church was torn down in 1906, a small memorial chapel was built here on **Stille Nacht Platz**. Its stained glass windows honor school teacher Franz Gruber, who wrote the music, and Father Joseph Mohr, who wrote the text to the beloved Christmas carol. A painted, wooden garland illuminated with candles crowns a lovely nativity scene. Walking down the hill behind the chapel brings you to a peach-colored house where Mohr wrote the lyrics to the carol.

The new **St. Nicolas church** was constructed across the river at the other side of the hill on which the memorial is located. Visit the **Heimatmuseum** if you want to learn more about the history of *Silent Night, Holy Night*. The chapel is open daily from 8 a.m. to 5 p.m. The museum is located at *7 Stille Nacht Platz. Tel. 6272-7569.* Admission is 35 schillings for adults and 20 schillings for children. Open Tuesday through Sunday, 9 a.m. to noon and 1 p.m. to 5 p.m.

Oberndorf is about 13 miles north of Salzburg and can be reached by car by taking the autobahn north. Exit signs are marked for the town. Trains also are available from Salzburg to the local station. **Oberndorf Tourist Information**, *Stille Nacht Platz, A-5110 Oberndorf. Tel. and fax 6272-7569.*

St. Florian

One of Austria's most famous landmarks, the Augustine monastery **St. Florian**, is just outside of Linz. The huge baroque edifice is the work of architects Carlo Carlone, Jakob Prandtauer, and Gotthard Hayberger. The monastery is dedicated to the saint martyred in 304 A.D. Composer **Anton Bruckner**, who worked here for several years of his life, is buried in the crypt of the church. Concerts are still held in the monastery and the boy's choir is as renowned in Austria as the **Vienna's Boy's Choir**. You'll also find the only secular building, the **Hohenbrunn castle**, constructed by master builder Jakob Prandtauer. For more information, *call 7224-56-90; fax 7224-5690.*

St. Florian is just 20 kilometers from Linz, and two kilometers off the A1 autobahn. A train station is two kilometers away in Asten. **St. Florian Tourist Information**, *A-4490 St. Florian bei Linz. Tel. 7224-4255; fax 7224-5278.*

Scharding

Scharding is known for its "Silver Row," brightly painted, gothic terraced houses on the main town square. The gabled houses were once owned by the town's wealthy merchant class, hence the name: the merchant class was the one with the "silver in their pockets." The merchants made their money trading Austrian salt, wood, limestone, marble and Venetian wine.

The local **museum** is open Tuesdays and Wednesdays from 3 p.m. to 5 p.m. and Thursdays, Fridays and Saturdays from 10 a.m. to noon. Admission is 10 schillings. Guided tours of the Baroque town are available in English for 500 schillings. Contact the **tourist office** at *Tel. 7712-4300; fax 7712-4320.* River cruises on the Inn are also possible. Roundtrip tickets cost 95 schillings for adults and 45 schillings for children. For more information, *call 7712-3231.*

To get to Scharding, take the A-8 autobahn heading west from Linz. Express trains also run between the town and Vienna.

On a visit to Scharding, make a detour to the 700-year-old Trappist Monastery of **Engelszell** where you can taste the liqueur made by the monks. During the summer, guided tours of the monastery built on the banks of the Danube are available Wednesdays at 2:15 p.m.Seventeen kilometers south of Scharding is the Augustiner Chorherren Baroque monastery. From Easter to November 1, free guided tours of the monastery are led daily at 3 p.m.

Scharding Tourist Information, *A-4780 Scharding. Tel. 7712-4300; fax 7712-4320.*

Steyr

Located where the Enns and Steyr rivers converge, **Steyr** is a charming town well worth a detour. The old section is filled with Gothic, Renaissance, and Baroque buildings. If you're going to be in Upper Austria during the winter holiday season, you should definitely make plans to stop in Steyr. The self-proclaimed town of *Christkindl*, which literally means the "Christ child," is known for its Christmas festivities. A special post office has been set up in the town to handle the letters sent by children from around the world to the Christ child.

Legend has it that the wax Christ figure at the pilgrimage church supposedly glows during the Advent season. The **Pottmesser creche**, displayed in the Kripperl-Roas from late November through January 6, is one of the largest in the world.

Steyr is 50 kilometers outside of Linz, and 18 kilometers off the A1 autobahn taking the Enns exit. The town also has a train station. **Steyr Tourist Information**, *A-4400 Steyr. Tel. 7252-53229; fax 7252-53229-15.*

Wels

Austria's "last knight" Maximilian I died in **Wels** in 1519. Visitors can savor the city's medieval history with a visit to the **Burgmuseum**. Cyclists will enjoy the city's flat countryside. Wels also has a large outdoor swimming facility with sauna and solarium and a sports and fitness center.

Wels is 15 kilometers outside of Linz, and 4 kilometers off the A8 autobahn. The town also has a local train station. **Wels Tourist Information Office**, *A-4600 Wels. Tel. 7242-43495; fax 7242-47904.*

PRACTICAL INFORMATION

American Express
• **American Express Travel Service**, *Buergerstrasse 4, PO Box 264, A-4021 Linz. Tel. 732-669013.*

Credit Cards
The following numbers can be called 24 hours a day if you lose your card. The numbers are located in Vienna, so first dial area code *0222.*
• **American Express**, *Tel. 51-29-714*
• **Diners**, *Tel. 50-1-35*
• **Mastercard**, *Tel. 71-7-01-0*
• **Visa**, *Tel. 53-4-87-77*

Exchanging Money
Banks in Linz are open in general Monday, Tuesday, and Wednesday from 8 a.m. to 4:30 p.m.; Thursdays 8 a.m. to 5:30 p.m.; Fridays 8 a.m. to

2 p.m. Many close as well for lunch. You can change money at the **Post Office**, *Domgasse 1, A-4010 Linz*. Opening hours are Monday through Friday from 7:30 a.m. to 6:30 p.m. and Saturday from 8 a.m. to noon.

Money can also be changed at **Sparda Bank Linz** *at the train station*. The bank is open Monday through Friday from 8 a.m. to 6 p.m. Change machines are located at the Sparda Bank, the Oberbank, Zweigstelle Landstrasse 37, and Raiffeisenkasse, Zweigstelle Landstrasse 26.

Emergency Phone Numbers
• **Ambulance**, *Tel. 144*
• **Police**, *Tel. 133*
• **Fire Department**, *Tel. 122*

Guided Tours

Guided **walking tours** are available from April to October. For more information and tickets, contact the **Tourist Information Office**, *Hauptplatz, A-4010 Linz. Tel. 732-2393-1777*. There also are several guided tours of Linz available through the following operators: Anita Froschl, *Tel. and fax 60-42-02*; Gundi Grabner, *Tel. and fax 732-65-77-57 or 664-34-09-047*; Josef Kreilmeier, *Tel. and fax 79-09-82 or 664-10-03-136*; Ernst Wiesinger, *Tel. and fax 60-23-60*.

Parking

Linz has several large free parking lots, including: **Urfahrmarkt-Gelande**, **Stadion Parkplatz**, and **Brucknerhausparkplatz**.

Pharmacies

Several pharmacies are open 24 hours a day in case of emergencies. The address of the nearest open pharmacy will be posted in the window of each closed shop. For pharmacy assistance, *call 1550*.

Post Offices

Most post offices are open Monday through Friday from 8 a.m. to noon and 2 p.m. to 6 p.m.; Saturdays from 8 a.m. to 10 a.m.

Tipping

A service charge is added to your hotel and restaurant bill. However, if you are pleased with the service, it is customary to tip an additional 5 to 10 percent of the check. Taxi drivers and hair dressers also are generally tipped the same amount.

Weather

For the latest weather information, *call 15-66*.

15. THE LAKE DISTRICT

INTRODUCTION

The **Lake District**, or **Salzkammergut**, is the country's number one honeymoon destination. The Lake District is made up of parts of Styria, Upper Austria, and Salzburg and is easily accessible from all three areas.

Tourists flock here in the summer to take advantage of the abundance of regional lakes, about 40 in all, including the **Wolfgangsee**, the **Attersee**, the **Mondsee**, the **Altaussee** and the **Traunsee**, which the Romans called "the happy lake." If you can, make sure to visit **Hallstatt**, which has proven to be an important archaeological site. It is also one of the most picturesque towns in the whole of Austria and is well worth the detour.

The region gets its name from its most famous product, salt, which was once dubbed white gold, because it was so precious and valuable. There are several salt mines which can be toured by the public. In fact, the oldest salt mine in the world still in active operation is in Hallstatt. This is a fun thing to do with children, with their underground lake boat rides, miners' slides, and underground railways.

The curative power of salt and thermal waters are promoted in many cities around the region. If you want to restore your spirits after some hectic sight-seeing, head to the nearest spa.

ORIENTATION

Summer is obviously high season for the lake district when honeymooners, Austrian families, and tourists alike descend in droves. The crystal clear waters are surrounded by splendid mountain scenery.

If you can avoid it, it's best not to hit the lakes during a weekend when they are swarmed with people. Plan a trip during the week. You'll have fewer people to deal with. The area is also lovely and quieter during the rest of the year, although the water will probably be too cool for swimming.

SALZKAMMERGUT TOURIST INFORMATION

If you're planning a trip to the lake district be sure to contact the local tourist office. They have maps, hotel information and recreation activities to make your visit a memorable one. Here is a list of local tourist offices to get you started.

    Ferienregion Almtal, A-4644 Scharnstein. Tel. 7615-2340; fax 7615-25530.

    Ferienregion Attergau, A-4880 St. Georgen. Tel. 7667-386; fax 7667-8448.

    Ferienregion Attersee, A-4861 Schorfling. Tel. 7662-8547; fax 7662-3860.

    Ferienregion Dachstein-Hallstattersee, A-4822 Bad Goisern. Tel. 6135-8329 or 7201; fax 6135-8329-74.

    Ferienregion Mondseeland Und Irrsee, A-5310 Mondsee. Tel. 6232-2270; fax 6232-4470.

    Tourismusverband Steirisches Salzkammergut, A-8990 Bad Aussee. Tel. 3622-54873; fax 3622-54890.

    Ferienregion Wolfgansee, A-5360 St. Wolfgang. Tel. 6138-2239; fax 6138-2239-81.

ARRIVALS & DEPARTURES

By Air

    The nearest airport to the Lake District is in **Salzburg**, about 53 kilometers away. The **Linz Airport**, which is approximately 75 kilometers away, is another option. From there, there are train and bus connections to the various resort towns. If you plan to see several of the towns along the way, renting a car is advisable.

By Bus

    There is **Bundesbus**, or mail bus, service from Salzburg to many Lake District locations including Bad Ischl, Fuschl, and St. Wolfgang. The bus schedules are posted outside the main train station. The buses leave from here as well. Tickets cost about 50 schillings one way. Be careful though. The buses do not run that frequently, so be sure to check the schedule and plan accordingly.

By Car

    Getting to the Lake District from Salzburg is very easy. Just take Route 158 east out of the city. The way is well marked and you should see signs with *See*, or lake, so you'll know you're heading in the right direction. Route 158 leads to Fuschl, St. Gilgen and Bad Ischl.

If you're coming from Graz, you can take the Autobahn A-9 until you hit Route 145 going west, which will lead you to Bad Aussee.

From Vienna or Linz, get on the A1 heading east until you reach the juncture with Route 145, which will take you directly into the region.

By Train

You can reach many of the resorts here, like Hallstatt, Bad Aussee, and Durchstein, by rail. Trains leave frequently from the Salzburg and Linz train stations.

If you're traveling by train to Hallstatt, be forewarned that you'll have to take a **ferry** across the lake to get to the city. The ferries are timed to correspond with the train's arrival, so you shouldn't have long to wait going there. Tickets cost 20 schillings. Make sure you get a ferry schedule before leaving the boat so you don't get marooned without a way to get back to the train depot.

This is actually a lovely way to approach Hallstatt, since the trip across the lake provides a picture postcard view of the city.

GETTING AROUND THE LAKE DISTRICT

Most of the lake district resorts have public parking lots. This is probably your best option, since parking is often difficult to find or restricted. The sights are in easy walking distance from the parking lots.

If you have car troubles, you can call the **Automobile, Motorcycle, and Touring Association** for help around the clock at *120*, or the **Automobile, Motorcycle, and Bicycle Association** of Austria at *123*.

WHERE TO STAY

Many of the hotels in the Lake District are located right on the waterfront, so when reserving your room make sure to ask for a room with a view. Most of the hotels have their own restaurants, many of superior quality. If you're not here just to see the sights or splash around in one of the myriad lakes, you can take the cure and have your body prodded and plumped into shape.

Bad means bath in German, so any town with Bad in its name will have spa facilities in the area.

Altaussee

HOTEL KOHLBACHERHOF, *Puchen 87, A-8992 Altaussee. Tel. 3622-71-6-45 or 71-6-51; fax 3622-71-6-51-17. Doubles start at 510 schillings per person, including breakfast. All credit cards accepted.*

Manfred and Martina Kohlbacher run this classically rustic hotel. Rooms are furnished in traditional country style and most have balconies.

Guests can use the hotel's beach on the lake. A sauna, fishing, and biking are also available. Children and pets are welcome.

HOTEL SEEVILLA, *Fischerndorf 60, A-8992 Altausee. Tel. 3622-71-3-02; 3622-71-3-02-82. Doubles start at 1000 schillings per person, including breakfast. American Express and Diners accepted.*

The Hotel Seevilla is like a breath of fresh air amid the trees. Klau Gulewicz operates the 45 room country-style hotel located directly on the lake. Be sure to ask for a room with a balcony overlooking the water. The hotel also has a sauna, solarium, swimming pool, fitness room, private beach and biking services for guests. Pets are welcome as well.

LANDHAUS HUBERTUSHOF, *Puchen 86, A-8992 Altaussee. Tel. 3622-712-80; fax 3622-712-80-80. Doubles start at 500 schillings per person. All credit cards accepted.*

High above Lake Altaussee, this hotel once served as a hunting lodge for Prince Moritz von Schillinsfurst. The landhaus is decorated with hunting trophies, Biedermeier secretaries, and hand-etched chandeliers. Rooms are comfortably appointed with country classic furnishings. Owner Countess Rose Marie Stasoldo Graffemberg also extends a warm welcome to guests at the hotel.

Bad Aussee

GASTHAUS LEHMGRUBE, *Paulngasse 85, A-8990 Bad Aussee. Tel. 3622-52190. Doubles start at 400 schillings, including breakfast. No credit cards.*

This is a real down-home guest house. You may find yourself invited into the kitchen where Frau Rastl prepares the evening *Schnitzel*. But despite its small size, this joint is jumping, probably because of the reasonable prices, good home cooking and inviting atmosphere. Rooms are comfortable and clean, but don't expect elegance. This is a good, basic guest house where they treat you like a long lost member of the family.

HOTEL ERZHERZOG JOHANN, *Jurhausplatz 62, A-8990 Bad Aussee. Tel. 3622-52-5-07; fax 3622-52-5-07-680. Doubles start at 720 schillings per person, including breakfast. Mastercard accepted.*

You won't be able to miss the eye-popping yellow of the Hotel Erzherzog in the center of Bad Aussee. The 62 room hotel is run by Regina Stocker and boasts an excellent restaurant with innovative cooking rather than the same old rehash of Austrian specialties. For those who come to Bad Aussee for the curative waters, the hotel offers guests access to a spa, sauna, solarium, fitness room and swimming pool.

KALSSWIRT BAD AUSSEE GASTHAUS-RESTAURANT, *Unterkainisch 58, Bad Aussee. Tel. 8990-03622-55215. Restaurant open daily noon to 2 p.m. and 6 p.m. to 9 p.m., closed Thursday. The guest house is closed during Easter week. No credit cards accepted.*

The Kalsswirt Bad Aussee is a bright green guest house and restaurant, decorated with baskets of red and pink geraniums. Run by the Gassner family, this is a down-home style guest house with stick-to-your-ribs cooking. If you're there when the weather is nice enjoy a stein of beer outside in the guest garden. The cheery guest house is filled nightly with locals eating and drinking. The staff is not unfriendly but a bit harried. Rooms are simple but comfortable. Don't expect glamour, but if you're looking for simple accommodations for a good value, this is the place for you.

Bad Ischl

HOTEL GOLDENES SCHIFF, *Stifterkai 3, A-4820 Bad Ischl. Tel. 6132-24241; fax 6132-242-4158. Doubles start at 420 schillings. All credit cards accepted.*

The Hotel Goldenes Schiff is located in the heart of downtown Bad Ischl overlooking the Traun River. The Gruber family runs this comfortable hotel furnished with a nice blend of modern and classic touches. The hotel also has a garage for guests. The restaurant features a large breakfast buffet and Austrian specialties for lunch or dinner.

HOTEL SCHENNER, *Schulgasse 9, A-4820 Bad Ischl. Tel. 6132-24600; fax 6132-24600-6. Doubles start at 463 schillings per person. Visa, Diners and American Express accepted.*

This 30 room hotel has a fitness room, solarium and rooftop pool to pamper their guests. Rooms are basically furnished and although comfortable, they lack a certain charm. But the staff is helpful and gracious. The hotel also has an outdoor restaurant with grilled meats a specialty.

KURHOTEL, *Voglhuberstrasse 10, A-4820 Bad Ischl. Tel. 6132-204; fax 6132-27682. Doubles start at 780 schillings per person, including breakfast. Visa, Diners and American Express accepted.*

The Kurhotel is a modern 112 room hotel with a staff that goes out of their way to serve their guests. The hotel's restaurant serves both regional and international specialties and even features a light menu.

If you're a golfer, this is the hotel for you. The Kurhotel sponsors several golf programs for guests and has spa facilities, too. A pool, sauna, solarium, and massages are also available to guests. The hotel also has a private beach for guests on St. Wolfgang.

SONNHOF, *Bahnhofstrasse 4, A-4820-Bad Ischl. Tel. 6132-23078 or 25298; fax 6132-230785. Doubles start at 450 schillings per person, including breakfast. All credit cards accepted.*

This bed and breakfast is located right across from the train station, but you'd never know it while staying there. The pension is located on a wooded hill, which gives every impression of being in the heart of the forest although you're only a stone's throw from town. The staff is friendly although they speak no English. Rooms are light-filled and cozy, furnished with lots of light furniture and country prints. Several of the rooms also have balconies to enjoy the view of the garden.

Fuschl Am See

HOTEL MOHRENWIRT, *A-5330 Fuschl Am See 10. Tel. 6226-228; fax 6226-628-88. Doubles start at 525 schillings per person, including breakfast. All credit cards accepted.*

The elegant Hotel Mohrenwirt is run by the Schmidlechner family and is on the city's "main street" within easy walking distance to the lake. Guests can use the hotel's whirlpool, sauna, and fitness room. The hotel also has a private beach on the lake at their guests' disposal. Rooms are furnished in dark woods and floral prints. The rooms are comfortable but lack warmth.

The restaurant, though, is a real find with inventive dishes that go far beyond the standard Austrian fare. Dishes include a delicious pairing of tartare of smoked fish with mushroom risotto and medallions of veal with nut cream sauce and leek noodles.

HOTEL SCHUTZENHOF, *A-5330 Fuschl Am See. Tel. 6226-208-0 or 565; fax 6226-565-44. Doubles start at 420 schillings per person. No credit cards but traveler's checks accepted.*

The Vogl family runs this cozy hotel on the banks of the Fuschl Lake. Rooms are comfortably furnished with light colored wood pieces and rich fabrics. The hotel also has a good restaurant with seating on the patio overlooking the water. The menu features a good selection of fish dishes like smoked trout fillet with horse radish cream and trout with saffron sauce.

Gmunden

PARKHOTEL AM SEE, *Schiffslande 17, A-4810 Gmunden. Tel. 7612-4230; fax 7612-4230-66. Doubles start at 570 schillings per person. All credit cards accepted.*

Located right on the lake, the Parkhotel am See has a spectacular view and is a prime summer vacation spot. The 48 room hotel is comfortably furnished and well-appointed. Guests can enjoy the hotel's beach facilities, play tennis, or bike. The hotel has a fine restaurant featuring Austrian and international favorites. Guests can also unwind in the hotel's bar.

SEEHOTEL SCHWAN, *Rathausplatz 8, A-4810 Gmunden. Tel. 7612-3391; fax 7612-3391-13. Doubles start at 600 schillings per person. All credit cards accepted.*

The 40 room Seehotel Schwan is run by the Best Western hotel chain. The hotel is located right in the heart of downtown Gmunden on the City Hall Square. Parking is available for guests so you won't have any hassle finding a space. Rooms are comfortable but lacking a bit in the charm department. The restaurant has both Austrian specialties and low calorie alternatives.

Hallstatt

BRAUGASTHOF, *A-4830 Hallstatt. Tel. 6134-8221; fax 6134-8224. Doubles start at 540 schillings per person. All credit cards accepted.*

This a charming guest house decorated with lots of rustic furniture and quaint touches. The staff goes out of their way to be helpful and welcomes you like a member of the family. The restaurants serves the typical Austrian favorites in a cozy dining room. There is also outdoor seating overlooking the water during warm weather.

GASTHOF BERGFRIED, *A-4830 Hallstatt. Tel. 6134-248-502; fax 6134-248-33. Doubles start at 350 schillings per person. All credit cards accepted.*

The Scharf family runs the Gasthof Bergfried, just off the main highway entering Hallstatt. The guest house is cozy and its down-home atmosphere is very welcoming. A sauna, steam room, solarium, and fitness facilities allow guests to unwind. The guest house's restaurant features the usual stick-to-your-ribs Austrian classics in ample portions. The bar in the guest house is small and intimate and a nice place to have a drink before or after dinner.

GASTHOF ZAUNER, *Marktplatz, A-4830 Hallstatt. 6134-8246; 6134-8246-8. Doubles start at 530 schillings per person, including breakfast. Mastercard, Diners and Visa accepted.*

This is a delightful guest house on the main square of one Austria's most picturesque towns. Rooms are decorated with beautiful light-wood furniture that is both comfortable and charming at the same time. Views from the hotel's balconies are breathtaking, looking over the Hallstatt's rooftops at the lake below. The vine-covered dining room is panelled in rich woods making the traditional Austrian fare and even better dining experience. The staff is welcoming and friendly, ensuring a pleasant stay.

GRUNER BAUM SEEHOTEL, *Marktplatz 104, A-4830 Hallstatt. Tel. 6134-263; fax 6134-420. Doubles start at 1,000 schillings, including breakfast. Visa, Mastercard and Diners accepted.*

The Gruner Baum is located right on the water. The staff welcomes you like a long lost friend. Rooms are cozy and inviting, decorated with cheery floral fabrics and light wood furniture. The restaurant dining room has a spectacular view of the nearby lake. The kitchen serves Austrian specialties and is so good that it is frequented by a large local clientele. Baby cribs can be rented for an additional 90 schillings and your dog can also stay in your room for 50 to 80 schillings more depending on height. For stays of seven days or more, the hotel offers a 10 percent discount.

HOTEL BAYRISCHER HOF, *Schropferplatz 1, Hallstatt. 6132-6350. Doubles start at 760 schillings. Visa, Diners and American Express cards accepted.*

The Hotel Bayrischer Hof is in the heart of town and is managed by the Lindmayr family. The rooms are basic and simply furnished. The decor lacks character and the rooms are rather cold, but a good value for the money. The cafe-restaurant features the standard Austrian dishes. Like the hotel, the dishes are basic. There are no real surprises here, but nothing falls completely flat either.

Mattsee

IGLHAUSER SCHLOSSBRAU, *Schlossbergweg 4, A-5163 Mattsee. Tel. 6217-205; fax 6217-20-5-33. Doubles start at 600 schillings per person. All credit cards accepted.*

This castle brewery first appeared in archives dating from the year 1200. The castle became a "court tavern" in 1398 and has been under the management of the Iglhauser family since 1780. The hotel was a favorite for traveling nobility, and guests today will also receive the royal treatment. The Schlossbrau also has a gourmet restaurant with an excellent selection of regional wines to choose from.

SCHLOSSBRAU MATTSEE, *A-5163 Mattsee. Tel. 6217-205; fax 6217-205-33. Doubles start at 900 schillings per person. Visa cards accepted.*

This impressive castle was built right on the water, and has been transformed into a sophisticated hotel by the Iglhauser family. The hotel combines old world charm with modern elegance. The staff is friendly and goes out of their way to help their guests. The restaurant at the hotel specializes in traditional Austrian cuisine with fresh ingredients from the region featured.

St. Gilgen

HOTEL GASTHOF ZUR POST, *Mozartplatz 8, A-5340 St. Gilgen. Tel. 6267-7509 or 7510; fax 6227-698. Doubles start at 350 schillings per person, including breakfast. Mastercard and American Express accepted.*

The Hotel Gasthof Zur Post is conveniently located across from the tourist office on the town square. You won't be able to miss it because of the distinctive hunting mural painted on the outside. The service is friendly and the rooms are comfortable and charming.The restaurant features traditional Austrian favorites including the ubiquitous *Schnitzel* and goulash. The specialty of the house is the *Post Knodel*.

HOTEL RADETZKY, *A-5340 St. Gilgen. 6227-232 or 7356. Doubles start at 1,000 schillings, including breakfast. No credit cards but traveler's checks accepted.*

This charming hotel run by the Schweinitzer family has a long history serving as an inn since 1590. Located on St. Gilgen's town square, the hotel has a patio where guests can sit and watch the crowds walk by. Rooms are a bit austere, but clean and comfortable. The restaurant specializes in traditional Austrian cuisine. The cooking is a bit predictable, but there are no real disasters on the menu.

HOTEL TRAUBE, *A-5340 St. Gilgen. 6227-254. Doubles start at 370 schillings per person. Open May through September. No credit cards accepted.*

The Hotel Traube is run by the Ramsauer family and is a good, basic guest house. Rooms are furnished with sturdy, heavy furniture, although the dark brown colors are a bit oppressive. The hotel has a guest garden and garage for guests, and a taxi service is at your disposal. The restaurant features the standard favorites like *Schnitzel*, grilled cutlets, and Braten. Don't expect any surprises. The food is basic but satisfying.

St. Wolfgang

LANDHAUS ZU APPESBACH AM SEE, *Au 18, A-5360 St. Wolfgang. Tel. 6138-2209; fax 6138-220914. Doubles start at 550 schillings per person. All credit cards accepted.*

This a lovely 24 room hotel on the banks of St. Wolfgang. Tucked away on tree-filled grounds, the hotel is a converted private residence imbued with charm. The Kozma-Eidlhuber family provide exceptional service. Sports enthusiasts will like the wide range of activities available, including golf, sailing, tennis, fishing and wind surfing. Children and pets are welcome. The hotel also has a good restaurant with both low-calorie and traditional dishes, plus a bar.

WHITE HORSE INN, *Markt 74, A-5360 St. Wolfgang. Tel. 6138-2306-0; fax 6138-2306-41. Doubles start at 1,200 schillings. All credit cards accepted.*

The White Horse Inn is itself one of the principle sights to see in St. Wolfgang. It was here that the film by Gustav Kadelburg and Oskar Blumenthal *At the White Horse Inn* was made. The film is shown daily in the local cinema during the summer. The inn is right on the lake, and diners can eat on a terrace overlooking the water at the inn's first class restaurant serving Austrian dishes. The inn is tastefully decorated with dark wood paneling. Rooms are cozy but elegant.

WHERE TO EAT

As in most other parts of Austria, outside the big cities most of the good restaurants are attached to hotels, inns, and guesthouses, which are listed and reviewed above in *Where to Stay*. Below are two recommended restaurants not attached to hotels:

Bad Ischl

KURHAUS, *Kurhausstrasse 8, A-4820 Bad Ischl. Tel. 6132-23420; fax 6132-28428. Moderate. Open 9 a.m. to 10 p.m. No credit cards accepted.*

Dining at the Kurhaus restaurant is like stepping back into another century. It's easy to imagine the emperor walking through the doors at any minute. The restaurant's band plays Austrian classics as diners enjoy their meals outside near the restaurant fountains. The restaurant features the usual Austrian specialties like *Schnitzel* and roast chicken but they are served with a certain flair. The service is meticulous and enhances the old world atmosphere, which really makes this restaurant special.

St. Gilgen

SEE RESTAURANT FISCHER, *A-5340 St. Gilgen. Tel. 6227-304; fax 6227-7415. Moderate. Open from 8 a.m. to 10 p.m. All credit cards and traveler's checks accepted.*

The See Restaurant Fischer overlooks the water of the Wolfgangsee. The cooking is basic and the portions large. But the value is good and the selection enormous. There are a wide variety of fish dishes to choose from, plus turkey with mushroom sauce, game ragout, and a vegetable plate.

SEEING THE SIGHTS

The main attraction in the Lake District is, of course, the crystal-clear water of the lakes themselves with their dramatic background of mountains. Visitors flock to their beaches for sunning, swimming, and boating. But many of the towns also have special attractions beyond their natural splendor.

Altaussee

The **Altaussee** is on the western boundary of the Lake District in Styria. From its pristine waters you can see the **Dachstein Glacier** looming in the distance. Like many cities in the region, Altaussee has a salt mine. Here during World War II, the Nazis stored valuable art treasures pilfered from the country. You can now tour where the booty was hidden.

Altaussee is 55 kilometers from Salzburg, three kilometers off the A-1 and accessible by train. **Altaussee Tourist Information**, *Kurhaus, A-8992-Altaussee. Tel. 3622-71643; fax 3622-71187.*

Bad Aussee

Nature lovers and health seekers will enjoy a visit to **Bad Aussee**, near the **Grundlsee** and **Altausee lakes**. The hiking is excellent here during the summer months. Make sure to stop off at the tourist office for maps, tours, and tips on hiking in the area. Salt and thermal water **spas** have also grown up around the region. The market town has an important footnote in the country's history, since Hapsburg Archduke Johann married a local postmaster's daughter.

Bad Aussee is 80 kilometers southeast of Salzburg. **Bad Aussee Tourist Information,** *Hauptstrasse 48, Bad Aussee A-8990. Tel. 3622-54720; fax 3622-52323-23.*

Bad Ischl

Bad Ischl is home to the summer residence of Emperor Franz Josef and his wife Elisabeth, who resided at the **Imperial Villa,** *Tel. 6132-23241,* in the town. The villa is definitely worth a visit, with its collection of the emperor's hunting trophies, austere sleeping quarters, and other royal memorabilia. You really get a sense of the imperial lifestyle touring the royal residence. Information on the villa is also available in English. The grounds are lovely and open to the public for a stroll. The Imperial Villa is open May through September, from 9 a.m. to 11:45 a.m. and 1 p.m. to 4:45 p.m. Admission to the villa is 88 schilling for adults and 40 schillings for children; admission to the park is 35 schillings for adults and 20 schillings for children.

The **Museum of the Township of Bad Ischl,** *Hotel Austria at Esplanade 10,* has a fine collection of folk art and exhibitions on local history. Open Tuesdays, Thursday, Fridays, Saturdays and Sundays from 10 a.m. to 5 p.m.; Wednesdays open 2 p.m. to 7 p.m.; closed Mondays. Bad Ischl is also known for its **spas**, where visitors can seek cures using mineral mud and salt, sulphur springs, electrotherapy and inhalations.

Bad Ischl is 56 kilometers east of Salzburg. **Bad Ischl Tourist Information Office,** *Bahnhoffstrasse 6, A-4820 Bad Ischl. Tel. 6132-27757; fax 6132-2775777.*

Gmunden am Traunsee

Gmunden is linked to the mainland by a 130 meter wooden bridge. The Archduke Salvator, the nephew of Emperor Franz Josef I, acquired the heavily fortified **fortress** in 1878. The Gothic chapel of the chateau also is worth seeing. Admission is free.

Gmunden is 45 kilometers east of Salzburg. **Gmunden Tourist Information Office,** *Am Graben 2, A-4810 Gmunden. Tel. 7612-4305; fax 7612-71410.*

Grunau im Almtal

The attraction of the lake resort of **Grunau Im Almtal** at the foot of the **Toten Gebirge** is its natural setting in the heart of the forest. You can hike the scenic valley or climb the nearby mountains. This is a must stop for nature lovers. Grunau im Almtal is also the home of the **Alm Lake's Nature and Natural Game Preserve**.

Grunau is 60 kilometers south of Linz. **Grunau Tourist Information Office**, *A-4645 Grunau im Almtal. Tel. 7616-8268; fax 7616-8895.*

Hallstatt

Salt is still being mined in the 4,500-year-old town of **Hallstatt**. The salt mines are the oldest in the world. The prehistoric age from 800 B.C. to 400 B.C. is dubbed the Hallstatt Age, because of the significant archaeological finds made in the area. In 1734, miners discovered a corpse here that had been preserved by salt for more than 2,000 years. Many of the artifacts discovered in the area are on display in the **Prehistoric Museum** and the **Regional Museum**. Admission to the two museums is 40 schillings for adults, 35 schillings for groups and 20 schillings for children. They're open from 10 a.m. to 4 p.m.

The **market square** is charming with 16th century homes bordering cobbled streets. The local **parish church**, perched precariously on the hillside, is worth a visit. Two beautiful altar pieces from 1450 and 1520 decorate this small Gothic church crowning the city. Next door is the **Chapel of St. Michael**. Because of a lack of space in the graveyard, the bones of the dead were stored in the chapel. You'll notice the rather morbid tradition of painting the skulls of the dead.

Hallstatt is 80 kilometers southeast of Salzburg. **Hallstatt Tourist Information Office**, *Seestrasse 169, A-4830 Hallstatt. Tel. 6134-8352; fax 6134-8352.*

Mondsee

Mondsee's central **market square** is bordered by houses in candy-colored pastels preserved in all their former glory. Be sure to visit the magnificent Baroque **Staffelkirche** which you may recognize from the movie *The Sound of Music* – the church was used as the site of Maria's wedding. Formerly a Benedictine abbey, the church was consecrated in 1487. The bright-yellow facade was remodelled in 1730. The ornate Baroque interior contains seven altars sculpted by M. Guggenbichler.

Mondsee is 35 kilometers east of Salzburg. **Mondsee Tourist Information Office**, *Mondseeland, Dr. Franz Muller Strasse 3, A-5310 Mondsee. Tel. 6232-2270; fax 6232-4470.*

St. Gilgen

St. Gilgen is considered the gateway to the lovely Lake District. The town is also famous for being the birthplace of Mozart's mother, Anna

Maria Walburga Pertl, who was born here on Christmas day in 1720. She left St. Gilgen in 1724 and later married the violinist Leopold Mozart. Only two of their seven children survived, a daughter, Nannerl, and a son, Wolfgang, who became one of the greatest musicians the world has ever known. Nannerl lived in St. Gilgen after her marriage to Baron Johann Baptist Berchtold Sonnenburg.

The home of Mozart's mother now houses the local museum, **Mozart Gedenkstatte,** *off the Ischlerstrasse,* which has a collection of lace bobbins and glassware dishes, for which the town is renowned. Exhibitions on the Mozart family are also featured. Tickets are 10 schillings for adults and 5 schillings for children. The **town square** also features a **fountain** dedicated to Wolfgang Amadeus Mozart.

Winter sports abound in St. Gilgen. Downhill skiing is available at the nearby **Zwolferhorn,** 1,522 meters high. The area also has 20 kilometers of cross-country skiing trails. When the lake freezes, ice skating is possible. There is even a sledding run for the kids.

St. Gilgen is 35 kilometers east of Salzburg. **St. Gilgen Tourist Information Office,** *1 Mozartplatz, A-5340 St. Gilgen. Tel. 6227-7267 or 348; fax 6227-72679.*

St. Wolfgang

One of the major attractions in **St. Wolfgang** is the massive Gothic **altar** by Michael Pacher, created between 1471-1481 in the **parish church.** Also note the Wolfgang chapel and the pilgrimage fountain which attracts the faithful from around Austria.

St. Wolfgang came to the area in 976 where he lived as a hermit. Legend has it that St. Wolfgang grappled with the devil, and when he threw his ax into the valley, he made a divine promise that he would build a church wherever it fell. The resort town later became a playground for the Hapsburg emperors, from Maximilian I to Leopold I. Kaiser Franz Joseph often journeyed to St. Wolfgang from Bad Ischl to meet his mistress, Katharina Schratt.

The town's **central square** is especially picturesque, leading to the historic **White Horse Inn,** the site of the operetta of the same name by Ralph Benatzky. If you plan to visit the resort during the high season, try to go during the week. The resort is mobbed on the weekends (see *Where to Stay,* above).

St. Wolfgang is 50 kilometers east of Salzburg. **St. Wolfgang Tourist Information Office,** *Pilgerstrasse 28, A-5360 St. Wolfgang. Tel. 6138-2239; fax 6138-223981.*

Scharnstein Im Almtal

This resort town on the **River Alm** has fine scenic views of the Alps. A highlight is surely the 16th century **Sharnstein Chateau**, which contains a **criminal museum** and a **reptile zoo**. The **Viechtwang parish church** was consecrated in 1691. **Fortress ruins** from the 11th century are also available for a visit.

Scharnstein is 58 kilometers south of Linz. **Scharnstein Tourist Information Office**, *A-4644 Scharnstein/Almtal. Tel. 7615-2340; fax 7615-224430.*

Traunkirchen am Traunsee

Located on the western side of the **Traun Lake**, the town center is dominated by the **Johannesberg** castle and a former **monastery**. Also worth seeing are the Baroque **parish church** with its Fisherman's pulpit and the calvary chapel.

Traunkirchen is 5 kilometers north of Ebensee. **Traunkirchen Tourist Information Office**, *A-4810 Traunkirchen 56. Tel. 7617-2234; fax 7617-3340.*

NIGHTLIFE & ENTERTAINMENT

Because of the Lake District's close proximity to **Salzburg**, your best bet for nightlife and entertainment is to make the short drive into the festival town. Many local churches also feature concerts, and the intimate setting can provide a really memorable setting for the music. Local tourist offices can provide information on the times, locations, and ticket prices.

For operetta fans, **Bad Ischl** hosts its annual **Operata Festival** during July and August. The town was once home to Franz Lehar, who composed several operettas, including *The Merry Widow* and *The Land of Smiles*.

You could also opt to take an evening boat trip on the **Wolfgangsee** from June through September, on the **Romantic Classics cruise** between St. Gilgen and St. Wolfgang. You can have dinner and drinks on the boat. The kitschy cruises feature the all-women orchestral group *Fledermaus* playing classics from such composers as Mozart and Strauss – but again, these are really only for diehard tourists. The cruise costs 390 schillings per person. The cruise leaves St. Gilgen at 8 p.m. and return at 10:30 p.m. For reservations, *call 6227-348 or 7267.*

SPORTS & RECREATION

Summer Sports

There is extensive hiking, biking, swimming, sailing and other water sporting opportunities in the **Salzkammergut**. Most of the tourist offices have hiking maps available with hikes already mapped out for you.

Guided tours and hikes are often also available for a fee. Reservations should be made through the local tourist offices. Golfers can keep in form at golf courses in Bad Ischl, Fuschl, and two in Mondsee.

If you'd like to enjoy a mountain view, but don't want to deal with the rigors of climbing or hiking, try taking the **Schafberg railway**. The railway was constructed in 1892. Construction materials had to be toted up the mountain by more than 6,000 mule-loads and a viaduct, and several stone bridges had to be constructed and two tunnels excavated. The railway has five old-time steam locomotives. Two diesel engines were also put into service in 1964. The steam locomotives take about an hour to get to the top of the mountain, and the diesel engine trip takes 40 minutes. You can get refreshments on the mountain plateau, at a height of 1,780 meters, at the **Schbergspitze Hotel** operated by the railroad.

Or you might prefer touring the **Wolfgangsee** by **boat**. A paddle-steamer was first put into operation in 1873 and is still running. Today, several other boats are in operation, run by the Austrian Federal Railways. The boat service runs between St. Gilgen, Furberg, Lueg, Ferienhort, Riedfalkenstein, St. Wolfgang, Gschwendt and Strobl. For more information on the rail or boat trips, *call 6138-22320; fax 6138-223212.*

Winter Sports

The Salzkammergut **ski areas** have gentle slopes for beginners and challenging runs for more experienced skiers. **St. Gilgen** has eight kilometers of runs and **Strobl** has 12 kilometers of runs. The Wolfgangsee and the Salzkammergut-Tennengau ski passes are valid in 21 ski areas. There are also opportunities for cross country skiing, winter hiking, ice skating, ice sailing, curling, snowboarding, ice disco and horse-drawn sleigh rides.

For more information on skiing possibilities, contact the following ski slopes:
• **St. Gilgen**, *Tel. 6227-348 or 7267; fax 6627-72679*
• **Strobl**, *Tel. 6137-255; fax 6137-5958*
• **Fuschl Am See**, *Tel. 6226-250; fax 6226-650*

THE OBERTAUERN SNOW GUARANTEE!

*The **Obertauern** offers 150 kilometers of prepared runs and guarantees snow from November to May. There are four downhill schools and snowboard instruction. Cross country skiing, touring, winter hiking, mono, swingbo, freestyle, tobogganing, curling, timed races and bowling are also possibilities.*

*For **Ski Information**, contact Obertauern A-5562. Tel. 6456-252 and 320; 6456-515.*

DAY TRIPS & EXCURSIONS

Dachstein Caves

A great day trip with children is to the **Dachstein Caves**. Scientists believe the caves are are at least one million years old, and could be up to 25 million years old. There are more than 13,000 cubic meters of ice in the caves, which form dramatic peaks and gorges that you can explore on guided tours.

You can also tour the **Mammoth Cave**, the deepest in Austria. The cave descends some 37 kilometers beneath the earth's surface. In the **Koppenbruller Cave**, stalactites are being formed by the fast flowing **Dachstein River**. The **Dachstein Museum** allows you to get up close and personal to eyeless cave insects and other creatures that once lived in the caves. The museum also has models and exploring equipment on display.

The ice cave and the Mammoth Cave are open daily from May through October 15; the Koppenbruller Cave is open May through September. Make sure to wear practical shoes and bring warm clothes for exploring the caves. Tours take approximately one and a half hours. The Koppenbruller Cave is located just outside the Obertraun heading in the direction of Bad Aussee. You can take the Dachstein cable car to reach the Mammoth and ice caves. For more information, *call 61-31-273; fax 61-31-531.*

Mauterndorf Castle

Mauterndorf Castle was once a toll station, but was later used as a summer residence of the Archbishops. The chapel, court with arcades, and medieval halls can be visited on guided tours of the castle. It's also possible to enjoy a medieval style dinner with minstrel music and dancers.

To get to the castle from Salzburg or Vienna, take the Tauern motorway heading south towards Villach and exit at St. Michael. If you prefer the scenic route via an ancient Roman road, take the federal road in the direction of Hallein and Golling. For more information, *call 6472-6426; fax 6472-7426.*

Salt Mines

Many of the local **salt mines** have guided tours open to the public. Children and their parents alike can race down the slides the miners used to access the caves, cruise across underground lakes, or ride the rails down to the mines. No children under four years old admitted. For general information on area mines, *call 4504-9393365.*

For specific salt mines, try:
• **Bad Ischl Salt Mines**, *Tel. 6132-23948-31.* Open daily from April to June from 9 a.m. to 4 p.m.; July through September, 10 a.m. to 5 p.m.

Admission for adults 120 schillings; children 60 schillings; tour escorts 40 schillings.

- **Hallstatt Salt Mines**, *Tel. 6134-8251-72 or 46*. Open June through September, 9:30 a.m. to 4:30 p.m.; October through May, 9:30 a.m. to 3 p.m. Admission for adults is 130 schillings; children 60 schillings.

PRACTICAL INFORMATION

Credit Cards

If your credit cards are lost or stolen, you can call the following numbers 24 hours a day to make a report. The numbers are located in Vienna, so first dial area code 0222.

- **American Express**, *Tel. 51-29-714*
- **Diners**, *Tel. 50-1-35*
- **Mastercard**, *Tel. 71-7-01-0*
- **Visa**, *Tel. 53-4-87-77*

Emergency Phone Numbers

- **Ambulance**, *Tel. 144*
- **Police**, *Tel. 133*
- **Fire Department**, *Tel. 122*

Money Exchange

You can change money at most local banks, which are open Monday to Friday, 8:30 a.m. to 12:30 p.m. and 2 p.m. to 4:30 p.m. Banks are closed Saturdays, Sundays and public holidays.

Pharmacies

Several pharmacies are open 24 hours a day in case of emergencies. The address of the nearest open pharmacy will be posted in the window of each closed shop. For pharmacy assistance, *call 1550*.

Post Offices

Most post offices are open Monday through Friday from 8 a.m. to noon and 2 p.m. to 6 p.m.; Saturdays from 8 a.m. to 10 a.m.

Tipping

A service charge is added to your hotel and restaurant bill. However, if you are pleased with the service, it is customary to tip an additional 5 to 10 percent of the check. Taxi drivers and hair dressers also are generally tipped the same amount.

Weather

For the latest weather information, *call 15-66*.

16. SALZBURG

INTRODUCTION

Alexander Humboldt called **Salzburg** the Rome of the North although most Americans might know it better as the setting for the movie *The Sound of Music* or the hometown of composer Wolfgang Amadeus Mozart.

Salzburg was once a Roman stronghold and called *Juvavum*. But after the fall of the empire, the city went into decline until **St. Rupert** came on the scene. He was given the remains of the old Roman city in 696 by the Archduke Theodo, whom he had baptized. St. Rupert later erected St. Peter's Abbey.

Salzburg continued to increase in prestige over the centuries. The archbishops owed their wealth and political power to the tremendous salt reserves in the region, which in earlier times was called white gold because of its extraordinary value. Even when the Hapsburg's empire stretched across Europe, the archbishops managed to maintain their sovereignty through diplomatic and political manipulation.

Today, the province of Salzburg stretches 2,761 square miles and has 483,727 inhabitants. The region includes the **Limestone Alps**, the lakes of the **west Salzkammergut**, part of the **Kitzbuheler Alps** and parts of the **Hohe Tauern** and the **Nieder Tauern**. For information on Salzburg's portion of the Salzkammergut, see Chapter 15, *The Lake District*.

ORIENTATION

The Salzburg tourist bureau offers a **Salzburg Card**, which entitles card holders to free admission to city tourist attractions, public transportation, and a guide explaining the principal sights in the city. The cards are available for 24 hours for 180 schillings, 48 hours for 260 schillings or 72 hours for 350 schillings. You can buy the cards at local tourist offices, hotels and travel agencies.

The **area code** for Salzburg is 662. Remember to dial a zero before the area code if you are trying to reach the city from inside Austria.

ARRIVALS & DEPARTURES

By Air

The **Salzburg Airport** is located at *Innsbrucker Bundesstrasse 95. Tel. 662-80-550 or 662-85-2091; fax 662-80-5529; telex 633133.* For **Salzburg Airport Services**, *call 662-8055-251*. For **charter flight information**, *call 662-851-212; fax 662-851-215*. For **Austrian flight information**, *call 662-8529-00*.

The airport is open from 7 a.m. to 10 p.m. Taxis are available and can get you downtown in about 20 minutes, or you can catch bus number 77, which will take you to the old town.

If you're flying into Munich International Airport, you can take a train to Salzburg. But a better bet may be to reserve a seat with the Salzburger Mietwagen. The service takes you from the airport directly from the Munich airport to your hotel in Salzburg. Be aware, though, that you may be in for a wait at the airport, because there may be other passengers that will be riding with you. **Salzburger Mietwagen Service**, *Ignaz Harrer Strasse 79A, A-5020 Salzburg. Tel. 662-8161-0; fax 662-436324.* One way fare costs 440 schillings; roundtrip fare costs 730 schillings.

By Car

If you're coming from Vienna, the A1 west will get you to Salzburg.

By Train

The **Main Train Station** is located at *Sudtiroler Platz 1* and is within walking distance from the old section of the city. There are rail connections with all major cities in Austria and around Europe. For **train information**, *call 17-17*.

GETTING AROUND TOWN

By Bike

Touring Salzburg by bicycle is a great way to get around, especially to see important sights just outside the city like Hellbrun, the archbishop's former palace. There are 135 kilometers of bicycle paths around the city and along the river. The bike trails are marked with a bike and rider on the paths and by blue and white signs. Watch out for shared pedestrian and biker paths, which are also marked with signs.

If you don't have your own bicycle, you can rent them at several shops around town:

- **Hager Albert**, *Furnstenalle 39. Tel. 823-723*. Rents year round.
- **Salzburg Main Train Station**, *Sudtiroler Platz 1, counter seven or eight. Tel. 8887-5377*. Year round rental, 24-hours a day.
- **Velo-Acti**ve, *Willibald-Hauthaler Strasse 10. Tel. 435-595 or 663-868827.*

Rents year round. Velo-Active, Residenzplatz. Rentals from April to October.

• **Zweirad Frey**, *Willibald-Hauthaler Strasse 4. Tel. 431-682.* Rents year round.

By Bus

Bus schedules are posted at each stop. Buses are punctual and reliable, but they don't run very late so you may end up getting stuck after a concert or other performance. Tickets can be purchased from the driver, at machines located at selected stops, at **tabak-trafik** (stores selling cigarettes), and at some newsstands. Buying your ticket in advance will save you a few schillings. You can purchase individual tickets or in multiple packs. Make sure you validate your ticket inside the bus. If you are caught with a ticket that has not been validated, you will be subject to a fine. Children under six years old can travel for free. All-day passes and passes for 72 hours are also available if you plan to spend several days in the area.

If you want to take a trip outside the city to Hellbrun, Hallein, or the Lake District, the Bundesbus leaves from in front of the **Main Train Station**, *Sudtiroler Platz 1.*

By Car

If you're planning to confine your visit to just seeing the sights in Salzburg's old town, leave your car at your hotel or park it in one of several public parking lots located around the city. Most of the **Altstadt** (Old Town) is confined to pedestrian walkways or bike paths. Or park at the city limits in a public lot and you can take a bus into the city.

If you plan to rent a car, remember to make arrangements back home if at all possible to save yourself a bundle. Here are the local car rental offices serving Salzburg:

• **Avis**, *5020 Ferdinand-Porsche Strasse 7. Tel. 662-87-72-78; fax 662-88-02-35; at the airport, Tel. 662-87-72-78.*

• **Euro Car**, *Gabelsbergerstrasse 3. Tel. 662-87-42-74; fax 662-87-87-62; at the airport, Tel. 662-85-29-49.*

• **Hertz**, *Rainerstrasse 17. Tel. 662-87-34-52; fax 662-88-23-87; at the airport, Tel. 662-85-20-94.*

Local automobile associations include the **Salzburger Automobile, Motorcycle, and Touring Association**, *Tel. 662-639-990.*

For **emergencies**, 24 hour help is available by calling *120*. You can also call the **Automobile, Motorcycle, and Bicycle Association of Austria**, *Tel. 662-433-601 or 662-433-631*; their 24 hour emergency service is *123*.

Trying to **park** on the street can be problematic in Salzburg. If you do find a space, make sure that you pay for a parking voucher at machines on the sidewalks. For longer periods and greater peace of mind, your better bet is to park your car in one of the public lots around the city. Salzburg has ample public parking throughout the city to reduce congestion on crowded thoroughfares and encourage drivers to use public transportation.

Some of the bigger lots are:

- **Park and Ride Sud**, *Alpenstrasse*. Open year round with 440 spaces available.
- **Airport Park and Ride**, *Salzburg Airport*. Paid parking available year round with 715 spaces.
- **Park and Ride SAZ**, *Salzburger Ausstellungszentrum, exhibition center*. Paid parking available during the festival season in July and August with 2,600 spaces. Direct access to the autobahn.

If you want to put your rental car in an **indoor garage**, try some of these:

- **Altstadt-Garage**, *in Monchsberg*. Open 24 hours a day in heart of Salzburg's old city section. Paid parking with 1,500 spaces available.
- **Hypo-Garage**, *Nonntal*. Open daily June to September from 7 a.m. to 11 p.m.; October to May, Monday to Saturday 7 a.m. to 11 p.m.; closed Sundays and public holidays.
- **Mirabell Garage**, *Mirabellplatz*. Paid parking with 660 places available from 7 a.m. to midnight.
- **Parkgarage Auersperg**, *Auerspergstrasse 4*. Paid parking with 70 spaces available from 7 p.m. to midnight.
- **Raiffeisen Garage**, *Schwarzstrasse 13-15*. Paid parking with 179 spaces available from 7 a.m. to midnight.
- **REWAG-Garage**, *Ramada Hotel, Fanny-von-Lehnert Strasse 7*. Paid parking with 7,500 parking spaces available 24-hours a day.
- **WIFI-Garage**, *Julius Raab Platz*. Paid parking with 2,220 parking spaces available Monday to Friday from 7:30 a.m. to 11 p.m.; Saturday 7:30 a.m. to 6 p.m.; closed Sundays and public holidays.

By Horse-Drawn Carriage

For a romantic way to see the city or if you'd just prefer to sit back and enjoy the view, you can enjoy Salzburg from the comfort of a horse-drawn carriage.

Drivers line-up at **Residenzplatz**, beside the cathedral. Make sure you ask your driver if he can speak English, since most will explain the historical significance of the main sights. Also, agree on the price of the trip before hand. A 25 minute trip will cost approximately 350 schillings for four people; a 50 minute ride costs about 680 schillings for four people.

By Taxi

Taxi stands are located around the old city at the Hanuschplatz, Residenzplatz, Rudolphsplatz *(Tel. 662-843-344)*, Tomaselli *(Tel. 662-844-345)*, Monchsburg-Aufzug, at the main train station *(Tel. 662-872-680)*, Hofwirt *(Tel. 662-877-164)*, Markartplatz, Unfallkrankenhaus and the Wirtschaftsforderungsinstitut.

You can call or fax to order a taxi, for a surcharge, although if you're near the old part of the city this shouldn't be necessary. Try **City Taxi**, *Hannakstrasse 11, A-5020 Salzburg. Tel. 662-661-066; fax 662-661-019;* or **Salzburger Funktaxi-Vereinigung**, *Rainerstrasse 27, A-5020 Salzburg. Tel. 662-81-11.* To reserve a taxi in advance, *call 662-874-400; fax 662-882-505.* Taxis are allowed to drive in the pedestrian-only parts of the *Altstadt* (Old Town) to take you and your luggage from the airport or train station to your hotel.

CALLING ALL INTERNET ADDICTS!

If you want to check your electronic mail or need to send one yourself, head over to the Internet Cafe Am Rainberg, Rainbergerstrasse 3A, A-5020 Salzburg. Tel. 662-886483. The cafe is open from 9 a.m. to midnight.

WHERE TO STAY

The hotels in Salzburg and the surrounding area, as in the rest of Austria, boast quite a few good hotel restaurants. In addition to the *Where to Eat* section below, consider some of these restaurants when choosing a place to eat.

Salzburg

HOLIDAY INN CROWNE PLAZA, *Rainerstrasse 6-8, A-5020 Salzburg. Tel. 662-889-78; fax 662-87-88-93. Doubles start at 2,400 schillings, including buffet breakfast. All credit cards accepted.*

Salzburg's Holiday Inn offers the height in comfort and a lot of American touches that tourists may find welcome. There are non-smoking rooms, and special accommodations designed for easier access by the disabled are offered. Children under 19 can stay free with their parents. The hotel also has fitness facilities, a pool, a sauna, and a solarium.

Guests have their choice of two restaurants: the family-style restaurant **Auersperg**, open from 6:30 a.m. to 6 p.m., and the more upscale **Rainer Stube**, open from 6 p.m. to midnight.

HOTEL ALTSTADT SALZBURG, *Rudolfskai 28, A-5020 Salzburg. Tel. 662-84-85-71-0; fax 662-84-85-71-6 or 8. Doubles start at 1,900 schillings per person. All credit cards accepted.*

Run by the Radisson hotel chain, the Hotel Alstadt combines American hospitality and service with old world charm. Located in the heart of Salzburg's old section, the former brewery dates back to the Middle Ages. The building has been renovated to pamper guests with the best in modern amenities, while preserving its architectural past from wood beams to stucco work.

HOTEL BRISTOL, *Makartplatz 4, A-5020 Salzburg. 662-73-5-57; fax 662-73-55-76. Doubles start at 2,300 schillings. Mastercard, Visa, and American Express accepted.*

The Hotel Bristol was built in the 1800's and continues in the tradition of a fine old grand hotel. Just off the Mirabell Gardens, many of the rooms offer a vantage of the Hohensalzburg fortress, so be sure to ask for a room with a view. Children, up to 10 years old, also can stay free with their parents. The hotel also boasts an excellent restaurant, **The Polo Lounge**, where Austrian specialties are handled with a lighter hand than you usually find. The hotel staff, however, tends to be cold and less than helpful, unforgivable at a luxury hotel like this.

HOTEL GOLDNER HIRSCH, *Getreidegasse 37, A-5020 Salzburg. Tel. 662-84-85-11; fax 662-84-33-49. Double rooms start at 3,300 schillings per person. All credit cards accepted.*

The Hotel Goldner Hirsch has the reputation as one of Salzburg's premier hotels, and it's no wonder. The hotel manages to perfectly balance Austrian rustic charm with all of the modern amenities. Several of the rooms are furnished with local antiques, providing the right blend of elegance and style.The hotel's award winning restaurant, tastefully decorated in green and white linens, offers several Austrian favorites. But be forewarned, you're going to have to dig deep into your pocketbook for the privilege of dining here. A full-dinner menu also is available for 490 schillings per person.

HOTEL-RESTAURANT ELEFANT, *Sigmund Haffner Gasse 4, A-5020 Salzburg. Tel. 662-84-33-97 or 662-84-34-09; fax 84-01-09. Doubles start from 1,450 shillings. All credit cards accepted.*

This elegant hotel is located in one of Salzburg's ancient architectural treasures. The building, over 700 years old, is just off the busy Getreidegasse. For 400 years, the building has served as an inn and is suffused with old world charm. Tucked away in a quiet side street, the Hotel Elefant is minutes by foot from most of the city's principal sights. The restaurant features the usual hearty Austrian fare. You can also have a drink in the hotel's historic **Ratsherrnkeller** which the Mayr family, the hotel's proprietors, say was called the wine cellar of Salzburg during the 17th century.

TEIN, *Giselaki 3, A-5020 Salzburg. Tel. 662-874-346; fax 662-
s start at 880 schillings, including buffet breakfast. All credit*

The family-run Hotel Stein is slightly rough around the edges. The rooms are somewhat dark with a lot of heavy, somber furniture. Staying at the Hotel Stein is like being in somewhat's guest room – a bit worn but comfortable. The hotel boasts a great rooftop cafe, which has a spectacular view of the spires of the city with the fortress hovering over them and is definitely worth a detour.

OSTERREICHISCHER HOF SALZBURG, *Schwarzstrasse 5-7, A-5020 Salzburg. Tel. 662-88-977; fax 662-88977-14. Doubles start at 3,900 schillings. All credit cards accepted.*

Founded as the Hotel d'Autriche in 1866, this hotel has housed a string of such notables as Richard Strauss and Max Reinhardt. The hotel, on the banks of the Salz River, was acquired in 1988 by Peter Gurtler, the owner of the famed Hotel Sacher in Vienna, who conducted extensive renovations in 1990. The hotel is richly and uniquely decorated, and guests will be pampered by an incredibly accommodating staff.

The **Theaterkeller** is decorated with antique signs and medieval goblins. The gourmet restaurant **Zirbelstube** was designed by masters from Southern Tirol. Or order something from the grill at the **Salzachgrill**. The hotel also boasts a traditional restaurant, **The Red Salon**, and a coffee house cafe.

PENSION ERNA, *Gaisbergstrasse 43, A-5020 Salzburg. Tel. 662-641415. Doubles start at 460 schillings, including breakfast. No credit cards accepted.*

The Pension Erna is about as basic as you can get. But for the money, there is no better bargain in Salzburg. Rooms are clean, comfortable, and simply furnished. Make sure to request that you are not put in a room under the television room, which can get noisy. Parking is available for guests. There is no restaurant in the pension, and none nearby, so make sure to eat in town before you return for the night.

PENSION STRUBER HOTEL-GARNI, *Nonntaler Haupstrasse 35, A-5020 Salzburg. Tel. 662-84-92-74, Fax 662-84-37-28. Doubles start at 1,000 schillings, including breakfast. Visa, American Express and Mastercard accepted.*

Located at the back of the fortress and just a 10 minute walk from the heart of Salzburg's old town, the Pension Struber is a comfortable, small hotel simply furnished with traditional Austrian crafts. The lovely Schloss Leopoldskron palace is close by and within easy walking distance.The Illmer family runs the 24 bed hotel, and the staff is helpful and speaks English.

A breakfast buffet is available for guests, but there are no other restaurant facilities. Parking is available in front of the hotel so you won't be forced to pay for a space on the street or in a lot.

SCHLOSS NEUHAUS, *Kuhbergstrasse 1, A-5023 Salzburg. Tel. 662-64-36-16; fax 662-64-36-16. Apartments start from 2,000 schillings per person. All credit cards accepted.*

Dr. Nikolaus Topic runs this castle hotel with its three private apartments. Each apartment is decorated in its own specific style, from a modern New York loft to a traditionally romantic and classic Biedermeier salon. The castle was formerly a bishop's residence and was built by Eberhard III. Chamber music concerts are held here, too. Be sure to savor the spectacular view of Salzburg from the castle garden.

SHERATON SALZBURG, *Auerspergstrasse 4, A-5020 Salzburg. Tel. 662-889-990; fax 662-881-776. Doubles start from 3,100 schillings. All credit cards accepted.*

Located behind the famed Mirabell Gardens, the Sheraton is understatedly elegant and the staff bends over backwards to help you. You can eat around the clock here dining on haute cuisine at the **Mirabell Restaurant**, getting a light snack at **The Bistro**, or having a pre-concert drink in the piano bar. If you want to bring Fido or Fifi along, the Sheraton accepts pets for an extra charge of 250 schillings for your dog or cat.

WEISSES KREUZ HOTEL-RESTAURANT, *Bierjodlgasse 6, A-5020 Salzburg. Tel. 662-84-56-41, Fax 662-84-56-49. Doubles start from 800 schillings, with breakfast. All credit cards accepted.*

The Weisses Kreuz is located at the foot of the Festung Hohensalzburg. This small hotel definitely gets high marks for its charm with its delightful roof-top garden and carefully furnished rooms. The hotel is within a stone's throw of the heart of the old town, but you'll feel like you've escaped to an alpine inn where the staff treats you like a long lost friend. The hotel also has a very good restaurant featuring Balkan and Viennese specialties. You can dine in the dark panelled dining room or on the small outside terrace. Private garage parking is available to guests at the hotel.

Anif

HOTEL GARTENAUER, *A-5081 Anif 40. Tel. 6246-724-65; fax 6246-725-08-42. Doubles start at 1,150 schillings. All credit cards accepted.*

The Hotel Gartenauer is run by the Wieser family in what was once a farmhouse. The hotel has an extensive garden with a swimming pool for guests. The hotel is cozy rather than elegant. You'll feel like you've been invited to a friend's country home. Rooms are simply but tastefully furnished. There is a restaurant at the hotel with the usual Austrian favorites. The cuisine is basic; don't expect any surprises.

HOTEL-RESTAURANT FRIESACHER, *A-5081 Anif. 6246-8977; fax 6246-89-77-49. Double rooms start at 1,060 schillings, including breakfast buffet. All credit cards accepted.*

The Hotel-Restaurant Friesacher has a long tradition of serving travelers dating all the way back to 1515. Today, the hotel is furnished with lots of over-stuffed chairs, traditional wood burning stoves, and dark wood throughout. Rooms are beautifully decorated with elegant floral fabrics and rich wood furniture. Guests are also invited to use the hotel's sauna, turkish bath, and fitness room. The restaurant serves traditional Austrian cuisine as well as fish and pasta dishes. The wine list also features an excellent selection of Austrian vintages.

STAY IN A PRIVATE HOME OR FARM!

*The Salzburg Tourist Office publishes a list of **Zimmers**, or rooms, in private residences. Prices for rooms start at 250 schillings per person, usually including a hearty breakfast. Another option is stay at a **farm** where you can relax in the tranquil countryside or, if you prefer to be more active, you can lend a hand. There are farms for bikers and with lake access, horseback riding and special services for children.*

*You can receive information on farms in the Salzburg province by contacting the **Salzburg State Board of Tourism**, Alpenstrasse 96, A-5033 Salzburg. Tel. 662-8191; fax 662-623070. Bookings can be made through **Trumer Tourismus GmbH**, POB 3, A-5163 Mattsee. Tel. 6217-6080; fax 6217-7421.*

Anthering bei Salzburg

WALDPENSION HAMMER SCHMIEDE, *Acharting 22, A-5102 Anthering bei Salzburg. 6223-2503; fax 6223-25033-77. Doubles start at 790 schillings. All credit cards accepted.*

This lovely hotel is about 10 miles outside of Salzburg, but worth the trip. The hotel is tucked away in the woods. You'll feel as though you've discovered the pot of gold at the end of the rainbow. The hotel has rabbits, ducks, and even a peacock strutting around the garden. Rooms are elegant but at the same time very cozy with lots of rustic furniture in dark wood and floral fabrics. The service is impeccable, unobtrusive but always helpful.

No trip to the Hammer Schmiede would be complete without a visit to the restaurant that has delicious home cooking. Do not pass up dessert. The strudel is made on the premises with eggs from their own chickens. You'll have a meal to remember.

Dorfgastein

HAUSERBAUER, *A-5632 Dorfgastein. Tel. 6433-339; fax 6433-339-33. Doubles start at 440 schillings per person. All credit cards accepted.*

This alpine guest house is run by the Rohrmoser family and that friendly touch is apparent from the rooms to the restaurant. Perched on a hilltop overlooking the town, the Hauserbauer has modern, light-filled rooms. Guests can dine or have a drink on the wooden terrace or sit inside the traditional wood-panelled dining room. The hotel also is conveniently located to hiking and caving trails.

Maria Plain

GASTHOF PLAIN, *Plainbergweg 41, A-5101Maria Plain. Tel. 50701-0; Fax 63-2801. Doubles start at 1,300 schillings. Diners and American Express accepted.*

The Gasthof Plain is filled with cozy, comfortable rustic furnishings and local antiques, just the right touch for this country-style inn. The restaurant has the standard fare from *Wiener Schnitzel* to Cordon Bleu in ample portions served either in the dining room or on the outside terrace with a spectacular view overlooking Salzburg. There is also a menu for children. Ample parking is available on site for 60 schillings per day. Bringing your dog will cost an extra 65 schillings per day.

Oberalm bei Hallein

SCHLOSS HAUNSPERG, *A-5411 Oberalm bei Hallein. Tel. 6245-80-6-62; fax 6245-856-80. Apartments start from 850 schillings per person. All credit cards accepted.*

The Haunsperg Castle hotel has six luxurious apartments. The castle, bordering the Salzach river between Salzburg and Hallein, dates back to the Renaissance. The Von Gerneth family lovingly manages the hotel furnished with antiques from daguerreotypes to the Bosendorfer grand piano in the palace's music room. The castle is even reported to have a ghost! If you're looking for romance in the truest sense, the Schloss Haunsperg is an ideal lodging for you.

Wald im Oberpinzgau

HOTEL JAGDSCHLOSS, *A-5742 Wald im Oberpinzgau. Tel. 6565-6417; fax 6565-6920. Doubles start at 620 schillings per person. All credit cards accepted.*

Located at the outskirts of the Hohe Tauern National Park, this former hunting lodge castle is filled with hunting trophies. Cozy, comfortable rooms are decorated in rustic motifs. Count Graf vond der Recke owns the hotel and considers his clients his own personal guests. Ask him to whip you up a "Secret of the Woods" cocktail to unwind.

WHERE TO EAT

Salzburg's most celebrated dish is probably *Salzburger Nockerl*, a souffle filled with cream, egg whites, and sugar. Another sweet treat is

Kletzenbrot, a type of fruit cake made with dried pears. Salzburg also has a wide variety of cafes, restaurants, and pastry shops. Some of my selections are known throughout the country, and others are well-kept secrets.

AUGUSTINER BRAU, *Kloster Mulln, Augustinergasse 4, A-5020 Salzburg. Tel. 431-246; fax 431-246-20. Open daily 3 p.m. to 11 p.m.; Saturdays, Sundays and holidays 2:30 p.m. to 11 p.m. No credit cards accepted.*

The restaurant and beer garden is situated in what once was a former Augustinian monastery. You can still see signs of its religious roots in a lot of the architecture. Counters serve different Austrian specialties from huge slabs of pork to fish spreads to flaky pastries. This is a great place to go with children, since finicky eaters can pick and choose what they like. They atmosphere is relaxed and genial.

You'll also get a real sense of an authentic beer garden. Wash down your meal with steins of beer, which you can purchase in various sizes. Indoor seating is communal style at benches and tables, so if you don't like rubbing shoulders with some of the locals, this place may not be for you. The crowd can get pretty raucous as the night goes on, too.

BACKEREI JOSEF FUNDER, *29 Nonntaler Haupfstrasse, A-5020 Salzburg. Inexpensive. Open Monday through Friday, 6 a.m. to 12:30 p.m. and 3 p.m. 6:30 p.m.; Saturday 6 a.m. to noon. No credit cards accepted.*

This bakery is one of Salzburg's finest. If your hotel does not provide breakfast, head over here for some freshly baked rolls still warm from the oven. Or try something a little more caloric. The bakery has an excellent selection of tempting and tasty pastries.

BURGERWEHR EINKEHR, *Monchsberg 19, A-5020 Salzburg. Tel. 662-84-17-29. Moderate. Open 10 a.m. to 10 p.m. No credit cards, but dollars accepted.*

This cozy restaurant is perched up at the top of the Monchsberg with an amazing view of the city. The small kitchen serves the standard fare of Cordon Bleu, *Wiener Schnitzel,* and roast beef. But the meals are satisfying and the portions ample. If you're looking for some down-home cooking overlooking Salzburg's spires, this restaurant makes a nice stop.

CAFE KONDITOREI FURST, *Brodgasse 13, A-5020 Salzburg. Tel. 662-84-37-59. Inexpensive. Open Monday through Saturday 8 a.m. to 9 p.m.; Sundays 9 a.m. to 9 p.m.*

Founded in 1884, the Cafe Furst was the original creator of the *Mozart Kugel,* a delicious candy concoction with chocolate, marzipan, and hazelnuts. You'll see the ubiquitous red *Mozart Kugels* being sold over the city, but head to the source for the authentic candy in its silver and blue wrapping. The cafe also features a wide variety of cakes and pastries to tempt even the most jaded palate.

CAFE TOMASELLI, *Alter Markt 9, A-5020 Salzburg. Tel. 84-44-88. Inexpensive. Open Monday through Saturday 7 a.m. to 9 p.m.; Sundays 8 a.m. to 9 p.m. No credit cards.*

You may feel like you've entered a traditional Viennese coffee house when you walk into the Cafe Tomaselli, owned by the family since 1852. You can catch up with the latest news over your coffee and cake since the cafe provides complimentary newspapers.The cafe serves up to 50 different cakes and basic cafe fare, like omelettes. The outside seating and balcony make ideal people-watching perches.The Tomaselli house was once home to Mozart's widow and her second husband. The two are now buried in St. Sebastian's cemetery.

CAFE WINKLER, *Monchsberg 32, A-5020 Salzburg. Tel. 847-738; fax 847-738-30. Moderate. Open Tuesdays through Saturday 11 a.m. to 11 p.m. and Sundays 11 a.m. to 5 p.m.*

The Cafe Winkler offers an extraordinary, panoramic view of the city atop the Monchsberg. The cafe serves standard fare and pastries, but seeing the city's spires, either during the day or evening, from this vantage point is the real attraction. There is extensive outdoor seating if you happen to be in Salzburg during the balmy months. And after you've finished your dinner or coffee and cake, you can head next door to the casino.

If you don't want to climb the mountain, an elevator is available at 13 Gstattengasse. Roundtrip tickets cost 25 schillings, 15 schillings one way; children, 13 schillings roundtrip, 8 schillings one way.

DIE WEISSE, *Virgilgasse 2, A-5020 Salzburg. 87-64-81. Moderate. The beer garden is open daily 11 a.m. to 11 p.m. Open daily 5 p.m. to midnight; closed Sundays. No credit cards accepted.*

This beer garden and restaurant is far from the tourist hordes. Guests are served in the dark paneled dining rooms plates full of hearty Austrian fare, from goulash to various types of *Wurst*, at communal benches. Of course, huge steins of beers are readily available, and the crowd definitely gets more jovial as the night wears on.

GLOCKENSPIEL CAFE-RESTAURANT, *Mozartplatz 2, A-5020 Salzburg. Tel. 84-14-03-0; fax 84-21-659. Moderate. Open daily 11 a.m. to 6 p.m.; during the festival season, 11 a.m. to midnight. All credit cards accepted.*

Overlooking the Mozart place, the Glockenspiel Cafe-Restaurant is right smack in the heart of the city. The outside seating in the summer is an ideal place for people watching. The upstairs terrace affords a great view of the fortress. The menu offers the usual standard Austrian dishes, desserts, and coffees and is definitely a tourist restaurant. The cooking is not inspired, but you also won't be faced with any disasters either. The cafe is a great place for a quick stop for a cup of coffee and a pastry, but try somewhere else for lunch or dinner.

MIRABELLGARTEN CAFE, *Mirabell Gardens, A-5020 Salzburg. Tel. 87-33-19. Inexpensive. Open during park hours. No credit cards accepted.*

Relax with a cool drink or a coffee and a piece a cake in this outdoor cafe in the Mirabell Gardens. The tree-shrouded cafe has an excellent view of the formal gardens and fountains. A good place to get your second wind before continuing your sight-seeing adventure.

RESTAURANT LEITER, *Paris-Lodron Strasse 13, A-5020 Salzburg. Tel. 88-13-96. Inexpensive. Open Monday through Friday 9 a.m. to 6 p.m. No credit cards accepted.*

The Restaurant Leiter is one of the city's best kept secrets. Tucked away in a dark alley, this tiny restaurant only has a few tables. But the strudel is out-of-this-world and is one of the best bargains in town. The restaurant also has great pizza and unusual salads ideal for a light lunch. You can also get something to go for a picnic.

ST. PETER STIFTSKELLER, *St. Peter District 1/4, A-5020 Salzburg. Tel. 84-84-81, Fax 84-12-68-75. Moderate. Monday to Saturday 11 a.m. to midnight, Sunday 10 a.m. to midnight. Visa, American Express and Diners accepted.*

The St. Peter Stiftskeller purports to be Europe's oldest restaurant with its first mention appearing in 803 A.D., when Emperor Karl the Great visited Salzburg. A visit to the restaurant's stone hewn, Romanesque courtyard, next to St. Peter's church, is like stepping back into the Middle Ages. Sample such specialties as St. Peter's fish in shrimp and cream sauce and *Salzburger Nockerl* egg souffle. Be sure to try the *Pralatenwein* grown in the convent's own vineyards in the Wachau. The restaurant is also a local favorite for wedding receptions and has facilities to cater to large groups.

SCHATZ-KONDITOREI, *Getreidegasse 3, A-5020 Salzburg. Tel. 84-27-92. Inexpensive. Open Monday through Friday 8:30 a.m. to 6:30 p.m.; Saturdays 8 a.m. to 1:30 p.m. No credit cards accepted.*

This is a real old-style cafe with marble counter tops that your great aunt would feel right at home in. A great place to relax with a cup of tea and a slice of cake or a dish of ice cream.

SPAGHETTI AND CO., *Geitreidegasse 14, A-5020 Salzburg. Tel. and fax 841-400. Inexpensive. Open daily 10:30 a.m. to midnight. All credit cards accepted.*

If your children are threatening to rebel if you order them another *Schnitzel*, then this restaurant may be just the ticket. The food is unremarkable, but straightforward and a good value. A wide variety of pasta and pizza are served until midnight, so it's ideal for a quick bite to eat after going to a late-night performance.

STIEGEL KELLER, *Festungsgasse 10, A-5020 Salzburg. Tel. 84-00-82. Moderate. 11 a.m. to midnight. All credit cards accepted.*

This restaurant and beer garden is located in the shadow of the Festung, the medieval fortress above the city. The beer garden has extensive outdoor seating with a great view of the cathedral. From this height, it looks like ants are playing chess on the giant board below you. The restaurant serves the typical favorites, and there is even an infamous *Sound of Music* dinner (and you thought you'd have some respite from the musical in the dining room.) You'll swear that the curtains decorating the dining room are straight from the movie lot. You remember, the ones out of which Maria made the children's play clothes.

ZUM GOLDENEN ZIRKEL, *Papagenoplatz, A-5020 Salzburg. Tel. 84-11-06. Moderate. Open Monday through Friday 9:30 a.m. to 11 p.m.; Saturdays 9:30 a.m. to 2 p.m. All credit cards accepted.*

This guest house run by owner Manfred Wretschnig, serves up rib-sticking Austrian fare. You'll find more of the local crowd here, too, in the traditionally furnished dining room.

ZUM GULENSPIEGEL, *Hagenauerplatz 2, A-5020 Salzburg. Tel. 84-31-80; fax 84-31-80-6. Moderate. Open daily noon to 2 p.m. and 6 p.m. to 10:30 p.m. American Express, Visa, and Mastercard accepted.*

This cozy, flower-bedecked restaurant is across the square from the bright yellow house where Mozart was born. The dining room is traditionally decorated. Diners may feel like they are eating in a private home rather than in a restaurant. There are some some unusual spins on traditional dishes here, like calf's liver with white bread dumplings and poached salmon with saffron noodles.

SEEING THE SIGHTS

Historic Salzburg is very compact and can be easily managed on foot for most visitors. Many of the streets in the old town are only accessible by foot, so leave your car at your hotel or at one of the many public parking lots which surround the old section.

No trip to Salzburg would be complete without a visit to the **Hohensalzburg Festung**, *Monchsberg 34, Tel. 662-80-42-21-23 or 21-33; fax 662-80-42-29-24,* the medieval fortress that rises over the city. The fortress is well-preserved and you'll get a real feel for life in the time when the prince archbishops reigned here. You can visit the fortress' torture chamber, the **Salzburger Stier** mechanical organ, medieval state rooms, and the **Reckturm** tower with a fantastic view of the city below. Around the castle, you'll notice there are several stone-carved beets, which were part of the coat-of-arms of Archbishop Leonhard.

Legend has it that the archbishop was not the most diligent of young men and preferred to loll away his days. One day, in frustration, his uncle threw a beet at him to try to motivate him. It apparently worked, since his mark on the architecture of the city is apparent through much of the city.

At the back of the castle, be sure to notice while gazing out over the scenic overlook the house sitting all by itself in a field behind the fortress. Locals say that the lonely house was home to the neighborhood executioner. Since no one wanted to live with a man with blood on his hands, he was forced to take up residence in isolation. I don't know how much credence you can give the legend, but it does make a romantic story.

If you don't want to tackle the somewhat steep path leading up to the fortress, a funicular runs from the base of the mountain to the fortress. The funicular, which starts running at 8 a.m., costs 32 schillings for an adult roundtrip ticket, 22 schillings one way, 16 schillings for a child's roundtrip ticket, and 11 schillings for a child's one way ticket. The last ride up the mountain is at 9 p.m. The last ride down is at 10 p.m. Admission to the castle is 30 schillings for adults and 15 schillings for children. Free entry after 7 p.m.

Tours of the fortress, which include a free trip to the **museum**, cost 30 schillings for adults, 25 schillings for seniors and groups, students 20 schillings and children 15 schillings. The tours, which last about 50 minutes, are available January through March between 10 a.m. and 4:30 p.m.; April through June from 9 a.m. to 5 :30 p.m.; September and October 9:30 a.m. to 5 p.m. and November and December from 10 a.m. to 4:30 p.m.

Also on the fortress grounds is the **Rainer Museum** and its **Sound and Vision Show**, open November through March from 9 a.m. to 5 p.m.; during April, May, June and October, the festung is open 9 a.m. to 6 p.m.; and during July, August, September 8 a.m. to 7 p.m. The fortress also has a small restaurant with soup, hamburgers, and salads. No credit cards accepted, but you can pay with traveler's checks. The restaurant is open from 10 a.m. to 10 p.m. during the summer and from 10 a.m. to 8 p.m. during the rest of the year.

If you continue along the path, behind the fortress, you'll get to the **Nonnberg Convent**. The convent's first abbess was St. Erentrud, the niece of St. Rupert, who founded the city of Salzburg. The Gothic-style convent has a lovely chapel with a carved altarpiece dating back to the Middle Ages. St. Erentrud's tomb is also here. If you are at the chapel at 5:15 p.m., the nuns sing vespers. If the convent already looks familiar to you, you may have seen it already in *The Sound of Music*, which also has scenes at the Residenzplatz, St. Peter's cemetery, and the Mirabell Gardens.

If you walk down from the fortress, be sure to notice the view over the huge chess set next to the *dom*, or **cathedral**. The original cathedral was built by St. Virgil, the abbot of St. Peter's and Bishop of Salzburg. A fire destroyed the cathedral in 1598, and the only thing that remains from the Romanesque cathedral is the baptismal font from 1321. Most people believe that the archbishop himself, Wolf Dietrich, was behind the blaze

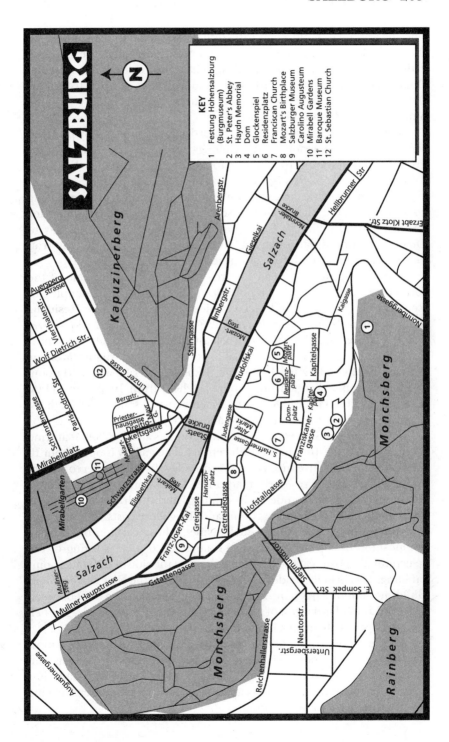

since he wanted to build a new cathedral, but lacked popular support for the plan. The Italian architect Santino Solari designed the baroque cathedral, which was consecrated in 1628. The cathedral's museum, **Domplatz**, housing clerical treasures and artworks, is open from May through October, Monday through Saturday from 10 a.m. to 5 p.m.; Sundays and holidays, 11 a.m. to 5 p.m.

Tours of the museum are held Saturdays at 3 p.m. and by previous arrangement. Admission is 40 schillings for adults, 30 schillings for groups and seniors and 10 schillings for children and students. For more information, *call 662-84-41-89 or 662-84-25-91-120; 84-04-42.*

You can also visit the cathedral's **archaeological excavation**s being conducted on-site. Tickets cost 20 schillings for adults, 15 schillings for groups, and 10 schillings for children. The site is open from May to October, Wednesday through Sunday from 9 a.m. to 5:00 p.m. Tours can be reserved. For more information, *call 662-84-52-95.*

From the cathedral, head towards the **Residentzplatz**, one of the former residences of the archbishops. The palace has examples of Renaissance, Baroque, and Neo-Classical architecture. The **Residenz State Rooms**, *Residentzplatz 1, Tel. 662-80-42-26-90; fax 662-80-42-29-78,* can only be seen by guided tours for at least three people. The tours, which last for about 40 minutes, are available during July and August, Monday through Friday at 10 a.m., 10:30 a.m., 11:00 a.m., 11:30 a.m. and noon. From September through June, tours are held from 10:00 a.m., 11:00 a.m., noon, 2:00 p.m. and 3:00 p.m. Tickets cost 45 schillings for adults, 35 schillings for seniors and groups and 15 schillings for children.

The **Residenz Gallery**, *Residenzplatz 1,* houses an art gallery featuring paintings from the 16th to the 19th century. The gallery is open from 10 a.m. to 5 p.m. The museum is closed Wednesdays from October to March. Guided tours can be reserved in advance. Admission costs 45 schillings for adults, seniors and students 35 schillings and children 15 schilling. A combined ticket for the state rooms and the gallery costs 70 schillings.

Across the square is the **Glockenspiel**, whose carillon bells play a composition by Mozart at 7 a.m., 11 a.m., and 6 p.m. A listing of the selections are posted at the Residentzplatz, on the side of the state rooms building. The 35 bells, made in 1688, are housed in the **New Government Building**, commissioned by Archbishop Wolf Dietrich and built between 1588 and 1602. The largest of the bells weighs about 840 pounds. The bell tower is open daily from 11 a.m. to 4 p.m.

In the adjoining square, is a **statue** dedicated to Salzburg's most famous son, **Wolfgang Amadeus Mozart**, designed by Ludwig von Schwanthaler and erected in 1842. During his lifetime, Mozart had a less than idyllic relationship with the city, and headed to Vienna after breaking his ties with his archbishop boss.

Circle around the Mozartplatz, crossing the Domplatz, which will lead you to the **Franciscan Church** dating back to the eighth century. Through the years several changes have been instituted to the church including the high altar, which incorporates Michael Pacher's gothic madonna. Also note the lion at the base of the pulpit, which dates back to Romanesque period.

Continuing down the street, you'll see a passageway leading to **St. Peter's Abbey**. The Benedictine abbey was founded by St. Rupert in 696 A.D. and has a Romanesque and Gothic cloister. But the abbey underwent extensive renovations and retains much of these Baroque and Rococo elements. The altar paintings are by Krems' artist J.M. Schmidt. It is also possible to visit the **Johann Michael Haydn Memorial** in the court of St. Peter's. From July to September it is open daily, except Wednesdays, from 10 a.m. to noon and 2 p.m. to 4 p.m. Tours are available. The cost of admission is 20 schillings for adults and 10 schillings for seniors, groups and children. For more information, *call 662-84-45-76-19.*

Through an archway adjoining the abbey is the **St. Peter's Cemetery**, which was used first by the Romans. Enclosed by arcades and festooned with wrought-iron markers and gates, the cemetery has served as a dramatic background for legendary productions of *Faust*. Mozart's sister, Nannerl, is also buried here. While in the cemetery make sure to visit the **catacombs**. Tours for a minimum of five people are conducted hourly from 10 a.m. to 5 p.m., May through September. From October to April, tours, which last about 20 minutes, are available at 11: a.m., noon, 1:30 p.m., 2:30 p.m. and 3:30 p.m. The cost is 12 schillings for adults and eight shillings for children. For more information, *call 84-45-78-0; 84-45-76-80.*

If you exit St. Peter's through the same street you came in and continue away from the cathedral, you'll find yourself at the back of the **University Church**. Enter the church, consecrated in 1707, from the **University Square**. The church is Fischer von Erlach's masterpiece and one of the most important Baroque churches in Europe.

Coming out of the University Church, head down one of the myriad alleys leading off the right side of the square. On the other side, you'll find yourself on the **Getreidegasse**. This is Salzburg's main shopping street, and is often swarming with people, so you might want to visit later in the evening. Restaurants and shops along the narrow, charming street, are marked with ornate, wrought-iron signs which make the Getreidegasse picture-postcard perfect.

Here, too, you'll find **Mozart's birthplace**, *Getreidegasse 10*. It was in this bright yellow house that on January 27, 1756 little Wolfgang Amadeus Mozart was born. The museum contains several of the young genius' musical instruments, portraits of the family, and a room recreated in the style of the period of Mozart's childhood. Open Monday through Saturday 9 a.m. to 6 p.m.; from July to September, 9.m. to 7 p.m. Adults 65 schillings; students and seniors 50 schillings; children 15-18, 25 schillings; children six to 14, 20 schillings; families 160 schillings. Conducted tours are available. For more information *call, 662-84-43-13; fax 662-84-06-93.*

At the end of the Getreidegasse is the **Archbishop's Horse Pond**, decorated with a rearing, marble horse and colorful horse frescoes. Built in 1700, the archbishop's horses were led through the water to wash them. Walk down one of the alleys off the Getreidegasse towards the river, cross the pedestrian bridge, and you'll find yourself at the **Mirabell Gardens**. Archbishop Wolf Dietrich constructed the palace for his mistress Salome. The archbishop did not take his vows of chastity too seriously. He and Salome had between 14 or 16 children, depending on who is explaining the history. The palace is open to the public. The extravagant marble staircase festooned with frolicking cherubs is a favorite for wedding pictures, so you'll often see newly married couples getting their picture snapped here.

The gardens were designed by the Baroque master Fischer von Erlach in 1690 in magnificent patterns in plants and flowers. The figures around the central fountain represent the four elements of earth, air, fire, and water, as well as scenes from mythology. There is also a maze and a **hedge theater**, where performances are held during the summer months. Make a stop in the **garden of the dwarfs**. Here you'll seen larger than life versions of dwarfs once kept at the court of the archbishops as curiosities.

Head back towards the river until you reach the **Linzer Gasse**, another famous shopping street, although less upscale than the Getreidegasse. Bearing off to the right is the medieval **Steingasse**. The narrow, quaint street will make you feel as if you've just stepped back in time several centuries. If you continue up the Linzer Gasse, you'll find **St. Sebastian's church**. St. Sebastian's cemetery, in the church courtyard, was designed by Andreas Berteleto in 1600 in the Italian *campo santo* style.

The cemetery provides an interesting contrast to the one belonging to St. Peter's. Mozart's wife, Constanze, and his father, Leopold, are both buried here as is one of the father's of modern medicine, Paracelsus. You'll also see a **mausoleum** dedicated to the Prince Archbishop Wolf Dietrich in the center of the cemetery. The mausoleum is covered in brightly colored tile. The effect is dramatic rather than bizarre, and just one more example of Wolf Dietrich's flamboyance.

Off the Linzer Gasse are several paths leading up the mountain. Lining the path are life-size **Stations of the Cross**, which lead up to the **Kapuzinerberg** mountain. The path is steep, but the view of the city across the river is spectacular.

Museums

If you have time, Salzburg has several smaller, specialized museums. The **Museum of Natural History** and **The Toy Museum** (below) are especially good for children.

The **Carolino Augusteum**, *Museumsplatz 1*, features important archeological finds including mosaics and sculptures from the times of the Romans. The museum also has religious artifacts and paintings from the Middle Ages and Romanesque periods. Five hundred years of musical instruments are also on display. The museum is named for Emperor Franz I's widow, Caroline Augusta. The emperor was fascinated by the local archaeological finds from the garden of the Burglstein Palace, where the earliest Roman artifacts were discovered. The collection was purchased in 1852 for the museum. The museum is open Tuesdays from 9 a.m. to 8 p.m. and Wednesday through Sunday 9 a.m. to 5 p.m. Tours are possible. Tickets cost 40 schillings for adults, 30 schillings for groups and 15 schillings for children. For more information, *call 662-84-31-45; fax 662-84-11-34-10.*

Mozart's Residence, *Mozartplatz 8, Tel. 662-84-43-13; fax 662-84-06-93*, has been newly renovated and recently reopened to the public. Admission is 55 schillings for adults; 45 schillings for seniors and students; 20 schillings for children; 120 schillings for a family ticket. The **Mozart Sound and Film Museum**, *Getreidegasse 14/2, Tel. 662-84-13-69; fax 662-84-06-93*, is open free to the public Tuesday and Friday 9 a.m. to 1 p.m. and Wednesday 1 p.m. to 5 p.m. Guided tours can be arranged in advance.

The **Museum of Natural History**, *Museumsplatz 5, Tel. 662-84-26-53; fax 662-84-79-05*, has a reptile and amphibian house, an aquarium and dinosaur models to entertain children young and young at heart. The museum is open daily from 9 a.m. to 5 p.m. Tours can be arranged. Admission is 45 schillings for adults, 40 schillings for groups and 30 schillings for children and students.

The **National Costume Museum**, *Greisgasse 23/1, Tel. 662-84-31-19*, has traditional Salzburg costumes from the past and present on display. The museum is open Monday through Friday from 10: a.m. to noon and 2 p.m. to 5 p.m. and Saturdays from 10:00 a.m. to noon. Tours available. Tickets cost 30 schillings for adults and 20 schillings for children.

The **Rupertium**, *Wiener-Philharmoniker Gasse 9, Tel. 662-80-42-23-36 or 25-41; 662-80-42-25-42*, features 20th century graphic art, sculpture, photography and painting. The museum is open Tuesdays, Thursdays, Fridays, Saturdays and Sundays from 10 a.m. to 5 p.m. and Wednesdays 10 a.m. to 9 p.m. Conducted tours are available upon request. Adults pay 40 schillings; seniors, students and groups pay 20 schilling; children are free.

The **Salzburg Baroque Museum**, *in the Mirabell Gardens, Tel. 662-87-74-32*, has paintings and models on display from the height of the Baroque period. The museum is open Tuesday through Saturday from 9 a.m. to noon and from 2 p.m. to 5 p.m.; Sundays and holidays 9 a.m. to noon. Guided tours are available. Tickets for adults cost 40 schillings and 20 schillings for seniors, groups and students. Children are free.

The **Toy Museum**, *Burgerspitalgasse 2, Tel. 662-84-75-60*, has a wide variety of toys, arts and crafts, and musical instruments on display to entertain even the most jaded tyke. Every Wednesday afternoon the museum puts on a Punch and Judy puppet show for its youngest visitors. The museum is open Tuesday through Sunday from 9 a.m. to 5 p.m. Tours can be reserved. Tickets cost 30 schillings for adults, 20 schillings for groups and 10 schillings for children.

NIGHTLIFE & ENTERTAINMENT
Concerts

Since Salzburg has the reputation as a city of music, rarely a night goes by without a performance by its most famous son, Mozart. Several concert series feature works by the composer.

The Best of Mozart, *Gotischer Saal, Blasius, Burgerspitalplatz 2*. From the end of May to early November, Thursdays and Saturdays. Concerts begin at 7:30 p.m.; during July and August, performances start at 8:30 p.m. 280 schillings per ticket, including a drink during intermission. These are chamber music concerts by candlelight featuring compositions by Mozart. Another good series is the **Eine Kleine Nachtmusik...**, *Gotischer Saal, Blasius, Burgerspitalplatz 2*. Advent and Christmas concert series. Concerts begin at 7:30 p.m. 270 schillings. Folk music and classical pieces are featured.

If you're in Salzburg during the Christmas season, try the **Mozart-Orchesterkonzerte**, *Grosser Saal, Mozarteum*. December 25, 30, and 31 and January 1. Concerts begin at 7:30 p.m. Tickets range from 280 to 480 shillings. Musicians in period costumes play Mozart movements from his symphonies and instrumental concertos.

For more information on these or other concerts, contact **Salzburger Mozart-Serenanden**, *Lieferinger Hauptstrasse 136. Tel. 662-43-68-70; fax 43-69-70*. Additional information on entertainment is available at local tourist offices, which have monthly list of events in Salzburg and the surrounding region.

If you have the opportunity, try to get tickets to one of the concerts staged in the **Hohensalzburg fortress**. The chamber music is enhanced by the regal surroundings and the grand view of the city behind the musicians. But these concerts generally feature classical standards and may disappoint more serious music lovers. Tickets cost from 300 to 330 schillings. The concerts begin at 8 p.m. in March, April, September and October; 8:30 p.m. from May to August; 7:30 p.m. November through January. For more information, call **Salzburger Festungskonzerte**, *Anton-Adlgasser Weg 22, Tel. 82-58-58; fax 82-58-59.*

Concerts are also held in the **Mirabell Palace** and in the **Archbishop's former residence** as part of the **Salzburger Schlosskonzerte** series. The concerts showcase the talents of many young artists and those of more established international stars. The concerts begin at 8 p.m. in January, February, March, October, November and December; 8:30 p.m. in April, May, June, July, August and September; matinee performances begin at 11 a.m. Tickets range from 300 to 360 schillings. Seating is on a first come, first serve basis. For more information, *call 662-84-85-86; fax 662-84-47-47.*

Performances also take place in the **Mozarteum conservatory** throughout the year. For more information, *call 662-87-29-96; fax 662-87-31-54.* Everyday at 5 p.m. (5:30 p.m. Sundays and holidays) during the summer months, the **Johann Michael Haydn Society** and **St. Peter's church** sponsor concerts highlighting the career of this famous composer. The concerts are held in the Haydn memorial, across from St. Peter's, and are performed by various young artists. For more information, *call 662-841268-0 or 848481.*

Puppet Theater

The **Salzburg Marionette Theater**, *Schwarzstrasse 24, A-5024. Tel. 87-24-06; fax 88-21-41,* is a treat for the entire family. Marionettes perform full-length operas by such renowned composers as Mozart, Strauss, and Rossini. This is an ideal way to introduce youngsters to the joys of opera, but the theater may be inappropriate for very young children, who may not be able to sit through an entire foreign language performance. The theater was founded by the sculptor Anton Aicler. His son Hermann expanded the theater into a world-famous institution. Today, his daughter continues the family tradition, expanding the program and touring around the world with the theater. The box office is open Monday through Sunday 9 a.m. to 1 p.m. and two hours before performances, which begin at 7:30 p.m. All credit cards are accepted.

Gambling

Perched at the top of the **Monchsberg** mountain, the **Salzburg Casino**, *Klessheim Palace, Monchsberg,* offers French and American roulette, black jack, poker, red dog, wheel-of-fortune, sic bo and Baccarat. The palace was originally built for Prince Archbishop Johann Ernest Count Thun in 1700 and designed by the Baroque master Fischer von Erlach. Open daily 3 p.m. until midnight. Free hourly shuttles to the casino are available from the Monchsberg to the Mirabellplatz. An elevator can whisk you from 13 Gstattengasse up through the mountain to the casino. Roundtrip tickets 25 schillings, 15 schillings one way; children 13 schillings roundtrip, 8 schillings one way.

Dinner Shows

Of course, what entertainment section on Salzburg would be complete without at least a mention of the **Sound of Music dinner show**. The menu includes Clear Soup with Cream-Colored Ponies, Schnitzel with Noodles, and Crisp Apple Strudel. And if you stay for the show, you'll be treated to a full rendition of all the schmaltzy favorites from the musical. Although most locals don't seem to have ever actually seen the Julie Andrew's musical, the dinner show is a big favorite with tourists. But expect to dig deep into you pockets for this spectacle.

Dinner, which starts at 7:30 p.m., and the show will set you back 520 schillings for adults and 320 schillings for children ages six to 15. For the show only, tickets cost 360 schillings for adults and 220 schillings for children. Tickets are sold at the door of the Steiglkeller, Festungsgasse 10, from 7 p.m. to 8 p.m. The shows starts at 8:15 p.m. To reserve a place, write to The New Sound of Music, *Petersbrunnstrasse 3 or Tel. 662-84-00-82; fax 662-84-50-21*.

Movies

Like most of Austria, Salzburg doesn't have much in the way of American movies in their original form. But if you're dying to see a movie that hasn't been dubbed head to **Das Kino**, *Gisela-Kai 11. Tel. 87-31-00*, an art house-type theater that presents films in their original languages. A monthly schedule of films is posted at the theater.

SHOPPING

Salzburg has a wide variety of shops, so you can stock on everything from Liederhosen to designer dresses. Be forewarned though, according to Austrian news reports, Salzburg is the most expensive city in the country. You might want to put off your shopping spree to Vienna, where you'll find a better variety and more reasonable prices.

The most famous of Salzburg's shopping street is the **Getreidegasse**, where ornate wrought-iron sign posts set off the shops lining this ancient, narrow street. Even McDonald's is marked with an elaborate wrought-iron sign with a lion, a wreath, and an eagle setting of the famed golden arches. This street is often swarming with tourists and is so crowded that you may have a difficult time making your way through during the festival months of July and August. Try visiting early in the morning or in the evening, after the tourist throngs have died down. Also, when it rains, which is quite often in Salzburg, the crowds thin.

Other shopping areas include **Mozartplatz**, the **Alter Markt**, **Kaigasse**, **Mirabell Square** and the **Linzer Gasse**, across the river dividing the city. Shops are generally open Monday to Friday from 8 a.m. to 6 p.m. Some stores close for lunch, so check the opening hours usually posted on the door. Businesses close early on Saturdays and are usually only open from 8 a.m. to noon. During the festival season, some shops remain open Saturday afternoons, but you'll need to check individual shops for their weekend hours. On the first Saturday of each month, shops keep their doors open until 5 p.m. Shops are closed Sundays and public holidays.

Salzburg has two open air **markets** where you can find local produce, farm-fresh cheeses, fresh baked goodies, sausages and flowers, not to mention kitschy souvenirs galore. A visit to one of the markets is the ideal stop to stock up for a picnic or for a light lunch or dinner if you're tired of eating out. The two markets are **The Grunmarkt**, *Universitatsplatz and Weiner-Philharmoniker Gasse*, Monday to Friday, 6 a.m. to 7 p.m.; Saturday 6 a.m. to 1 p.m; and **The Schranne**, *Andra Church, near the Mirabell Gardens*, Thursdays, 6 a.m. to 1 p.m.

SPORTS & RECREATION

Golf

Golfers won't have to deprive themselves of the game during their trip to Salzburg. **Altentann Golf and Country Club**, *5302 Henndorf. Tel. 6214-60-26; fax 6214-61-05-81*, is 20 kilometers from the city and was designed by the American golf great Jack Nicklaus. Open from April to November.

At the **Klessheim Palace**, *5071 Wals bei Salzburg. Tel. 85-08-51*, the site of the local casino, there is a 9-hole course, which is where the Salzburg Festival Tournament is held. Open from March through November.

Hiking

The Salzburg Tourist Office publishes extensive information on hiking in the city and the surrounding province, including maps and suggested routes. One of the favorite hiking spots of locals is **Untersberg Mountain**. The mountain rises 1,853 meters on the border between Germany and Austria and offers a breath-taking view of Salzburg. Legend has it that the French Emperor Charlemagne, who once ruled over what is now Austria, sleeps deep in the heart of the mountain. Locals claim he will awaken when the empire needs him, and the ravens no longer fly over the mountain. Until then, cable car service will whisk riders to the top of the mountain.

More adventurous travelers may like the challenge of climbing the mountain. Well-marked paths will help you find your way. Be sure to bring your passport, as the mountain straddles the Austrian-German border and depending on which side you descend, you may find yourself across the German border. There are several *Hutte*, or huts, along the way offering fresh milk and cheese to weary hikers for just a few schillings. You'll pass the cows, who provided the milk for your snack, along the way. If a beer or a *radler*, a concoction of beer and lemonade which is actually a lot better than it sounds, is more your speed, there is a guest house at the top of the mountain. The proprietor speaks English since he spends half of his year in Austria and half in Colorado.

The cable car up Untersberg Mountain is operated on the half hour and runs from March through June 9 a.m. to 5 p.m.; July through September from 8:30 a.m. to 5:30 p.m.; October 9 a.m. to 5 p.m. Round-trip tickets for adults cost 200 schillings, ascent only 120 schillings, descent only 100 schillings; children's round-trip tickets cost 90 schillings, ascent only 60 schillings, descent only 50 schillings. For more information, *call 87-12-17.*

The **Pinzgau regional tourist office** also sponsors a program called "Hiking without Luggage." Your things are transported daily to your next accommodations so you can enjoy your day hiking without worrying about logistics. Three week-long tours are available. Contact **Fremdenverkehrsverband**, *A-5760 Saalfelden. Tel. 6582-2513; fax 6582-5398.*

Horseback Riding

If you prefer to see Salzburg on horseback, two places you should contact are: **Reiterhof Moos**, *Moosstrasse 135. Tel. 83-06-90.* The office is open Tuesday through Friday from 3 p.m. to 6 p.m. Closed Mondays; and **Reitzentrum Doktorbauer**, *Eberlingasse 5. Tel. 82-20-65.* Closed Sundays and holidays.

Ice Skating

The ice skating season runs from September 17 to April 1. The best place to go skating is the **Stadtische Kunsteisbahn**, *Hermann Bahr Promenade 2. Tel. 62-34-11-0 or 80-72-22-10; fax 62-34-11-21.*

Skiing

The Salzburg province has some excellent skiing with several resorts within an easy drive of Salzburg. You can do your sightseeing one day and then take a turn at the slopes the next.

Here is a broad selection of great skiing possibilities:

In **Bad Durrnberg**, the **Durrnberg ski area** near Hallein extends into neighboring Germany. There are 20 kilometers of runs ranging from moderate to challenging. The Salzkammergut-Tennengau ski pass can be used here. There is a downhill ski school here if you need to brush up on

your skills. Cross-country skiing, winter hiking, ice skating, paragliding, tobogganing and curling are also possible.
• Contact *Ski Information, Hallein/Bad Durrnberg, A-5400. Tel. 6245-85394; fax 6245-85185-13*

Dachstein-West/Tennengau is a region for serious skiers with more than 100 kilometers of slopes. The Salzkammergut-Tennengau ski pass is valid for all slopes. There are several down hill ski, cross-country ski and snowboarding schools here. for those who would rather try their hand at other winter sporting activities there are ski touring, winter hiking, monoski, swingbo, skibob, paragliding, hang-gliding, horseback riding, tobogganing, curling, ice skating horse-drawn sleigh rides and an indoor pool in Golling.
• In **Abetnau**, contact *Ski Information, Abetnau, A-5441. Tel. 6243-2293-0; fax 6243-2293-20*
• In **Annaberg**, contact *Ski Information, Annaberg, A-5524. Tel. 6463-8125; fax 6463-8118-85*
• In **Russbach**, contact *Ski Information, Russbach, A-5442. Tel. 6242-206; fax 6242-244*
• In **St. Martin**, contact *Ski Information, St. Martin, A-5522. Tel. 6463-7288; fax 6463-7488*
• In **Tennengau-Gesamtinformation**, contact *Tennengau-Gesamtinformation, A-5400 Hallein, Postfach 7. Tel. 6245-84259-0; fax 6245-84259-14*

The area of **Forstau/Fageralm** has 14 kilometers of runs. The resort has a downhill ski school and snowboard instruction and rental. Cross-country skiing, winter hiking, ski races, tobogganing, curling and horse-drawn sleigh rides round out the activities here.
• *Ski Information, Forstau A-5550. Tel. 6454-8325; fax 6454-8439*

In the **Gastein Valley-Grossarl Valley**, a vacation here allows you to go straight from the slopes to a thermal bath. There are 60 groomed runs totalling 200 kilometers. The Gastein Valley-Grossarl Valley region has schools for downhill skiing, cross-country and snowboarding. Ski tour areas, winter hiking, skibob, monoski, swingbo, Telemark, tobogganning, paragliding, hang gliding, horse-back riding, ski races and ice skating can also be done.
• In **Badgastein**, contact *Ski Information, Badgastein A-5640. Tel. 6434-2531-0; fax 6434-2531-37*
• In **Bad Hofgastein**, contact *Ski Information, Bad Hofgastein A-5630. Tel. 6432-7110-0; fax 6432-7110-31*
• In **Dorfgastein**, contact *Ski Information, Dorfgastein A-5632. Tel. 6433-277; fax 6433-637-37*

• În **Grossarl**, contact *Ski Information, Grossarl A-5611. 6414-281 or 625; 6414-8193*

In **Hochkonig**, there are 70 kilometers of slopes with guaranteed snow at the Hochkonig resort. If you need instruction, there are downhill, cross-country and snowboarding lessons available. Ski touring, winter hiking, swingbo, monoski, ice skating, tobogganing, inner tube sledding, curling and horse-drawn sleigh rides all take place here.
• In **Dienten**, contact *Ski Information, Dienten A-5652. Tel. 6461-263; fax 6461-521*
• In **Muhlbach/Hochkonig**, contact *Ski Information, Muhlbach/Hochkonig A-5505. Tel. 6467-7235; fax 6467-7811*

In **Hohe Tauern National Park**, which includes parts of neighboring Tirol and Carinthia, you can take your pick of the following ski resorts: the **Rauris**, the **Uttendorf Weissee**, the **Mittersill, Neukirchen, Wildkogel, Hochkrimml, Gerlosplatte, Wald** and **Konigsleiten**. Downhill ski, cross-country and snowboarding instruction are offered. Winter hiking, ski touring, Telemark, tobogganing, ice skating, paragliding, horseback riding, curling, children's snow parties and races, ski safari, snowrafting, horse-drawn sleigh rides and hay rides can also be enjoyed.
• In **Konigsleiten**, contact *Ski Information, Konigsleiten A-5742. Tel. 6564-8224-0; fax 6564-8224-4*
• In **Krimml**, contact *Ski Information, Krimml A-5743. Tel. 6564-239; fax 6564-550*
• In **Neukirchen Am Grossvenediger**, *contact Ski Information, Neukirchen Am Grossvenediger A-5741. Tel. 6565-6256; fax 6565-6550-74*
• In **Mittersill**, contact *Ski Information, Mittersill A-5730. Tel. 6562-4292 or 93; fax 6562-5007*
• In **Rauris**, contact *Ski Information, Rauris A-5661. Tel. 6544-6237; fax 6544-7049*
• In **Uttendorf/Weissee**, contact *Ski Information, Uttendorf/Weissee A-5723. Tel. 6563-8279; fax 6563-8585*

The **Krispl-Gaissau/Hintersee** ski area is ideal for less advanced skiers. There are 40 kilometers of groomed slopes. You can use the Salzkammergut-Tennengau ski pass to access the trails. There are downhill ski schools in Faistenau, Hintersee, Hof and Krispl Gaissau. Other winter sports you can participate in include snowboarding, cross country, winter hiking, monoski, mini-bob sledding, sledding, horse-drawn sleigh rides and adventure programs.
• In **Hintersee**, contact *Ski Information, Hintersee, A-5324. Tel. 6224-344; fax 6224-217*

• In **Krispl-Gaissau**, contact *Ski Information, Krispl-Gaissau, A-5421. Tel. 6240-414; fax 6240-213-14.*

The **Lofer/Unken-Heutal** is a family-style ski resort featuring 20 runs totalling 47 kilometers. Instruction is offered in downhill skiing, snowboarding and cross- country skiing. Ski touring, winter hiking, tobogganing, swingbo, monoski, Telemark, freestyle, ice skating, curling, ski racing, horse-drawn sleigh rides and ski parties for children are available.
• Contact *Ski Information, Lofer A-5090. Tel. 6588-321-0; fax 6588-7464*

The **Langau** resort is located in the sunniest basin in the country and is easily accessible from the Tauern motorway. There are 200 kilometers of runs in four different areas. Downhill, cross-country and snowboarding instruction are possible. Ski touring, winter hiking, swingbo, Telemark, tobogganing, ice skating, night skiing, horse-drawn sleigh rides and curling are all available here.
• In **Mariapfarr**, contact *Ski Information, Mariapfarr A-5571. Tel. 6473-8278; fax 6473-7347*
• In **Mauterndorf**, contact *Ski Information, Mauterndorf A-5570. Tel. 6472-7279; fax 6472-7657*
• In **Ramingstein-Karneralm**, contact *Ski Information, Ramingstein-Karneralm A-5591. Tel. 6476-290; fax 6476-527*
• In **St. Michael**, contact *Ski Information, St. Michael A-5582. 6477-342; fax 6477-309*
• In **Weisspriach**, contact *Ski Information, Weisspriach A-5571. Tel. 6473-7034*

The **Maria Alm/Saalfelden** area has new snow-making equipment in case Mother Nature fails to cover its 90 kilometers of slopes. Students can take lessons in downhill skiing, cross country skiing and snowboarding. Ski touring, winter hiking, swingbo, monoski, Telemark, ice skating, tobogganing, curling, horse-drawn sleigh rides and inner tube sledding possible.
• In **Maria Alm**, contact *Ski Information, Maria Alm A-5761. 6584-7816; fax 6584-7600*
• In **Saalfelden**, contact *Ski Information, Saalfelden A-5760. 6582-2513; fax 6582-5398*

The **Pongauer Sonnenterrasse** combines skiing and winter recreation with cultural events at the Goldegg Castle and spa facilities. There are 12 kilometers of ski runs in the area, and schools in the area for down hill, cross country and snowboarding. You can also participate in winter

hiking, ice skating, horseback riding, tobogganing, curling and ice disco.
• Contact *Ski Information, Goldegg A-5622. Tel. 6415-8131; fax 6415-8580*

The world-famous ski area of **Saalbach Hinterglemm-Leogang Ski Circus** is the host of the World Championships in Alpine Skiing. There are 280 kilometers of runs for every level. The Ski Circus allows visitors to use interconnected lift systems in Leogang and Viehhofen. Downhill, cross-country, and snowboarding instruction are available. Other sporting opportunities include ski touring, winter hiking, monoski, swingbo, Telemark, freestyle, ice skating, tobogganing, snow rafting, curling and horse-drawn sleigh rides.
• In **Leogang**, contact *Ski Information, Leogang A-5771. Tel. 6583-234; fax 6583-7302*
• In **Saalbach Hinterglemm**, contact *Ski Information, Saalbach Hinterglemm A-5753. Tel. 6541-7272; fax 6541-7900*

In the **Salzburger Sport Amade**, one pass enables you to use the 120 lifts at this enormous ski area. There are 320 kilometers of runs connecting three valleys. Schools for both downhill and cross country are available. Winter hiking, snowboarding, monoski, freestyle, ice skating, horseback riding, paragliding, timed slalom course, racing, night-skiing, snowrafting, curling, horse-drawn sleigh rides, curling and hot air ballooning are all possible.
• In **Altenmarkt/Zauchensee**, contact *Ski Information, Altenmarkt/Zauchensee A-5541. Tel. 6452-5511 or 5611; fax 6452-6066*
• In **Eben/Pongau**, contact *Ski Information, Eben/Pongau A-5531. Tel. 6464-8194; fax 6464-8595*
• In **Filmoos**, contact *Ski Information, Filmoos, A-5532. Tel. 6453-235 or 500; fax 6453-685*
• In **Flachau**, contact *Ski Information, Flachau A-5542. Tel. 6457-2214; fax 6457-2536*
• In **Kleinarl** , contact *Ski Information, Kleinarl A-5602. Tel. 6418-206; fax 6418-364*
• In **Radstadt**, contact *Ski Information, Radstadt A-5550. Tel. 6452-305 or 7472; fax 6452-6702*
• In **St. Johann-Alpendorf**, contact *Ski Information, St. Johann-Alpendorf. Tel. 6412-6036-0; fax 6412-6036-74*
• In **Wagrain**, contact *Ski Information, Wagrain A-5602. Tel. 6413-8265 or 8448; fax 6413-8449*

Tennenbebirge is where Olympic gold medalist Petra Kronberger learned to ski. There are 40 kilometers of slopes at varying levels of difficulty. Downhill and cross-country skiing and snowboarding instruction are possible. Touring, winter hiking, monoskiing, paragliding, hang gliding, curling, tobogganing, bowling and horse-drawn sleigh rides also are available.

• Contact *Ski Information, A-5453 Werfenweng. Tel. 6466-420; 6466-581-72*

The **Untersberg** run in Grodig may be the ideal choice if you're staying in Salzburg and don't want to travel too far for your skiing. The 7.5 kilometer run is challenging. Salzburg has a ski school which also offers instruction in snowboarding. Cross-country skiing, winter hiking, ice skating, tobogganning, curling and horse-drawn sleigh rides are available, too.

• Contact *Ski Information, Grodig A-5083. Tel. 6246-73570; 6246-74795*

You can go glacier skiing (on the Kitzsteinhorn) year round at the **Zell Am See-Europa Sport Region Kaprun**. Ski runs in the area total 130 kilometers. Free ski buses run between Kaprun, Zell am See, Bruck, Fusch, Niedersill, Piesendorf and Maishofen. Several downhill ski, cross country and snowboarding schools are available. Visitors can participate in ski touring, winter hiking, Telemark, monoski, freestyle, horse-back riding, ice skating, saunas, tobogganning, horse-drawn sleigh rides, curling, bowling, sightseeing plane rides, skiing play grounds and ski races.

• In **Kaprun**, contact *Ski Information, Kalprun A-5710. Tel. 6547-8643-0; fax 6547-8192*
• In **Zell Am See**, contact *Ski Information, Zell Am See A-5700. Tel. 6542-2600-0; fax 6542-2032*

Tennis
If you're in Salzburg in warmer weather, several courts are available. **Salzburger Tennis Club**, *Ignaz-Rieder Kai 3, A-5020 Salzburg. Tel. 662-62-24-03*, is open May through October; and the **Salzburger Tennis Courts Sud**, *Berchtesgadener Strasse 35, A-5020 Salzburg. Tel. 662-82-03-26*, is open April through October.

DAY TRIPS & EXCURSIONS
Anif
Although you won't find it in the information from the tourist office, **Anif** is the home of the famed **Water Castle**, which look likes it stepped out of the pages of a fairytale. From 1693 to 1814, the castle was the summer residence of the Prince-Archbishop of Chiemsee. The castle was later reconstructed in the romantic style. Unfortunately, the castle is privately owned, so you won't be able to get a close-up view, but you can

see it through a clearing from the roadway. Just look for the other tourists snapping their pictures.

Take the Salzburg-Sud autobahn in the direction of Anif. The castle is right in the center of town near the tourist office. Anif is also the home of several lovely hotels listed in the *Where to Stay* section above if you'd like to be away from Salzburg's crowds during the high season. If you don't have a car, the city is easily accessible by Bundesbus, which leave for Salzburg every 30 minutes.

Anif is seven kilometers south of Salzburg. **Anif Tourist Information Office**, *Alpenstrasse, A-5081 Anif. Tel. 6246-2365; fax 6246-432522.*

Hallein

Hallein is in the heart of the Tennegau region of the Salzburg province. The city used to be the ancient salt capital of the area. Hallein was home to an important Celtic settlement because of its salt and its location along the prehistoric route through the Salzach Valley. Today, visitors can visit an open air museum on the Durrnberg mountain with a reconstruction of how life may have once been for these early people. A **Celtic Museum** is located in the city.

Of course, many people visit Hallein's **Durrnberg mountain** to see the salt mines. You'll be given a change of clothes to protect you from the cold, take a miners' "railroad" into the mountain, slide down a mineshaft and sail an underground lake. The philosopher Stendhal reportedly developed his theory of crystallization after visiting the mines here in 1810. You can also take the cure at several different sites in Hallein from bathing in brine to inhalations for respiratory ailments.

If you're driving, take the Tauern motorway south towards Villach and take the Hallein exit, which is about 15 kilometers outside of Salzburg. The federal road also runs between Salzburg and Hallein. A Bundesbus, leaving from in front of Salzburg's train station, will also take you to Hallein. Trains also run between the two cities For more information, contact the **Hallein Tourist Information**, *Unterer Markt 1, A-5400 Hallein. Tel. 6245-5394; fax 6245-85-185-13.*

Hellbrun

If you are traveling with children, **Hellbrun**, the summer residence of Salzburg's archbishops, is a destination not to be missed. Prince-Archbishop Markus Sittikus commissioned the Italian architect Santino Solari to build him a Renaissance palace in the Italian style. The palace has a reputation of one of the most remarkable Renaissance buildings north of the Alps, noted for its main hall and octagonal room with wall and ceiling paintings by Arsenio Mascagni.

But the residence is not the major attraction. Most visitors come to see the famed **Wasserspiele**, or water games, which continue to amaze modern visitors. The water games can only be seen through guided tours. The first thing you'll see is a stone banquet table and stone chairs. The Prince-Archbishop had a sense of humor, having rigged the benches to shoot out water to the seats of his unsuspecting guests, who were not allowed to stand until the archbishop got up. Intricate city scenes magically come to life, propelled by the water flowing from springs from nearby Hellbrun mountain. Other surprises await you in shell encrusted rooms, grottos, and water-rigged statues. Be prepared to get wet.

Be sure to walk around the extensive gardens, which make the perfect spot for a picnic on a nice day. Bring along some extra bread to feed the ducks and swans in one of the several palace pools. The white gazebo you see here was used in *The Sound of Music* for the scene where the eldest Von Trapp daughter danced and sang with her Nazi boyfriend. The castle and trick fountains are open in April and October from 9 a.m. to 4:30 p.m. and May to September from 9 a.m. to 5 p.m. Evening tours during July and August are held hourly from 6 p.m. to 10 p.m. Tours last about 40 minutes. Tickets cost 48 schillings for adults, 43 schillings for groups and 24 schillings for children. The park and orangerie are open free to the public. For more information, *call 82-03-72-0; fax 82-03-72-31. The area code is the same as Salzburg's: 662.*

If you visit the Hellbrun on a Friday from May to mid-September, stay to enjoy a concert featuring chamber pieces, arias, and duets by Mozart performed inside the palace. The concerts begin at 7:30 p.m.; during July and August performances start at 8:30 p.m. Music lovers can get a bite to eat during intermission at a buffet included in the ticket price. A nighttime tour of the water gardens is available after the concert for an additional 50 schillings. Concert tickets sell for 300 schillings a piece.

Paths lead from Hellbrun's park to the nearby **Folklore Museum**, *Monatsschlosschen, Tel. 82-03-72-21,* and the **Hellbrunn Zoo**. The museum is housed in the "Month Castle," nicknamed for the few months it took to build under the direction of Archbishop Markus Sitikus. Traditional costumes, religious folk art, and folk medicine are displayed in the collection here. The view of the Hellbrun gardens is also spectacular. The museum is open from April through October from 9 a.m. to 5 p.m., and tours are available upon request. Admission to the museum is 20 schillings for adults, groups 15 schillings and children 10 schillings. The zoo, which has a variety of native Austrian animals on display, is open from October through March 8:30 a.m. to 4 p.m. and from April through September 8:30 a.m. to 6 p.m. Tours are available. Ticket cost 60 schillings for adults, 50 schillings for groups, 35 schillings for students and 25 schillings for children.

Krimml Waterfall

The **Krimml Waterfall** is Europe's highest, with the falls starting at 1,470 meters up the mountain. You can take an easy four kilometer hike to the top of the falls, which has several overlooks along the way if you need to take a breather. The view of the enormous stream of rushing water is really quite spectacular and worth a side trip if you have the time. For sports enthusiasts, Krimml offers 60 kilometers of marked hiking trails, the beginning of the Tauern bike path, fishing, miniature golf, paragliding, tennis courts, swimming, sailing and surfing.

The Krimml Waterfalls are 153 kilometers southwest of Salzburg. **National Park Information, Salzburg Regional Office,** *5741 Neukirchen am Grossvenediger Nr. Tel. 306. 6564-239.*

Leopoldskron

The Rococo palace of **Leopoldskron** was built by the Prince Arch-bishop Leopold Anton Firmian in 1736. Musical buffs will also recognize it as yet another set from *The Sound of Music* used as the family home. Max Reinhardt, one of the founders of the famed Salzburg Festival, later owned Leopoldskron. The palace is now used as a conference center and is available for rental for seminars, banquets, and other large events.

During the festival, at Christmas and Easter, the palace functions as a hotel. If you're not lucky enough to be staying there, you still can get a good view of it across the lake where there are benches set up. Skating is possible on the lake during the winter. Leopoldskron is one of the few sights in Salzburg accessible by car and is located behind the Hohensalzburg Fortress. The palace is also easily reached, too, by either foot or bike with well-marked paths.For more information, contact **Schloss Leopoldskron,** *Conference Center, Leopoldskronstrasse 56-58, A-5010 Salzburg. Tel. 662-839830; fax 662-839837.*

Maria Plain

Finished in 1674, this two-towered baroque church is perched on a hill just outside the city limits in Bergheim bei Salzburg. The interior is decorated in blue and gold with lots of ornate Rococo sculptures, paintings, and the usual flourishes. The view from the church yard affords a spectacular view of the city.

Maria Plain is just outside Salzburg's city limits and is easily accessible by car. Or you can take local bus number 6 to the end of the line and walk about a kilometer to the church. You can stay just next door in style at the **Gasthof Plain** (see *Where to Stay,* above).

Mautendorf Castle

The **Mautendorf Castle** is in the Langau region in the southeastern tip of the Salzburg province. The site was on an ancient Roman road and was first used as a customs point a thousand years ago. The Salzburg archbishops later built a castle here in the 13th century.

The castle is open during July and August, 10 to noon and 3 p.m. and 5 p.m. (closed Tuesdays); June and September, open Saturday and Sunday, 3 p.m. to 5 p.m. It is possible to tour the castle with an advance reservation; call 6472-7425. For more information, contact A-5580 Tamsweg, POB 57. Tel. 6474-6284; fax 6474-7434.

Werfen

The **Hohenwerfen fortress** and the Eisriesenwelt are in the Pongau region of Salzburg province. The incredibly preserved fortress built for the clergy in the 11th century rises over the Salzach Valley. The fortress contains a chapel, torture chamber, and bell tower that makes an especially good tour if you're traveling with children. Trainers in period costume put on daily demonstrations with birds of prey. The fortress is open April and November from 9:30 a.m. to 4 p.m.; May, June, September, October, 9 a.m. to 5 p.m.; July and August 9 a.m. to 6 p.m.; closed Mondays. Admission is 100 schillings for adults; 90 schillings for seniors and 50 schillings for children. The bird of prey demonstrations are at 11 a.m. and 3 p.m.; July and August, 11 a.m., 2 p.m. and 4 p.m. For more information, call 6468-7603; fax 6468-7603-4.

The **Eisriesenwelt** is the largest ice cave in the province. You can only visit the caves with a guided tour, which takes a bit more than an hour to complete. You'll also need to take a cable car up to the caves. A roundtrip ticket including admission to the cave costs 180 shillings; 90 shillings for children. Or you can hike up the mountain. Admission to the caves is 80 shillings for adults and 40 shillings for children. Make sure to wear warm cloths and sturdy shoes no matter what time of year you make your visit. You can park at the cable railway valley station if you drive. If you're coming by train, there is a taxi-bus service to the cable car. Or you can walk from Werfen to the station, but it takes about an hour and a half. For more information about the caves, contact Getreidegasse 21, A-5020 Salzburg. Tel. 662-842690 or 291.

The Pongau region is also is home to the **Goldegg Castle**. If you prefer to see the glories of nature, then visit the **Gastein Waterfall**. Perhaps you need to seek the cure after all this sightseeing. The thermal baths in Bad Hofgastein will sooth away aching muscles and relax you. From Salzburg, take the Tauern motorway south in the direction of Villach and take the Werfen exit. The federal road going south towards

Hallein and Golling will also take you past Werfen. For more information, contact the **Salzburg State Board of Tourism**, *A-5033 Salzburg, POB 8/II. Tel. 662-620506-0; fax 662-623070.*

Wildpark Ferleiten

If you're traveling with children, the **Wildpark Ferleiten**, *Tel. 6546-220*, makes a nice detour. Here you can see alpine animals, from deer to bears to birds of prey. Paths take you through the park to the various animals on display. There is also a children's playground with bumper cars, a kiddie train, and a carousel. This is really only an attraction for children, so skip it otherwise.

To get to the park, take the Grossglockner road south of Salzburg, get off at Ferleiten and follow the signs.

PRACTICAL INFORMATION

American Express Office

You can change money, buy tickets, and book bus tours through the office here. **American Express**, *Mozartplatz 5, A-5020 Salzburg. Tel. 662-842-501; fax 662-842-501-90*. Open Monday to Friday 9 a.m. to 5:30 p.m.; Saturday 9 a.m. to noon.

Babysitting

Babysitting services are available through the **Austrian Students' Association**, *Kaigasse 28, A-5020 Salzburg. Tel. 662-8044-6001 or 02*

Bookstores

You won't have any problems in Salzburg finding a good selection of English-language publications from newspapers to magazines to best sellers. Here are a few bookstores to browse, but most bookstores will have some English-language selections.

- **American Discount**, *Alter Markt 1, A-5020 Salzburg. Tel. 843-89-32*
- **Bucher Stierle**, *Kaigasse 1, Mozartplatz, A-5020 Salzburg. Tel. 840113 or 14*
- **Buch und Press Ambahnhof Salzburg**, *Filiale S1 Bahnohof, main train station, A-5020 Salzburg. Tel. 87-73-32; fax 87-73-32-4*
- **Hollrigl**, *Sigmund Haffner Gasse 10, A-5020 Salzburg. Tel. 84-11-46 or 84-26-51*

Consulates

- **United States Consulate**, *Herbert Von Karajan Platz 1, A-5020 Salzburg. Tel. 84-87-76; fax 84-97-77*. Open Monday, Wednesday and Friday from 9 a.m. to noon.
- **British Consulate**, *Alter Markt 4, A-5020 Salzburg. Tel. 84-81-33*. Open Monday through Friday from 9 a.m. to noon.

Credit Cards

If your credit cards are lost or stolen, you can call the following numbers 24 hours a day to make a report. The numbers are located in Vienna, so first dial area code *0222*.
- **American Express**, *Tel. 51-29-714*
- **Diners**, *Tel. 50-1-35*
- **Mastercard**, *Tel. 71-7-01-0*
- **Visa**, *Tel. 53-4-87-77*

Emergency Phone Numbers
- **Ambulance**, *Tel. 144*
- **Police**, *Tel. 133*
- **Fire Department**, *Tel. 122*

Exchanging Money

In general, local banks are open Monday to Friday, 8:30 a.m. to 12:30 p.m. and 2 p.m. to 4:30 p.m. Banks are closed Saturdays, Sundays and public holidays.

You can also change money at the following places:
- **Main Train Station**, *Sudtiroler Platz 1, A-5020 Salzburg. Tel. 662-871-377.* Summer daily 7:30 a.m. to 9 p.m. Winter daily 7:30 a.m. to 9 p.m. Money transfers can be made using Diners, Eurocard, Mastercard, Visa or Western Union.
- **Salzburg Airport**, *Salzburger Sparkasse, Innsbrucker Bundesstrasse 95. Tel. 852-088.* Open daily 8 a.m. to 4 p.m. Money transfers can be made using Eurocard, Mastercard and Visa. After business hours, exchanges can be made at the airport information counter *(Tel. 662-852-091)*.

Guided Tours

City tours, lasting an hour, in English and German are available through the local **tourist office** at *Mozartplatz 5. Tel. 889-87-332; fax 889-87-342.* The tours begin at 12:15 p.m. daily except for Sundays. Tours in German cost 1,320 schillings and 1,450 schillings in other languages.

Several private companies operate walking and bus tours of Salzburg, including the ubiquitous **Sound of Music tours**. Since the principal sights in Salzburg are best explored by foot, a bus tour is recommended only if your time is extremely limited. Try the following:
- **Panorama Tours**, *Schrannengasse 2/2/25, A-5020 Salzburg. Tel. 83-32-11-0; fax 87-16-18*; also at *Mirabellplatz, St. Andra Kirche. Tel. 87-40-29; fax 63-24-17.* In the U.S., you can call toll free at *1-800-982-7969*. Cancellations can be made up to four hours in advance. Hotel pick-up is possible.

• **Salzburg Guide**, *Mozartplatz 5, A-5020 Salzburg. Tel. 842501-8080.*
• **Salzburg Sightseeing Tours**, *Mirabellplatz 2, A-5020 Salzburg. Tel. 88-16-16; fax 87-87-76.*

Laundry

If you need to do your laundry in Salzburg and your hotel does not have the facilities, you can visit the following laundromats:
• **Constructa**, *Kaiserschtzenstrasse 10, A-5020 Salzburg, opposite the main train station. Tel. 876-253*
• **Team Textil Reinigung**, *Paris-Lodron Strasse 16, A-5020 Salzburg. Tel. 876-381*
• **Westinghouse Laundromat**, *Kaiserschutzenstrasse 18, A-5020 Salzburg opposite the main train station. Tel. 873-390*

Luggage Storage

You can leave your luggage at the **Main Train Station**, *Sudtiroler Platz 1, A-5020 Salzburg. Tel. 872-746.* The luggage storage desk is open 24 hours a day.

Medical Treatment

If you have a medical emergency in Salzburg during off-hours when a regular doctor may not be available, help is available at *Paris-Lodron Strasse 8a*. Medical staff is on duty from 7 p.m. on Friday to 7 a.m. on Monday and on public holidays.

Pharmacies

Pharmacies are typically open Monday to Friday from 8 a.m. to 12:30 p.m. and 2:30 to 6 p.m.; Saturdays 8 a.m. to noon. Some pharmacies are open during lunch, at night and on weekends and holidays. Closed pharmacies post in their windows the name, address and number of the nearest open pharmacy in case of emergencies.

Police

• **Police Headquarters**, *Alpenstrasse 90. Tel. 63-80-0; fax 6383-4409*

Post Offices

Post offices are located at **Makartplatz** and at **Residentzplatz**. Not only can you find the stamps to send your postcards home, but you can also send faxes, buy phone cards to use at pay phones so you don't have to hunt for change, or make calls and pay the fee after you've finished. Post offices are open from 8 a.m. to 7 p.m.

The post office at **Sudtiroler Platz**, *next to the Main Train Station*, is open 24 hours a day if you need to post something after hours.

Religious Services

The Salzburg tourist office publishes a listing of religious services, addresses, and times. A Lutheran service in English is held at 11 a.m. every second and fourth Sunday in the common room of the **Parish House**, *Evangelische Kirche, Scwarzstrasse 25. Tel. 519902 or 621412.*

Weather

For the latest weather information, *call 15-66.*

Winter Vacation Information

If you need information on snow conditions or other winter holiday tips, contact the **Winterlauber Information**, *Tel. 81-91-0.* Open December through April, Monday to Saturday from 7:30 a.m. to noon.

17. INNSBRUCK & TIROL

INTRODUCTION

When you think of **Innsbruck** and the province of **Tirol**, images come to mind of snowcapped mountains, Alpine chalets, and great skiing. That stereotypical picture is in fact the reality. No wonder Hapsburg Emperor Maximilian I decided to move Austria's capital to Innsbruck. *Tirol is a coarse peasant's dress with lots of folds, but it keeps you nice and warm*, the emperor proclaimed.

The Romans first settled the region more than 2,000 years ago, calling the area *Veldidena*. What would become Innsbruck was strategically important because of its location on the Via Claudia Augusta, the important north-south trading route. Innsbruck gets its name from the first bridge, or *Bruck* in German, over the **River Inn**, which was constructed more than 800 years ago. The Hapsburg monarch Maximilian fell in love with the city and made it his royal seat.

The region is a skier's paradise. Tirol was the site of the 1964 and 1976 Winter Olympics. Today, the province attracts hordes of tourists, and, in fact, Tirol takes in more foreign tourist dollars than any other part of Austria. But don't worry, there are more than enough slopes for everyone. There are nearly 600 mountains in the province, the highest being the **Wildspitze** rising 3,774 meters into the heavens.

Don't feel shortchanged if you visit during the summer. There is extensive hiking, biking, golfing, and other recreational activities in Tirol during the summer months, not to mention castles and monasteries.

Tirol is 4,882 square miles wide and has a population of 639,701 residents. The province is the third largest in the country. Because of its mountainous terrain, only 13 percent of the land is inhabited and most inhabitants are concentrated in the **Inn Valley** and neighboring valleys.

ORIENTATION

If you stay overnight in Innsbruck, you can ask for a **club card** from your hotel or pension which entitles you to various discounts at museums, restaurants and other sites throughout the city. The **Innsbruck-Igls Visitor's Card**, offered through the *Innsbruck Tourist Office, Burggraben 3, Tel. 512-53-56,* will enable you to visit all museums, use free public transportation for one day, and take a round-trip on either the Patscherkofel Cable Car or the Nordkette Cable Car to Seegrube.

The **area code** for Innsbruck is *512.* You need to dial a zero before the area code if you are calling from another region in Austria.

SPECIALTY LODGING IN TIROL: KIDS, FARMS, & ZIMMERS

*If you are traveling with children, the **Tirol Information Office** publishes a brochure listing hotels in the province catering specifically to kids. There are also specialized brochures for fishermen, bikers, golfers, hikers and, of course, skiers. Tirol Information, Wilhelm Greil Strasse 17, A-6020 Innsbruck. Tel. 512-5320; fax 512-5320-174.*

*If you're interested in staying at a Tirolean farm house, contact **Holidays on a Farmstead**, Information and Reservations, Adamgasse 3-7, A-6020 Innsbruck. 512-Tel. 561882.*

*Accommodations in private homes are also available. **Zimmers**, or private rooms, are usually a bargain. You'll receive a warm welcome and a hearty breakfast and a chance to see how real Austrians live. For more information, contact **Verband der Privatzimmervermieter Tirols**, Adamgasse 2A, A-6020 Innsbruck. Tel. 512-587748.*

ARRIVALS & DEPARTURES

By Air

Innsbruck has its own **airport** at *Furstenweg 180, Tel. 512-25252.* Bus F takes you from the airport into the city. If you need a taxi, *call 1718.* The taxi trip into the old town will cost you between 100 to 150 schillings.

For international travelers, the closest airport is in Munich. It takes about two hours to drive from Munich to Innsbruck taking the A1 autobahn.

Shuttle bus service is also available through the **Four Seasons Travel Company**, *Mullerstrasse 14. Tel. 58-41-57; fax 58-57-67.* Reservations are recommended. Buses leave from the Olympic Ice Stadium at 2 a.m., 3 a.m., 4:30 a.m., 10 a.m.. 11:30 a.m. and 4 p.m. Shuttles leave from Munich airport at 7 a.m., 9 a.m., 11 a.m., 2 p.m., 3 p.m. and 8 p.m. A one way ticket costs 420 schillings.

By Train

There are daily train connections to Innsbruck from Vienna, Salzburg, and other major cities around Austria. The **Westbahnstrecke** running from Bregenz to Vienna is operated at two hour intervals. Most major European cities have direct train service to the city as well. For Austrian railway information, *call 1717*.

The **train station** is within walking distance to the old section of Innsbruck. There is also a taxi stand just outside the station to whisk you to your hotel if you prefer.

By Bus

The **bus terminal** is next to the Main Train Station in Innsbruck.

By Car

Innsbruck is easily accessible by car. Take the Brenner motorway if you are traveling north from Italy. The Inn Valley Motorway enters the city if you are coming from the east, north, or west. Coming from Salzburg, 118 miles northeast, or Vienna, 293 miles northeast, take the autobahn heading west. You will actually pass through part of Germany on your way to Innsbruck, so make sure you have your passport with you.

GETTING AROUND INNSBRUCK

By Bike

Riding your bike is a great way to get around Innsbruck (See the *Sports & Recreation* section later in this chapter). If you haven't brought your own set of wheels, you can rent one from:
- **Innsbruck Main Railway Station**, *Innsbruck. Tel. 503-53-85*
- **City Mountainbikerental**, *Insstrasse 95, Innsbruck. Tel. 28-65-15*

By Car

It's best to make arrangements to rent a car back home, where the rates are substantially cheaper. Here are the local car rental offices in Innsbruck.
- **Avis**, *Tourist Center, 6020 Salurner Strasse 15. Tel. 57-17-54; fax 57-71-49; at the airport, Tel. 57-17-54.*
- **Budget**, *Michael-Gaismayr Strasse 7. Tel. 58-84-68; fax 58-45-80; at the airport, Tel. 28-71-81.*
- **Europcar**, *Salurnerstrasse 8. Tel. 58-20-60; fax 58-20-60-9; at the airport Tel. 58-20-60.*

If you need emergency car help, you can call 24 hours a day the **Automobile, Motorcycle, and Touring Association** at *120*, or the **Automobile, Motorcycle, and Bicycle Association of Austria** at *123*.

If you're traveling during the winter months, some roads may be closed because of snow or ice conditions. Others will be open only to vehicles with snow chains. The automobile clubs listed above can give you the latest road information, so check before setting off.

Short-term **street parking** for up to 90 minutes is available in posted parking zones in Innsbruck. A half an hour of parking costs 5 schillings. Tickets can be purchased from vending machines or at the *Innsbruck Information Office, Burggraben 3.*

There are several **parking garages** in Innsbruck where you can leave your car and then explore the city.
- **Hotel Maria Theresia**, *Erlerstrasse. Open 24 hours a day*
- **Sparkassen Garage**, *Sparkassenplatz 1. Open Monday through Friday 7 a.m. to 8 p.m.; Saturday 8 a.m. to 1 p.m.*
- **Tourist Centre**, *Salurnstrasse 15. Open 24 hours a day*
- **Landhausplatz Garage**, *Wilhelm Greil Strasse. Open daily 7 a.m. to 1 a.m.*

By Horse-Drawn Carriage

If you'd like to see Innsbruck from a horse-drawn carriage, you can rent a ride in front of the **Landestheater** in the square. A half-hour carriage trip will cost about 300 schillings.

By Public Transportation

In Innsbruck, you can purchase tickets on **street cars** or **buses** from the driver. Single tickets cost 18 schillings, a block of four tickets costs 44 schillings, an all-day ticket costs 23 schillings and a weekly ticket costs 105 schillings. Tickets are slightly discounted if you buy them ahead from a Tabak-Trafik, a news kiosk, or the tourist information office. Zone 1 tickets are good for the city center. Tickets for zone 2 are good also in Hungerburg, Igls, Rum, and Thaur.

You are entitled to reduced ticket prices if you traveled to Innsbruck by train, Bundesbus, or a bus run by the national railway system.

Buses to other parts of Tirol leave regularly from the **main bus terminal**, *Kaiserjagerstrasse*, which is located next to the main train station. Tickets can be purchased from the driver.

For skiers, buses are also operated between the various resorts and Innsbruck so you can leave your car behind. Ski bus service is available to and from 185 Tirolean ski villages.

By Taxi

To order a cab in Innsbruck, *call 5311 or 45-5-00.* Elsewhere in Tirol, *call 17-18.*

WHERE TO STAY

Tirol has a wide range of accommodations depending on what you are looking for. You can find a good selection of luxury hotels and more intimate inns in Innsbruck if you want to use the provincial capital as your base, which is a nice way to get to know the area. You can explore this important historic city and then head to the mountains for hiking or skiing. Of course, there are ski chalets, pensions, and even *Schloss*, or castle hotels, servicing the various resorts across Tirol.

Below are a selection of hotels from around the region, beginning with Innsbruck. Many local tourist offices at your destination can also help you find accommodations. Many of the hotels listed below have fine restaurants attached to them. In addition to the *Where to Eat* section below, consider some of these restaurants when choosing a place to eat.

Innsbruck

GASTHOF HOTEL WEISSES KREUZ, *Herzog Friedrich Strasse 31, A-6020 Innsbruck. Tel. 512-59479; fax 512-594-7990. Doubles start at 370 schillings per person. Mastercard, Visa and American Express accepted.*

Wolfgang Amadeus Mozart arrived at this hotel on December 15, 1769, before traveling to Italy. You will be equally welcomed today when you visit the Weisses Kreuz in the heart of the city's historic section. The hotel is decorated with traditional, sturdy rustic furnishings. Rooms are comfortable and light filled. The hotel also has a good restaurant serving stick-to-your-ribs Austrian specialties in a cozy, homey setting. The dining room is filled with lots of carved wood furniture and folk art. Parking is available at the hotel's garage for an additional 100 schillings.

HOTEL CENTRAL, *Gilmstrasse 5, A-6020 Innsbruck. Tel. 512-5920; fax 512-58-03-10. Doubles start at 1,400 schillings, including breakfast. All credit cards accepted.*

The Hotel Central is a delightful 87 room establishment. The staff bends over backward to help guests. The hotel is furnished with modern and art deco touches and achieves an understated elegance. A sauna, steam bath, and fitness room are also available to guests.

In addition, the hotel has a delightful cafe, open from 8 a.m. to 11 p.m., with a real old-world atmosphere where you can leisurely linger over coffee and a piece of cake. The hotel restaurant serves such dishes as sliced beef with ham and mushrooms, cheese fritters with cabbage salad and three different kinds of *Knodels*.

HOTEL EUROPA TYROL, *Sudtiroller Platz 2, A-6020 Innsbruck. Tel. 512-5931; fax 512-587800. Doubles start at 1,350 schillings per person, including breakfast. All credit cards accepted.*

The only five-star hotel in Innsbruck, the Hotel Europa Tyrol is located just across from the main train station. The 125 rooms of the hotel, which originally opened in 1869, are elegantly furnished with thick carpets, tasteful fabrics, and comfortable furniture. The hotel also has a sauna, steam bath, and solarium for their guests to unwind.

Europa Stuberl, the hotel's award-winning restaurant, is decorated in a traditional Tirolean style and features regional specialties using local ingredients – a must for both local and foreign gourmets.

HOTEL INTERNATIONALES STUDENTENHAUS, *Rechengasse 7, A-6020 Innsbruck. Tel. 512-501-0; fax 512-501-15. Doubles start at 420 schillings. All credit cards accepted.*

If you're planning your trip to Innsbruck during the summer months through October and you're looking for a real bargain, the International Student House is the place for you. The rooms are clean and comfortable, but have all the charm of a dorm room, which they are during the rest of the year. Breakfast is available, and the staff is cheerful and helpful. There is even free parking on-site. The hotel is about a 10 minute walk from the sights in the old town.

HOTEL MARIA THERESIA, *Maria Theresien Strasse 31, A-6020 Innsbruck. Tel. 512-5933; fax 512-575619. Doubles start at 1,500 schillings, including breakfast. American Express, Visa and Diners accepted.*

The Hotel Maria Theresia is a member of the Best Western chain, but doesn't live up to the usually high standards of service found at most of their hotels. The staff is brusque and inattentive. The large rooms are pleasantly furnished. Each has a minibar, radio, hairdryer, and cable television. The hotel's restaurant, serving standard Austrian cuisine, is open from 7:30 a.m. to 6:30 p.m. The hotel has a private garage for guests at an additional cost of 140 schillings a day.

HOTEL MAXIMILIAN, *Marktgraben 7-9, A-6020 Innsbruck. Tel. 512-59967; fax 512-577450. Doubles start at 520 schillings per person, including breakfast. All credit cards.*

The Hotel Maximilian is run by the Penz family and is located just outside the old city. The rooms are somewhat small though comfortably furnished, but are lacking in character. However, the hotel staff is courteous and attentive, and ready to help with even the smallest detail.

HOTEL-RESTAURANT-TAVERNE-HAPP, *Herzog Friedrich Strasse 14, A-6020 Innsbruck. Tel. 512-582980; fax 512-58298011. Doubles start at 450 schillings per person, including breakfast. All credit cards accepted.*

The Hotel Happ is just down the street from the "Golden Roof." The hotel, which has been in operation for more than 200 years, has an old world charm preserved in its architecture and the attention of its helpful staff. Rooms are tastefully furnished with modern, light-wood furniture. The hotel also has a fine restaurant featuring Tirolean and pasta favorites, including mushroom strudel, homemade ravioli and gnocchi and roast beef with onion sauce.

HOTEL SAILER, *Adamgasse 6-10, A-6020 Innsbruck. Tel. 512-5363; 512-53637. Doubles start at 600 schillings per person, including breakfast. All credit cards accepted.*

Joschi and Maria Sailer manage the Hotel Sailer tucked in a quiet street in the heart of town. The hotel is furnished with rustic folk pieces. There is a lounge off the reception area where guests can relax and read the paper or watch television. Service at the hotel was somewhat lacking, however, and the staff can be imperious and dismissive.

PENSION SIGRID, *Hottingergasse 27, A-6020 Innsbruck. Tel. 512-28-19-05. Doubles start at 800 schillings. All credit cards accepted.*

The Pension Sigrid is across the river from the Altstadt (old town) but within easy walking distance. Rooms are simply furnished and basic. The staff is helpful and attentive. Street parking is available near the pension.

WEISSES RÖBL HOTEL, *Kiebachgasse 8, A-6021 Innsbruck. Tel. 512-583057; fax 512-583057-5. Doubles start at 1,200 schillings. All credit cards accepted.*

The Plank family runs this charming 14 room hotel on a quiet street in the old city. You'll feel as if you're a member of the family. Rooms are comfortably furnished, light, and airy. The hotel also runs a very good restaurant on the premises featuring a 90 schilling menu. Specials change each day.

Berwang

SPORT SINGER, *A-6622 Berwang. Tel. 5674-8181; fax 5674-818183. Doubles start at 1,380 schillings. American Express, Diners and Visa accepted.*

Gunter and Gerti Singer run this chalet hotel in the heart of the mountains. The hotel is filled with lots of rustic charm decorated with floral fabrics, painted ceilings and carved wood. Rooms are light-filled, and guests can enjoy the spectacular view off their balconies. The restaurant has a menu starting at 330 schillings per person. Specialties include foie gras made on site, lamb with rosemary sauce and local game. The restaurant also has a good selection of Austrian and Italian wines.

Ellmau

HOTEL DER BAR, *Kirchbichl 9, A-6352 Ellmau. Tel. 5358-2395; fax 5358-239-556. Doubles start at 2,100 schillings. All credit cards accepted.*

Joachim and Heike Strickrodt own the Hotel Der Bar just a few miles down the road from the Kitzbuhel resort. Rooms are decorated with modern furniture and most have balconies or terraces from which you can gaze out at the peaks of the Wilder Kaiser.

Guests can play tennis, practice their golf swing on the indoor and outdoor courses, or go for a swim. Or you can indulge yourself with a trip to the beauty salon, a massage, a sauna, or a steam bath. The restaurant features a wide variety of Austrian, French, and Italian wines. Diners can enjoy international cuisine, seafood, and local dishes.

Hall In Tirol

HOTEL MARIA THERESIA, *A-6060 Hall in Tirol. Tel. 5223-56313-0; fax 05223-44685. Doubles start at 860 schillings. All credit cards accepted.*

The Zoschg family runs the Hotel Maria Theresia in Hall in Tirol. The staff is personable and helpful. Rooms are sparsely furnished but comfortable, although they tend to be a bit dark. The hotel has a fine restaurant featuring traditional Tirolean dishes. There is also an extensive wine cellar from which to choose a bottle of wine to complement your dinner.

HOTEL RESTAURANT HEILIGKREUZ, *Reimmichlstrasse 18, A-6060 Hall In Tirol. Tel. 5223-57114; fax 5223-571145. Doubles start at 400 schillings per person, including breakfast. Visa accepted.*

This 70 room hotel run by the Eisendle family is only a 10 minute walk from the town center and a 15 minute drive to Innsbruck. Rooms are comfortable, and the staff is very attentive. Sports lovers will like the hotel's immediate proximity to a heated outdoor swimming pool, tennis courts free for guests, bowling, and mini-golf. The hotel's bar features ping-pong and billiards. Bike rentals are also possible. The restaurant offers diners a good selection of Tirolean cuisine.

Hintertux

DER RINDERERHOF, *A-6294 Hintertux. Tel. 5287-501; fax 5287-502. Doubles start at 630 schillings per person. No credit cards but traveler's checks accepted.*

Der Rindererhof is run by the Krajnc family. Some rooms are furnished with canopied beds, a welcoming and cozy touch after a hard day of skiing. You can also warm up before a roaring fire in the hotel lounge. The hotel also has a sauna, solarium, whirlpool and turkish bath at guests' disposal to help you relax. The restaurant is passable, but nothing special. But there are vast quantities of food for hefty appetites.

HOTEL NEU HINTERTUX, *A-6294 Hintertux. Tel. 5287-325 or 367; fax 5287-318409. Doubles start at 690 schillings per person. No credit cards but traveler's checks accepted.*

This 45 room hotel is run by the Tipotsch family. Rooms are discreetly furnished in blond wood and pastel fabrics. The staff also is courteous and attentive. If you don't have ski equipment with you, the hotel can fit and rent your skis before you head to the nearby glacier. The hotel has a good restaurant with the usual regional dishes and an excellent selection of wines to complement your dinner.

You can unwind in the evenings playing your favorite games in the hotel's lounge with pinball machines, bowling, billiards, ping-pong and an exercise room.

Igls

SCHLOSS IGLS, *Viller Steig 2, A-6080 Igls. Tel. 512-377217; fax 512-378679. Doubles start at 3,400 schillings. All credit cards accepted.*

This 19th century castle hotel overlooks Innsbruck and has a great view of the Patscherkofel mountains. A baroque fireplace welcomes guests in from the cold during the winter months. Rooms are elegantly furnished in muted fabrics. The Beck family makes sure that guests are pampered. The Schlosshotel Igls also has an indoor swimming pool, sauna and hairdresser on the premises. The hotel's restaurant is equally elegant and tantalizing with caviar, salmon dishes, and for dessert, Salzburg souffle.

Imst

SCHLOSS SPRENGENSTEIN ROMANTIK HOTEL POST, *A-6460 Imst. Tel. 5412-2554; fax 5412-2519-55. Doubles start at 650 schillings per person. All credit cards accepted.*

The Hotel Post's distinctive onion-domed architecture has become a landmark in Imst. The former Sprengenstein Palace was built in 1450 and has a splendid park to pass the hours away. The palace was transformed into an inn originally in the 17th century. Today the hotel has a rustic charm tempered with elegantly appointed rooms. The restaurant is a must for gourmands who want to taste the best of what Tirol has to offer. Try their special spinach dumplings. Diners can choose from a number of international selections as well.

Kitzbuhel

FAMILIENHOTEL ERIKA, *Josef-Pirchl Strasse 21, A-6370 Kitzbuhel. Tel. 5356-4885; fax 5356-467413. Doubles start at 960 schillings per day. All credit cards accepted.*

Uschi and Benedikt Schorer run this bright orange hotel near the center of town. The charming 19th century-style building is surrounded by a large, well-tended guest garden. Rooms are furnished in turn-of-the-century style and bright fabrics. Activities like wine tasting, carriage rides, cycling tours, mountain hikes and culinary evenings are sponsored by the hotel. The hotel also has swimming, a sauna, a steam room, massages and a fitness room available for guests.

ROMANTIKHOTEL, *Griesenauweg 26, A-6370 Kitzbuhel. Tel. 5356-3181; fax 5356-3181-70. Doubles start at 1,290 schillings per person. All credit cards accepted.*

Kitzbuhel may be known for fantastic skiing, but it also has good golf available. The Romantikhotel offers week-long golf packages to its guests including room and board and lessons for beginners or advanced players.

There is also a swimming complex which includes sauna, steam bath, solarium, and whirlpool. This former manor house is elegant in a beautiful country setting. Such guests as the Duke of Windsor and the Aga Khan have enjoyed its accommodations. Rooms are comfortably furnished in floral fabrics. The restaurant is a must for gourmets, earning two chef toques from the Gault Millau gourmet guide. Vegetables are raised on the hotel grounds for the freshest produce possible.

SPORTHOTEL REISCH, *Franz Reisch Strasse 3, A-6370 Kitzbuhel. Tel. 5356-33660; fax 5356-3291. Doubles start at 850 schillings per person. All credit cards accepted.*

The 80 bed Sporthotel Reisch is in the heart of Kitzbuhel. Guests can enjoy the hotels steam room, massage facilities, sauna, and tennis. Private parking is also available for guests. The hotel is justifiably known for the excellence of its Austrian cuisine and a well-stocked wine cellar with regional vintages. Barbecues and buffets are held in the hotel garden during warmer weather.

Kuhtai

JAGDSCHLOSS KUHTAI, *A-6183 Kuhtai. Tel. 5239-201 or 225; fax 5239-2814. Doubles start at 1,060 schillings per person. All credit cards accepted.*

Originally built in 1280 as a royal hunting lodge, the hotel still bears witness to its former Hapsburg owners, including engravings of family trees owned by Princess Marie Louise, Napoleon's wife, and royal hunting trophies. You'll be treated like royalty by the congenial staff. The hotel is high up in the mountains and conveniently located to ski areas. You can warm up in the hotel's bar after a hard day on the slopes.

Lienz

HOTEL TRAUBE, *Hauptplatz 14, A-9900 Lienz. Tel. 4852-64444; fax 4852-64184. Doubles start at 1,740 schillings. All credit cards accepted.*

The Vergeiner family has been running this cheery hotel since 1868. Rooms are furnished with a selection of charming examples of regional antiques. The hotel also has a rooftop swimming pool and sauna. The restaurant offers a good choice of fresh-water fish and lamb dishes. Dinners are served by candlelight and you will often be serenaded with live music. The wine list has a wide variety of vintages from Tirol and the rest of Austria.

Meran

HOTEL SCHLOSS LABERS, *I-39012 Meran. Tel. 473-23-44-84; fax 473-23-41-46. Doubles start at 1,050 schillings per person. All credit cards accepted.*

The Hotel Schloss Labers is picture-postcard perfect. The former castle overlooks the vineyards with the mountains as a backdrop. Guests can enjoy a heated swimming pool and the hotel's tennis courts. The castle is secluded and appears to be far away from civilization, although Meran is only a five minute drive away. Hikers will enjoy the paths leading into the vineyards and nearby mountains. Inside, beyond the castle's meter-thick walls, rooms are cozily furnished with comfortable elegance.

HOTEL SCHLOSS RUNDEGG, *Schennastrasse 2, I-39012 Meran. Tel. 473-23-41-00; 473-23-72-00. Doubles start at 1,800 schillings per person. All credit cards accepted.*

The former Rundegg castle dates back to the 12th century, as attested by the ancient towers, alcoves, and balconies adorning the architecture. Today, guests flock to the hotel to pamper themselves with the spa facilities. Doctor-supervised treatments include lymph drainage, underwater massage, facial treatments and medicinal baths. Rooms are warmly furnished with burnished wood detailing, oriental rugs, and sumptuous draperies.

KURHOTEL PALACE, *Cavourstrasse 2-4, I-39012 Meran. Tel. 473-21-13-00; fax 23-41-81. Doubles start at 1,500 schillings per person. All credit cards accepted.*

The Kurhotel Palace is an elegant hotel with lots of old world charm. As the name implies, guests can come here to "take the cure." Facilities include a spa complex, sauna, solarium, fitness room and beauty farm. The hotel also has a swimming pool and large garden. Rooms are tastefully furnished and most have balconies. The Kurhotel Palaces restaurant features regional specialties and diet dishes for those watching their figures.

Pertisau am Achensee

HOTEL FURSTENHAUS, *A-6213 Pertisau am Achensee. Tel. 5243-5442 or 5443. Doubles start at 750 schillings per person. All credit cards accepted.*

The Hotel Furstenhaus is situated on the banks of Lake Achen, favored by Emperor Maximilian I for its fine fishing. The lake today still attracts fishermen and hunters as well as more modern pursuits, like windsurfers and paragliders.

The hotel is decorated with a huge fresco of the royal hunt scene from Maximilian's fishing guide. Sigmund Freud came to the hotel to unwind, and guests today can follow suit in a stone-oil bath at the beauty farm adjoining the hotel. This fine hotel combines modern luxury with centuries old tradition.

St. Anton in Tirol

HOTEL-RESTAURANT ADLER, *A-6771 St. Anton in Tirol. Tel. 5552-67118; fax 5552-67118-50. Doubles start at 690 schillings per person, including breakfast. All credit cards accepted.*

The Hotel-Restaurant Adler is run by the Battloff family, who welcome you with open arms. Rooms are large and simply furnished. The family style atmosphere extends to the restaurant where heaping platters of food are the norm. There is also a *Keller* where you can relax and have a drink. If you're looking for entertainment at the end of your day, the hotel offers ping-pong, dancing, bowling, a sauna, billiards, and a solarium to their guests. Parking is available.

St. Johann in Tirol

HOTEL CRYSTAL, *Hornweg 5, A-6380 St. Johann in Tirol. Tel. 5352-2630; fax 5352-62-6-30-13. Doubles start at 780 schillings per person. All credit cards accepted.*

The Hotel Crystal is operated by the Lagler family and is an example of Austrian hospitality at its finest. The hotel has large, comfortable rooms with modern furnishings. The lounge and restaurant have big, cozy furniture for relaxing. There is also a playroom for children. The restaurant has a selection of local and national specialties, although the cuisine can be a bit ordinary. Nothing is added to the usual dishes and some fall flat entirely.

HOTEL GOLDENER LOWE, *A-6380 St. Johann. Tel. 5352-2251; fax 5352-2981. Doubles start 660 schillings per person, including half-pension. All credit cards accepted.*

This flower-bedecked hotel stands out in the center of town. The staff is gracious and welcoming despite handling hordes of visitors. Rooms are comfortable and large and most have balconies. Children under 10 get a 25 percent reduction if they stay with their parents. The food is basic, but good. And if you're ravenous after tackling the slopes all day, second helpings are free.

HOTEL POST, *A-6380 St. Johann In Tirol. Tel. 5352-2230; fax 5352-22303. Doubles start at 620 schillings per person, including breakfast. All credit cards accepted.*

The Hotel Post has been serving visitors for more than 750 years. The hotel is decorated in the classic Tirol style with lots of rich wood panelling, painted ceilings, and sturdy wood furnishings. The hotel's restaurant is open from 8 a.m. to midnight and half-board is possible for guests for an additional fee. The staff is friendly and helpful, ensuring that your stay will be a memorable one.

Seefeld

GARTENHOTEL TUMMLERHOF, *A-6100 Seefeld. Tel. 5212-2571-0; fax 5212-2571-104. Doubles start from 1,340 schillings per person. All credit cards accepted.*

The Zorn family runs this delightful hotel and first-class restaurant just a short walk from the center of town. The chalet-style rooms all have balconies where you can enjoy the view. Gourmets are in for a treat, since the restaurant has earned two toques from the Gault Millau gourmet guide. There is a children's Club-Kinderkarten to look after the kiddies. For parents, there is a putting green, tennis, swimming, and sauna available.

HOTEL ASTORIA, *Geigenbuhel 185, A-6100 Seefeld. Tel. 5212-22720; 5212-2272-100. Doubles start at 830 schillings per person. All credit cards accepted.*

The Hotel Astoria is about 10 minutes outside of Seefeld. Rooms are elegantly furnished and most have balconies. The hotel also has a restaurant featuring regional specialties and a good group of Austrian wines. Golfers will enjoy the hotel's private putting green. Guided hikes in the surrounding mountains are also possible. The hotel has a large sauna, steam bath, solarium, fitness room, massages and an indoor pool at guests' disposal.

HOTEL KLOSTERBRAU, *Klostrstrasse 30, A-6100 Seefeld. Tel. 5212-2621-0; fax 5212-3885. Doubles start at 1,300 per person. All credit cards accepted.*

This five-star hotel is located in the heart of Seefeld, the site of two winter Olympics. The hotel is run by the Seyrling family, who have operated it for 180 years. The building was originally constructed in 1516 by Emperor Maximilian I as a monastery, but has been expanded and renovated into a luxury hotel. Guests can unwind in the hotel's underground swimming facility or in the large outdoor swimming pool. The hotel also houses an elegant restaurant with a fine selection of local and international wines.

HOTEL HOCHEDER, *Moserer Strasse 121, A-6100 Seefeld. Tel. 5212-2469; fax 5212-20-39-47. Doubles start at 680 schillings per person. All credit cards accepted.*

The Tauber family runs this 60 bed hotel as well as the Hotel St. Peter just down the street. The Hotel Hocheder's restaurant is known for its first-rate cuisine served in its homey dining room. Rooms are comfortably appointed and tastefully furnished in muted tones. A golf instructor is on staff. The hotel is also located within walking distance of a tennis school, riding facilities, the casino, and a paragliding school. Excursions are possible on the hotel's old-style bus.

Zell im Zillertal

HOTEL GASTHOF, *A-6280 Zell im Zillertal. Tel. 5282-2313-0; fax 5282-2313-17. Doubles start at 590 schillings per person. No credit cards accepted.*

The Hotel Gasthof, run by the Kolbitsch-Herbst family, is richly furnished with dark wood, complimenting fabrics, and folk art. Rooms are elegant but comfortable with more dark wood furniture and crisp white bedding. The service, however, is less than exemplary. The reception staff is brusque if not downright rude. There is, however, an excellent restaurant featuring local cuisine with rich and delicious desserts.

HOTEL TIROLER HOF, *A-6280 Zell im Zillertal. 5282-2227; fax 5282-2227-351. Doubles start at 390 schillings per person, including breakfast. All credit cards accepted.*

The Waidhofer family welcomes you to their hotel with open arms. Rooms are plain but comfortable. The Hotel Tiroler Hof also has a restaurant with international specialties and a selection of Tirolean dishes. The wine cellar has a good selection of Austrian vintages. The hotel has a heated outdoor swimming pool for guests. You can also rent a bike to better explore the area. Every week, music is performed at the hotel for guests. There is also a library, sauna, solarium, and massage available.

HOTEL PENSION VIERJAHRESZEITEN, *A-6294 Zell im Zillertal. Tel. 5287-326; fax 5287-695. Doubles start at 600 schillings per person. No credit cards, but traveler's checks accepted.*

The Hotel Pension Vierjahreszeiten is traditionally decorated with lots of wood panelling and beige fabrics, although the overall effect is a bit drab. The restaurant features traditional dishes and a good selection of regional wines. After a hard day on the slopes, relax in the hotel's whirlpool, sauna, or solarium. Or try some liquid refreshment in the hotel bar.

SPORT HOTEL THERESA, *A-6280 Zell Am Ziller. Tel. 5282-2286; fax 5282-4235. Doubles start at 900 schillings per person. All credit cards accepted.*

The Sport Hotel Theresa is in the business of pampering guests body and soul. The hotel is lovingly run by the Egger family. Rooms are modern and understatedly elegant with muted colors and discreet lighting. A playroom is available for children. The restaurant offers lighter fare, a relief after the heaviness of much of the local cuisine. Fresh produce and regional ingredients are emphasized. The hotel also has a modern fitness room, indoor swimming pool, tennis, and massage for guests.

WHERE TO EAT

There are a wide variety of dining choices in Innsbruck, so you won't go hungry if you're in the mood for Austrian dishes or want to venture farther afield for international cuisine. The smaller towns and resorts have fewer selections, but the good news is that several hotels have very good restaurants and wine cellars – so make sure to take a look at the *Where to Stay* section above when looking for dining options.

Tirolean cooking usually means simple cuisine using local seasonal products. Look for Tirolean bacon dumplings served "in water," really clear broth with chives or "on land" on a bed of salad greens or sauerkraut. *Flecksuppe* is flavored with tripe and will keep you warm on a cold winter's day. The province's most famous dish is *Grostel*, a combination of potatoes, meat, bacon, and eggs. Pasta dishes are also frequently on the menu. Noodles are topped with cream sauce with eggs and lots of butter. Spinach, potato, or cabbage can also be added. To finish your meal, try a *Blattlstock*, a tiered cake with poppyseed filling and dribbled with honey.

No need to head into town to eat if you're on the slopes. Most ski areas have rustic restaurants along the way down the mountain. On one run in Harschbichl, there are eight mountain restaurants before you get down to the village. The food in these restaurants is basic but will stick to your ribs – a good refueling stop so you don't need to interrupt your day of skiing.

Of course, if you really want to warm yourself after a day in the cold, you must try some of the region's *schnapps*. There are many fruit-based varieties, including apricot, pear, berry, or plum. Be careful though – the schnapps pack a serious punch and a little goes a long way.

Innsbruck

FISCHERHAUS, *Herrengasse 8, A-6010 Innsbruck. Tel. 58-35-35. Moderate. Open daily 10 a.m. to 2 a.m. All credit cards accepted.*

This restaurant with a separate beer garden and bar is tucked next to the cathedral. The restaurant has a cozy atmosphere and is tastefully decorated in earth tones with lots of nooks to nestle in with that special someone. The Fisherhaus serves traditional Austrian specialties and several varieties of pasta.

HERZOG FRIEDRICH, *Riesengasse 6, A-6010 Innsbruck. Tel. 512-582-309. Moderate. Open Monday through Saturday, 10 a.m. to 10 p.m.; closed Sundays. No credit cards accepted; there is a 25 schilling fee for traveler's checks.*

Tea is the specialty at this cafe restaurant, with more than 70 different varieties in stock served in the restaurant's Gothic interior, which dates from 1434. Diners won't be disappointed either. Dishes include pork with mushroom sauce, game ragout with flour dumplings, and Viennese-style boiled beef served with roasted potatoes and spinach.

JORGEL, *Herzog Friedrich Strasse 1, A-6010 Innsbruck. Tel. 57-10-06. Moderate. Open from 11 a.m. to 2:30 p.m. and 6 p.m. to 11 p.m.; closed Mondays from January to April. All credit cards accepted.*

This restaurant and wine house is right in the heart of the city's old town. Specialties like liver with bacon and tomatoes, rabbit with cream and bacon, and game stew with mushrooms and spinach dumplings are served up nightly in the rustic dining room. There's an extensive wine list with selections from Tirol, France, Italy, Argentina and California.

GASTHAUS GOLDENES DACHL, *Altstadt, A-6010 Innsbruck. 512-58-93-70. Moderate. Open 7:30 p.m. to midnight. All credit cards accepted.*

The food is basic and satisfying at the Gasthaus Goldenes Dachl. Selections include leg of lamb, grilled pork cutlet, fried pike and sauerkraut with all the fixings. The restaurant's cozy setting and cheerful waitresses enhance the dining experience.

HOF GARTEN RESTAURANT, *Rennweg 6A, A-6010 Innsbruck. Tel. 588-871; fax 589-957. Moderate. Open Tuesday through Saturday 6 p.m. to 2 a.m.; Sundays, 10 a.m. to 2 a.m.; closed Mondays. All credit cards accepted.*

As the name suggests, this restaurant is located in the Hof Garden, whose history extends back to the Middle Ages to 1410. Four hundred years later, King Maximilian commissioned a restaurant for the park. A new restaurant was constructed in 1924, which is the site of the current establishment. The restaurant's large garden is lit with tiny white lights giving it a fairytale quality. But the decor of the interior falls flat, trying too hard to be chic. The restaurant is known for its grilled ribs.

RESTAURANT CHILI'S, *Bozner Platz 6, A-6010 Innsbruck. Tel. 56-73-30. Inexpensive. Open daily 10 a.m. to midnight. All credit cards accepted.*

When your children refuse to face one more plate of *Wiener Schnitzel*, head over to Chili's for a festive evening. Part of the American chain, the restaurants have the standard Tex-Mex favorites. You can even order a Marguerita.

RESTAURANT OTTOBURG, *Herzog Friedrich Strasse 1, A-6010 Innsbruck. Tel. 512-574652; fax 512-589765. Moderate. Open 10 a.m. to midnight. All credit cards accepted.*

The Restaurant Ottoburg has a good selection of local wines to accompany such specialties as fried veal liver with apples, wild boar medallions with dumplings and cranberries, and ox with pepper sauce. But the restaurant is somewhat cramped with tables tightly packed together. The staff, too, can be surly and unresponsive.

STIFTSKELLER, *Burggraben 31, A-6010 Innsbruck. Tel. 512-583-490; fax 512-567-293. Moderate. Open daily from 10 a.m. to midnight. All credit cards accepted.*

The Stiftskeller is a huge family-style restaurant and beer garden with a festive atmosphere. The restaurant features a large selection of traditional Tirolean specialties served in large portions, from fresh trout to liver to dumplings. Several of the restaurant's dining rooms also have a history dating back to the time of Maria-Theresa.

Kitzbuhel

WIRTSCHAUS UNTERBERGER STUBEN, *Wehrgasse 2, A-6370 Kitzbuhel. Tel. 5356-2101; fax 5356-71996. Expensive. Closed Tuesdays and Wednesdays during lunchtime. No credit cards accepted.*

This 19th century chalet is decorated in rich wood panelling and lots of rustic wooden furnishing and folk art. Chef Josef Unterberger goes out of his way to make guests feel at home. Unterberger's mother was herself a "Cordon Bleu" chef. Her son cooks regional specialties but with a flair all his own that transforms dishes from just good to spectacular. The wine list includes white wines from Austria and the Rhine Valley as well as a good choice of Bourgognes, Bordeaux, and Italian reds.

SEEING THE SIGHTS

Like most of Austria's imperial cities, **Innsbruck** is easily seen on foot. In fact, since many of the streets in the old city are restricted to pedestrian traffic, walking is the only way to really get a good look at the city. The old section is very compact, so you can make a brief visit and still get a sense of what Innsbruck is like or, if you have more time, meander around the old, narrow streets. The city is charming and the people are very friendly, so no matter how long you stay you're sure to have an enjoyable time.

The easiest place to begin your visit is at the city's most famous landmark, **The Golden Roof** or **Goldenes Dachl**, *Herzog Friedrich Strasse*. The late Gothic bay window was constructed as a court box for the Emperor Maximilian, who ruled from 1494 to 1496. Maximilian liked to watch dancing and tournaments in the city square from the royal box. A total of 2,657 gilded copper tiles adorn the roof. Frescoes of coats of arms and dancers also decorate the bay and interior of the court box.

While you're here, stop off at the **Olympic Museum**, *Herzog Friedrich Strasse 15*. The museum has a video collection with scenes from the 1964 and 1976 Winter Olympics, which were held in Tirol. The museum is open daily from 9:30 a.m. to 5:30 p.m. Admission costs 22 schillings for adults and 11 schillings for seniors, children and students. The museum is closed on Mondays November through February.

Heading down Herzog Friedrich Strasse, you'll see the **City Tower**, which you can climb for a great view over the old city. The tower was built between 1442 and 1450. The pointed roof of the tower was replaced by a round one in 1560. The tower is open from March 1 through October 31 from 10 a.m. to 5 p.m. and in July and August from 10 a.m. to 6 p.m. Tickets cost 20 schillings for adults and 10 schillings for students and children. You can also purchase a combined ticket for entrance to the Olympic Museum and Tower for 32 schillings for adults and 16 schillings for students and children.

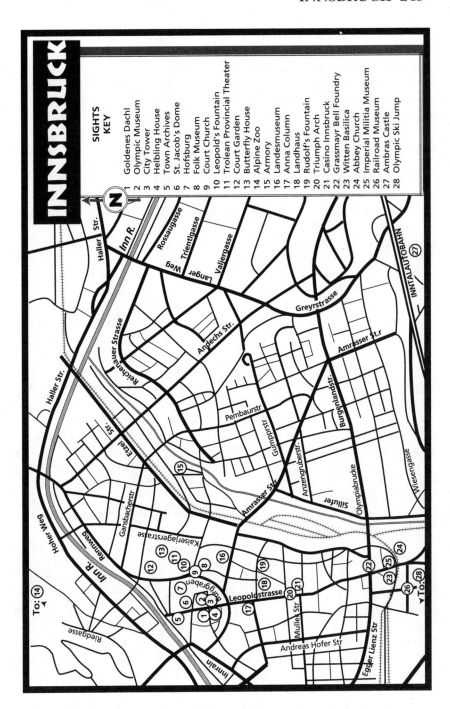

INNSBRUCK

SIGHTS KEY

1 Goldenes Dachl
2 Olympic Museum
3 City Tower
4 Helbling House
5 Town Archives
6 St. Jacob's Dome
7 Hofsburg
8 Folk Museum
9 Court Church
10 Leopold's Fountain
11 Trolean Provincial Theater
12 Court Garden
13 Butterfly House
14 Alpine Zoo
15 Armory
16 Landesmuseum
17 Anna Column
18 Landhaus
19 Rudolf's Fountain
20 Triumph Arch
21 Casino Innsbruck
22 Grassmayr Bell Foundry
23 Witten Basilica
24 Abbey Church
25 Imperial Militia Museum
26 Railroad Museum
27 Ambras Castle
28 Olympic Ski Jump

Across the street is the **Helbling House**, which was originally a Gothic residence built during the 15th century. Today, the facade is decorated with late Baroque stucco work that was added in 1730. The blue house looks like it has been glazed with a thick layer of wedding cake icing. Down the street, *at 31 Herzog Friedrich Strasse*, is a plaque marking the building were the composer Wolfgang Amadeus Mozart once lived. In fact, as you travel around the city, you'll see a cornucopia of plaques and signs marking Mozart's meanderings.

If you head back down towards the Golden Roof, turn right and make your first left you'll wind up in front of **St. Jacob's Dom**, or cathedral. The Baroque cathedral was built between 1717 and 1724. The interior has a famous altar by Lukas Cranach the Elder depicting the Virgin Mary and ceiling paintings by C.D. Asam.

Behind the cathedral is the **Hofburg Palace**, *Rennweg 1, Tel. 587-186; fax 587-186-13*. You may recognize the faces of Marie Antoinette and her husband, the French King Louis XVI, who both later lost their heads during the French Revolution, in the portrait gallery of the palace. On the ceiling is an allegorical fresco, painted by Franz Anton Maulbertsch, glorifying Maria Theresa and the Hapsburg monarchy. The Hofburg was built under Archduke Siegmund the Rich in 1460, enlarged by Emperor Maximilian I after he transferred the seat of government to Innsbruck, and remade in the Rococo style by Empress Maria Theresa, who also had it painted in her trademark yellow. Inside there are opulently decorated state rooms with ceiling frescoes by F.A. Maulbertsch, gold candelabras, tapestries, and lots of other royal knickknacks.

The Hofburg Palace is open from 9 a.m. to noon and 1 p.m. to 5 p.m. daily; mid-October to mid-May, open Monday through Saturday 9 a.m. to 4 p.m. Tours of the state rooms, lasting about 35 minutes, are available. Admission to the palace costs 50 schillings for adults, 30 schillings for students and 10 schillings for children.

On the nearby *Rennweg* is **Leopold's Fountain**. The equestrian statue of Archduke Leopold V (1619-1632) is the oldest depiction of a rearing horse to be found north of the Alps. The great Baroque architect Christoph Gumpp designed the **Dogana**, *Rennweg 3*, in 1630 on what was once the site of the court theater. It has served as a library, a riding school, a banquet room, and a customs hall. Today it has been integrated in Innsbruck's Congress Center. The **Tirolean Provincial Theater**, *Rennweg 2, Tel. 512-520-7401* was constructed between 1844 and 1846. The classically styled theater with its Corinthian columns was built to replace the former court theater. Archduke Ferdinand Karl built the theater in 1655 to stage baroque operas.

The **Tirolean Folk Museum**, *Universitatsstrasse 2, Tel. 512-584302*, has a variety of regional folk art from the middle ages to the 18th century including masks, instruments, toys, sleighs and iron work. Several rooms are recreated with traditional furnishings. The museum building itself was constructed between 1553 and 1563 as an abbey. Tickets to the museum cost 40 schillings for adults, 25 schillings for students and 15 schillings for children. The museum is open Mondays through Saturday, from 9 a.m. to 7:30 p.m.; Sundays 9 a.m. to noon. Don't miss the **Christmas creche museum** downstairs, which has an incredible collection. Whole villages have been recreated. The detail and craftsmanship is really remarkable.

Across the Renaissance arcaded court of the museum is the **Court Church**, built between 1553 and 1563, and one of the must-see sights in Innsbruck. Inside the church is a huge sarcophagus with a statue of the kneeling Emperor Maximilian I. The sarcophagus is actually empty, however, since Maximilian later chose Wiener Neustadt as his final resting place. Massive statues of Maximilian's royal relatives and ancestors stand around the sarcophagus. You'll notice England's King Arthur among the funeral cortege. Albrecht Durer was among the hordes of artists and craftsmen who worked on the elaborate sculptures. The church's **Silver Chapel** is the final resting place of the Archduke Ferdinand II and his wife. The wooden organ in the church dates from 1600 and is still used today.

The **Tiroler Landesmuseum Ferdinandeum**, *Museumstrasse 15, Tel. 512-59489-87; fax 512-5948988*, has an impressive collection of Roman artifacts that have been discovered in the area. There are also fine examples of medieval and Dutch works, although the more modern pieces are a bit disappointing. There is also an interesting relief map of Tirol in the basement so you can get your bearings on the geography of the region. Entrance to the museum costs 50 schillings for adults, 40 schillings for seniors, 30 schillings for students, 20 schillings for children and free for children under six. The museum is open January through April, 10 a.m. to noon and 2 p.m. to 5 p.m.; Sunday and holidays 10 a.m. to 1 p.m. May through September, the museum is open daily from 10 a.m. to 5 p.m.; Thursdays the museum stays open until 9 p.m.

The **Tirolean Armory**, *Zeughausgasse, Tel. 512-587439; fax 512-587439-18*, originally was built by Emperor Maximilian in 1506 and served as the emperor's central arms storehouse. The museum has exhibitions on natural science, technology, mining, hunting, musical instruments, coaches and locomotives. The museum is open from May through September from 10 a.m. to 5 p.m.; Thursdays, 10 a.m. to 9 p.m.; from October through April, 10 a.m. to noon and 2 p.m. to 5 p.m.; Sundays and holidays 10 a.m. to 1 p.m.; closed Mondays.

The **Anna Column**, *Maria Theresien Strasse*, was erected after the province successfully thwarted a Bavarian invasion during the War of the

Spanish Succession in 1703. The nearby **Landhaus** Baroque palace was built by G.A. Gumpp between 1725 and 1728.

The **Rudolf Fountain**, *Bozner Platz*, was constructed in 1877 to commemorate the 500th anniversary (1363-1863) of Tirol's unification with the rest of the country.

The **Triumphal Arch**, *Salurner Strasse*, was originally commissioned in 1765 to commemorate the betrothal of Maria Theresa's son, the future emperor Leopold II, to a Spanish princess. But his father, Emperor Francis I, died unexpectedly during the celebrations. So on one side of the arch shows nuptial scenes, and on the other are symbols of mourning.

The Rococo-style **Wilten Basilica**, *Pastorstrasse*, has long been a favorite pilgrimage site. The church was built between 1751 to 1755. Inside the church is a 14th century statue of the Virgin Mary. The **Wilten Abbey Church**, *Klostergasse*, is a Baroque church consecrated in 1665. The nearby monastery was constructed in 1138.

You don't need to be a royal to tour the **Court Garden** these days. The public can visit the concert and art pavilions and outdoor chess boards in the gardens, which were completed in 1710. The Hof Gardens are open from 6 a.m. to 10 p.m. If you're traveling with children, make sure to stop by at the **Butterfly House** in the Hof Gardens. Hundreds of tropical butterflies are allowed to fly free in the exhibition. The Butterfly House is open daily from 10 a.m. to 5 p.m. from June through September. Admission is 40 schillings for adult, 25 schillings for students and seniors and 15 schillings for children.

Specialty Museums

If you have the time, there are some other specialty museums in Innsbruck that may interest you.

Grassmayr Bell Foundry, *Tel. 59416*. Open Monday through Friday, 9 a.m. to 6 p.m.; Saturdays, 9 a.m. to noon. Admission is 20 schillings for adults and 10 schillings for children. The museum features displays explaining how ores are used to make bells. The foundry has been in operation for more than 400 years.

Town Archives, *Badgasse 2. Tel. 587-380*. Open Monday through Thursday from 8 a.m. to noon and 2 p.m. to 6 p.m.; Fridays 8 a.m. to 1 p.m. The museum has displays and documents on local history on exhibit.

Tirolean Imperial Militia Museum, *Klostergasse 1. Tel. 583-386*. Open May through September 10 a.m. to 4 p.m.; Sundays and holidays 9 a.m. to noon. The museum houses equipment used by the Tirolean Imperial Militia in World War I.

Tirolean Railway Museum, *Stubai Valley Station*. Open May through October only on Saturdays from 9 a.m. to 5 p.m. The museum has a variety of historic locomotives on display.

NIGHTLIFE & ENTERTAINMENT

During the summer, Innsbruck hosts the **Festival of Early Music** at the **Ambras Castle**. Reservations can be made through the **Festival Ticket Office**, *Ambraser Schlosskonzerte, Scopfstrasse, 20, A-6020 Innsbruck*. Tickets can also be reserved through the **Box Office**, *Innsbruck Information, Burggraben 3, A-6020 Innsbruck, Tel. 512-5356-21; fax 512-5356-43*. On the day of the performance, leftover tickets can be purchased at the Innsbruck Information office between 2 p.m. and 5 p.m. Tickets can not be reserved over the phone. You must pick them up in person. Some tickets may be sold at the door on the night of the performance from 7 p.m. for concerts and 8 p.m. for operas.

There are also informal pre-concert talks given by the musicians about their music before the concerts at 7 p.m. Special buses to the concerts leave from Bozner Platz at 7:30 p.m. and return to Innsbruck after the concert finishes. Trams 3 and 6 also go to the palace.

Take a romantic cable car into the mountains to see the **Seegrube** by night. The **Nordkette Cable Car** runs Thursday nights from 6 p.m. to 11 p.m. during the summer. Information is available at the Nordkette Cable Car lower station, *Tel. 512-29-33-44*.

If you are looking for a current listing of available entertainment, the Tourist Information offices in Innsbruck publish a monthly program describing events in the city and the surrounding region.

Gambling

Gamblers can stake their bets on roulette, baccarat, blackjack, poker, red dog, Sic Bo, slot machines or the wheel of fortune at the **Casino Innsbruck**, *Landhausplatz, Tel. 512-587-040*. The casino also features live entertainment after 3 p.m. Admission is free, but if you pay 210 schillings, you'll receive chips amounting to 250 schillings. Parking is free for casino patrons.

SHOPPING

There are several department stores in the Innsbruck town center and on the outskirts of the city. Most specialty shops are found in the Old Town area. The primary shopping streets are **Maria Theresien Strasse** and the squares and streets running between the train station and the river. Stores are open, in general, Monday through Friday from 8:30 a.m. to 6 p.m. and Saturdays from 8:30 a.m. to noon. On the first Saturday of every month, shops stay open until 5 p.m.

There are several different **markets** around Innsbruck for intrepid shoppers to browse and find that special hidden treasure or just a nice lunch:

- **Farmers' Market**, *Innrain in the covered market*. Open Monday to Saturday 7 a.m. to 1 p.m.
- **Farmers' Market**, *Wiltener Platzl*. Open Saturday 7 a.m. to noon.
- **Christmas Market**, *Old Town*. Open last Saturday in November through December 22.
- **Bring 'n' Buy Sale**, *Adolf Pichler Platz*. Open first and third Saturday morning of each month.
- **St. Hubert's Market**, *in front of the covered market*. Open last week of October through mid-November.
- **Flea Market**, *Innrain*. Open Saturday mornings.

SPORTS & RECREATION
Archery/Shooting Ranges
- **Arzl Shooting Range**, *Eggenwaldweg 60, Innsbruck. Tel. 26-23-25*. Open April through November, Monday through Friday 1 p.m. to 7 p.m.; Saturdays, Sundays, and holidays, all day. Admission costs 60 schillings. Bow or rifle hire costs 50 schillings. Reservations must be made in advance.
- **Igls Shooting Range**, *Club House*. Reservations should be made through the **Igls Tourist Office**, *A-6080 Igls. Tel. 37-71-01*.

Biking
Tirol is the ideal vacation site for bikers young and old. If you didn't bring your own cycle but want to take advantage of the trails and excellent scenery available, you can rent bikes from the Austrian Federal Railway. The stations participating in the program are in Hall, Innsbruck, Jenback, Kirchberg, Kitzbuhel, Kufstein, Lienz, Otztal, Reutte, Scharnitz, Seefeld, Sillian, Steinach and St. Johann. Bikes are also available in sizes fit for children.

You are not required to return the bicycles to the stations from which you rented them and can instead drop them off at the nearest participating station. Bikers can also purchase reduced price train tickets. Special train cars are geared for bikers. You can even ship your bike ahead and pick it up when you arrive.

There are several biking events held in the province. The **Cycling World Cup** takes place in August. The 40 kilometer course starts off in St. Johann and winds its way through Gasteig Kossen, Erpfendorf, and Kirchdorf. For more information, contact the **St. Johann Tourist Board**, *A-6380 St. Johann. Tel. 5352-2218*.

The 120 kilometer **Dolmites Round Tour**, beginning in Lienz, takes place in June. For more information, contact the **Lienz Tourist Board**, *A-9900 Lienz. Tel. 4852-65265*.

In September, the **Otztal Valley Bicycle Marathon** is held. The 235 kilometer race is for serious sportsmen and women and goes through the Timmelsjoch, Jaufenpass, Brenner, and Kuhtai passes. For more information, contact the **Solden Tourist Board**, *A-6450 Solden. Tel. 5254-2212-0.*

The **Family Bicycle Marathon** is a 25 to 50 kilometer race. To be eligible, at least one parent and one child between six and 14-years old must register for the race which starts on the **Mieminger Plateau**. For more information, contact the **Mieming Tourist Board**, *A-6414 Mieming. Tel. 5264-5274.*

At the end of August, there is an annual **Mountain Bike Festival** in Ischgl. For more information, contact the **Ischgl Tourist Board**, *A-6561 Ischgl. Tel. 5444-5266.*

The **Tirol Information Office**, *Tel. 512-5320-170 or 171,* can give you further information on regional bicycle maps, resort brochures, accommodations, and a calendar of events. They also have additional details on mountain biking, including routes and course details.

Billiards
- **Billiard-Club**, *Burggraben 31/I, Innsbruck. Tel. 512-56-73-45.* Open daily from 3 p.m. to midnight. Table rental for one hour is 90 schillings.

Bobsledding
An unforgettable experience is to try your hand down the bobsled run with an experienced pilot at the Olympic Stadium in **Igls**. Reservations are a must. The cost is 300 schillings per person. Rides are possible Tuesdays from 9 a.m. to noon and Thursdays from 7 p.m. For more information, *call 512-37-75-25 or 37-71-60.*

Bowling
- **Gasthof Tengler**, *Hottinger Au 60, Innsbruck. Tel. 28-37-89*
- **Igls Congress Center**. *Tel. 37-71-73*
- **Rettung Bowling Alley**, *Sillufer 3. Tel. 36-00-34*
- **Gasthof Eller**, *Hohenstrasse 16. Tel. 28-41-66*

Fishing
The lakes and rivers throughout Tirol have a wide variety of fish to attract anglers including brook and rainbow trout, brook char, and grayling. Emperor Maximilian was an avid fisherman, and today many local inns cater to the needs of modern-day fishermen. The **Tirol Tourist Office**, *Wilhelm Greil Strasse 17, A-6010 Innsbruck*, publishes a guide in English called *Fish and Fly* with fishing locations, accommodations, and tips for fishermen. For more information, *call 512-5320; fax 512-532-0150.*

Golf

At the foot of the **Patscherkofel mountain** just outside of Innsbruck are two golf courses, the nine-hole **Sperberegg Course**, *Tel. 37-71-65*, and the 18-hole **Rinn Course**, *Tel. 5223-8177*. Or you can practice your swing at the **Igls Target Golf/Driving Range** *at the Hotel Gruberhof. Tel. 37-71-42*. Advance reservations are strongly recommended.

Seefeld has two golf courses: **The Golfclub Seefeld-Wildmoos**, *Postfach 22, A-6100 Seefeld. Tel. 5212-30030; fax 5212-3722-22*. Green fees for the 18-hole course cost 630 schillings during the week and 730 schillings on the weekend. A 30 minute lesson costs 250 schillings. The course is open from May through October.

The **Golf Academy Seefeld**, *A-6100 Seefeld, Tel. 5212-3797; fax 5212-3355*, is a 6-hole course. Green fees start at 190 schillings. This course is also open from May through October. **Kitzbuhel** also has two golf courses. The 18-hole **Golfclub Kitbuhel Schwarzsee**, *Golfweg Schwarzsee 35, A-6370 Kitzbuhel, Tel. 5356-716-45; fax 5356-71685*, is open from May to October. Weekday green fees start at 500 schillings; 600 schillings for the weekend. A 50-minute lesson will cost 60 schillings.

The 9-hole **Golfclub Kitzbuhel**, *Castle Kaps, A-6370 Kitzbuhel, Tel. 5356-3007; fax 5356-247-47*, is open from April through October. Weekday green fees are 450 schillings; 550 schillings weekends. A 30-minute lesson costs 280 schillings.

Hiking

The tourist office sponsors a mountain hiking program for visitors to Innsbruck. Anyone staying overnight here or in Igls can participate for free when you present a guest card obtained from your hotel. Individuals don't need to register in advance.

The **Alpinschule Innsbruck** has 40 different hiking routes mapped out for you in the Stubai Alps, Tux Alps, Karwendel Mountains, and the Mieminger Mountain Chain. The hikes take between three and five hours. Hiking experience is not necessary. The hikes are appropriate for children over eight years old and for adults of all ages. The program includes free guided hikes, bus transportation, hiking guidebook, and insurance. If you're lacking equipment, you can borrow boots and a backpack. The tours begin daily at 8:30 a.m. in front of the Innsbruck Congress Center regardless of weather conditions. If you're staying in Igls and don't have a car, hop on the number 6 tram to Maria Theresien Strasse. It's about a three-minute walk to the center. The bus leaves the center at 9 a.m. and returns between 4 p.m. and 5 p.m.

In **Igls**, hikes are organized from Monday to Friday. Those interested should meet at 9 a.m. in front of the local tourist office, *Hilberstrasse 15, Tel. 512-377101*. You should register at least a day in advance for the hike.

Lantern tours, available every Tuesday evening, travel from Igls to the Gasthof Heiligwasser for an Alpine hut party. The bus leaves at 7:45 p.m. from the Innsbruck Congress Center or 8 p.m. from the Igls Tourist Office returning at 11:30 p.m. There is no charge for the hike.

Or you could try the **Innsbruck Panorama Climbing Trail**. Divided into two sections, the hike takes approximately three hours to complete.

A three-day **Mountain Hiking Pass** is also available through the tourist office. The pass can be used for entrance to the Hungerburg Funicular Railway, Nordkette Cable Car, and Patscherkofel Cable Car. The passes cost 420 schillings for adults, 260 schillings for children, and children under six free.

The **Zirbenweg Round Trip Pass** allows hikers to use the Patscherkofel Cable Car in Igls, the Glungezer lift in Tulfes, or the Bundesbus Igs Tufles. You can buy the pass from the bus or cable car operators.

Ice Skating

Innsbruck has premier ice skating facilities, having hosted two Winter Olympic Games.

The **Olympic Ice Stadium**, *Tel. 33-8-38* features two rinks. The **outdoor ice rink** is open from mid-November to the beginning of March, Monday through Saturday, 1:30 p.m. to 4:30 p.m. and 8 p.m. to 9:45 p.m.; Sundays 1:30 p.m. to 4:30 p.m. The **indoor ice rink** is open Wednesday and Saturdays 2 p.m. to 5 p.m. and 8 p.m. to 10 p.m.; Fridays 8 p.m. to 10 p.m.; Sundays 2 p.m. to 5 p.m.

Admission for adults is 46 schillings and for children is 23 schillings. Skates can be rented for 50 schillings.

Winter Skiing

For many visitors to Tirol, the region means skiing. If you're looking for skiing information, *call 512-5320-175*, Monday through Friday from 9 a.m. to noon, or write **Alpine Auskunft**, *Wilhem Greil Strasse 17, A-6010 Innsbruck*. Resorts for every taste are available from small, family-style places to super-sophisticated resorts.

Here is a list to get you started on planning your skiing adventure; the sidebar on the next page gives you all the area phone numbers you'll need:

Fieberbrunn only has an altitude of 3,000 feet, but the resort is located in a snow pocket so it has excellent snow coverage.

The **Glungezer ski region** has the longest downhill run in Tirol totalling more than 15 kilometers. Skiing is possible across the Inn Valley on the peaks of the "North Chain" mountains near Innsbruck. The season extends well into the spring season.

Innsbruck-Igls has six ski areas: Axamer Lizum, Mutterer Alm, Stubaier Gletscher, Seegrube-Nordkette, Glungezer and Patscherkofel, conveniently located near Innsbruck. The local tourist office is sponsoring a **Club Card**, which you receive from your hotel or pension after staying one night. Then, you can ride the ski buses free of charge. The card also entitles you to reductions on ski passes, mountain railways and sightseeing flights. The **Innsbruck Gletscher Ski Pass** lets you ski the above resorts and gives you free public transportation in Innsbruck and Igls. A three-day pass costs 940 shillings for adults and 570 shillings for children.

FOR THE LATEST SNOW CONDITIONS & SKI RESORT INFO ...

If you want to find out the latest snow conditions, try a new resort or book a hotel room, you can contact the local tourist offices. They'll be happy to help you plan the next stop in your ski vacation.

Axamer Lizum Tourist Office, Tel. 5234-8240; fax 5234-7158
Brixlegg Tourist Office, Tel. 5337-62581; fax 5337-63882
Fieberbrunn Tourist Office, Tel. 5354-6304; fax 5354-2606
Hungerburg-Seegrube-Hafelekar Tourist Office, Tel. 512-29-33-44
Imst Tourist Office, Tel. 5412-2419; fax 5412-4783
Innsbruck Tourist Office, Tel. 512-59-8-50; 512-598-507
Igls Tourist Office, Tel. 512-37-71-01; fax 512-37-89-65
Kolsass Tourist Information, Tel. 5224-8124; fax 5224-67434
Kitzbuhel Tourist Office, Tel. 5356-182; fax 5356-2307
Landeck Tourist Office, Tel. 442-62344; fax 5442-67830
Lienzer Bergbahnnen Information, Tel. 4852-63975-17; fax 4852-63975-13
Mutters Tourist Office, Tel. 512-573744; fax 512-580563
Reutte Tourist Office, Tel. 5672-2336; fax 5672-5422
Schwaz Tourist Office, Tel. 5242-63240-0; fax 5242-65630
Seefeld Tourist Information, Tel. 5212-2313; fax 5212-3355
St. Johann Tourist Office, Tel. 5352-2218; fax 5352-5200
Telfes im Stubai Tourist Office, Tel. 5225-2750; fax 5225-4171
Westendorf Tourist Office, Tel. 5334-6230 or 6550; fax 5354-2390

Kitzbuhel is one of Austria's most famous ski resorts and has the high prices that go along with its worldwide reputation. The resort is part of the ski safari linking it to its neighbors Kirchberg and Pass Thurn. The "safari" literally allows you to ski for miles. The city itself is charming with cobbled, medieval streets and brightly painted houses. Covered with a layer of snow, Kitzbuhel is really transformed into a winter wonderland. The town has a wide range of shopping and restaurants, too.

The two villages of **Kolsass-Weer** are far from the crowds. You'll be skiing with local Austrians on the resorts' 20 kilometers of groomed runs. There is also a good beginner's area for those new to the slopes. The villages offer hourly bus service into Innsbruck and nearby ski resorts.

Many people don't consider the **Lienzer Dolomiten** area around the city of **Lienz** for skiing, but it is conveniently located to the **Zettersfeld** and **Hochstein** ski resorts. Snowboarding, ski, and ski-kindergarten schools are available if you want to sharpen your techniques. Equipment can be rented.

St. Johann was first settled 3,000 years ago by Celts attracted by the salt and copper found in the region. The Romans later took control of the area around 15 AD, but were defeated by the German barbarians about 500 AD. Historians surmise that St. Rupert, Salzburg's founder, established the first Catholic parish here in 738. St. Johann later became a popular playground for the archbishops of Chiemsee. Today, modern day revelers flock to the ski region, which is smaller and more charming than its more famous neighbor Kitzbuhel.

Seefeld has some of the country's best skiing accommodations, so if you want to be pampered after you're finished with the slopes stay here when the day is through. It's also the cross-country capital of Austria with 125 miles of prepared tracks, but only 15 miles from Innsbruck near the German border. Seefeld's sophisticated hotels, restaurants, shopping, and casino are for those who are as interested in what goes on off the slopes as on them.

For those who prefer a calmer pace than in the more frenetic Kitzbuhel, neighboring **Westendorf** is the place for you. Well-manicured runs crisscross gentle scenery, ideal for the beginner to intermediate skiers, although there are some more challenging runs for more advanced skiers. Westendorf is part of the **Wilder Kaiser**, made up of the medieval market towns of Hopfgarten, Brixen, Soll, Ellmau, Scheffau, Itter, Kelchsau and Going with 90 lifts. Cross country skiing, tobogganing, curling, ice skating, bowling and sleigh rides are also possible.

Summer Skiing

Glacier skiing is available in Tirol all year round. The **Innsbruck Information Office**, *Burggraben 3, Tel. 53-56*, sponsors a one-day trip to the Stubai Glacier. The bus trip, ski rental, and ski pass cost 660 schillings. The trip is best for less-experienced skiers. Year-round skiing is also available on the glaciers in the Kauner, Pitz, Otz, and Ziller valleys.

Sleigh Rides

What could be more romantic than a **horse-drawn sleigh ride** through the snowy streets surrounded by majestic mountains? Reservations can be made through the **Igls Tourist Office**, *Tel. 512-37-71-01*. The sleigh rides cost 600 schillings per hour.

Swimming

There are several lovely **lakes** in Tirol where you can swim during the warmer months. The lakes are open to swimmers from May to September.
- **Tivoli Outdoor Swimming Pool**, *Pfurtschellerstrasse 1. Tel. 42-3-44*
- **Rossau Recreation Area**, *Tel. 34-87-78*
- **Lansersee Alpine Lake**, *Tel. 37-73-36*
- **Natterer See**, *Tel. 54-67-32*

In **Innsbruck**, there are several indoor swimming pools, saunas and solariums that you can use. Pools are open from 9 a.m. to 8 p.m.; saunas from 10 a.m. to 8 p.m.
- **Indoor swimming pool and sauna**, *Amraser Strasse 3. Tel. 512-42-5-85*
- **Indoor swimming pool and sauna**, *Hottinger Au. Tel. 512-28-23-39*
- **Olympic Village indoor swimming pool and sauna**, *Tel. 512-26-13-42*

Tennis/Squash Courts

Court prices range from 90 schillings to 280 schillings per hour rental. Advance reservations are suggested.
- **Sparkassen Squash and Tennis Center**, *Stadlweg 40, Innsbruck. Tel. 512-34-55-14*
- **Allround Tennis Club**, *Wiesengasse 16, Tel. 512-36-01-10, Innsbruck*
- **Outdoor Tennis Courts**, *Olympic Ice Stadium, Innsbruck*

Tobogganing

There are **toboggan runs** from Heiligwasser, Muttereralm, Birgitzalm, Kemateralm and Rangger-Kopfl. If you don't have your own sled, you can rent one. Prices range from 30 to 70 schillings per day.
- **Kaserer Sports Shop**, *Bilgeristrasse 18, Igls. Tel. 512-37-72-47*
- **Platzer Sports Shop**, *Eichlerstrasse 16, Igls. Tel. 512-37-73-77*
- **Raich Sports Shop**, *Bilgeristrasse 12A, Igls. Tel. 512-37-72-75*

DAY TRIPS & EXCURSIONS

Alpine Zoo

A fun side trip to make, especially if you are traveling with children, is to the **Alpine Zoo**, *Weiherburggasse 37, A-6020 Innsbruck, Tel. 512-29-23-23; fax 512-2930-89*. The zoo is home to more than 2,000 alpine creatures, some of them endangered, and is open daily from 9 a.m. to 6 p.m. Admission is 60 schillings for adults and 30 schillings for children. The **Innsbruck Information Office**, *Burggraben 3*, offers an "environmental ticket" for admission to the zoo and free public transportation.

Getting to the zoo is half the fun. You can take the **Hungerburgbahn**, a cog railroad affording a lovely view of Innsbruck below. Trains leave every 20 minutes from the station adjacent to the **Rundgemalde**, which can be reached by tram or bus 1, C, 4, D, and E. It takes about 20 minutes to walk to the zoo from the center of the town. A special bus line Z runs from May through September leaving from Maria Theresien Strasse 45, Hofburg.

If you have time, on your way to the zoo, stop off at the giant panoramic painting covering 1,000 square meters of canvas. The painting shows a scene of the Battle on the Bergsiel from 1809, and open to the public from April through October from 9 a.m. to 4:45 p.m. Take the Tram 1 in the direction of Hungerburg Funicular Railway Station.

Ambras Castle

This medieval castle is just outside Innsbruck's city limits. The castle was originally built between the 11th and 15th century. Archduke Ferdinand II rebuilt the castle in the Renaissance style, and gave it to his wife Philippine Welser of Augsburg. The castle houses Europe's oldest collection of arms. Ferdinand was a great collector and the castle has pieces from the archduke's museum on display from scientific items to bizarre curiosities.

The **Spanish Hall** was built by Ferdinand between 1570 and 1572. Painted on the walls of the Renaissance hall are portraits of the Tirolean sovereigns of the Hapsburg line. The castle's **portrait gallery** contains about 250 paintings of the royal families from the 14th to the 19th centuries. During Emperor Maximilian's reign, the **Giant's Hall** contained paintings of giants. But Empress Maria Theresa commissioned painter Franz Maulpertsch to decorate the ceiling with allegorical frescos depicting the alliance between the Hapsburg and Lothringen houses.

The castle is open daily from April through October, 10 a.m. to 5 p.m.; closed Tuesdays; from the end of December through March, guided tours are held Monday through Friday from 2 p.m. to 3:30 p.m. Admission for adults is 60 schillings; 30 schillings for children. For an additional 20 schillings, you can take a guided tour from April through October, Wednesday to Monday, after 10 a.m.; from December through March, Monday to Friday, 2 p.m. *Tel. 512-3412154 or 348446; fax 512-361542.*

You can take a local Innsbruck bus to the castle departing from Maria Theresien Strasse on the hour and from the castle on the half hour.

Hall in Tirol

Hall in Tirol, 10 miles east of Innsbruck, is probably most famous for the **Hasegg Castle** where Emperor Maximilian I held his wedding reception to his second wife Bianca Maria Sforza of Milan. Hasegg Castle, which dates back to 1306, originally served as a fortress protecting the nearby salt mines. The Hapsburgs later used the castle as the **Tirolean Mint** starting in 1567. The mint produced silver-talers, from which the American word "dollar" is derived. Today you can mint your own coins on a tour of the castle.

The old town is lovely with many other medieval attractions. The Town Hall, or **Rathaus**, was once the residence of the Tirolean dukes. The building was donated by Duke Leopold IV of Hapsburg in 1406 to serve as a town hall. The building was destroyed by a fire in 1447 but rebuilt soon after.

The **Parish Church of St. Nikolas**, with an enormous collection of relics appropriated by Florian Waldauf, made a knight by Emperor Maximilian I, is also worth a look. The statue of the Virgin Mary inside the church was carved by the famous Tirolean sculptor Michael Pacher. There is also a salt mining museum, Jesuit Monastery, and St. Magdalena's Chapel to visit if you have time.

For more information, contact **Hall in Tirol Tourist Information**, *Wallpachgasse 5, A-6060 Hall in Tirol. Tel. 5223-56269; fax 5223-562-6920.* Open Monday through Friday 8:30 a.m. to noon and 2 p.m. to 6 p.m.; Saturdays 8:30 a.m. to noon.

Highest European Bridge

You didn't realize that the continent's highest bridge is in Austria, did you? The bridge, part of the **Brenner Autobahn**, traverses the Wipp valley 190 meters above the **Sill River**. It is over 777 meters long and 657 meters wide and is supported by hollow pylons.

Lienz

Lienz, not to be confused with the capital of Upper Austria, Linz, is in **East Tirol**. It was first settled during the Roman times and the first written notation was recorded in 1022. Although the city has suffered several fires over the centuries, there are some well-preserved houses from the Middle Ages that still remain in the main square or **Hauptplatz**.

Also worth a visit is the **Brucke Castle**, which formerly was home to the counts of Gorz and today houses the municipal museum with early historical relics, local artworks, and farming tools. **St. Andrews Church**, overlooking the town, was built about 1450. The church has several impressive Romanesque elements from the lions guarding the door to column capitals decorated with masks and flowers. The **Isel Tower** dates from the 16th century.

The **Dominican Convent and Church** were founded in 1220 and is one of the oldest buildings in Lienz. The Romanesque church contains the fresco *The Virgin Mediatress* by Hans Andre and the wooden sculptures *Visitation of Mary* and *Saint Hyazinth*, by Hans Troyer who founded the convent.

Just four kilometers outside of Lienz on the left bank of the Debant river is the former town of **Aguntum**, originally an Illyrian settlement dating from 1100 B.C. The town grew into a thriving Roman provincial trading center at the time of Christ's birth. Today, ruins of the former town walls and an early Christian burial church can be visited.

Contact **Lienz Tourist Information**, *Europaplatz 1, A-9900 Lienz. Tel. 4852-65265; fax 4852-65265-2.*

Olympic Ski Jump

Tourists can visit the **Olympic Ski Jump** and **The Olympic Ice Stadium** with its speed skating rink year round in Innsbruck.

The **Olympic bobsled run** is in Igls. The run is still used for international bobsled and luge competitions. You can make your own run with an experienced driver for 300 schillings per person. Reservations can be made Tuesdays from 9 a.m. to noon and Thursdays from 7 p.m. until closing. *Call 512-37-75-25 or 71-60.*

Schwaz

According to local lore, the **silver deposits** in **Schwaz** were accidentally discovered by a servant girl in 1409 when her bull extracted a silver nugget with its horn. The mine helped to finance Emperor Maximilian I's numerous wars and political campaigns. Supposedly, the Hapsburgs would not have been able to maintain their power after Maximilian's death without the money generated from Schwaz from which to bribe their electors. At its height in the 16th century, Schwaz was the biggest mining town in Central Europe, and was second only to Vienna in size. You and your family can visit the mine today, taking the underground railway and exploring how silver and copper were taken from the earth through the centuries.

Contact **Schwazer Silberbergwerk**, *Besucherfuhrungs, Alte Landstrasse 3A, A-6130 Schwaz. Tel. 5242-72372-0; fax 5242-72372-4.* Open daily during the summer from 8:30 a.m. to 5 p.m.; wintertime 9:30 a.m. to 4 p.m. Guided tours last approximately two hours. Coats and helmets provided. Wear sturdy shoes.

The town also is home to an impressive Gothic **Parish Church** built during the height of the town's influence. Maximilian was also a frequent guest in Schwaz after a mining operator had the nearby **Tratzberg Castle** renovated in the Renaissance style.

During the summer months, **concerts** are held at the **Franciscan Monastery**.

PRACTICAL INFORMATION

American Express Office

You can change money, cash traveler's checks, and take care of your other financial needs at the local **American Express**, *Brixnerstrasse 3, A-6020 Innsbruck. Tel. 512-582-491; fax 512-573-385.* Open Monday to Friday 9 a.m. to 5:30 p.m.; Saturday 9 a.m. to noon.

Babysitting

If you need a babysitter, most hotels can refer you to an appropriate service – or contact the local tourist office or university. There are also kindergartens for visiting children available in Innsbruck and Igls:

• **Children's Day Care Center**, *Pradler Platz 6A, Innsbruck, Tel. 512-34-52-82*
• **Igls Visitors' Kindergarten**, *Kurpack, Igls. Tel. 512-37-89-08*

Consulate

• **British Consulate**, *Matthias-Schmid Strasse 12/1, A-6020 Innsbruck. Tel. 512-58-83-20*

Credit Cards

If your credit cards are lost or stolen, you can call the following numbers 24 hours a day (in Vienna, so first dial area code *0222*).

• **American Express**, *Tel. 51-29-714*
• **Diners**, *Tel. 50-1-35*
• **Mastercard**, *Tel. 71-7-01-0*
• **Visa**, *Tel. 53-4-87-77*

Emergency Phone Numbers

• **Ambulance**, *Tel. 144*
• **Police**, *Tel. 133*
• **Fire Department**, *Tel. 122*

Exchanging Money

Banks in general are open from 8 a.m. to noon and 2:30 p.m. to 4 p.m.; closed Saturdays, Sundays, and bank holidays. If you get caught without cash when banks are closed, there are several automatic money exchange machines throughout the city. Or go to the **Main Railway Station**, which is open daily from 7:30 a.m. to 8 p.m. or at the *Innsbruck Information Office, Burggraben 3*, which is open daily from 8 a.m. to 7 p.m.

Flightseeing

You can see the majestic alpine scenery from a different vantage point on high from a plane window. Try these folks:

• **Tiroler Flughafenbetriebs**, *Furstenweg 180, Innsbruck. Tel. 22-5-25-390 or 395.* A 25-minute flight over the Alps costs 750 schillings. A glacier flight costs 950 schillings for 30 minutes or 1,350 schillings for 50 minutes.

Guided Tours

The local tourist office sponsors guided tours of Innsbruck. A "long bus tour" includes a visit to the old town on foot and lasts about three hours. The tour starts daily at noon from the **Hotel Information tourist office** *at the Main Train Station* or at 12:10 p.m. from the Bozner Platz in front of the Hypobank.

A "short bus tour" takes about one hour and leaves from across the street from the Hofkirche at 10:15, noon, 2 p.m. and 3:15 p.m. from mid-May through October. Tickets for both tours can be purchased from local tourist offices, travel agencies, or on the bus. There are also day trips to points outside the city available. For more information, *call 53-56.*

Private guided tours can be arranged through the **Innsbruck Information Office**, *Burggraben 3. Tel. 53-56.*

Bus tours of Innsbruck are also possible through **Luftner Reisen**. Tours leave daily from the train station at 10 a.m., noon and 2 p.m.; and at Bozner Platz at 10:10 a.m., 12:10 p.m. and 2:10 p.m. The cost of the tours are a 150 schillings; children 70 schillings; children under six free. Tickets can be booked at the Innsbruck Information Office.

A 3-hour sightseeing tour on an old-style tram is also possible. The tour takes you through Innsbruck's Old Town, the Court Church, Wilten Basilica, the Abbey Church and Igls. The tours leave Thursdays at 9:30 a.m. during the summer from the tourist office. Tickets cost 190 schillings for adults and 95 schillings for children.

Laundromats

If you need to do your wash, you can head to the following coin-operated laundry in Innsbruck.

• **Waltraud Hell**, *Amraserstrasse 15. Tel. 552-341367.* Open Monday through Friday 8 a.m. to 6 p.m.

Lost & Found

The lost and found office in Innsbruck is located at the **main police station**, *Kaiserjagerstrasse 8. Tel. 59-00.*

Luggage Storage

You can check your luggage at the **Main Train Station** *in Innsbruck. Tel. 56-27-35.* Open from September through May 6:30 a.m. to midnight; June through August, open 24 hours a day.

Medical Treatment

If you need medical assistance you can go to the following locations in Innsbruck.

- **University Clinic**, *Anichstrasse 35. Tel. 552-504-0*
- **Ambulance Service**, *Sillufer. Tel. 552-33-444*
- **Dr. Pierer Private Clinic**, *Leopoldstrasse 1. Tel. 552-59-0-90*

Pharmacies

Several pharmacies are open 24 hours a day in case of emergencies. The address of the nearest open pharmacy will be posted in the window of each closed shop. If you have a pharmacy emergency, *call 1550.*

Post Office

The **Main Post Office**, *Maximilianstrasse 2. Tel. 500-0.* The post office is open 24 hours a day so you can post a letter, send a fax or make a phone call any time you want. The post office in the **train station**, *Bruneckerstrasse 1-3*, is open Monday through Friday from 7 a.m. to 9 p.m.; Saturday and Sunday 8 a.m. to noon.

Ticket Offices

If you need to buy ticket for entertainment events in Innsbruck or the surrounding area, you can visit the following locations in Innsbruck.

- **Innsbruck Information Office**, *Burggraben 3. Tel. 552-53-56-21*
- **Rindfleisch Autoreisen**, *Innrain 1. Tel. 57-72-81*
- **Tiroler Landesreiseburo**, *Bozner Platz 7. Tel. 59-8-85*

Tipping

A service charge is added to your hotel and restaurant bill. However, if you are pleased with the service, it is customary to tip an additional 5 to 10 percent of the check. Taxi drivers and hair dressers also are generally tipped the same amount.

Toll Roads

You'll have to pay a toll on the Brenner Motorway. Other toll roads include the Arlberg Tunnel, the Gerlos Road, the Timmelsjoch Road, the Felbertauern Road and the Silvretta Road.

Weather

You can get the latest weather information for Innsbruck from 6 a.m. to 8 p.m., *Tel. 512-28-17-38.* A recorded message is available *at 512-1566.*

For Alpine weather conditions from February through September, *call 512-291600* between 1 p.m. and 6 p.m. A recorded message can be heard *at 512-1567.*

18. VORARLBERG

INTRODUCTION

Vorarlberg sticks out like a sore thumb out of the western part of the country. The province is a study in contrasts. Its provincial capital, **Bregenz**, lies on **Lake Constance**, where swans, ducks and brightly colored boats painted in primary colors skim across the water. Visitors are just a leisurely boat ride away from Switzerland or Germany.

The province was first settled by the Illyrians, Celts, and Romans. By the fifth century, Rhaeto-Romanic and Alemannic peoples inhabited the region. The Hapsburgs eventually acquired the area of Vorarlberg (meaning "before the Arlberg"), but the province managed to keep its autonomous self-government. In 1918, Vorarlberg became an independent federal Austrian state after World War I.

Vorarlberg is also the home of some of the most fabulous skiing in the Alps. Ice age glaciers formed the landscape of Vorarlberg with its high mountain peaks and narrow valleys. Altitudes range from between 1,300 and 11,000 feet above sea level. The highest mountain is **Piz Buin**.

Vorarlberg enjoys mild to temperate summers and lots of snow for winter, turning the area into a sports wonderland. The mountains dividing Vorarlberg from neighboring Tirol have an international reputation for great skiing. The world's first ski resort was opened in **Arlberg** in 1906, and that tradition continues today with trails rising up to 8,500 feet high. The region also promotes other winter sports like snowboarding, paragliding, and cross-country skiing.

Each summer, Bregenz is brought to international cultural prominence with its music festival featuring the largest lake stage in the world. And the music of Schubert is celebrated annually in the medieval city of **Feldkirch**.

Vorarlberg is the smallest Austrian province, after Vienna, with an area of only 1,004 miles and 322,551 residents.

> ### VORARLBERG TOURIST TIPS
> *The Vorarlberg Tourist Office can provide hotel information, maps and much more, whether you're planning a skiing sojourn or a hiking adventure. Contact Vorarlberg Tourismus, Romerstrasse 7, P.O. Box 302, A-6901 Bregenz. Tel. 5574-42525-0; fax 5574-42525-5.*

ORIENTATION

There are several discounted passes for making your way around the region. The **Vorarlberg Tariff Verbund** can be purchased for 70 schillings per region and 120 schillings for the entire area per day. A one-day family pass costs 100 schillings per region and 160 schillings for the entire area. Tickets can be purchased for the day, week, month, or year. You can even ride to Buchs and St. Margarethen in Switzerland, Lindau in Germany, and St. Anton am Arlberg in Tirol.

The **Lake Constance Pass** allows you to buy an unlimited number of half-price tickets for all boat lines on Lake Constance, Untersee and the Rhine, train lines, bus lines and mountain cablecars around the lake. A set of three one-day passes costs 231 schillings. Children up to age six can travel for free. The passes can be bought through the **Vereinigte Schiffahrtsunternehmen**. Make sure to carry your passport with you, because you don't want to get caught going on a day-trip over the border without it.

Families will feel especially welcome in Vorarlberg. The province has 34 hotels and restaurants that participate in the **Family Club**. During the summer months, Vorarlberg hosts 200 events geared for children, including the international **Milka Giant Chocolate Festival** and **Lech Adventure for Children and Young People** with river rafting, climbing, camping and fishing.

Vorarlberg also has 400 participating farms where families can pitch in and enjoy the tranquility of country living. The tourist office publishes a catalogue with farm lodgings. The address is **Vorarlberg Tourismus**, *Romerstrasse 7, P.O. Box 302, A-6901 Bregenz. Tel. 5574-42525-0; fax 5574-42525-5.*

ARRIVALS & DEPARTURES

By Air

Vorarlberg is accessible from several international airports. The **Zurich Airport** is only 75 miles away from **Bregenz**, the provincial capital of the region. You can drive from the airport in about an hour and a half. Direct rail connections between Zurich and Bregenz take about two hours.

During the winter months, a ski transfer bus is available weekends between Zurich Airport and the Arlberg and Montafon resorts. Reservations for the service can be booked through Swissair, the Vorarlberg Tourist Office, or the Arlberg and Montafon tourist offices.

From **Munich International Airport**, it takes about three hours to make the 120 mile drive or three and a half hours by train. The German airport in **Friedrichschafen** is about 20 miles away. Motorists can expect an hour's drive to reach Vorarlberg. The ride by train takes about 40 minutes.

Flights to and from **Vienna** are also operated daily by **Rheintalflug**, which you can reach by telephone *at 48800*.

By Bus

You can travel to and from even the smallest towns in Vorarlberg by the **Bundesbus**, the bright orange buses operated by the Austrian postal service. Travel by Bundesbus is ideal if you want to get off the beaten track. But remember that the buses don't always run frequently and connections can be complicated. Be especially careful on the weekends and on holidays when service is often sporadic at best.

On Saturdays and Sundays during the winter, a ski transfer bus service runs between Zurich Airport and the Arlberg and Montafon winter sports regions.

By Car

Getting around the region is probably easiest by car if you want to see more than the major cities. You can reach Vorarlberg by taking A14 on the Austrian autobahn. Coming from Switzerland, take the N13 motorway.

By Train

Direct train connections run between Bregenz and **Munich**, **Innsbruck**, and **Friedrichshafen** in Germany. Innsbruck is about 125 miles away and train travel will take approximately two hours. There are also direct trains travel to **Feldkirch** from London, Brussels, and other European cities.

If you need **train information**, you can reach the Austrian railway system *at 1717*.

GETTING AROUND VORARLBERG

By Car

If you need to rent a car in Vorarlberg, Hertz and Avis both have offices in the province. Try to make advance reservations in from the states where you can get a much better deal.

• **Avis**, *Schwefel 53A, Dornbirn A-6850. Tel. 5572-29780*

• **Hertz**, *Immler Schneeweiss, Am Brand 2, A-6900 Bregenz. Tel. 5574-44995*

Having a car makes getting around Vorarlberg a lot easier. The mountains that blanket much of the province make train travel more difficult and time consuming than in other parts of the country.

If you have car problems, you can call the **Automobile, Motorcycle, and Touring Association** for help around the clock at *120*, or the **Automobile, Motorcycle, and Bicycle Association of Austria** at *123*.

By Public Transportation

For those of you have come to the region for a skiing holiday, Vorarlberg has **ski buses** and **trains** to the major resorts. Ski passes to the Lech and Zurs runs are limited to 14,000 at any one time. The limit though means that there is less congestion both on the slopes and on the roads. Holiday guests and visitors who come by train or bus are guaranteed an all-day ski pass.

Ski buses are available to resorts in Montafon, Brandnertal, Bregenzerwald, Klein Walstertal, Klostertal, Laternsertal and the Rhine Valley. Lech/Zurs and Klein Walsertal also have night taxis to get you to and from your hotel. Special buses catering to hikers are also available to drop off and pick up passengers at popular hiking trails. Contact the local tourist office for details.

By Taxi

If you need a taxi, *call 1718*.

WHERE TO STAY

Vorarlberg offers a wide variety of accommodation choices from luxury castle hotels to alpine huts and farms to *Zimmers* in private residences. Your choice of accommodation will depend on how you plan to spend your vacation. Local tourist offices can also help you choose and reserve a room.

Many hotels feature excellent restaurants, too. As mentioned below in the *Where to Eat* section, most of the better restaurants are attached to hotels, inns, and guesthouses, and they are reviewed as part of each hotel below. The few restaurants independent of hotels are reviewed separately in *Where to Eat*.

Below is a selection of hotels from around the province, beginning with **Bregenz**, the provincial capital:

Bregenz

HOTEL BONDENSEE, *Kornmarktstrasse 22, A-6900 Bregenz. Tel. 5574-42356; fax 5574-42356-6. Doubles start at 700 schillings, including breakfast. All credit cards accepted.*

The Hotel Bondensee, just minutes from the banks of Lake Constance, is run by the Guttler family. The light-filled rooms are large and comfortably furnished with a combination of modern and antique pieces. The staff bends over backwards to serve you and is ready with a helping hand whenever guests need it.

HOTEL MERCURE BREGENZ, *Platz der Wiener Symphoniker 2, A-6900 Bregenz. Tel. 5574-461000; fax 5574-47412. Doubles start from 720 schillings per person. All credit cards accepted.*

This 94 room hotel, with non-smoking rooms and those equipped for the disabled, is right on the banks of Lake Constance and within easy walking distance of the casino and the Festival Hall. Rooms are stylish and modern, although a bit cramped. The staff is discreetly helpful and accommodating. The hotel's restaurant **Symphonie** has a garden terrace for dining and a wide selection of regional and international cuisine.

KAISER HOTEL, *Kaiserstrasse 2, A-6900 Bregenz. Tel. 5574-52-9-80; fax 5574-52-9-82. Doubles are 1,290 per person, including breakfast. All credit cards.*

The Kaiser Hotel has recently undergone extensive renovations after being acquired by Veronika and Werner Brugger in the summer of 1995. The renovations have successfully blended an eclectic mix of Old World antiques and modern flair. This hotel may not be for traditionalists, but if you enjoy a slightly funky, hip atmosphere this is the place for you. Rooms have whirlpool tubs, televisions and VCRs, CD-players and minibars.

There are three places in the hotel where you can fuel up for a fun day of sight-seeing, skiing, or whatever you have in mind: the **Cafe Wien**, modeled after a typical Viennese cafe; the **Segafredo** espresso bar; and **Cafe Restaurant Heitinger**, featuring Italian specialties.

MESSMER HOTEL, *Kornmarktstrasse 16, A-6901 Bregenz. Tel. 5574-42356; fax 5574-42-3-56-6. Doubles start at 1,340 schillings, including breakfast. All credit cards accepted.*

The elegant Messmer Hotel is filled with modern touches from the light wood and chrome in the lobby to the rooms decorated in neutral colored wood, metal, and fabrics. The hotel, one of the oldest in Bregenz, has a good restaurant serving both classical Austrian favorites and international cuisine.

Ausserbraz

GASTHOF TRAUBE, *Klostertalestrasse 12, A-6751 Ausserbraz. Tel. 5552-8103; fax 5552-8103-40. Doubles start at 430 schillings per person. All credit cards accepted.*

The Gasthof Traube, run by the Lorunser family, has been renovated and enlarged to accommodate 44 guests. You can relax in front of the fire or take a break in the rustic Hunter's parlor. This guesthouse knows how to take care of guests with a sauna, solarium, massages, and sun deck available. There is also a swimming pool and a tennis court. The restaurant here showcases light, local cuisine. The guest house also hosts a weekly fondue dinner, a zither evening, and a candlelit dinner.

Bezau

GASTHOF GAMS, *A-6870 Bezau. Tel. 5514-2220; fax 5514-2220-24. Doubles start at 530 schillings per person, including breakfast. No credit cards accepted.*

If you're looking for some pampering in an elegant, but comfortable atmosphere, then the Gams Hotel is for you. The hotel, which has been in existence since 1648, is operated as a labor of love by the Nenning family. Rooms are charmingly furnished with a variety of rustic and antique pieces. Guests can rent the hotel's tennis courts for 150 schillings an hour. A heated outdoor swimming pool, whirlpool, sauna, fitness room, and solarium is also available for guests.

The hotel also has an excellent restaurant, which even offers a selection of diet and vegetarian cuisine. Traditional Austrian fare is also available, including garlic soup and *Zweibelrostbraten*, or pot roast smothered with onions. Children under three can stay free with their parents. Children six and under cost 220 schillings per night, and 12 and under cost 240 schillings per night. You can even take Fido along for the trip. Dogs cost 60 schillings per night. A shuttle service is also available. To Bregenz or Dornbirn, the cost is 580 schillings, and to Lindau or Feldkirch, the cost is 680 schillings.

GASTHOF HIRSCHEN, *Bregenzerwald, A-6870 Bezau. Tel. 5514-2382; fax 5514-3470. Doubles start at 360 schillings per person, including breakfast. No credit cards, but traveler's checks accepted.*

The Albrecht family runs this traditional guest house in the heart of Bezau. Although the family doesn't speak much English, their hospitality is evident in everything they do at this alpine-style chalet. The rooms are simply but cozily furnished. The gasthof also has a family-style restaurant featuring traditional Austrian favorites. In warm weather, you can have a beer or eat outdoors.

POST KUR AND SPORT HOTEL, *A-6870 Bezau. Tel. 5514-2207; fax 5514-2207-22. Double rooms start at 950 schillings per person. Visa, MasterCard and Diners Club accepted.*

If you want to pamper yourself, this hotel is the place for you. Furnished with lots of dark wood panelling and furniture, the hotel is comfortable and elegant. The Post Hotel also features tennis courts, swimming pools, saunas, massages, and other perks to refresh the body and spirit.The hotel has a restaurant open from 11:30 a.m. to midnight, although the offerings are less than inspiring. You might be better off looking for a better place to indulge in all those calories you've burned off "taking the cure."

Bludenz

HOTEL ALTDEUTSCHE STUBEN, *Werdenbergstrasse 40, A-6700 Bludenz. Tel. 5552-62005; fax 5552-620056. Doubles start at 400 schillings per person. All credit cards accepted.*

Located in the heart of the pedestrian zone in the historic heart of the city, the hotel is a five minute walk from the train station. The hotel also offers free ski bus transportation to Brandnertal. Rooms are spacious and comfortably furnished. The Hotel Altdeutsche Stuben's restaurant is furnished to look like an old-style German guest house. Or you can have a drink in the rustic bar in the cellar.

HOTEL LOWEN, *Mutterstrasse 7, A-6700 Bludenz. Tel. 5552-62206; fax 5552-622063. Doubles start at 480 schillings per person. All credit cards accepted.*

Under the capable management of the Neyer family, the Hotel Lowen is located just outside the city's historic center and a 10 minute walk from the train station. The hotel has only room for 12 guests; you'll feel as if you've been invited to someone's private country home. A playroom is available, if you're traveling with children. The hotel's restaurant features a selection of Austrian and international cuisine. The menu changes daily. If you prefer, you can eat in the garden.

Brand

HOTEL SCESAPLANA, *A-6708 Brand. Tel. 5559-221; fax 5559-445. Doubles start at 760 schillings per person. All credit cards accepted.*

The Hotel Scesaplana is operated by the Schwarzler family and has room for 72 people. Relax in front of the fire after a long day on the slopes. Rooms are elegant but welcoming. The hotel's restaurant is bounteous, with a daily buffet of appetizers and desserts offered with country classics. Guests can relax by using the hotel's pool, sauna, solarium, massage, tennis or billiards. Parking is also available for guests.

Burserberg-Tschengla

BERGHOTEL SCHILLERKOPF, *A-6700 Burserberg-Tschengla. Tel. 5552-63104; fax 5552-67487. Doubles start at 500 schillings per person. All credit cards accepted.*

The Berghotel Schillerkopf is in the shadow of the nearby ski lifts. The hotel underwent renovations in 1984, and rooms are large and comfortably furnished with rustic pieces. The lounge has a fireplace to warm yourself after a day on the slopes. There is also a television room and disco. If you prefer to relax in a more healthful way, there is a pool, sauna, solarium, and massage available for guests as well as table tennis and billiards. The restaurant has a buffet where you can refuel with Austrian specialties.

Feldkirch

ALPENROSE, *Rosengasse 6, A-6800 Feldkirch. Tel. 5522-721575; fax 5522-72175. Doubles start from 575 schillings per person, including breakfast. All credit cards accepted.*

The Alpenrose is located in the heart of Feldkirch's old town. The hotel, which has been in operation for several hundred years, is lovingly run by the Hefel-Gutwinski family. Rooms are elegantly furnished with the right balance of old world charm with modern amenities. Parking is available for guests.

CENTRAL LOWEN HOTEL, *Neustadt 15-21, Schlossgraben 13, A-6800 Feldkirch. Tel. 5522-720700; fax 5522-720705. Doubles start from 1,020 schillings. Diners, Mastercard and Visa accepted.*

The General Lowen hotel boasts that it has 136 beds. But you get the sense that the hotel specializes in moving large numbers of people in and out, losing sight of the personal touches. The hotel even has bus parking available. It could also do with a good renovation, since the furnishings are beginning to look a little dreary.

The hotel does, however, feature a sauna and steam room for guests to relax in, and a large restaurant with a super selection of regional specialties and international favorites.

HOTEL POST, *Schlossgraben 5, A-6800 Feldkirch. Tel. 5522-72820. Doubles start at 940 schillings, including breakfast. No credit cards accepted.*

The Hotel Post is centrally located right next to Feldkirch's cathedral. The hotel, run by the Sturzenbaum family, is filled with dark panelling and comes off as a bit somber and a little worn around the edges. But the staff is congenial and helpful. Rooms are comfortable, but ordinary.

JEGENDHERBERGE, *Reichsstrasse 111, A-6800 Feldkirch. Tel. 5522-73181; 5522-79399. 130 schillings per person, including breakfast. No credit cards.*

Feldkirch's youth hostel deserves mention since it has its own significant place in history. The building dates back to the 13th century and was originally a hospital serving victims of the plague. The old-fashioned beamed building is worth a look even if you don't want to stay here. The romantic setting and well-preserved building allows visitors to relive a bit of history.

Klosterle

SPORTHOTEL KLOSTERTALER HOF, *A-6754 Klosterle. Tel. 5582-535; fax 5582-5368. Doubles start at 460 schillings per person, including breakfast. All credit cards accepted.*

The Sporthotel Klostertaler is a family-style hotel with room for 40 guests. The rooms are comfortably sized and furnished, and many have balconies. The restaurant serves Austrian specialties in ample portions. Guests can unwind in the hotel's television room or in the hotel whirlpool. There is also a guest garden. Parking is available for clients only.

Lech

HOTEL ARLBERG, *A-6764 Lech. Tel. 5583-2134-0; fax 5583-2134-25. Doubles start 1,880 schillings per person. Diners, American Express and Visa accepted.*

The sprawling Hotel Arlberg manages to blend rustic charm with elegant style. Rooms are comfortably appointed and filled with light. Many have spectacular views of the nearby mountains. Guests can treat themselves to a swim, a game of tennis, a sauna, or a massage. The Hotel Arlberg's restaurant has been awarded two toques by Gault Millau. The restaurant specializes in game and fish dishes.

HOTEL GASTHOF POST, *A-6764 Lech. Tel. 5583-22060; fax 5583-220623. Doubles start at 2,000 schillings. Credit cards accepted at the restaurant but not in the hotel.*

The hotel was once the site of the city's post office. After a hard day on the slopes, you can relax in the hotel's lounges decorated with rustic furnishings, hunting trophies, and old-fashioned clocks. Rooms are also furnished in rustic-style with carved canopy and sleigh beds. The Moosbrugger family makes sure each guest's needs are met promptly. The guest house is also known for its restaurant, whose specialties include game and strudel. The wine list features a good selection of Austrian and French vintages.

St. Christoph

HOSPIZ HOTEL, *A-6580 St. Christoph. Tel. 5446-2611; fax 5446-3545. Doubles start at 1,300 schillings. All credit cards accepted.*

This mountain hotel has been in existence since 1386, located on the Arlberg Pass separating the Inn and Rhine valleys. Rustic open fireplaces and comfortable leather armchairs welcome skiers back from the slopes. Rooms are light-filled and beautifully decorated. Guests can relax in the hotel's swimming pool, whirlpool sauna and solarium. The Hospiz Hotel's restaurant specializes in fish and game dishes. The hotel also has one of the country's biggest wine collections.

Schruns

HOTEL TAUBE, *Am Kirchplatz, A-6780 Schruns. Tel. 5556-72384; fax 5556-72145-8. Doubles start at 350 schillings per person, including breakfast. All credit cards accepted.*

The family-style Hotel Taube is charming and well-run by the Nels family. Rooms are cozy and welcoming. The hotel also has a large garden for guests and outdoor seating where you can enjoy a drink and watch the world go by during warmer weather. The Hotel Taube's restaurant offers a selection of classic Austrian and international dining. Parking is available for guests.

KURHOTEL MONTAFON, *Ausserlitzstrasse, A-6780 Schruns. Tel. 5556-72791; fax 5556-72791-70. Doubles start at 700 schillings per person. All credit cards accepted.*

The Kurhotel Montafon is the place to go if you want to be pampered with the latest in beauty treatments. The staff bends over backwards to serve you. The rooms are elegantly furnished with rich fabrics and light wood furniture and most have balconies. The restaurant also caters to discriminating pallets. The hotel also has dancing, ping-pong, a solarium, a swimming pool and a sauna for guests.

WHERE TO EAT

Vorarlberg is known also for its light regional cuisine emphasizing the province's fresh ingredients from local farms, forests, and lakes. Fresh fish from one of the province's myriad lakes, streams, and rivers is often on menus. Cheese plays a big part in the cuisine here and is often added to soups, tops noodles and stuffed into dumplings. Try a *Kraphen*, a doughnut filled with cream or fruit puree, for a snack.

As in most other regions of Austria, most restaurant choices are part of hotels and guest houses. But try one of these places if you don't want to eat in a hotel setting:

Bregenz

LA TAVERNA, *Kirchstrasse 32, A-6900 Bregenz. Tel. 5574-44022. Inexpensive. Open 11:30 a.m. to 2 p.m. and 5 p.m. to midnight. No credit cards, but traveler's checks accepted.*

You wouldn't know you were outside of Italy in La Taverna. The waiters go out of their way to make sure your evening is exceptional. The atmosphere is festive but still warm and cozy. The restaurant has a wide variety of pizza and pasta selections to choose from and a good wine list. Seating is also available on an outside terrace.

MAURACHBUND, *Maurachgasse 11, A-6900 Bregenz. Moderate. 5574-44020. Open from 10 a.m. to midnight. Visa and Mastercard accepted.*

The Oriental rugs, rich wood panelling, and beautifully set tables make dining at the Maurachbund feel like you've been invited into someone's elegant private home. A glassed-in porch also makes it possible to "eat outdoors" in all different types of weather. The Maurachbund has a selection of traditional Austrian dishes and a good variety of fish to choose from. The staff, however, seems to be a bit harried.

WIRTSHAUS AM SEE, *Seeanlagen, A-6900 Bregenz. Tel. 5574-42210; fax 5574-42210-4. Moderate. Open 11 a.m. to midnight. No credit cards but traveler's checks accepted.*

You can't miss the Wirtshaus Am See. The pyramid-shaped restaurant borders Lake Constance and is lit with white lights like a Christmas tree. There is also an extensive terrace where you can enjoy your dinner while looking out over the water. You won't find any surprises on the menu. The restaurant offers typical Austrian fare from *Knodels* to *Schnitzel* to *Bratwurst*. But the scenic location enhances every meal.

GELATERIA DOLCE VITA, *Eispavillion am Molo, A-6900 Bregenz. Tel. 5574-4633. Open March through September, 10 a.m. to 11 p.m. No credit cards accepted.*

This old fashioned ice cream parlor is just a stone's throw away from Lake Constance and the ideal place to take a break from you sight seeing in Bregenz. Lots of delicious ice cream to choose from and all sorts of rich concoctions to savor.

Bezau

GASTHOF ENGEL, *Platz 29, A-6870 Bezau. Tel. 5514-2203; fax 5514-22034. Moderate. Open 11:30 a.m. to 2 p.m. and 5:30 p.m. to 11 p.m.; closed Wednesdays and in November. Traveler's checks or cash only.*

You won't find tired plates of pasta with watery tomato sauce here. This is Italian food at its best. Lorenzo de Gaetano, who left his native Italy for Austria after falling in love with his Austrian wife, prepares fresh, flavorful pasta dishes with a loving hand. Fish and meat dishes are also featured, from *Soglioa* in orange and lemon sauce with capers to veal in Marsala sauce. There's also a good selection of Italian antipastas, salads, and cheeses, plus a small but excellent choice of wines. Your tastebuds are in for a treat here.

Dornbirn

BELLA NAPOLI, *Schillerstrasse 2, A-6850 Dornbirn. Tel. 5572-21107. Moderate. Open daily 5 p.m. to midnight. All credit cards accepted.*

Pasta is king at Bella Napoli. This authentic Italian restaurant offers classic veal and poultry dishes from Naples. Choose a bottle of vino from Austria's southern neighbor to complement your meal. There are also the standard Austrian specialties if you prefer.

Feldkirch

BAHNHOFRESTAURANT, *Bahnhofstrasse 40, A-6800 Feldkirch. Tel. 5522-78070; fax 5576-780704. Moderate. Open daily 6:30 to 11 p.m. All credit cards accepted.*

As the name implies, this simple restaurant is within a stone's throw of the train station. You won't find any surprises on the menu, just the usual stick-to-your-ribs classics from Schnitzel to *Leberknodel Soupe* at very reasonable prices. The service is outgoing and adds to the atmosphere.

SEEING THE SIGHTS

Arlberg

Arlberg is a skiers paradise, and it should be since it was the site of the world's first ski resort, established in 1906. The peaks rise up to 8,250 feet with 79 mountain railways and lifts and 125 miles of ski trails. Vorarlberg's winter season officially begins here in early December. Ski passes are limited to 14,000 at any one time so you won't be bothered by overcrowding.

The **Arlberg Ski Pass** is valid for the region's 79 lifts and the nine lifts on neighboring **Sonnenkopf/Klosteral**. Passes are available from one to 15 days, or 21 and 30 days.

But don't worry if you're planning to visit during the summer months, since the area sponsors a wealth of summer activities for the whole family, including fishing, hiking, and swimming. Contact **Arlberg Tourist Information**, *Verkehrsamt, A-6764 Lech. Tel. 5583-2161-0; fax 5583-3155.*

Bludenz/Brand

Bludenz is a well-preserved medieval city on the **River Ill**, which marks the beginning to five different valleys and four mountain ranges. One of the oldest settlements in western Austria, the city still maintains its historic charm, especially in the pedestrian quarter with its cobbled streets, pastel homes, and wrought-iron signs. The Baroque **Gayenhofen Palace**, now regional administrative offices, and **Saint Laurentius Church**, with its massive onion spire, are the town's landmarks.

If you're here for a skiing holiday, there are 10 resorts with a total of more than 250 lifts within a 25 mile radius. The city offers free bus service to Brandnertal and Klostertal. The **Montafon Railway** travels between Bludenz and Schruns. Cross-country ski trails include the five-mile-long **Braz Trail** and the nine-mile-long **Rona Trail** on the Tschengla Plateau above Burserberg. A large natural ice rink is at the **Hinterplarsch**.

The local tourist office has information on hikes on the 250 miles of hiking trails and the 14 mountain refuges in the five valleys. Guided hikes are also possible. There are about nine miles of cycling paths in Bludenz and about 30 miles in the **Upper** and **Lower Walgau**. Guided cycling excursions and bike rentals are possible. Other sporting opportunities include tennis, swimming, fishing, and golf.

Only a few miles outside Bludenz is the Alpine village of **Brand**, where visitors can hike, ride horses or play tennis or golf. Hikers can follow routes leading into the Ratikon Mountains on the Swiss border. In the winter months, ski passes, valid for 13 lifts to the 28 miles of runs, are available from one to 20 days. During the off-season passes are good for six, seven, 13, and 14 days.

For more information, contact **Brand/Bludenz Tourist Information**, *A-6708 Brand. Tel. 5559-555-0; fax 5559-555-20.*

Bondensee

Nine miles of lake shoreline provide the backdrop for a variety of water sports and cycling. You can also head to the nearby mountains for some hiking and spectacular views.

For more information, contact **Bondensee-Rheintal Tourist Information**, *A-6900 Bregenz, Anton Schneider Strasse 4A. Tel. 5574-43391-0; fax 5574-43391-10.*

Bregenz

If you're visiting **Bregenz**, you'll want to take advantage of one of Vorarlberg's major attractions, **Lake Constance**, and possibly venture into neighboring Germany or Switzerland. The Austrian Federal Railways runs daytime excursion trips to the flower Island of Mainau, Konstanz, Meersburg, Unteruhldingen, Wasserburg, Rorschach, Rheineck and Walzenhausen. Or dance the night away on a dancing cruise in Bregenz Bay. Tickets are available at the harbor ticket office.

But if you're sticking to Bregenz, you can easily see the town on foot. Start your walking tour along the lake shore at the **Weather Column**. The column, with its meteorological instruments, was erected in 1887. Note the base where the distances to major European cities are listed in kilometers. Leaving the lake walking left along the **Seestrasse**, you'll come to the **Main Post Office**. The neoclassical building was built in 1893 by the Viennese architect Friedrich Setz. Because of the region's marshy soil, the post office was built on wooden pilings. To the right of the post office, is a statue of Anton Schneider, who led Vorarlberg in the fight against France and Bavaria in 1809.

Behind the post office is the **Nepomuk Chapel**, built in 1757 to serve fishermen and boatmen. If you make a left into **Kornmarktstrasse**, you will see the Baroque **Kornmesser Inn** built in 1720. The **Vorarlberg**

Provincial Museum, *Kornmarkt, Tel. 46050*, has a fine collection of ancient artifacts, including objects dating from Roman times, folk art, and paintings and graphics from the romantic period to modern times. The museum is open 9 a.m. to noon and 2 p.m. to 5 p.m.; closed Mondays except during the Bregenz Festival. Left of the **Rathausstrasse** is the **City Hall**, built in 1686. The building was originally used as a municipal granary. In 1898, the facade was remade in the late-Renaissance style and the gabled tower was added.

Near the city hall, is the **Lake Chapel**, dedicated to St. George. Legend has it that the chapel was built on the graves of Swiss soldiers who tried to take the city in 1408. Inside the chapel is a Renaissance altar. Head up the hill into the medieval old town passing through the **Oberstadt Gate**. The **Epona Stone** on the outside of the gate shows the Celtic-Roman horse goddess; the original is in the provincial museum. The coat of arms of the Bregenz and Montfort counts are also depicted.

If you walk left, you'll see **St. Martin's Church**, built in 1362. Fourteenth century frescoes adorn the church interior. **St. Martin's Tower**, constructed in 1599, has the largest onion dome in Central Europe. The tower today houses the province's **military museum**. If you continue along **Martinsgasse** you can see part of the old city wall. The Old City Hall is also found here. The half-timber building was constructed in 1662 by the Baroque architect Michael Kuen.

The house at Eponastrasse 4 used to be the Ehreguta Inn, named for the woman who supposedly saved the city during the Appenzell War. On **Ehreguta Square** is a fountain where on Ash Wednesday the traditional "purse washing" takes place, where carnival revelers wash out their now empty pocketbooks. To the left of the fountain is the **Deuring Castle** built by Michael and Johann Kuen in 1680. Descend the Meissner Stairway and continue about 50 meters to the **Thalbach Monastery** and the parish church of **St. Gallus**. The church grounds afford a good view of the old city wall and the **Baker Tower**, where bakers who baked too small loaves of bread were imprisoned. The church was originally constructed in 1097 but later Romanesque, Gothic, and Baroque elements were added.

For more information, contact the **Bregenz Tourist Office**, *Anton Schneider Strasse 4A, Postfach 187, A-6900 Bregenz. Tel. 5574-43391-0; fax 5574-43391-10.*

Bregenzerwald

Bregenzerwald is Vorarlberg's largest vacation hot-spot with 22 resorts, including several medium-sized downhill skiing sites. The **Three Valleys Super Pass** is good for 89 lifts in Bregenzerwald, Grosses Walsertal, and Lechtal in neighboring Tirol. Passes are good for between three and 21 days.

The area is also a mecca for cross-country skiing and hiking. Free guided hikes are available in Au, Schoppernau, Schrocken, and Warth from the end of June through October. Resorts in the area cater specifically to families, including holiday packages pitching in on the farm. The Bregenzerwald sponsors the **Nature and Life** program, uniting farmers and the tourism industry. Enjoy farm fresh milk and meat products here. Other attractions include a cablecar ride up Bezau's Sonderdach mountain, a summer sled run in Bezau, and a visit to the parish church in Schwarzenberg, with frescoes by the artists Angelika Kauffmann painted when she was only sixteen.

For more information, contact the **Bregenzerwald Tourist Information**, *A-6863 Egg. Tel. 5512-2635; fax 5512-3010.*

Dornbirn

Dornbirn is called Vorarlberg's *Garden City*. The **Rappenloch** in the city is one of the biggest and most spectacular gorges in the Eastern Alps. You can hike along the gorge to the romanticmountain valley of **Ebnit**. A cablecar can take you up to the top of the **Karren**, where you can gaze over the **Rhine Valley**, **Lake Constance**, and the **Alps**.

For more information, contact the **Dornbirn Tourist Information**, *A-6850 Dornbirn. Tel. 5572-22188; fax 5572-31233.*

Feldkirch

Feldkirch is an incredibly picturesque medieval town that looks like it could have stepped out of the pages of a storybook. The primary landmark in the town is the **Schattenburg Fortress**, once the seat of the Dukes of Montfort. The first mention of the city appeared in 842. The town charter dates to 1218, when Count Hugo of Montfort built the fortress. When Rudolph the Last died without an heir in 1377, Feldkirch came under Hapsburg control. Many of the city's former fortifications are still in existence.

Feldkirch is alive with history, from the **Katzentum tower** to the **Churertor gateway** and the **town hall** covered with colorful frescoes. Narrow winding streets are bordered by old-fashioned burghers' houses, preserved through the centuries. The town also has an impressive gothic cathedral and the **Liebfrauenkirche**.

For more information, contact the **Feldkirch Tourist Information**, *Herrengasse 12, A-6800. Tel. 5522-23467 or 73467; fax 5522-29867 or 79867.*

Fraxern

Fraxern is blessed with a sunny climate, which helps to nurture the cherries that are grown here. More than 20 different varieties can be found and many are then turned into the *Fraxner Schnapps*, which is distilled from the fruit. Fraxern is particularly beautiful in the spring when the cherry trees are in bloom.

For more information, contact the **Fraxern Tourist Information**, *A-6833 Fraxern. Tel. 5523-4511; fax 5523-53189.*

Grosses Walsertal

This Alpine valley places an emphasis on preserving the region's traditional way of life. The area has smaller ski resorts and cross-country skiing. You're also more likely to make less of a dent in your pocketbook with the valley's lower-cost accommodations. Tobogganning parties, lantern hikes, dances, and folklore evenings can be taken advantage of when you're finished with the slopes. Gourmands should visit one of the Alpine dairy farms here where traditional mountain cheeses are made from fresh milk. Farms in Sonntag, Raggal, Fontanella, and Thuringerberg can be booked during the winter months.

Grosses Walsertal was originally settled in 941 by the hermit Gerold, where he lived a life of prayer. Around 1300, the Valaisan farmers moved into the region from what is now Switzerland. Their traditions have survived into the present day in local dialect and colorful folk costumes, which you may be surprised to see worn on the streets.

For more information, contact the **Grosses Walsertal Tourist Information**, *A-6741 Raggal. Tel. 5553-228; fax 5553-380.*

Hohenems

Hohenems has a **Jewish museum** with exhibitions documenting Jewish life in the Lake Constance area and day-to-day existence in a Christian-dominated society. The museum is located in the historic **Heimann-Rosenthal Villa**. There is also a Jewish cemetery that you can visit. Hohenems can be reached from Bregenz via Dornbirn.

For more information, contact the **Jewish Museum**, *Schweizer Strasse 5, A-6845 Hohenems. Tel. 5576-73989-0.* Open Thursday through Sunday 10 a.m. to 5 p.m.; Wednesdays 10 a.m. to 9 p.m. Admission is 30 schillings.

Klein Walsertal

The three large skiing regions here are within Austrian territory, but use Deutsche marks as they're in the German customs area. Forty miles of groomed ski trails are available with 57 lifts. The **Klein Walsertal/ Oberstdor pass** is valid for one to 31 days. Cross-country skiing, snowboarding, tobogganing and hiking are also popular. When you get off the slopes, you can try your luck at the local **casino**.

Kids will enjoy the ski kindergartens, children's ski races, group tobogganing, story telling hours, horse-drawn sleigh rides and video afternoons. A ski bus service runs every 15 minutes. A night bus service is also available from 8 p.m. to 3 a.m. for night owls to get home.

For more information, contact the **Verkehrsamt Klein Walsertal Tourist Information**, *A-6992 Hirschegg. Tel. 5517-5114-0; fax 5517-5114-21.*

Klosertal

The **Klosteral valley** connects the eastern and western Alp, linking Vorarlberg and Tirol. Between the Arlberg Pass and Bludenz, the region is known as the **Valley of the Post**. This postal tradition is celebrated every summer with post coach rides and trips on the old post bus. During the winter, the post buses are transformed into free buses for skiers. Skiing on the **Sonnenkopf** is reasonably priced and is made for family vacations. The **Sonnenkopf Ski Pass** is valid for nine lifts and 39 trails and is available for one to 15, 21, or 30 days. Snow-boarders should head to the **Glattingrat**, which has a half-pipe trail.

For more information, contact the **Klostertal Tourist Information**, *A-6752 Dalaas. Tel. 5585-244; fax 5585-590.*

Lech

Snow depth of two meters is not unusual here in **Lech**, even in the valley. Until 1939, only intrepid skiers on foot could conquer the virgin slopes. Today, however, the region has a worldwide reputation as a skier's paradise. Snow surfing, paragliding, and skiing via helicopter are also possible. Lech's districts include the romantic hamlet of **Zug**, car-free **Oberlech**, and beautiful **Stubenbach**. In the summer, there are lots of opportunities for hiking, biking, swimming and tennis.

For more information, contact the **Lech Tourist Board**, *A-6764 Lech Am Arlberg. Tel. 5583-2161-0; fax 5583-3155.*

Montafon

Ernest Hemingway was a frequent visitor to this Austrian alpine valley with its four large skiing areas and extensive cross-country trails. **Montafon** boasts 148 miles of groomed ski runs with about 73 lifts. Passes are available from three to 14 days or 21 days. During the off-season, passes are issued for six, seven, 13, and 14 days. Your ski pass entitles you to use any bus and the Montafon Railway between Bludenz and Schruns for free. In the summer, hikers can take their pick from leisurely strolls to climbing glaciers in the **Silvretta Mountains**. Tennis, golf and cycling opportunities also abound.

For more information, contact the **Mountafon Tourist Information**, *A-6780 Schruns, Silbertalerstrasse 1. Tel. 5556-72253; fax 5556-74856.*

Oberland

The **Laterns-Gapfohl** ski region in Oberland is a popular family vacation spot. There are more than 27 kilometers of ski runs and a natural toboggan run that is four kilometers. The ski area is only 20 minutes away from the Rhine Valley. Ski buses run between the Laternsertal from nearby Feldkirch and Rankwell.

For more information, contact the **Oberland/Feldkirch Tourist Information**, *Herrengasse 12, A-6800 Feldkirch. Tel. 5522-73467; fax 5522-79867.*

Schruns

Excellent hiking is just a cable car away from **Schruns**. The **Hochjochbahn** will transport you up to the **Kapellalpe** (1,850 meters high) and to the **Sennigrat** (2,300 meters high). Panoramic views await you along the **Verwall** mountain range. There are a variety of cable car tickets available ranging in price from 37 to 230 schillings.

For more information, contact the **Schruns Tourist Information**, *A-6780 Schruns 1. Tel. 5556-2166; 5556-72554.*

Zurs

Viktor Sohm opened the first public ski course in **Zurs** in 1906 in the Arlberg region. A year later Hannes Schneider started the Arlberg Ski School and an industry was born. The resorts really took off in the 1920s, when skiers from around Europe discovered this skiing mecca. The region's first ski lift appeared in 1937.

Today, the lifts and cable cars in Zurs, Lech, St. Anton, and Stuben can carry up to 105,000 people an hour. The area has excellent snow conditions, and the season extends from late November through April. Locals say that every run begins and ends at your front door with the snow "reaching right up to your bed." After a hard day on the slopes, you can relax with a massage, sauna, or Turkish bath.

For more information, contact the **Zurs Tourist Board**, *A-6763 Zurs. Tel. 5583-2245; fax 5583-2982.*

NIGHTLIFE & ENTERTAINMENT

The **Bregenz Festival** is held from the last week in July through the month of August and features the best in opera, drama, and concerts with internationally renowned performers. The stage for the event on Lake Constance provides a dramatic backdrop to the nightly performances. Be sure to bring along a raincoat and hat. Performances are usually still held on the lake stage during inclement weather. If you are planning a trip to Bregenz for the festival, book your hotel well in advance as accommodations can be difficult to get if not already reserved.

The Bregenz Spring festival takes place from mid-March to mid-May and features concerts and ballet performances. For more information or to reserve tickets, contact **Bregenzer Festspiele GmbH**, *Platz der Wiener Symphoniker 1, A-6900 Bregenz. Tel. 5574-4920-223; fax 5574-4920-228.*

Each summer in **Feldkirch**, the **Schubertiade Festival** celebrates the genius of Schubert with piano recitals, chamber events, and orchestra concerts. You can book tickets in advance by telephone, mail, or fax. You cannot use credit cards, but must pay with a bank transfer or postal order. Tickets are then sent registered mail. No refunds are available. An invoice for hotel reservations will be sent with tickets if you would like them to be made for you.

For more information, you can contact the following tourist information offices where the concerts take place:

- **Feldkirch Tourist Office**, *Herrengasse 12, A-6800 Feldkirch. Tel. 5522-73467; fax 5522-79867*
- **Schwarzenberg Tourist Office**, *A-6867 Schwarzenberg. Tel. 5512-3570; fax 5512-2902*
- **Schloss Achberg**, **Wangen Tourist Office**, *Rathaus, D-88239 Wangen im Allgau. Tel. 7522-74211; fax 5722-74111*

Feldkirch is also the site in July of the annual **Wine Festival**, featuring the vintages from the slopes of the Ardentzenberg. If you're looking for some less highbrowed entertainment, perhaps the **Jugglers' Festival** is right up your alley. The festival takes place each August.

During the summer months, **Bludenz** hosts several different festivals from the largest chocolate festival in Europe to a festival of children's drama, a street magician's competition, the Alpinale film festival, and a contemporary music festival. Contact the local tourist office for details: **Bludenz Tourismus**, *Werdenbergerstrasse 42, A-6700 Bludenz. Tel. 5552-62170; fax 5552-67597.*

Every August in **Klostertal**, the **Valley of the Post** celebrates its heritage with a parade of horse and carriage teams.

For gamblers, there are two **casinos** in Vorarlberg, one in Bregenz and the other in the Kleinwastertal. Games include poker, red dog, French and American roulette, baccarat, slot machines and black jack and wheel of fortune. Head to the **Casino Kleinwalsertal**, *Riezlern*. Open daily from December 25 to March 31, 5 p.m. to midnight; April 1 to December 23, 7 p.m. to midnight.

SHOPPING

Be sure to pick up some chocolate if you traveling to **Bludenz**. The city is the home of **Milka chocolates**. You'll notice their purple packets of chocolate in almost any store you go to in Austria. If you're standing downwind, sometimes you can even detect the delectable odor of chocolate wafting from the factory near the train station.

Milka Factory Store, *Fohrenburgstrasse 3, Tel. 5552-609-304.* Open Monday through Friday, 9:15 a.m. to 11:30 a.m. and 1:30 p.m. to 4:30 p.m.

SPORTS & RECREATION

Most resorts offer skiing in winter and hiking in summer, so no matter what time of year you find yourself in Vorarlberg there will be something active to pursue.

Biking

Vorarlberg has more than 180 miles of biking paths from the plains between Lake Constance and the Rhine to steep mountain trails. Cycling maps are available at most local tourist offices and are sold in area book stores. Bike rentals are possible at several regional train stations, including **Bregenz**, **Dornbirn**, **Hohenems**, **Feldkirch**, **Grotzis** and **Rankweil**. The cost of bike rentals range from 50 schillings up to 140 schillings.

Cycling tour packages are also available for avid bicyclists. All the details of a perfect cycling vacation are taken care of including hotel reservations, bike rentals, luggage transport, and guides. Contact **Vorarlberger Landesreiseburo**, *Marktrasse 18D, A-6850 Dornbirn. Tel. 5572-27762-14; fax 5572-28356.*

Boating

If you want to take a spin around **Lake Constance** there are tours and excursions leaving from **Bregenz harbor**, which can be reached by calling *5574-42868.* If you prefer to go boating on your own, there are several options for renting. Electric boats can be rented for 200 schillings per hour and pedal and rowboats can be rented for 110 schillings per hour. Taxi speed boat tours for up to seven people are available for 700 schillings for half an hour. Motor boat tours are also available on the **Silvrettasee**. Tickets cost 40 schillings for adults and 20 schillings for children.

Contact **Illwerke Seilbahn Betriebsgesellschaft**, *A-6780 Schruns. Tel. 5556-701-3167; fax 5556-701-3370.*

Fishing

Anglers can fish in **Lake Constance**, **Bregenzerach**, **Subersach**, and **Weissach**. You must first obtain a permit, though, from the Bregenz

Tourist Office. Fishing is also possible on the Lunersee, Silvrettasee, Vermuntsee, and the Kopssee lakes. Fishing cards must be purchased each day, and four fish can be caught. The cards cost 250 schillings or 170 schilling with a guest card obtained from your hotel or the local tourist office.

Contact **Illwerke Seilbahn Betriebsgesellschaft**, *A-6780 Schruns. Tel. 5556-701-3167; fax 5556-701-3370.*

Hiking

Hiking maps are available from most local tourist offices and at bookstores. Mountain guides can be booked to lead you on your way. The region also has several **mountaineering schools** that provide instruction on hiking and climbing, including sites in **Arlberg, Wolfort**, and **Bregenzerwald.**

Alpine Associations in the province run 39 huts where you can get refreshments after your journey and even spend the night between May and October. Local tourist offices can provide you with logistical information. Reservations are essential. If you'd prefer to take the easy way out, there are more than 50 mountain railroads servicing Vorarlberg to get you up to those fantastic mountain views quickly. Hikers' buses also run at the most popular hiking areas.

For serious hikers, there are several tourist packages available from May to late September. Hikes last between almost four hours to more than nine hours each day. While you're out in the mountains, your luggage is brought to your next hotel. Experienced guides can you take you on special tours through the mountains. For example, you can join the program **Via Valtellina** following the historic route that was used to transport Veltliner wine to Germany or the program **On the Tracks of the Walsers** from Klein Walsertal across the Montafon into neighboring Switzerland.

Contact **Vorarlberger Landesreiseburo**, *Marktstrasse 18D, A-6850 Dornbirn. Tel. 5572-27762-14; fax 5572-28356.*

Horseback Riding

If you are interested in riding horses, you can contact the **Bregenz Riding Club**, *Achsiedlungsstrasse, A-6901 Bregenz. Tel. 5574-76162.* Riding is also possible in the **Grosses Walsertal**. Contact local tourist offices for information on stables that conduct tours of the neighboring countryside.

In **Schruns**, you can try **horse trekking**, which is riding with sturdy Haflinger horses carrying your packs. Meals around the campfire add to the charm of the adventure. Contact the **Schruns Tourist Information**, *A-6780 Schruns 1. Tel. 5556-2166.*

Nature Preserves

Besides skiing and hiking opportunities, Vorarlberg has a wealth of nature reserves, parks, animal preserves and recreational facilities.

In **Bartholomaberg**, you can take an eight or nine hour hike tracing the geological history of the valley with illustrated charts along the way. Of course, shorter hikes are also a possibility. You can also explore the geological history of the **Breitach Ravine** in **Kleinwalsertal**.

In **Bizau**, you can hike the nature path along **Hirsch Mountain** or take a ride down on the **Hirschberg Summer Sled Run**. Guided tours in July and August are available of the cave labyrinth and underground lake at **Schneckenlochhohle**.

Bregenz is not only home to the regional capital but also to the **Pfander Wildlife Park**, which you reach by taking a funicular. You can watch a bird of prey demonstration at 11 a.m. and 2:30 p.m. from May to September. Admission for adults is 40 schillings and for children 20 schillings. The **Burs Gorge** and **Scesa Ravine** boast the largest wash in Europe. In **Dornbirn**, the **Rappenloch** and **Alploch** gorges are two of the largest in the Eastern Alps. And **Feldkirch** has the **Ardentzenberg Wildlife Park** and nature path for the whole family to explore.

For information about specific events during your visit, contact the **Vorarlberg Tourist Office**, *Romerstrasse 7, P.O. Box 302, A-6901 Bregenz. Tel. 5574-42525-0; fax 5574-42525-5.*

Sailing

If you want to set sail, visit the **Lochau Sailing School**, *Alte Fahre*, or the **Lochau Tourist Office**, *A-6911, Tel. 45304.*

Skiing

Ski **rentals** are available at all the major resorts at sporting shops and through members of the Skibischuh system. Bindings can be fitted in a matter of minutes and you can head out to the slopes. There are ski schools for all ages at the major resorts, including ski schools for tiny tots. Most ski towns even have ski and guest kindergartens for children.

Some of the best skiing in Austria is in Vorarlberg. The Arlberg region is spectacular, as are other parts of this beautiful province. For more details on ski towns, see Seeing the Sights above.

For the latest information on the ski season in Vorarlberg, you can request a copy of the *Vorarlberg Winter Journal* from **Vorarlberg Tourism**, *P.O. Box 302, A-6901 Bregenz, Austria. Tel. 5574-425250; fax 5574-425255.*

Spas

Spas around Vorarlberg offer everything including water therapy, holistic beauty treatments, massages and diet regimes. Spas are located in

Bezau, Dornbirn, Feldkirch, Gaschurn, Krumbach, Koblach, Lingenau, Reuthe and **Schruns**. Beauty treatments can be arranged in **Bezau, Brand, Dornbirn, Gaschurn, Hirschegg, Lech, Reuthe, Schruns** and **Sulzberg**. Check *Where to Stay* above for more details on various spas.

Squash

Squash courts can be rented for 80 to 110 schillings per half hour. The courts are in **Lauterach**, *Badweg 5, A-6923 Lauterach. Tel. 5574-75350.*

Swimming

If you're in the mood to take a dip, there are a lot of options in **Bregenz** along **Lake Constance** where there is a municipal lakeside bath, lake promenade and lake parks. The facilities are open from 9 a.m. to about 8 p.m.; the indoor lake pool is closed Mondays. The sauna and fitness center is open Tuesday through Friday, 5 p.m. to 8 p.m. On Saturdays, the **Mili** bathing beach opens at 9 a.m.

Tennis

Courts are available for rent in Bregenz. You should make a reservation in advance to make sure a court is available. **Bregenz Tennis Club**, *Druckergasse 13. Tel. 5574-74540.* Courts cost 120 schillings per hour.

Try also the **Dopfer Tennis School** and indoor tennis courts, *Tel. 5574-77773.* Courts cost 130 schillings in the summer months and 180 to 250 schillings during the winter months.

Waterskiing

You can waterski in **Bregenz**, although advance booking is necessary. Contact the **Schneeweiss Waterskiing School**, *Am Brand 2. Tel. 5574-43333.*

Windsurfing

Windsurfing is possible only at the **Wocherhafen**, which is located outside of Bregenz.

DAY TRIPS & EXCURSIONS

If you're staying in Bregenz and want to take a walk on the wild side, you can take a **cable car** up the **Pfander**, the highest mountain at Lake Constance rising 1,064 meters high. The cable car is open from 9 a.m. to 6 p.m. A roundtrip ticket costs 110 schillings, 73 schillings for children.

Near the cablecar station at the top of the mountain there is a marked foot path with explanations of Alpine animals and a playground for kids. There are daily bird of prey demonstrations, including owls, vultures and eagles, from May through September, 11 a.m. and 2:30 p.m. Admission is 40 schillings for adults and 20 schillings for children. If you want to walk back into town, the hike will take you approximately two hours. You can get down the mountain by taking the Fluh or Gebhardsberg paths.

Or take a trip on an old-fashioned **locomotive**. The **Walderbahnle** travels from Bezau to Bersbuch and back again. Roundtrip tickets cost 55 schillings and 25 schillings for children. Contact **Verein BWB**, *A-6941 Langenegg 39. Tel. 5513-6192; fax 5513-6192-4.*

You can also make easy day trips to **Germany, Switzerland**, and **Liechtenstein** from Vorarlberg. The countries are literally a lake trip away and several boat are available from Bregenz.

PRACTICAL INFORMATION

Automobile & Touring Clubs

If you are traveling in Vorarlberg by car and need some information or assistance, you can contact the following local associations:
- **OAMTC**, *Brosswaldengasse, A-6900 Bregenz, Tel. 5574-44378*
- **OAMTC-Vorarlberg**, *Rossmahder 2, A-6850 Dornbirn. Tel. 5572-23692*
- **ARBO**, *Rheinstrasse 86, A-6900 Bregenz, Tel. 5574-78100*

Credit Cards

If your credit cards are lost or stolen, you can call the following numbers 24 hours a day to make a report. The numbers are located in Vienna, so first dial area code *0222.*
- **American Express**, *Tel. 51-29-714*
- **Diners**, *Tel. 50-1-35*
- **Mastercard**, *Tel. 71-7-01-0*
- **Visa**, *Tel. 53-4-87-77*

Emergency Phone Numbers
- **Ambulance**, *Tel. 144*
- **Police**, *Tel. 133*
- **Fire Department**, *Tel. 122*

Exchanging Money

You can change money at most bank branches and at the post office. In **Bregenz**, currency exchange machines are available at **Raiffeisenbank**, *Kornmarktstrasse 14* and **Volksbank**, *Bahnhofstrasse 12.*

Flightseeing

If you'd like to see a bird's eye view of Vorarlberg, you can take a sightseeing flight costing from 500 to 1,900 schillings depending on the excursion. For more information, contact **Rheintalflug**, *A-6900 Bregenz. Tel. 5574-48800.* Or perhaps you'd prefer to take a ride in a **hot air**

balloon. For more information, contact **G. Schabus**, *A-6833 Klaus. Tel. 5523-51121.*

Pharmacies

Several pharmacies are open 24 hours a day in case of emergencies. The address of the nearest open pharmacy will be posted in the window of each closed shop. If you have a pharmacy emergency, *call 1550.*

Post Office

If you're looking for a post office with extended hours to exchange money, mail letters, or make a phone call, go to the **Bregenz branch**, *Seestrasse 5, A-6900 Bregenz. Tel. 5574-4900-0.* The post office is open Monday to Saturday, from 7 a.m. to 9 p.m.; Sundays and holidays 9 a.m. to 9 p.m.

Tipping

A service charge is added to your hotel and restaurant bill. However, if you are pleased with the service, it is customary to tip an additional 5 to 10 percent of the check. Taxi drivers and hair dressers also are generally tipped the same amount.

Toll Roads

You'll be forced to pay a toll on the **Silvretta Alpine Road** from Partenen in Montafor to Galtur in the Paznaun Valley in neighboring Tirol. The road is open only in summer. The cost for adults is 40 schillings and for children 15 schillings.

Traveling through the **Arlberg Tunnel** from Langen in the Klosteral to St. Anton am Arlberg in Tirol will cost 150 schillings. Some other alpine routes also charge a toll so be prepared to pay along the way.

Traffic Restrictions

Trailers are not allowed on the **Arlberg Pass Road** from Langen. No trailers are permitted on the **Silvretta Alpine Highway** between Partenen and Galtur. Several mountain roads are also restricted, so check your route before you travel.

Winter Driving

Snow chains can be rented from most gas stations and garages. Several roads are closed in Vorarlberg during the winter, including the **Silvretta Alpine Highway**. Roads in Lech, Warth, Laterns, Damuls, Hittisau, Balderschwang and Allgau may also be shut down depending on weather conditions. If you are unsure of weather conditions, check your route with one of the local auto clubs.

19. CARINTHIA

INTRODUCTION

Carinthia, Austria's southernmost province, is surrounded by mountains, including the highest in Austria, the **Grossglockner**, rising 3,798 meters into the heavens. The **High Tauern Mountains** border the north and the **Karawanken Range** marks the south of Carinthia, which gets its name from the Celtic word *carant* for friend. In addition, Carinthia is splashed with more than 1,200 lakes and some 8,000 kilometers of meandering rivers.

The spectacular scenery makes Austria's sunniest province a perfect stop for hiking and biking in summer and skiing in winter. Carinthia is also a gateway into neighboring Italy and Slovenia. **Klagenfurt**, the provincial capital, was established about 850 years ago. Italian architects working in the 16th and 17th century gave the city its character with its arched courtyards liberally sprinkled throughout the old town. The 400 year-old waterway, the **Lend Canal**, leads from the city to the famous **Worther See**, and is bordered by villas constructed at the turn of the century. If you have the time, make a detour to the towering **Hochosterwitz Fortress**, one of the most impressive and well-preserved in Austria.

During the summer, Austrians head to the so-called **Carinthian Riviera**, around the Worther See. The alpine lake is Europe's warmest. Sun worshipers and water lovers bask in the warm glow of this lovely province during the summer season, so make sure to plan ahead and book your hotel reservations in advance. Other popular resort lakes are the **Ossiacher See**, the **Millstatter See**, and the **Weissensee**. If you'd like to find your own private getaway, Carinthia has hundreds of smaller lakes, thermal springs, and waterparks where you can sooth your aches and pains away.

With the first snows, Carinthia is transformed into a winter wonderland. The mountains provide a wealth of downhill runs for skiers and more than 1,500 kilometers of cross-country tracks. The lakes, where visitors sunned themselves during the summer, are converted into huge ice skating arenas when they freeze over during the winter. Other more unusual ice sports include an ice golf course on Lake Weissensee, ice surfing, curling and *ski-joring*, in which skiers are towed by ponies.

Carinthia has abundant natural resources. The timber-rich region provides much of the lumber for the rest of the country. Each year, Carinthia hosts a **timber fair** in the provincial capital of Klagenfurt. Iron ore, lead, tungsten, and zinc are also mined here. Carinthia is 3,680 square miles and has a population of 551,293 residents. The province is also home to a group of Slovenians who live in the Gail, Rosen, and Jaun valleys.

CARINTHIA TOURIST TIPS

You can write or call the province's main tourist office for additional information, or you can surf the Internet to plan your trip to Carinthia. The regional tourist offices provide a variety of useful help from finding a hotel to participating in water sports.

__Klagenfurt Tourismus__, Rathaus, Neuer Platz, A-9010 Klagenfurt. Tel. 463-537-223; fax 463-537-925. Open May through September, Monday through Friday 8 a.m. to 8 p.m.; Saturday and Sunday from 10 a.m. to 5 p.m.; October through April, Monday through Friday from 8 a.m. to 6 p.m.

__Information Office Minimundus__, Villacher Strasse 241, A-9020 Klagenfurt. Tel. 463-23651. Open daily May through mid-October, 10 a.m. to 8 p.m.

__Information Office Volkermarkter Strasse__, Volkermarkter Strasse 225, A-9020 Klagenfurt. Open daily mid-June through mid-September, 2 p.m. to 8 p.m.

You can send e-mail to the tourist office at: __Klagenfurt-Info@W-See.or.at__ or reach their Internet web site at: __http://WWW.W-See.or.at/ Klagenfurt/__

ORIENTATION

The Klagenfurt Tourist Office offers a **Guest Passport** to visitors staying in local hotels, pensions, and camping grounds. The card offers discounts to the local indoor swimming pool, the SSC Squash and Sauna Center, KLC Tennis, the Planetarium, Happ's Reptile Zoo, the Federal Museum, the Knoll Riding Stable and the Town Parish Church. The tourist office also publishes a listing of concerts taking place in the area. Contact them at **Klagenfurt Tourist Information**, *Rathaus, Neuer Platz, A-9010 Klagenfurt. Tel. 463-537-223; fax 463-537-295.*

If you're traveling to the Millstatter See, you can save using the **Inclusive Card**, with discounts on indoor swimming pools, shuttle buses, and free boat trips. Visit or call the **Millstatter See Tourist Office**, *Kongresshaus, A-9872 Millstatt. Tel. 4766-37000; fax 4766-37008.*

ARRIVALS & DEPARTURES

By Air

The **Klagenfurt Regional Airport** is located about five kilometers northeast of the town center.The main number at the airport for general information is *463-415000*. Flights between Klagenfurt and Vienna take about an hour.

By Train

Klagenfurt is accessible from all the major cities in the country and from other locations around Europe. The trip takes about three and a half hours from Graz, four hours and 26 minutes from Innsbruck, two and half hours from Salzburg and four hours and 42 minutes from Vienna.

Smaller cities in the province are often difficult to reach by train. If you want to get off the beaten track, you should consider taking a car to explore Carinthia to its best advantage.

By Car

If you're traveling to Carinthia by car, Klagenfurt is 334 kilometers southwest of Vienna, 153 kilometers southwest of Graz, 318 kilometers southeast of Innsbruck and 231 kilometers south of Salzburg.

If you're approaching Carinthia from the east from either Graz or Vienna, take the A2 Sudautobahn. If you're traveling from Salzburg, take the A10 Autobahn traveling south. From Innsbruck and other points west, take the Kufstein-Sud exit at the Inntal Junction. Be prepared to pay a toll of 190 schillings for these two routes.

The scenic route into the province is the **Grossglockner Alpine Pass**, in the heart of the Hohe Tauern National Park. The toll is 350 schillings per car. The pass is closed from 10 p.m. to 5 a.m. The mountain scenery is beautiful, but take an alternate route if you're afraid of heights. The view of the nearby glaciers, mountains, and local flora and fauna is unforgettable. For more information, *call 4826-2212.*

GETTING AROUND CARINTHIA

By Boat

There's no better way to explore the sights around Carinthia's lakes than by boat. Ship cruises are available from May through September. Moonlight cruises are also offered during July and August. Two places to try are:

• **Weissensee Cruises**, *Mosel 2, A-9714 Stockenboi. Tel. 4761-242; fax 4761-657*. A roundtrip ticket costs 90 schillings.

• **Worther See Ship Cruises**, *Freidelstrand 3. Postal address: St. Veiter Strasse 31, A-9020 Klagenfurt. Tel. 463-21155; fax 463-21155-15.* A roundtrip ticket costs 170 schillings for adults and 85 schillings for children.

By Bus

The **Bundesbus**, or mail buses, go to even the smallest villages in Carinthia. But check bus schedules so that you won't get stranded in some remote area. Allot plenty of time between destinations since this is definitely a time consuming way to travel.

By Car

Reserve your rental car back home ahead of time if you can where the rates are a fraction of what they are in Austria. Here are the local rental car offices in Klagenfurt.
• **Avis**, *9020 Villacherstrasse 1C. Tel. 55-9-38; fax 50-40-32. at the airport Tel. 55-9-38*
• **Budget**, *at the airport, Flughafen Annabichl. Tel. 46-226; fax 47-924*
• **Europcar**, *Volkermarkter Ring 9. Tel. 51-45-38; fax 51-18-67; at the airport, Tel. 475-35*

If you have auto trouble, call the **Automobile, Motorcycle, and Touring Association** for help around the clock, *Tel. 120*, or the **Automobile, Motorcycle, and Bicycle Association of Austria**, *Tel. 123*, in an emergency. For touring information, call the local offices in Klagenfurt at *Tel. 463-23448 or 463-32523*.

By Foot

If you've decided to take a walking tour of **Klagenfurt**, just follow the green arrows starting at the City Hall on the Neuer Platz. They'll lead you to all the major sights in town.

WHERE TO STAY

Many of the hotels featured here have fine restaurants where you can dine in style. So you have the option to eat in or venture out. The first hotels listed are in **Klagenfurt**, and remaining hotels are listed by town.

Klagenfurt

HOTEL EUROPAPARK, *Villacher Strasse 222, A-9020 Klagenfurt. Tel. 463-537-223; fax 463-537-295. Doubles start at 580 shillings per person. All credit cards accepted.*

The 29 room Hotel Europapark pays careful attention to the smallest details from the well-appointed rooms to the pink linens in its dining room. Rooms are pleasingly furnished in pastel fabrics and unpretentious pieces. The hotel restaurant has both light fare and traditional dishes served with a gourmet flair. An extensive wine list is also featured, or you can have a drink in the hotel bar.

HOTEL MOSER VERDINO, *Domgasse 2, A-9020 Klagenfurt. Tel. 463-57-8-78; fax 463-51-67-65. Doubles start at 650 schillings per person. All credit cards accepted.*

Located in the heart of the old town, the Hotel Moser Verdino looks as if it was moved straight out of the 19th century. The 74 rooms in this Art Nouveau building are light-filled. But make sure to ask for a room off the street if quiet is important to you. There is no restaurant in the hotel although you can eat breakfast on the premises. You can also have a drink in the hotel bar before heading out on the town.

The adjacent cafe sponsors "Coffeehouse Shows" with 40 different ways to make coffee, as well as homemade cakes and pastries to sample.

HOTEL SCHLOSS ST. GEORGEN, *Sandhofweg 8, A-9020 Klagenfurt. Tel. 463-468-49-0; fax 463-468-49-70. Doubles start at 750 schillings per person. All credit cards accepted.*

The 400 year-old Hotel Schloss St. Georgen is conveniently located near the Klagenfurt airport. But you'll feel like you've left the modern world behind when you pass through the castle's gates. Each room has a different theme. One room's walls are whimsically painted with landscapes giving the effect of sleeping outside under blue skies and fluffy clouds. Other themes include a Renaissance room and an Oriental room. Look for the lifesize figure of a praying monk in the palace chapel.

Bad Kleinkirchheim

BERGHAUS RAUNIG, *A-9546 Bad Kleinkirchheim 2. Tel. 4240-357; fax 4240-8314. Doubles start at 445 schillings per person. All credit cards accepted.*

The Berghaus Raunig's motto is "make yourself at home." You'll feel like you're staying at a good friend's in this secluded hotel tucked high on the mountain slope. This is a good place for families, with a children's playground and a rustic lounge.

The hotel also has delicious Carinthian cooking in the restaurant to prepare you for your favorite sporting activities. An ample breakfast buffet is served until 11 a.m.

VITAL HOTEL ESCHENHOF, *Bach 45, A-9546 Bad Kleinkirchheim. Tel. 4240-8262; fax 4240-8262-82. Doubles start at 870 schillings per person. All credit cards accepted.*

You won't see cookie-cutter hotel decorations at the Vital Hotel Eschenhof. Rooms are richly furnished with light wood panelling, jewel colored fabrics, and brass lamps. The ski lifts are right in front of the front door. The hotel offers daily gymnastic classes or more leisurely cosmetic treatments and massages at Eva's Beauty Refugium. A delightful restaurant on-site has regional dishes treated with a lighter touch.

Feld am See

HOTEL LINDENHOF, *Dorfstrasse 8, A-9544 Feld Am See. Tel. 4246-2274; fax 4246-227450. Doubles start at 520 schillings per person. All credit cards accepted.*

The Hotel Lindenhof has all sorts of accommodations available from regular rooms to full-service apartments. Rooms are furnished with blond wood and rustic, solid furniture for lots of cozy comfort.

It's easy to pamper yourself with the hotel's Temple of Health, with its steam bath, sauna, solarium, Kneipp treatments, massage, fitness program and curative baths. Health food is an option at the restaurant as well as heartier, traditional fare. There's also a pub, with a traditional tiled stove to warm you, and a cafe.

Heiligenblut

HOTEL GLOCKNERHOF, *A-9844 Heiligenblut 3. Tel. 4824-2244; fax 4824-22-44-66. Doubles start from 890 schillings per person. All credit cards accepted.*

You only need to walk a few steps to the ski slopes from the Hotel Glocknerhof. After a hard day of skiing, you can relax in the hotel's indoor swimming pool, get a massage, or read in front of the fireplace in the reception hall. The hotel also sponsors a variety of activities, such as night hiking with a picnic around a campfire. The rooms are large and comfortably furnished. Apartments are also available. Most rooms have balconies where you can admire the dramatic mountain scenery.

HOTEL POST, *Hof 1, A-9844 Heiligenblut. 4824-2245; fax 4824-22-45-81. Doubles start at 770 schillings per person. All credit cards accepted.*

If you want to sharpen your skiing technique, the Hotel Post has a skiing instructor on staff. And the hotel also offers guided skiing tours to their own private cottage. After hours, take a swim in the hotel's indoor pool, enjoy a steam bath, or have a drink in the town's oldest tavern on the premises. There's a fitness room for those who want to continue their workout. The 100 bed hotel has guest parking, and reductions are offered for children. Rooms are modestly furnished with rustic touches. The hotel offers a breakfast buffet and a choice of menus with lots of hearty food to fuel up for the slopes.

VILLA KAISER FRANZ-JOSEF, *A-9844 Heiligenblut. Tel. 4824-2084; fax 4824-2084-13. Doubles start at 800 schillings per person. All credit cards accepted.*

The Villa Kaiser Franz-Josef looks like a ski chalet out of a storybook. The hotel has eleven individually furnished apartments in imperial grandeur that would have made the most picky member of the Hapsburg family proud. A breakfast buffet is served through lunchtime. Guests can also take it easy in the villa's sauna, fitness rooms, or steam bath.

Hermagor

ERLEBNISHOTEL HUBERTUSHOF, *Kameritsch 1, A-9620 Hermagor. Tel. 4285-280; fax 4285-280-50. Doubles start at 500 schillings per person. All credit cards accepted.*

The Erlebnishotel Hubertushof caters to families with a children's playroom, handicrafts, and adult supervision. Located outside of the village center, the hotel is near free ski bus service, cross-country trails, and a natural sled run. The 60 bed hotel, run by the Hubmann family, offers a breakfast and salad buffet and a choice of menus with the usual Austrian classics.

HOTEL-PENSION KAISER VON OSTERREICH, *Hauptplatz, A-9620 Hermagor. Tel. 4282-2263; fax 4282-3821. Doubles start from 420 schillings per person. All credit cards accepted.*

Smack in the middle of the Carnic ski region, the Hotel-Pension Kaiser Von Osterreich was built in 1838. You'll fall in love with the romantic arcaded courtyard just as Emperor Franz Josef and his Empress Elisabeth did when they stayed here in 1856. The 68 bed hotel caters to groups, but hasn't lost individual attention to service. The hotel is only 100 meters away from a free ski bus shuttle stop to get you to the slopes.

Kotschach-Mauthen

HERRENHAUS RESTAURANT AND LANDHAUS KELLERWAND, *A-9640 Kotschach-Mauthen. Tel. 4715-269; fax 4715-378-16. Doubles start at 700 schillings per person. All credit cards accepted.*

The Herrenhaus is a charming hotel, but it is really renowned for its food. Owner Sissy Sonnleitner has been awarded three chef toques and was named Chef of the Year by the Guide Gault Millau. Gourmets come from miles around to dine here.

The country manor is at the foot of the Kellerwand mountain. Suites, with circular stairways separating the living areas from the bedrooms, are arranged around a covered courtyard. Baths are equipped with whirlpools where you can relax after a long day.

Mallnitz

FERIENHOTELS ALBER TAUERNHOF, *A-9822 Mallnitz 25. Tel. 4785-525; fax 4784-527. Doubles start at 450 schillings per person. All credit cards accepted.*

If you've come to Mallnitz for cross-country skiing, the Tauernhof is within a stone's throw of this resort's cross-country trail. Many of the 25 rooms have balconies. Guests can unwind in the in-house library, take a sauna or whirlpool, or exercise in the fitness room. The rooms are nothing fancy but comfortably furnished, and the Alber-Haub family makes sure each visitor receives a warm welcome. Children up to six can stay free with their parents; older children can get up to a 70 percent reduction on room rates.

The hotel's kitchen serves up both traditional Austrian dishes and regional classics. Guests can fuel up at the breakfast buffet and then later choose from a variety of menus.

FERIENHOTELS ALBER ALPENHOTEL, *A-9822 Mallnitz 26. Tel. 4784-525; fax 4784-527. Doubles start at 590 schillings per person. All credit cards accepted.*

Run by the same family as the Tauernhof, the Alpenhotel has an equally welcoming atmosphere. Guests can choose to stay in the main building or in the nearby guest house. Make sure to request a room with a balcony so you can savor the view. The Alpenhotel has even more leisure activities from which to choose, including billiards, ping-pong, and curling. There's also a fitness center, sauna and whirlpool to relax in.

The restaurant features savory local favorites and dishes from the rest of the country as well. Like the Tauernhof, there is an extensive breakfast buffet to prepare you for the slopes.

Portschach

HOTEL SCHLOSS SEEFELS, *Toschling 1, A-9210 Portschach. Tel. 4272-2377; fax 4272-3704. Doubles start at 1,680 schillings. American Express accepted.*

This castle on the banks of the Worther See once belonged to Emperor Franz Joseph. The hotel is elegantly decorated with period pieces, and the staff is attentive and helpful. Guests can have a drink at the open air bar at the waterfront or have dinner on the Belle Epoch veranda. The hotel has a private beach and marina on the "Austrian Riviera" at their guests' disposal. Or perhaps you would prefer to play tennis, go swimming, or pamper yourself with a sauna or massage.

SCHLOSS LEONSTAIN, *A-9210 Portschach. Tel. 4272-28-160; fax 4272-28-23. Doubles start at 960 schillings per person. All credit cards accepted.*

The Schloss Leonstain can trace its history back to the Middle Ages. Located on Lake Worth, the castle was first mentioned in 1166. Legend has it that a nymph from the lake fell deeply in love with the lord of the castle. But when he married a human woman instead of her, the nymph avenged herself against the family. Famous guests have included Johannes Brahms who wrote a symphony, concerto, and a sonata while summering at the castle.

Today, guests can pamper themselves in the basement spa and sauna. The hotel is filled with antiques and manages to balance elegance with comfort. A fine restaurant and bar add to the ambience.

Seeboden

SPORTHOTEL ROYAL, *Seehofstrasse 23-33, A-9871 Seeboden. Tel. 4762-81714-0; fax 4762-81714-705. Doubles start at 540 schillings per person. All credit cards accepted.*

The Sporthotel Royal is located in the heart of a huge park right on the banks of the lake. Sports lovers can take advantage of the curling alley, three indoor tennis courts, and the ski and snowboarding school on the premises. There's even a practice slope for you to polish your moves. The rooms are somewhat bland, but comfortably appointed. The hotel also offers an extensive breakfast buffet to load up before all your exertions.

Spittal

HOTEL-RESTAURANT ERTL, *Bahnhofstrasse 26, A-9802 Spittal. Tel. 4762-2048 or 611200; fax 4762-611205 or 20485. Doubles start at 450 schillings per person. All credit cards accepted.*

Located in the heart of town off the Millstatter Lake, the Hotel-Restaurant Ertl has modern, spacious rooms and reasonable rates. Large windows let in the light, but you may want to request a room off the street. The 86 bed hotel also offers reductions for children staying with their parents. If you want to dine at the hotel, you can select from a variety of menus. And of course there's an ample breakfast buffet.

Velden

HOTEL ALTE POST, *Europaplatz 4-6, A-9220 Velden/Worther See. Tel. 4274-2141; fax 4274-51120. Doubles start at 660 schillings per person. All credit cards accepted.*

Located in the center of town near the Worther See, this is an old-fashioned establishment run with warm hospitality. The 70 bed hotel is owned by the Wrann Family. Make sure to ask for a room off the main street if quiet is important to you. Rooms are clean and bright but nothing overly luxurious. The hotel has indoor tennis courts available to guests and an instructor to help you perfect your backhand. The casino is just across the street if you'd prefer to gamble your night away.

Villach

GASTHOF KRAMER, *Italienerstrasse 14, A-9500 Villach. Tel. 4242-24953; fax 4242-249533. Doubles start at 400 schillings per person. All credit cards accepted.*

Just a five minute walk from the center of town, the Gasthof Kramer is a traditional guest house on the edge of Villach's old quarter. Rooms are somewhat dark, but clean and basic. You're also within easy reach of ski slopes in the area. The restaurant is surprisingly good, with a selection of Carinthian classics and seasonal specialties.

ROMANTIK HOTEL POST, *Hauptplatz, A-9500 Villach. Tel. 4242-26101-0; fax 4242-26101-420. Doubles start at 515 schillings per person. All credit cards accepted.*

The Romantik Hotel Post has all the charm of an old-style European hotel. The 140 bed hotel is right on the main square. The reception area has a blazing fire ready to warm you, and the service will also give you a healthy glow. The hotel has a sauna, solarium, and fitness room at guests' disposal. Children up to 12-years-old can stay free with their parents. The restaurant has updated traditional local cuisine with lighter variations, and the wine list offers both regional and national vintages.

Warmbad Villach

DER KARAWANKENHOF, *A-9504 Warmbad Villach. Tel. 4242-3002-0; fax 4242-3002-61. Doubles start at 660 schillings per person. All credit cards accepted.*

Der Karawankenhof is Austria's version of "Water World." Kids will love the indoor waterslide, pools, and whirlpools. Children between three and nine years old can be supervised at the hotel's Mini Club while their parents pamper themselves with beauty treatments, saunas, and exercise. There's a self-service restaurant at the hotel, and for more formal dining, the **Avocado** restaurant. Other organized activities and musical entertainment are also featured.

Weissensee

HOTEL AND APARTMENTS RONACHERFELS, *Neusach 40, A-9762 Weissensee. Tel. 4713-2172-0; fax 4713-2172-24. Doubles start at 620 schillings per person. All credit cards accepted.*

This resort offers the height of luxury. Perched on the banks of the lake, rooms are elegantly furnished. Be sure to ask for a room with a tiled stove for a cozy extra touch where you can snuggle during cold evenings. The restaurant has gourmet dining by candlelight. In the **Rauchkuchlstuberl** you can enjoy schnapps and wine-tasting in front of an open fire. There's even a Finnish-style sauna overlooking the lake.

WHERE TO EAT

If you're a fan of pasta, Carinthia will satisfy your cravings. Stuffed noodles like ravioli, called Nudeln, are often featured on the menu.

Fillings include cream, turkey, beef, pork or potato. During the Christmas season, a sweet variation, stuffed with dried, cooked pears, honey, and cinnamon, is served. *Reinling* is a cake made for Easter, weddings, and other special occasions that will satisfy any sweet tooth.

Another specialty is *Jauntaler Saumagen*, which may be a bit too exotic for many American palates. A pig's stomach is stuffed with highly spiced ground meat, boiled then baked, and served warm or cold. Other notable dishes include *Leberlan* a mixture of different types of liver and *Dempffleisch*, a variety of sliced meats and a casserole of minced veal, pork, and lamb seasoned with fine herbs.

If you're in the mountains during the summer months, stop off at one of the *huts* where local farm women look after the cows during the warm weather. They will sell you some of their homemade bread topped with fresh butter and cheese or perhaps a glass of cold milk. One of the most basic meals you can buy but simply delicious.

The Lavanttal Valley is famous for its sparkling cider. Take a detour at one of the orchard taverns or inns and have a glass or two with a cold meat and cheese platter. The cider, fermented in huge wooden barrels, was first produced by Benedictine monks who built the St. Paul Abbey in the valley.

As in other parts of Austria outside the big cities, most restaurants are attached to hotels and guesthouses. If you're a food lover, don't overlook the **Herrenhaus Restaurant and Landhaus Kellerwand** (listed above in *Where to Stay* in the town of Kotschach-Mauthen. Here are a few additional recommendations that are not part of a hotel, beginning with **Klagenfurt**:

Klagenfurt

A LA CARTE, *Kevenhullerstrasse 2, A-9020 Klagenfurt. Tel. 463-516651. No credit cards accepted.*

Chef Harald Fritzer was chosen as Austria's 1992 Cook of the Year, so it's no wonder that gourmets make this restaurant a place of pilgrimage. The lake fish is especially good. If you're interested in tasting Carinthia's version of haute cuisine, this is a must stop for your trip.

RESTAURANT LIDO, *Friedelstand 1, A-9010 Klagenfurt. Tel. 463-261723. Moderate. Open Wednesday through Monday, 6:30 p.m. to 10 p.m. All credit cards accepted.*

Austrian cuisine is showcased at both the bistro and the more formal restaurant housed here overlooking the Worther See. Fish caught from the nearby lake is a highlight here, innovatively prepared and artfully presented. The kitchen uses a light touch with other classic Austrian dishes, which can be relief from the heavy offerings at so many other restaurants.

Spital

CAFE-PUB MARIKKA RIEDL, *Bahnhofstrasse 15, A-9800 Spital. Tel. 4762-4750. Inexpensive. Closed Sundays. No credit cards accepted.*

If you need a place to take a break from your sight-seeing, then head to the Cafe-Pub Marikka Riedl. Open faced sandwiches are the house specialty – ideal for a light lunch or a quick snack. The cafe also has an ample salad bar, where you can create your own concoctions.

Villach

RESTAURANT DOBNER, *Dobrovastrasse 3, A-9500 Villach. Tel. 4242-3225. Moderate. Open Monday through Saturday 5 p.m. to midnight. Closed Tuesdays and Sundays. All credit cards accepted.*

Food from Carinthia's southern neighbor are featured on the menu here although you can also choose from classic Austrian fare as well. The wine list also has a strong selection of Italian wines to accompany your pasta, served by a friendly staff that goes out of its way to make you feel at home.

SCHMID, *Seestrasse 18, A-9500 Villach. Tel. 4242-421-49; fax 4242-42-68-28. Moderate. Open daily 11 a.m. to 2 p.m. and after 6 p.m. All credit cards accepted.*

Brigitte and Christian Kaufmann run this friendly guest house just outside the center of Villach. The main attraction here is the extensive wine cellar, with vintages from around the country. The restaurant also cooks up regional specialties, including delicious homemade noodles to enjoy with your wine. The guest house also has rooms to let if you'd like to stay the night.

SEEING THE SIGHTS IN KLAGENFURT

Start your tour of Klagenfurt at the **City Hall** on the **Neuer Platz**. Originally built in 1650, the Renaissance palace was the home to the Counts of Rosenberg. The square itself was the town center and was set up originally in 1518 outside the fortifications protecting the Spanheimer ducal family. The town's most famous landmark, a feisty dragon taken from the legend of Hercules, is located in the **Lindwurm Fountain** placed in the center of the square in 1636. A statue dedicated to the Empress Maria Theresa sits on the west side of the square.

At number 2 is a house built from the town's original stone fortifications dating from the 13th century. Next door, the house at number three was built in the 17th century and actually incorporates part of the city wall in its structure. Several of the other houses on the square, which you can wander through, have lovely arcaded courtyards built in the 16th century, reflecting the Italian influence throughout Klagenfurt.

Continue your walking tour down the pedestrian shopping street **Krammergasse** until you reach the **Alter Platz**. In the center of the square is a Trinity Column erected in 1680 after Klagenfurt was delivered from an outbreak of plague. The **Goess Palace**, *number 30 Alter Platz*, was completed in 1738 and is noted for its grilled staircase and stone balustrade. At the far west end of the square is the **Landhaus**, built for the provincial diet in 1574. (You can reach the arcaded Landhaus courtyards by passing through the Frank Passageway next to number 1 Herrengasse.) The site formerly housed the city's first fortress with a moat before it was replaced by the Landhaus. An incredible display of Carinthia's 665 coat of arms can be found in the Landhaus's huge arcaded hallway, further decorated with colorful ceiling frescoes and a multicolored marble floor.

Note also the house *at number 3 Alter Platz*, a Baroque building constructed in the 14th century that was used as headquarters for the salt and tobacco monopolies. Klagenfurt's oldest house, called the **Golden Goose**, can be found *at number 31* and was given to the emperor in exchange for the castle where the Landhaus is now located. The **Christalnig Palace**, *14 Herrengasse*, also has a decorated arcaded courtyard added during the 16th century.

Take a detour behind the Landhaus to the **Church of the Holy Ghost**, *Heiligengeistplatz*. The church was originally constructed in the Gothic style but Baroque elements were later added like in so many other Austrian churches. The adjacent monastery, adorned with six wooden coats of arms from 1623, has been under the jurisdiction of the Ursuline order since 1678.

Continue to the **Pfarrplatz**, or Church Square, which was the site of the city's first cemetery until 1677. The onion-domed topped spire of **St. Egyd's Church** rises majestically over the old part of Klagenfurt and dates from 1255. The three-aisled basilica once had two towers, but the other was destroyed. To get an even better view of the church, take the Alter Platz passageway next to number 20. You can look out to the church tower from the 16th century arcaded courtyard.

Next, head down **Wienergasse**, which is bordered by some lovely Gothic residences. The **Ossiacher Hof** is *at number 10*, which is the town residence of the local order of Benedictine monks. This is another richly decorated 17th century arcaded courtyard. The **Old Town Hall** here was formerly the Welzer Palace built in the 17th century. At the end of the street is the **Heu Platz**. The **Floriani Monument** in the center of the square was erected in 1781 to commemorate a fire that decimated the city four years earlier.

To reach the **cathedral**, head back to the Neuer Platz and walk down Karfeit Strasse. The cathedral is located on the grounds of the former Jesuit College, which was bombed during World War II. The country's oldest pilaster church was built by Protestant noblemen in 1581. The Jesuits took control of the church in 1604. The cathedral suffered considerable damage during a fire in 1723. The ornate Baroque stucco work was added in 1727. Also note the painting by Johann Martin Schmidt, called the *Kremser Schmidt*, located in the vestry. Across from the cathedral is the **Golden Fountain house** built as annex to the Jesuit barracks during the 17th century with its round arch gateway.

Museums & Galleries

Klagenfurt also has a variety of small museums and other attractions that you can visit if you have the time. Below are the opening times and admission fees for the attractions listed above on the walking tour:

Agricultural Museum, *Ehrental Castle, Ehrentaler Strasse 119, A-9020 Klagenfurt. Tel. 463-435-40; fax 463-48-17-65-10.* Open daily in May, September and October from 10 a.m. to 4 p.m. and June, July and August 10 a.m. to 6 p.m.; closed Saturdays. Admission for adults is 40 schillings, 30 schillings for seniors and students and 10 schillings for children.

Bergbau Museum, *Kinkstrasse 6, A-9020 Klagenfurt. Tel. 463-537-432; fax 463-537-636.* Open daily April through October from 9 a.m. to 6 p.m. Admission is 40 schillings for adults; 20 schillings for seniors and students; children under age six free.

Botanical Gardens, *Kinkstrasse 6, A-9020 Klagenfurt. Tel. 463-502715.* Open daily May through October from 9 a.m. to 6 p.m. Admission free.

Carinthian Gallery, *Burggasse 8, A-9020 Klagenfurt. Tel. 463-536-30542; fax 463-502829.* Open daily Monday through Friday 9 a.m. to 6 p.m.; Saturdays, Sundays and holidays 10 a.m. to noon. Admission is 20 schillings for adults and 5 schillings for seniors, students and children.

Diocesan Museum, *Linmanskygasse 10/3, A-9020 Klagenfurt. Tel. 463-57770-84.* Open Monday through Saturday 10 a.m. to 2 p.m. Admission is 30 schillings for adults, 10 schillings for students and 5 schillings for children.

Gustav Mahler House, *Worther See Sudufer Strasse, A-9020 Klagenfurt. Tel. 463-537-587 or 226.* Open daily July through September 10 a.m. to 4 p.m. Admission 10 schillings.

Koschat Museum, *Viktringer Ring 17, A-9020 Klagenfurt. Tel. 463-23-05-02.* Open May 19 through October 15, Monday through Friday from 10 a.m. to noon or by prior arrangement. Admission is based on voluntary donations.

Museum of the Province of Carinthia, *Museumgasse 2, A-9020 Klagenfurt. Tel. 463-536-305-71; fax 463-536-305-40.* Open Tuesday through Saturday from 9 a.m. to 4 p.m.; Sundays and holidays from 10 a.m. to 1 p.m. Admission for adults is 30 schillings and 15 schillings for students and children.

Robert Musil Museum, *Bahnhofstrasse 50, A-9020 Klagenfurt. Tel. 463-501429.* Open Monday through Friday from 10 a.m. to noon and 2 p.m. to 4 p.m.; Saturday 10 a.m. to noon. Admission free.

Spire of St. Egyd's Church, *Pfarrplatz. Tel. 463-537-293; fax 463-537-295.* Open April through September, Monday through Friday 10 a.m. to 5:30 p.m.; Saturdays, 10 a.m. to 12:30 p.m. Admission is 10 schillings for adults and 3 schillings for children.

Tramway Museum, *Lendkanal. Tel. 463-740368; fax 463-740208.* Open July and August, Saturdays from 4 p.m. to 7 p.m.; Sundays 10 a.m. to noon and 4 p.m. to 7 p.m. or by prior arrangement. Tickets are 40 schillings for adults, 20 schillings for children and 100 schillings for children.

Wappensaal, *Landhaus, A-9020 Klagenfurt. Tel. 463-536-305-52; 463-563-30-540.* Open April through September, Monday through Friday from 9 a.m. to noon and 12:30 p.m. to 5 p.m. Admission is 10 schillings for adults and 5 schillings for children.

NIGHTLIFE & ENTERTAINMENT
Klagenfurt

You can enjoy the local folk songs called *Karntner Lieder* any time of year, but the entertainment scene in Carinthia really comes alive during the warmer weather from summer concerts to open air plays. The **Cistercian Monastery**, *in Viktring, 4274-52-100,* founded in 1142, is host to an annual music festival during July and August. The **New Music Forum**, features both young performers and established stars playing everything from classical music to jazz.

Klagenfurt sponsors an annual **cultural festival**, with many performances staged in the city's arched courtyards dating from the 16th century. In June, authors from around Europe gather in the town for the **Ingeborg Bachmann Literature Competition**. Visitors can attend authors' readings.

If stars and planets are your thing, explore where no man has gone before at the **Planetarium**, *Villacher Strasse 239, A-9020 Klagenfurt. Tel. and fax 463-21700.* Presentations are made January through March and November through December, Saturday and Sunday at 3 p.m.; daily in May, 2 p.m and 4 p.m.; daily in June at 11 a.m., 2 p.m., 3 p.m. and 4 p.m.; July and August daily every hour from 11 a.m. to 5 p.m.; daily in September, 2 p.m., 3 p.m. and 4 p.m.; daily in October at 3 p.m. Admission is 75 schillings for adults, 65 schillings for seniors and students and 45 schillings for children. Or head to the **Kreuzbergl Observatory**, *Kreuzbergl, A-9020 Klagenfurt. Tel. and fax 463-21700.* The observatory is open April through November from dusk on Wednesdays and Fridays.

Guided tours are conducted no matter what the weather. Admission is 50 schillings for adults and 30 schillings for children.

Kids will enjoy the thrills and chills of **Happ's Reptile Zoo**, *Villacher Strasse 237, A-9020 Klagenfurt. Tel. 463-23425; fax 463-234-2514.* Open daily 8 a.m. to 6 p.m. Admission is 70 schillings for adults, 60 schillings for students and 30 schillings for children. Another highlight for families is the **Mageregg Castle Game Park**, *Mageregger Strasse 177, A-9020 Klagenfurt.* The park is a nice place to pack a picnic and spend a leisurely afternoon, and the best part is it's absolutely free. The park is open year-round Monday, Thursday, and Saturday from 9 a.m. to 10 p.m.; Sundays from 9 a.m. to 6 p.m.; closed Tuesdays and Wednesdays.

Wander around the most important sights in the world at the **Minimundus**, with 160 models of famous buildings from around the globe, from the Statue of Liberty to the Eiffel Tower. All the buildings, plus harbors, ships, and a railroad, are built to a scale of 1:25. Minimundus is located at *Vilacher Strasse 241, A-9020 Klagenfurt. Tel. 463-211-94; fax 463-211-94-60.* Open daily April 20 to October 13 from 9 a.m. to 5 p.m. Admission is 85 schillings for adults, 65 schillings for seniors, 55 schillings for students and 10 schillings for children.

For additional details on any of the above, contact the **Klagenfurt Tourist Information**, *A-9010 Klagenfurt. Tel. 463-537-223; fax 463-537-295.*

Elsewhere in Carinthia

Further afield, the **Finkenstein Ruins**, at the base of the **Mittagskogel**, *Fremdenverkehrsamt Faak/See, A-9583 Faak. Tel. 4254-2110-0; 4254-3855,* hosts concerts, plays, and other cultural events during July and August. The 16th century ruins and surrounding scenery provide a dramatic backdrop to the festivities.

Spittal's Renaissance **Porcia Palace** comes alive each summer with a series of performances in its beautiful arcaded courtyard. The castle is the setting for an **International Choir Festival** and the *Porcia Comedies.* Admission to the courtyard is free. The **Local Heritage Museum** in the palace has exhibits from around the province. Admission is 35 schillings for adults and 15 schillings for students and children. Contact **Schloss Porcia**, *Burgplatz, A-9800 Spittal/Drau. Tel. 4762-3420.* Open daily from 8 a.m. to 9 p.m.

The **Ossiacher See** provides a natural backdrop to the **Carinthian Summer Music Festival**. The concerts are held at the **Ossiach Abbey**, a Romanesque basilica finished in 1028. Contact **Carinthischer Sommer Ossiach**, *A-9570 Ossiach. Tel. 4243-2510; 4243-2353.* The **Landskron Ruins** tower high above the **Ossiacher Lake**, *A-9523 Landskron. Tel. 4242-41563; 4242-44208.* Daily falconry displays are put on each day from May to September at the ruins. The 40-minute spectacular shows the birds dramatically diving as they would for their prey. Admission is 40 schillings per person. The **Burg Sommeregg**, *Schlossau 7, A-9871 Seeboden. Tel. 4763-81391*, hosts concerts every Tuesday evening in the castle arena. Overlooking the **Millstatter See**, the fortress dates to 1237. Children will enjoy a visit to the **Torture Museum**. Open April through October. Closed Mondays. Admission to the castle is 65 schillings for adults and 35 schillings for children.

The **Millstatt Abbey**, *Kurverwaltung Millstatt, A-9872 Millstatt. Tel. 4766-2022*, is the site of a **Spring Music Festival**, an **Autumn Music Festival**, and an **International Music and Organ Festival**. The abbey, with Baroque, Gothic, and Romanesque elements, was founded by the Benedictine order before 1100. Or you can gamble the night away at the **Velden Casino**, *Am Corso 10, A-9220 Velden. Tel. 4274-2064 or 3093; fax 4274-2064-82*.

SHOPPING

Shops are open Monday through Friday from 9 a.m. to 6 p.m. However, many stores close during lunchtime hours. On Saturdays, shops are open in general from 9 a.m. to noon, except for the first Saturday of the month when they stay open until 5 p.m.

In tourist areas, stores are often open until 8 p.m. during the week and until 6 p.m. on Saturday, Sundays, and holidays. If you're interested in picking up a new pair of Lederhosen or some other souvenirs, head to the **Krammergasse** pedestrian zone off the main square in Klagenfurt. Krammergasse is actually Austria's first pedestrian zone, established in 1961. The market street was originally moved from Spitalberg hill. There are also shops on the **Alter Platz** pedestrian zone, another route created by Duke Bernhard.

Even if you're not a shopper, there are several arcaded courtyards and houses built during the Middle Ages, the Renaissance, and Art Nouveau periods worth taking a look at. If you're in the **Upper Drau Valley**, you can pick up a variety of fresh and dried herbs, medicinal remedies, and cosmetics made from the plants that grow wild along the hillsides. The village of **Irschen** is particularly renowned. One interesting store here is the **Nature and Herb Center**, *A-9733 Irschen 41*. Open May through September, daily from 3 p.m. to 5 p.m. and Tuesday and Friday from 3 p.m. to 5 p.m. In the **Rosental Valley**, you can pick up fresh honey and tools involved with beekeeping at the **Natur und Ferienregion Rosental**, *A-9170 Ferlach. Tel. 4227-5119*.

During the Christmas season, Klagenfurt and the surrounding towns all put on extravagant **Christkindl markets**, too.

SPORTS & RECREATION

Biking

One of the most popular places for cyclists in Carinthia is the **Keutschach Valley**. A **Historical Cycling Track**, takes you past many castles, churches, and other important historical landmarks. Nature lovers can savor the beauty of the lakeside scenery on the **Natural History Trail**, linking the lakes throughout the valley. In July, the valley is host to the **Carinthian Lakes Marathon** for serious bikers. Contact the **Seental Keutschach Tourist Office**, *A-9074 Keutschach am See. Tel. 4273-24500; fax 4273-3389.*

CYCLE LIKE CRAZY & WIN A FREE TRIP!

*The **Upper Drau Valley** has nine different cycling tours from which to choose. You'll get a medal for successfully completing one leg of the circuit, and if you finish all nine you'll receive a free holiday from the Tourist Office and can participate in the spring cycling festival. The **Drau cycle trail** winds 230 kilometers along the river. Contact **Gebietsverband Oberdautal,** A-9771 Berg. Tel. 4712-8212; fax 4712-8537.*

More leisurely cycling is possible around the **Millstatter See**. Biking enthusiasts can participate with world-class cyclists in **The Nockalm Cup** and the **Race of Legends** bike races. Contact **Mallstatter See Tourismus**, *Kongresshaus, A-9872 Millstatt. Tel. 4766-37000; fax 4766-37008.* Last but not least, is the **Giro d'Amore** cycling event for young couples in love and for those still on the lookout for Mr. or Ms. Right. The course leads through the countryside surrounding Villach.

The city's Director of Tourism has offered to serve as best man for anyone lucky enough to fall in love during the event and who plan to get married in Villach. Contact **Villach Tourist Office**, *Europaplatz 2, A-9500 Villach. Tel. 4242-244440; fax 4242-24444-17.*

Fishing

The **Lower Drau Valley** is an angler's paradise with the rich waters of the **Drau River** and **Lake Weissensee** as well as countless smaller lakes and streams. The country is pristine and unspoiled, and the water is full of trout, pike, carp, and other fish. The only thing that will disturb you is the whispering of the reeds and the ducks quacking. Check with the local tourist office for the necessary licenses needed to fish in the region. **Tourist Information Office**, *A-9762 Weissensee. Tel. 4713-222013; fax 4713-222044.*

In October, you can try your luck against local fisherman in the **Crystal Whitefish** angling competition in the Millstatter See. **Mallstatter**

See Tourismus, *Kongresshaus, A-9872 Millstatt. Tel. 4766-37000; fax 4766-37008.*

Golf

You may not think that you could tee off during the winter months, but golfing is still possible on the 18-hole ice golf course on Lake Weissensee. Upper Carinthia's first golf course is in **Berg** in the Drau Valley (**Gebeitsverband Oberdrautal**, *A-9771 Berg. Tel. 4712-8212; fax 4712-8537*). The modest 9-hole course still has some challenges even for seasoned golfers, such as the Eagle's Nest tee set high above the river.

Hiking

If all of Carinthia's hiking and walking trails were joined together they would stretch around the globe, so you won't be short of paths from which to choose. One of the most dramatic places to hike is the **Garnitzenklamm gorge**, *Moderndorf, A-9620 Hermagor. Tel. 4282-2043*. The trail documents the 600 million years of geological history of the area. This path, which takes you over ravines and past cascading waterfalls, is for more experienced hikers. You should also have proper equipment and not be afraid of heights. Open from June through September. The cost is 20 schillings per person.

The gorge along the **Ragga River** in the Molltal Valley is also spectacular. Walkways, steps and bridges line the gorge allowing you to get an up close and personal look at the effect of thousands of years of water wearing away rock. A roundtrip hike takes a little under two hours. Rafting, white water canoeing, hang-gliding, and paragliding are also possible. Contact the **Tourist Information Office**, *A-9831 Flattach. Tel. 4785-615; fax 4785-617*. Admission is 50 schillings for adults and 25 schillings for children.

In southern Carinthia, hikers can explore the **Tscheppaschlucht Gorge** near the town of **Ferlach**. The trail is well-marked and has bridges, steps, and walkways to take you up to the dramatic **Tschauko Waterfalls**, which tumble 26 meters into the gorge below. Contact **Tscheppaschlucht Gorge Information**, *Kirchgasse 5, A-9170 Ferlach. Tel. 4227-2600-31 or 41; fax 4227-2311*. Open from May to October. Admission is 30 schillings per person.

Botanical aficionados should hike the **Sonnenalpe Nassfield** in the Carnic region. The delicate, blue wulfenia flower can only be found on the **Garnerkofel** and in the Himalayas. The tiny flowers blanket the hillsides during June. Contact the **Carnic Region Tourist Information**, *A-9620 Hermagor. Tel. 4282-3131; fax 4282-2043-50*.

For more leisurely hikes, head to the **Weissensee** where you can take a chairlift up to the alpine meadows of the **Naggler Alm**. There is also an alpine hut at the top where you can get a bite to eat. **Weissensee Chairlift**, *A-9762 Weissensee. Tel. 4713-2269; fax 4713-2269.* Open mid-May to mid-October. Roundtrip tickets for adults cost 100 schillings and 60 schillings for children.

Ice Skating

Carinthia's myriad lakes turn into natural ice skating arenas during the winter months. If you're interested in speed skating, sharpen your blades and head over to **Lake Weissensee**. You can even win a medal or a certificate on the 6.5 kilometer lake.

For more information, contact the **Tourist Information Office**, *A-9721 Weissenstein. Tel. 4245-23850; fax 4245-2385-29.*

Skiing

If you don't have your own equipment, you can rent all your ski supplies for six days for 990 schillings at all resorts participating in the **Ski Top Class** program around Carinthia. The rental includes daily adjustments on bindings and skis if necessary.

Below are the major ski areas in Carinthia:

The **Bad Kleinkirchheim/Falkertsee resort** features about 100 kilometers of prepared trails as well as 70 ski instructors, cross-country trails, thermal baths and indoor golf, tennis, and squash. Probably the province's most famous resort, local ski legend Franz Klammer helped put Bad Kleinkirchheim on the map. The resort, at an altitude of 1,100 to 2,440 meters, caters to families, so children won't be left out of the fun. All-day supervision is offered through many hotels, as well as children's after-ski activities and snowman building. The **Children's Snowland** in St. Oswald is an especially good destination to bring the kiddies. There are also natural ice rinks in Bad Kleinkirchheim/St.Oswald and on Falkert.

If you want to sooth your tired muscles after a day on the slopes, head to the **Romerbad**, or Roman baths, where you can enjoy underwater massage, steam baths, and artificial rapids. The baths are open from 9 a.m. to 8 p.m. Admission is 115 schillings for adults and 70 schillings for children. Or visit the **St. Kathrein thermal baths** open from 8 a.m. to 8 p.m.. Admission is 115 schillings for adults and 70 schillings for children.

There are five Ski Top Class ski rental locations in Bad Kleinkirchheim, St. Oswald, Romerbad, Maibrunnbahn and Brunnachalmbahn. For more information, *call 4240-555 or 346; fax 4240-5555 or 648.* Courtesy ski buses run between 6 p.m. to 2 a.m. Several hotels are listed above in *Where to Stay*; for more details, contact the **Bad Kleinkirchheim Tourist Office**, *A-9546 Bad Kleinkirchheim. Tel. 4240-8212; fax 4240-8537.*

Another great ski area is the **Carnic Region**, near the Italian border, boasting Austria's first permanent cross-country course. But downhill lovers also flock to the resort with its 23 lifts and 43 slopes above 1,300 meters, which means more than 100 kilometers of trails. The longest trail, some 15 kilometers long, will take you right into Tropolach. Hotel guests can take advantage of the free ski bus to the slopes.

You can also sizzle on your skates on Europe's largest frozen lake, the **Weissensee**. Curling, ice hockey, speed skating, and of course ice skating are possible on the 6.5 kilometer lake, frozen from mid-December to March. The resort also has 34 lifts with 117 kilometers of trails, ice skating and toboggan runs. For the equestrian lovers among you, there are horse-drawn sleigh rides around the region. You can practice your dressage techniques in an indoor arena in Weissbriach in Gitschtal.

There are three Ski Top Class locations in the Carnic Region. *Call 4282-2068; fax 4282-2068-41* for resort information, or check out some of the area hotels listed above in *Where to Stay (see* Hermagor and Weissensee). For more area information, contact the **Tourist Information Office**, *A-9762 Weissensee. Tel. 4713-22200; fax 4713-2220-44.*

Due south of Villach is the **Dreilandereck**, or *Three Nations*, resort. As the name implies, you can ski above the Austrian village of **Arnoldstein**, and then head over into the neighboring resorts of Kranjska Gora in Slovenia or to Tarvisio or Sella Nevea in Italy. The resort is less demanding and a nice alternative for those who may not feel so confident in their skiing abilities. For more area information, contact the **Tourist Information Office**, *A-9601 Arnoldstein. Tel. 4255-2260-14; fax 4255-2260-33.*

The **Heiligenblut/Grossglockner resort** is at an altitude of 1,301 to 2,900 meters with 60 kilometers of downhill runs, 13 kilometers of cross-country runs, curling, and ice climbing. For children, the resort offers a playground where kids can learn to ski. The resort also features a tennis camp with video analysis and tournament prizes. The cost of the camp is 3,550 schillings per person. At **Hans Pichler** and **Heiligenblut**, you can rent skis through the Ski Top Class hire system. For more information, *call 4824-2256-45.* For more area information, contact the **Tourist Information**, *A-9844 Heiligenblut. Tel. 4824-200121; fax 4824-200143.*

The **Katschberg/Rennweg** area offers the **Katschberg ski circus**, extending into the Salzburg province and boasting 80 kilometers of runs with 15 lifts. The ski resorts of **Fanningberg**, **Speiereck**, and **Grosseck** are all linked to the circus with a total of 120 kilometers of runs and 30 lifts. Horse-drawn sleigh rides are possible at the **Gontal nature reserve** for 250 schillings per person during the day and 300 schillings per person at night. Many hotels have trained staffs to look after children and activities to keep the little ones happy and busy. The **Sport Erni**, *Tel. 4734-320; fax 4734-3204*, is a member of the Ski Top Class rental program. For more area information, contact the **Tourist Information Office**, *A-9863 Katschberg. Tel. 4734-630 or 3300; fax 4734-753 or 3305.*

The **Lavanttal Valley** is comprised of seven ski areas: Koralpe, Klippitztorl, Weinebeine, Petzen, Hebalm, Salzsteigel and Hirschegg. Skiers can take on 95 kilometers of slopes with 48 lifts. Ninety kilometers of cross-country trails are also a big draw for winter hikers. The frozen lake near **St. Andra** stretches 3.5 kilometers long for ice skating and curling. There's even an ice disco. Smaller frozen ponds and lakes for skating can also be found in the Lavanttal. For schnapps connoisseurs, you can see how local farmers make the powerful elixir from fruit mash. Take a bottle home with you to keep warm on a cold evening.

If you'd like to take a break from the slopes, make a visit to **Wolfsberg** with its charming old town sprinkled with boutiques and cafes to warm you after the cold. **Zentrasport in Loike**, *Tel. 4350-2888,* is a member of the Ski Top Class for ski rentals. For snowboard hires or course information, *call 4352-2878.* For more area information, contact the **Tourist Information Office**, *Minoriteplatz 1, A-9400 Wolfsberg. Tel. 4352-2878; fax 4352-52032.*

Mallnitz is the gateway to the **Hohe Tauern National Park**. The mountains, rising up to 2,650 meters high, guarantee snow well into spring. The Ankogel cable car will whisk you right to the top of the slopes. The **Molltal glacier** is also nearby, where skiing is possible even in summer. The resort has extensive ski school opportunities, including a ski kindergarten and snow boarding instruction. Other winter activities include a five kilometer toboggan run, cross-country skiing, ice skating, and curling. For those who prefer to take it easy, there are sleigh rides and cleared walking and hiking tracks. The train will drop you off at Mallnitz and you can take a free ski-bus up to the resort area. For more information, contact the **Tourist Information Office**, *A-9822 Mallnitz. 4784-290; fax 4784-635.*

Finally, consider **Villach**, Austria's southernmost resort right near the border of neighboring Italy. There are eight lifts servicing 75 kilometers of well-groomed trails. Cross-country skiers will like the 100 kilometers of trails, as well as walking and hiking tracks. Austrians also go to Villach to "seek the cure" with water treatments and indoor pools. For more information, contact the **Tourist Information Office**, *Europaplatz 2, A-9500 Villach. Tel. 4242-24444-0; fax 4242-24444-17.*

Tennis & Squash

Klagenfurt has 130 open air tennis courts, five indoor tennis centers, and two squash centers. Check with the local tourist office for the location nearest your hotel: **Klagenfurt Tourist Information**, *Rathaus, Neuer Platz, A-9010 Klagenfurt. Tel. 463-537-223; fax 463-537-295.*

Swimming

The clear, clean water in Carinthia's many lakes and rivers is ideal for swimming. Plus, the water temperature is much warmer than in the rest of the country, so you won't freeze.

If you're traveling with children, you might want to try some manmade water fun at the **Carinthian Fun Park** on the shores of **Lake Pressegger See**, *Presseger See, A-9620 Hermagor. Tel. 4282-3388; fax 4282-33884.* There's a giant water slide, loop-the-loop, Sky Dive, and lots more to please the young and the young at heart. Open from May to October, 9 a.m. to 7 p.m. Admission is 100 schillings per person.

DAY TRIPS & EXCURSIONS

Gerlamoos

Art lovers and history buffs visiting the Upper Drau Valley should make a stop in the **parish church** of this tiny village. Inside you'll find priceless frescoes by the Gothic artist Thomas Villach. **Ferienregion Oberdrautal**, *A-9771 Berg. Tel. 4712-667; fax 4712-713.*

Gurk Cathedral

Often described as the religious heart of Carinthia, the **Gurk Cathedral** is a two-spired Romanesque church. The cathedral houses the oldest Lenten veil in Carinthia dating from 1458. The church also has a famous crypt supported by a hundred pillars with the tomb of St. Hemma, a gilded high altar, and a bronze statue of the Virgin and Child by artist Raffael Donner.

Gurk Cathedral, *A-9342 Gurk*. Open daily 8 a.m. to 5:30 p.m. Guided tours available from mid-April through September. Tour fee is 30 schillings for adults, 15 schillings for children and students and 10 schillings for children under 10 years old.

Heft Open Air Museum

The 400-year old history of the iron works in the Huttenberg is explained here. Precious and semi-precious stones are also on display. The museum, which opened in 1984, has a mining trail that you can hike.

Huttenberg Show Mine and Mineral Museum, *Norevent Huttenberg, A-9376. Tel. 4263-427; fax 4263-8109.* Admission is 75 schillings for adults and 45 schillings for children.

Hohe Tauern National Park

The **Hohe Tauern National Park** stretches approximately 365 kilometers across Carinthia and the neighboring Tirol and Salzburg provinces. The park contains Austria's tallest mountain, the **Grossglockner**, towering 3,280 feet above sea level. The peak's biggest glacier is called the **Ostalpen**. The mountain also has the beauitful **Krimml Waterfalls** (see Chapter 16, *Salzburg*, for additional details). For more information, contact **Regionalverband Grossglockner**, *A-9844 Heiligenbut. Tel. 4824-2001-21; fax 4824-2001-43.*

You can choose from almost as many sporting activities as there are mountains in the park: climbing, tennis, riding, fishing, rafting, hanggliding, pony trekking and mountain biking. A man-made wonder on the way to the park is the **Kolnbrein Dam**, open from May to October. Drive the 18 kilometers along the **Malta Panoramic Route** into the mountains of the Hohe Tauern National Park. You'll then reach the dam, a part of the country's largest hydroelectric power station. Guided tours are possible upon request; contact **Reisseck-Maltatal Touristik**, *Kohldorfer Strasse 98, A-9020 Klagenfurt. Tel. 463-23716; fax 46-202256.*

For more information about the park , contact **Regionalverband Nationalpark Hohe Tauern**, *A-5722 Niedernsill POB 2. Tel. 6548-8417; fax 6548-8436.*

Hochosterwitz Castle

Many Americans already know the **Hochosterwitz Castle**, which inspired Walt Disney's version in the animated feature *Snow White*. No wonder: the fortress is everything one imagines a fairy tale castle should be. The fortress, with its myriad walls, portals, and gates stretching up the mountain, is one of Carinthia's most famous landmarks. You must pass through 14 different checkpoints just as knights of yore had to do before reaching your destination. Contact **Hochosterwitz**, *Burgverwaltung, A-9314 Launsdorf. Tel. 4213-202 and 2010.* Open daily May through October from 8 a.m. to 6 p.m. Admission is 40 schillings per person.

The surrounding area is rich in history with Celtic excavations, Roman artifacts, medieval castles and fortresses, and Carinthia's oldest towns **St. Veit** and **Friesach**. Guided tours are available through the historical section of St. Veit with its moat, arcaded courtyards, and well-preserved town squares. The local tourist office also publishes a map with information on some of the lesser known castles in the area. Contact **St. Veit Guided Tours**, *Stadtgemeinde St. Veit, A-9300 St. Veit. Tel. 4212-5555-13* or **Burgen und Schlosserregion**, *A-9300 St. Veit Glan. Tel. 4212-2374; fax 4212-2374-1.*

Find out how Austrian farmers lived off the land during the last century at the **Maria Saal Folk Museum**. A rural village is set up here with demonstrations. Contact the **Tourist Information Office**, *A-9063 Maria Saal. Tel. 4223-2812; fax 4223-2214-22.*

Magdalensberg Excavations

If you'd like to travel back in time to when Austria was a former Roman settlement, visit the excavations here. Displays document the region's early Celtic and later Roman occupations. The site is open from mid-April to the end of October. Guided tours are possible but should be reserved in advance through **Magdalensberg Roman Excavations**, *A-9064. Tel. 4224-2255 or 463-536-30552.*

Obir Caves

Just outside the town of **Eisenkappel** in the south of the province, the **Obir Caves**, *Hauptplatz 79, A-9315 Eisenkappel. Tel. 4238-8239; fax 4238-8374,* are open to visitors. You can take a fascinating tour to see the stalactites and stalagmites formed over the centuries. Open April through October from 9:15 a.m. to 3:30 p.m. Admission is 160 schillings for adults and 85 schillings for children. Children under age four are not admitted. Bus service to the caves is available from Eisenkappel.

Nockberg National Park

Almost a decade ago, the land bordering the **Nockalm panoramic route** was turned into a national park. Today, you can explore the pristine alpine countryside and learn about the environment at information centers along the route. You can even visit a *Karlbad,* a bathhouse with traditional wooden tubs.

The **Nockberg Mountains** and the region around **Bad Kleinkircheim** harbor an oasis of water therapies with Finnish saunas, Roman steam baths, and thermal waters.

For more park information, contact **Nockberge National Park**, *Grossglockner Hochalpenstrasse AG, Verwaltung Nockalmstrasse, Rainerstrasse 2, A-5020 Salzburg. Tel. 662-8736730; fax 662-87367313.* Open from May to October. The cost is 40 schillings per person.

Porsche Automobile Museum

You might be surprised to find out that the first car bearing the name Porsche actually originated here in Carinthia. Professor Ferdinand Porsche lived and worked in the province from 1944 to 1950. The Porsche 356 was in fact created here in **Gmund**. The museum has 44 coupes and 8 cabriolets on display.

For more information, contact **Porsche Automobile Museum**, *A-9853 Gmund. Tel. 4732-2471; fax 4732-2454.* Open daily mid-May through mid-September 9 a.m. to 6 p.m.; and mid-September to mid-May 10 a.m. to 4 p.m. Admission is 50 schillings per person.

Reisseck Funicular Railway

If you'd like to "climb every mountain," but don't think your hiking is quite up to speed, then hop aboard the **Reisseck Funicular Railway**, *Berghotel Reisseck. Tel. 4783-24200; fax 4783-2420220.* The cars leave from **Kolbnitz** rising up the mountain in three different stages. You'll climb through a mountain tunnel where you can enjoy a spectacular view of the lake below. A round trip ticket is 190 schillings for adults and 100 schillings for children.

Rosegg Wildlife Park

About 350 animals roam the **Rosegg Wildlife Park**, *Fremdenverkehrsamt Rosegg, A-9232 Rosegg. Tel. 4274-2712,* in areas mirroring their natural habitats from around the world. Ecological displays describe the lives of the animals, and the parts they play in their home environments.

Schloss Henckel-Donnersmarck

The **Schloss Henckel-Donnersmarck** looks like it could have been transplanted from the English countryside. The first written record of the **Wolf's Perch Castle** appeared in 1178. The lovely white-stone castle was rebuilt in the British Tudor style in 1846. For more information, contact the **Wolfsberg Tourist Information**, *Minoritenplatz 1, A-9400 Wolfsberg. Tel. 4352-537-274 or 2878; fax 4352-537-277 or 52032.*

St. Paul's Abbey

For a glass of some of the Lavanttal Valley's famous cider head right to the source at **St. Paul's Abbey**, *A-9470 St. Paul. Tel. 4357-201922.* There's even an orchard museum if you're curious how the cider is produced. The abbey also is home to the **Treasure House of Carinthia**, with ecclesiastical masterpieces from the Romanesque, Gothic, and Baroque periods, including the famous **Adelheid Cross**. The **Benedictine Cloister** is the only one still in full operation in the province. Admission is 70 schillings per person.

Worther See

The **Worther See** is so clear that locals brag that you can actually drink the water. The lake, with an average temperature of 23 degrees Celsius, is home to the "Carinthian Riviera" and is surrounded by resort facilities. You can tour the lake on Europe's only propeller-driven steamship. For lake area information, contact the **Worther See Information**, *A-9010 Klagenfurt. Tel. 463-54777; fax 463-54777.*

To get a good gander of the Worther See to the **Nock Mountains** and all the scenery in between, head up the **Pyramidenkogel View Tower**, *Tel.*

4273-2443 or 2291-0. Open April through October. Admission is 50 schillings for adults and 20 schillings for children.

PRACTICAL INFORMATION

American Express Office

The local **American Express** office can take care of your money and reservation needs at *Reiseburo Springer, Weisbadener Strasse 1, A-9020 Klagenfurt. Tel. 463-33520.*

Auto Club

The **Austrian Automobile, and Touring Club/Travel Department** is headquartered in Vienna. The club can answer your questions on touring the country by car.

You can contact them at *Schubertring 1-3, A-1010 Vienna. Tel. 0222-711-990; fax 0222-71199-1473.*

Banks

In general, banks are open Monday through Friday from 8 a.m. to noon and 2 p.m. to 3:30 p.m. Some banks maintain longer banking hours in resort towns.

Credit Cards

If your credit cards are lost or stolen, you can call the following numbers 24 hours a day to make a report. The numbers are located in Vienna, so first dial area code *0222.*
• **American Express,** *Tel. 51-29-714*
• **Diners,** *Tel. 50-1-35*
• **Mastercard,** *Tel. 71-7-01-0*
• **Visa,** *Tel. 53-4-87-77*

Emergency Phone Numbers

• **Ambulance,** *Tel. 144*
• **Police,** *Tel. 133*
• **Fire Department,** *Tel. 122*

Exchanging Money

Banks in general are open from 8 a.m. to noon and 2:30 p.m. to 4 p.m.; closed Saturdays, Sundays, and bank holidays.

If you get caught without cash when banks are closed, there are several automatic money exchange machines throughout the city.

Pharmacies

Several pharmacies are open 24-hours a day in case of emergencies. The address of the nearest open pharmacy will be posted in the window of each closed shop. For pharmacy assistance, *call 1550.*

Post Offices

Post offices are open, in general, Monday through Friday from 9 a.m. to 11 a.m. and 3 p.m. to 4:30 p.m. In larger towns and resort areas, many post offices have extended hours.

Road Conditions

To find out the latest traffic information, *call 459-299-299.*

Tipping

A service charge is added to your hotel and restaurant bill. However, if you are pleased with the service, it is customary to tip an additional 5 to 10 percent of the check. Taxi drivers and hair dressers also are generally tipped the same amount.

Weather

For the latest weather information, *call 15-66 or 463-41443.* For a recorded weather announcement, *call 463-1588.*

20. STYRIA

INTRODUCTION

Austrians call **Styria** the *green province*, since forests cover about half the region and vineyards cover an additional quarter. In contrast, Styria is also the mining capital of Austria. The mountains in the north of the province have extensive reserves of iron ore coming from the Erzberg, literally Ore Mountain. Lignite and magnetite are also mined in the province.

Styria's provincial capital, **Graz**, is Austria's second largest city with more than 250,000 residents. Graz once was home to the emperor in the late Middle Ages, although many Americans may be more familiar with the fact that the city is the birthplace of movie star Arnold Schwarzenegger. Graz has long been in the shadow of Vienna, but the city's narrow, meandering streets and picturesque buildings with their famous red tiled roofs surrounding the Schlossberg deserve attention in their own right. The medieval city center is one of the best preserved in Europe, earning an award for urban preservation from the Council of Europe.

Styria is also home to the famous **Lippizaner stallions**. They are raised in Piber just west of Graz. And more than 3,000 wine-growers grow their grapes in Styria, so if you are a wine lover the province is a good place for you to stop to savor the best vintages. For information on the Styrian portion of the Salzkammergut, see the Chapter 15, *The Lake District*.

ORIENTATION

Autumn is an especially nice time to visit Styria, when the apples begin to ripen and the grapes are being harvested for the year's vintage. There are several scenic roads where you can while away the day sampling the new wine at the vineyards along the way.

A good portion of Graz's old town is restricted to pedestrian traffic. Otherwise, the traffic patterns are somewhat confusing and complicated, so your best bet would be to park your car and either enter the old city on foot or catch a street car into town.

The **area code** for Graz is *316*. Remember to dial a zero before the area code if you are calling from inside Austria.

ARRIVALS & DEPARTURES
By Air
Styria's **airport** is just outside Graz, at *Flughafenstrasse 51, A-8073 Feldkirchen. Tel. 7233-291-541-0*. Flights arrive daily from airports around Austria.

By Car
If you're driving to Graz or other parts of Styria from Vienna, take the A2 autobahn south, which you pick up just outside of the city.

By Train
There is daily train service to Graz from all major cities in Austria. The main train station is within easy walking distance of the old town. For **train information,** *call 1717.*

STYRIA TOURIST INFORMATION
*If you're planning a trip to Styria, make sure you contact the **tourist information** office in Graz for information on hotels, sports, spas, or whatever else interests you. There are several locations around Graz:*
- *Hans Sachs Gasse 10, A-8010 Graz, Tel. 316-83-52-41-0; fax 83-79-87*
- *Herrengasse 16, A-8010 Graz. Tel. 316-835241-11*
- *Main Train Station, A-8010 Graz. Tel. 316-916837*

GETTING AROUND GRAZ
By Bike
You can explore the city on two-wheels as well as venture into the countryside or take a leisurely ride along the Mur River. In Graz, **green-lined parking areas** are reserved for cyclists.

If you don't have your own wheels with you, you can rent bikes at the following locations in Graz:
- **Main Train Station**, *Europaplatz, A-8010 Graz. Tel. 316-9848-508*
- **Verein Bicycle**, *Rechbauerstrasse 57, A-8010 Graz. Tel. 316-821-357* or at *Kaiser Franz Josef Kai 56, A-8010 Graz. Tel. 316-821-357*

By Car
Leave your car at your hotel or in a garage before venturing into Graz's old town. There are several **parking garages** scattered around town, including the following:

- **Andreas-Hofer Platz**, *A-8010 Graz. Tel. 316-829-191*
- **Burgring**, *A-8010 Graz. Tel. 316-822-488*
- **City Garage**, *Etenplatz, A-8010 Graz. Tel. 316-903-555*
- **Parkhaus**, *Schonaugasse 6, A-8010 Graz. Tel. 316-835-377*
- **Operngarage**, *A-8010 Graz. 316-829-575*

Blue Zoned parking spaces are also available on the street if you can find an empty space. You can park in such a zone for a maximum of three hours. Automatic machines located on the sidewalk allow you to purchase a parking voucher, which you should post in your front window.

As always, if you're planning to rent a car for your trip, try to make advance arrangements at home, where the rates will be significantly reduced. Here are the local **rental car offices** in Graz:
- **Avis**, *8010 Schlogelgasse 10, A-8010 Graz. Tel. 316-81-29-20; fax 316-84-11-78; at the airport, Tel. 7233-81-29-20*
- **Budget**, *Bahnhofgurtel 73, A-8010 Graz. Tel. 316-91-69-66; fax 316-91-66-834; at the airport, Tel. 7223-29-15-41-342*
- **Europcar**, *Wiener Strasse 15, A-8010 Graz. Tel. 316-91-40-80; fax 316-91-1929; at the airport Tel. 7223-29-67-57*

Getting around the rest of Styria really requires a car to visit the castles, spas, and vineyards scattered across the countryside. Some trains and **Bundesbus**, or post office buses, do go to remote locations, but you'll need to have the luxury of time. Scheduling can be tricky, so make sure you plan your itinerary accordingly.

If you get stuck and need emergency car help, you can call around the clock the **Automobile, Motorcycle, and Touring Association** at *120* or the **Automobile, Motorcycle, and Bicycle Association of Austria** at *123*.

By Public Transportation

You can get around Graz by **bus** and **street car**. Tickets can be purchased from the driver. You can also reach the top of the **Schlossberg**, or Castle Mountain, by **funicular** if you don't want to take on the challenge of trying to climb the stairs. The funicular runs every 15 minutes during the summer from 8 a.m. to 11:00 p.m. and during the winter from 10:00 a.m. to 10:00 p.m. The funicular departs from *Kaiser Franz Josef Kai 38, A-8010 Graz. Tel. 316-887-413.*

For more information and schedules, contact **Graz Public Transportation**, *Hauptplatz 14, A-8010 Graz. Tel. 316-887-411*; and at *Schlossbergbahn, A-8010 Graz. Tel. 316 887-413.*

By Taxi

To order a taxi throughout Styria or elsewhere in Austria, *call 1718.*

Some several local taxi companies in Graz include:
- **Funktaxigruppe**, *Tel. 2801*
- **Taxifunk**, *Tel. 983*
- **Funktaxi**, *Tel. 878*

WHERE TO STAY

Most people who visit Styria see the provincial capital of **Graz** and not much else. The city has a wide range of accommodations from which to choose.

One of the charms of this rural province is getting into the countryside, where you can enjoy many idyllic hotels and pensions, most of which have dining available using the best of regionally grown produce. As mentioned below in the *Where to Eat* section, most of the better restaurants are attached to hotels, inns, and guesthouses, and they are reviewed as part of each hotel below. The few restaurants independent of hotels are reviewed separately in *Where to Eat*.

Below is a selection of hotels from around the province, beginning with **Graz**, the provincial capital:

Graz

AUSTRIA TREND HOTEL EUROPA GRAZ, *Heinz Stefan, A-8020 Graz. Tel. 316-9076; fax 316-9076-606. Doubles start at 840 schillings per person. All credit cards accepted.*

You can't beat the Europa for its convenient location – directly across from the main train station. In fact, the hotel is connected directly to the station via an underground walkway lined with shops. The hotel is modern and well-appointed and the service efficient, making it popular with visiting business executives. But it's somewhat lacking in the charm department. The hotel's restaurant serves Austrian specialties, but the food is somewhat lack lustre.

ERZHERZOG JOHANN HOTEL, *Sackstrasse 3-5, A-8010 Graz. Tel. 316-811616; fax 316-811515. Doubles start at 825 schillings per person. All credit cards accepted.*

The Erzherzog Johann Hotel is right in the heart of the old town just off the main square. The former town palace's 70 rooms are filled with antique furniture and rugs. The hotel has been in operation for the past 140 years and is sumptuously furnished. One of the hotel's highlights is a Viennese-style bar designed by the Austrian artist Ernst Fuchs. The restaurant, serving traditional Austrian specialties with a novelle cuisine edge, is housed in the center of a glass-roofed Baroque winter garden. The green, light-filled space enhances the dining experience of guests.

GRAND HOTEL WIESLER, *Grieskai 4-8, A-8020 Graz. 316-9066-\
Tel. 316-9066-76. Doubles start at 1500 schillings per person. All credit card.
accepted.*

Graz's only five-star hotel, the Grand Hotel Wiesler overlooks the
River Mur so be sure to ask for a room with a view. The hotel has been
renovated in recent years and accommodations have been upgraded. The
rooms are filled with sumptuous fabrics and antique pieces. If you want
a quick bite to eat, you can select from the hotel's cafe, piano bar, or snack
bar. For more elegant dining, choose the Wiesler restaurant.

HOTEL GRAZERHOF, *Stubenberggasse 10, A-8010 Graz. Tel. 316-82-
43-58; fax 316-81-96-33. Doubles start at 700 schillings. Visa and Mastercard
accepted.*

The Hotel Grazerhof is in the heart of the old town. Located on a
quiet street just off Herren Gasse, you'll be in the thick of things without
having to subject yourself to the hustle and bustle of the streets. But the
hotel is a bit rough around the edges and looks as if it has seen better days.
Rooms are also somewhat dark, too.

HOTEL MARIAHILF, *Mariahilferstrasse 9, A-8010 Graz. Tel. 316-91-
31-63; fax 316-91-76-52. Doubles start at 490 schillings per person. All credit
cards accepted.*

The Hotel Mariahilf is a short stroll across the Mur River into Graz's
old town. The hotel is charming although a bit worn looking. But you can't
beat the price for its central location. Not all rooms have private baths, so
make sure to request one when you reserve your room. Pets are also
welcome.

Deutschlandsberg

HOTEL BURG DEUTSCHLANDSBERG, *Burgstrasse 19, A-8530
Deutschlandsberg. Tel. 3462-5656; fax 3462-5656-22. Doubles start at 480
schillings per person. All credit cards accepted.*

The Hotel Burg Deutschlandsberg resembles a castle out of the
Brothers Grimm with its massive drawbridge. The former fortress was
renovated by the Schick family. Rooms are filled with delightful rustic
furnishings. Guests won't want to miss the hotel's restaurant, a favorite
with local gourmets, in the former Hall of Knights. You can have an after
dinner drink in the **Steirerhof Bar** formerly located in Graz and reas-
sembled here. The **Cordon-Rouge Bar** is located in the 450 year-old
vaulted cellar of the fortress.

Irdning

HOTEL SCHLOSS PICHLARN, *Gatschen 28, A-8952 Irdning. Tel.
3682-228-410; fax 3682-228-416. Doubles start at 1,500 schillings per person.
All credit cards accepted.*

This former palace dates back to 1074. Over the years, the hotel has been expanded into a real recreational resort. Golfers will love the 18-hole course in the shadow of the Grimming Mountain. Riding is also possible in the Enns Valley. Three outdoor and two indoor tennis courts are also available. If your muscles need relaxing after playing all day, the hotel has spa facilities and a swimming pool. The hotel's restaurant is a treat for gourmets. The delicious Styrian cuisine earned a "Chef's Hat" from the Gault Millau Restaurant Guide.

Leibnitz

GASTHOF SAILLER, *Hauptplatz 5, A-8430 Leibnitz. Tel. 3452-72-5-16. Doubles start at 270 schillings per person, including breakfast. All credit cards accepted.*

The Gasthof Sailler is a tiny guest house run by Frau Gilda Karasek. Simple but comfortable, the guest house has a television room for guests as well as a garden and grill at their disposal. Savor a glass of wine on the terrace in front of this simple guesthouse and watch the world pass by.

HOTEL PENSION KARNTNERHOF, *Retzhoferstrasse 18, A-8430 Leibnitz. Tel. 3452-84-38-00; fax 3452-84-3-80-100. Doubles start at 280 schillings per person, including breakfast. All credit cards accepted.*

The Krassnig family operates this 46 bed, pink pension and welcomes you with open arms. However, don't expect the height of elegance; rooms are clean and basic, but not much else, other than satellite television. Children six and under can stay free with their parents. Parking is available for guests.

HOTEL-RESTAURANT ROMERHOF, *Marburger Strasse 1, A-8430 Leibnitz. Tel. 3452-82419 or 71-1-70; fax 3452-82-4-19-40. Doubles start at 317 schillings per person, including breakfast. All credit cards accepted.*

The Hotel-Restaurant Romerhof is run by Frau Irmgard Huss. For those who want to be pampered, the hotel has a beauty farm, sauna, solarium, and massage available. Guests can relax on the hotel's terrace or guest garden. The restaurant features the usual regional favorites with a good selection of local wines.

SCHLOSS SEGGAU, *Bildungshaus, A-8430 Leibnitz. Tel. 3452-82-4-35;fax 3452-82-43-5-10. Doubles start at 1,800 schillings per person. No credit cards accepted.*

The Schloss Seggau dates from the ninth century, but today offers modern amenities for weary travelers. The castle is perched above the wine producing town of Leibnitz and has a fantastic view of the village below. Half-pension starts at 300 additional schillings. The castle also has tennis courts, a sauna, indoor swimming pool, and a solarium available for guests.

Sebersdorf

ROMANTIKHOTEL SCHLOSS OBERMAYERHOFEN, *Bad Waltersdorf, A-8272 Sebersdorf. Tel. 3333-2503; fax 3333-2503-50. Doubles start at 720 schillings per person. All credit cards accepted.*

The Romanktikhotel Schloss Obermayerhofen has been delightfully restored maintaining its fairytale castle charm. Rooms are luxuriously furnished with perfectly coordinated pieces. The hotel's simple elegance is sure to please even the most exacting guest. The palace chapel with its Gothic touches is also a popular place for weddings. Be sure not to miss the red spot in the courtyard. According to local legend, the spot was created when a duchess with a passion for gambling was whisked away by the devil.

Seggauberg

GASTHOF-RESTAURANT HASENWIRT, *Seggauberg 27, A-8430 Seggauberg. Tel. 3452-82570; fax 3452-74-5-70-33. Doubles start at 330 schillings per person, including breakfast. All credit cards accepted.*

This cozy 40 bed guest house is operated by Herr Leo Kapper and is located right besides the vineyards. Children up to 15 years old can stay in their parents room. They can also amuse themselves at the guest house's playground. Enjoy a glass of local vino with your meal at the guest house's restaurant. There is also a guest garden and grill where you can relax.

WEINBAUERNHOF ASSIGAL, *Seggauberg 45, A-8430 Seggauberg. Tel. 3452-86-8-11. Doubles start at 250 schillings per person. No credit cards accepted.*

There are only 10 beds at the rustic Weinbauernhof Assigal, which only adds to its intimate charm. The Assigal family runs this guest house on the hills of their vineyards. You'll be treated like a member of the family. Of course, another reason to come is to sample the vintages produced here. You won't be disappointed by the quality or the quantity available. Make sure, however, to reserve well in advance since rooms are in relatively short supply.

WHERE TO EAT

Be sure to try the mushroom soup or beef consomme topped with *Sterz*. Lamb with mustard sauce is also a specialty. Styria is renowned for its pumpkin seed oil, a strong, nutty oil. Although many tourists turn up their noses, the distinctive flavor is really very good. The almost black oil is used to dress salads and in cooking.

But even more tempting are the wines from Styria's more than 3,000 vineyards. The *Welschriesling*, the sauvignon *Muskat-Sylvaner*, the pinot blanc chardonnay *Weisse Burgunder-Morillion*, the *Traminer*, the pinot gris *Rulander*, the *Muller-Thurgau* and the *Muskateller* are all cultivated here. Western Styria is also home to the *Schilcher* wine, which varies in color and flavor by region, from the light red *Onion Schilcher* from Stainz to the deep burgundy found in Eibiswald. True connoisseurs can take a trip down the **Kloch Wine Road** which runs from Bad Radkersburg to Fehring.

While you're sampling different wines, have a glass with some Styrian cheese; *Steirerkas*, a caraway spread or filling in *Krapfen* doughnuts; or *Verhackert*, a meat spread eaten on dark, country bread.

The smaller towns and resorts outside of Graz have fewer selections, butmost hotels have very good restaurants and wine cellars – so scan the *Where to Stay* section above when looking for a good place to eat.

Graz

GAMLITZER WEINSTUBE, *Mehlplatz 4, A-8020 Graz. Tel. 316-82-87-60. Moderate. Open Monday through Friday from 9 a.m. to 11 p.m. All credit cards accepted.*

If you want to find out where the locals go to sample Styrian culinary classics, head to the Gamlizer Weinstube. As the name implies, you'll also be able to sample some the delicious wine grown on the nearby hillsides. The atmosphere is friendly and boisterous.

GERLINDES GASTHAUS, *Abraham A Santa Clara Gasse 2, Graz. Tel. 316-81-38-30. Expensive. Open Monday through Saturday from 5 p.m. to 2 a.m. Diners and American Express cards accepted.*

Gerlindes Gasthaus is a charming restaurant with a wonderful combination of rustic charm and sophisticated style. The restaurant features a broad choice of Styrian favorites and international cuisine elegantly presented. The wine list boasts an excellent selection of regional wines as well.

HOFKELLER, *Hofgasse 8, A-8010 Graz. Tel. 316-83-24-39. Moderate. Open Monday through Saturday from 11 a.m. to 3 p.m. and 6 p.m. to midnight. All credit cards accepted.*

If you're tired of soggy pasta and watery tomato sauce, which sometimes passes for Italian cuisine, head to the Hofkeller. The restaurant specializes in Italian haute cuisine from Austria's southern neighbor. The restaurant also has a wide variety of Italian wines to complement your dinner.

KEPLERKELLER, *Stemfergasse 6, A-8020 Graz. Tel. 316-82-24-49. Moderate. Open Monday through Saturday 6 p.m. to 2 a.m. All credit cards accepted.*

If you've been out on the town and are in the mood for classic Styrian fare in a convivial atmosphere, then the Keplerkeller is the place for you.

Regional vintages are featured prominently on the wine list. And to finish off your evening, live music will entertain you while you dine.

OPERNCAFE, *Operring 22, A-8020 Graz. Tel. 316-82-13-83. Inexpensive. Open daily 7:30 a.m. to midnight; Sunday and holidays 9 a.m. to midnight. No credit cards accepted.*

If you need to take a breather from your sight-seeing, then the Operncafe could be just what the doctor ordered. A wide variety of the coffees and rich cakes flavored with chocolate, fresh fruit and cream will tempt you. You can also have light meals for lunch or a quick snack.

STAINZERBAUER, *Burgergasse 4, A-8010 Graz. Tel. 316-82-11-06. Moderate. Open Monday through Saturday 11 a.m. to midnight. American Express card accepted.*

If you're looking for a restaurant with classic Styrian fare, then head to the Stainzerbauer. The restaurant is cozily furnished and welcoming with its leaded glass windows and classic decor. The restaurant features a variety of regional and national favorites. And don't forget to have a glass of the local, fruity wine grown in the nearby countryside.

TEMMELS KAISERHOF, *Kaisergasse 1, A-8010 Graz. Tel. 316-83-0436. Inexpensive. Open 7:30 a.m. to 9 p.m. No credit cards accepted.*

The Temmels Kaiserhof is at the base of the Schlossberg near the stairs leading up to the tower and ideal for a big, cold beer, either before your trek up the hill or as a reward for your labor on the way down. The Temmels Kaiserhof is like your corner neighborhood bar, and the atmosphere is friendly and boisterous. The bill won't put too much of a dent into your pocketbook either.

ZUR GOLDENEN PASTETE, *Sporgasse 28, Graz. Tel. 316-82-34-16. Moderate. Open Monday through Friday from 11 a.m. to midnight; closed weekends and holidays. All credit cards accepted.*

The Zur Goldenen Pastete is a cozy dining experience, with its colorful red, green, and white exterior – perfect for a cold, winter evening. And the food is as good as the restaurant looks. Specialties include pork with pumpkin, black pudding, and Styrian dumplings.

Kapfenstein

WEINGUT WINKLER-HERMADEN, *Schloss Kapfenstein, A-8353 Kapfenstein 105. Tel. 3157-23 22. Moderate. Open noon to 9 p.m. All credit cards accepted.*

Part of the joy of a trip to Styria is tasting the many wines grown in the craggy hillsides. What better place than in a restored castle perched high above the vineyards in the southeastern part of the province? The Sauvignon Blanc and the Grauer Burgunder are especially good. The kitchen cooks up Styrian classics to complement your wine.

SEEING THE SIGHTS IN GRAZ

Graz was first mentioned in 1128 as *Gradec*, Slavic for "little fortress." The city's wall was erected about a century later. Graz became the imperial seat under Frederick III in 1440. The city was devastated by the plague in 1680, when over a quarter of the population was killed. In 1809, the city was besieged by the French during Napoleon's invasion of the country, and the Schlossberg fortress was destroyed. But the city managed to save its famous clock tower by paying a large ransom to the French army.

Despite these bouts with disaster, the city has managed to preserve its medieval character. Start your visit in the city's **Hauptplatz**, Graz's main square which has served as a market and trading center since its inception in 1164. The **Rathaus**, or City Hall, was erected in 1550 at the southern end of the square, but the facade reflects its German Renaissance roots after it was restored between 1887 and 1893. In the center of the square there is a fountain memorializing the Archduke John from 1878. The four female figures at the base of the fountain represent the Mur, Enns, Drau, and Sann rivers of Styria.

Head off the square to the **Franziskanergasse** and note the medieval houses that line the street. The **Church of the Franciscans** and the **Monastery** was built as early as 1240 next to the former city walls. The steeple was added in 1636 as part of Graz's fortification. The choir stalls have modern stained glass windows by Franz Felfer and the Benedictine nun Basilia. The Franziskanerplatz is also know as the **Butcher's Quarter** because of the meats and sausages sold here through the centuries.

Take the **Neue Welt Gasse** to the **Schmiedgasse**, where there are several preserved burgher's homes where blacksmiths, plumbers and cartwrights had their shops during the Middle Ages. This will take you to the **Landhausgasse** and **Herrengasse**, the main shopping street in the old town. On your left, you'll see the **Painted House**, which was originally a ducal residence that also served as the home away from home for the emperor whenever he was in town. The rococo house on the corner is one of the oldest chemists in town. Across the street is the **Styrian Parliament** building designed by Domenico dell'Allio of Lugano in the 16th century and modeled in the style of a Lombardy Renaissance palace.

Next to the parliament is the regional **arsenal**, *Herrengasse 16*, which houses an incredible **museum**, *Tel. 7031-2778*. If you're going to visit just one museum in Graz, make it this one. The armory houses more pistols, lances, coats of armor, and other artifacts of war than you've ever seen under one roof. In fact, over 30,000 pieces are on display from the 16th and 17th centuries. The staff is incredibly helpful and friendly, and they may even let you try on a helmet or two. Appropriately enough, everyone's favorite general Napoleon Bonaparte once spent the night across the

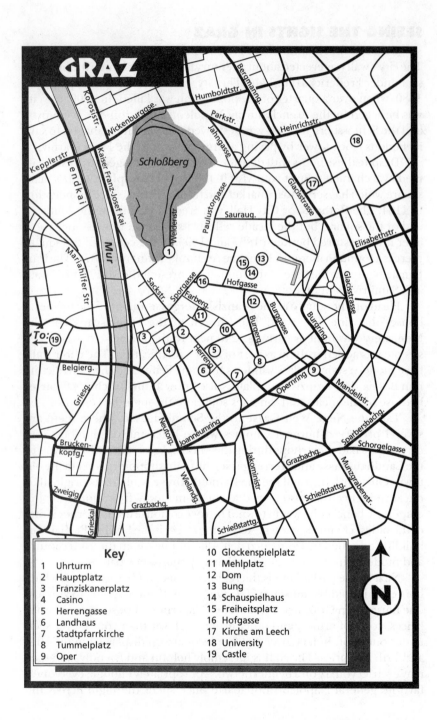

GRAZ

Key

1 Uhrturm
2 Hauptplatz
3 Franziskanerplatz
4 Casino
5 Herrengasse
6 Landhaus
7 Stadtpfarrkirche
8 Tummelplatz
9 Oper

10 Glockenspielplatz
11 Mehlplatz
12 Dom
13 Bung
14 Schauspielhaus
15 Freiheitsplatz
16 Hofgasse
17 Kirche am Leech
18 University
19 Castle

street at Zeughaus 13. The armory is open April 1 to Oct. 31, Monday through Friday from 9 a.m. to 5 p.m.; Saturdays, Sundays and holidays 9 a.m. to 1 p.m. Admission is 25 schillings for adults; seniors 10 schillings; free for students and children.

Down the street is the **Stadtpfarrkirche**, or city parish church, dating from the beginning of the 16th century. The church originally served as an abbey church for the Dominicans. Inside, you'll find Tintoretto's *Assumption of Mary*, which was brought to Graz in 1594. Also worth noting are the modern stained glass windows in the front of the church. The windows were heavily damaged during World War II and were replaced by the Salzburg painter Albert Birkle, who depicted Hitler and Mussolini as being among Christ's persecutors.

Leaving the church and crossing the Opernring, you'll see the **Thalia monument** designed by Viennese architect Rudolf Vorderegger. The **Opera House** was designed in the style of the Baroque master Fischer von Erlach, who was born in Graz. In front of the opera house is the **Lichtschwert**, or light sword, modeled after New York's Statue of Liberty by Styrian artist Hartmut Skerbisch. Crossing the Opernring, you'll see the **Tummelplatz**, which gets its name from breaking horses. Follow the Schlossergasse to the **Bishop's Square** where you'll see two palaces. On the left is the **Bishop's Palace** and across the street is the former **Earl Inzaghi's Palace**. In the nearby **Carillon Square**, at 11 a.m., 3 p.m. and 6 p.m. daily, the windows open and a life-sized Styrian couple dance to the music of the glockenspiel.

Head back to Abraham-A-Santa-Clara Gasse and walk up the hill to the **Crown of the Town**, which includes the Cathedral, Mausoleum, Castle, Theater and old university. **Ferdinand II's Mausoleum** was built by the architects Pietro de Pomis and by Pietro Valnegro. Fischer von Erlach was commissioned by emperor Leopold I to finish the inside in 1687. **St. Catherine's Chapel** has a barrel vault in the form of a Latin cross. The crypt chapel is elliptically shaped. On the cathedral exterior wall, notice the *Picture of the Scourge of God*, painted in 1485 showing the three plagues of 1480: the Turkish invasion, locusts, and the Black Death. Emperor Friedrich III commissioned the late Gothic **Cathedral** in 1438. Inside, you'll find two Renaissance chests designed by Andrea Mantegna and altar paintings by Pietro Pomis. Friedrich lived across the street in the castle, but most of it was demolished in the last century. The Gothic double spiral staircase from 1499 is still in existence, however.

Continuing down **Hofgasse**, you'll run into the theater and in the center of the square is a monument to Emperor Franz I. From here go down Ballhausgasse to **Sporgasse**, named for the craftsmen who molded arms here in the 14th and 15th century. On the left is the **Saurau Palace**. On the left gable is the figure of a Turk, who according to legend, represents the general Ibrahim Pascha. One night while he was eating in the palace occupied by the Turks, a cannon ball fired from the Schlossberg landed in his plate. He immediately withdrew his troops from the city and left Graz.

You can walk from the palace to the **Clock Tower,** Graz's most famous landmark. Notice that the clock's hands are reversed. Originally, there was only one large hand and the small one was added later. The tower used to serve as a lookout post for fires in the city. The whole city, with its red tiled roofs, stretches below you and is really worth the trek. You can descend the hill either by funicular or by the picturesque rock staircase.

Museums

There are several small museums in Graz to visit if you plan a longer stay. Admission for each is 25 schillings for adults, 10 schillings for seniors, and free for students and children.

Archives, *Sackstrasse 17, Palais Attems, A-8010. Tel. 316-83-03-35 or 82-53-17.* Open Monday, Tuesday and Thursday, 8 a.m. to 4 p.m.; Wednesday and Friday 8 a.m. to 1 p.m.

Austrian Aviation Museum, *Flughafen Graz-Thalerhof, A-8073. Tel. 316-32-95-32.* Open May through October, Sundays and holidays from 11 a.m.

Austrian Lock and Key Museum, *Griesgasse 14-16/Belgiergasse 3, A-8020 Graz. Tel. 316-91-16-200.* Open Thursday 3 to 6 p.m.

City Museum, *Palais Khuenburg, Sackstrasse 18, A-8010 Graz. Tel. 316-82-60-21 or 82-25-80.* Open Thursdays 10 a.m. to 9 p.m.;Wednesday through Saturday 10 a.m. to 6 p.m.; Sundays and holidays 10 a.m. to 1 p.m.

Diocese Museum, *Mariahilferplatz 3, A-8020 Graz. Tel. 316-91-39-94.* Open Monday through Wednesday 10 a.m. to 4 p.m.; Thursday to Saturday 10 a.m. to 5 p.m.; Sundays and holidays 10 a.m. to 1 p.m.

Early History Museum, Hunting Museum, and **Mint,** *Eggenberger Allee 90, A-8020 Graz. Tel. 316-58-32-64-21.* The Early History Museum is open February through November 9 a.m. to 1 p.m. and 2 p.m. to 5 p.m.

Folklore Museum, *Paulustorgasse 11-13A, A-8010 Graz. Tel. 316-83-04-16 or 80-17-48-80.* Open Monday through Friday 10 a.m. to 5 p.m.;Saturday, Sunday and holidays 2 p.m. to 5 p.m.

Garison Museum, *Schlossberg, A-8010 Graz. 316-82-73-48.* Open Easter through mid-October, Tuesday through Saturday 10 a.m. to 5 p.m.

Geology, Zoologie, Botanical, and **Mineral Museums,** *Raubergasse 10, A-8010 Graz. Tel. 316-80-17-47-00; fax 316 80-17-48-00.* Open Monday through Friday, 9 a.m. to 4 p.m.; Saturdays, Sundays and holidays, 9 a.m. to noon.

House of Architecture, *Engelgasse 3-5, A-8010 Graz. Tel. 316-323-500.* Open Monday through Friday 9 a.m. to 5 p.m.

Kunstgewerbe (Arts and Crafts Museum) and **Old Art Gallery**, Neutorgasse 45, A-8010 Graz. Tel. 316-80-17-47-80 or 70. Open Monday, Wednesday and Friday 10 a.m. to 5 p.m.; Saturday, Sunday and holidays 10 a.m. to 1 p.m.

New Gallery, *Sackstrasse 16, A-8010 Graz. 316-82-91-55 or 82-91-86.* Open Thursday through Saturday 10 a.m. to 6 p.m.; Sundays and holidays 10 a.m. to 1 p.m. Features modern art works.

Printing Museum, *Hans Brandstetter Gasse 12, A-8010 Graz. Tel. 316-47-16-53.* Monday through Friday 8 a.m. to 6 p.m.

Robert Stolz Museum, *Mehlplatz 1, A-8010 Graz. Tel. 316-81-59-51.* April 1 through September, Tuesday through Friday 2 p.m. to 5 p.m.; Saturday and Sunday 10 a.m. to 1 p.m.; October through March, Tuesday and Thursday 2 p.m. to 5 p.m.; Sundays 10 a.m. to 1 p.m.

Tramway Museum, *Endhaltestelle Mariatrost Strassenbahnlinie 1. Tel. 316-9070-0.* Open July through September, Friday 3 p.m. to 6:30 p.m.

NIGHTLIFE & ENTERTAINMENT

Graz is home to the **Steirischer Herbst**, one of the world's most important festivals featuring avant-garde works. Founded in 1968, the festival takes place every October. The **Styriarte Festival** summer program is directed by Graz's most famous conductor, Nikolaus Harnoncourt. Concerts are performed in the Conference Hall, in the Eggenberg palace park, and in numerous squares in the city's old town. The **Opera House** offers a seasonal program, which includes opera and ballet performances.

Graz also is home to Styria's **casino**, *Landhausgasse 10,* which opens its doors beginning at 3 p.m. daily. You'll have to pay 210 schillings to get in, but you receive 250 schillings in chips. Try your luck at roulette, baccarat, black jack, poker, red dog, sic bo, wheel of fortune and slot machines. The area around the **Mehlplatz** and the **Farberplatz** in Graz is known as the "Bermuda Triangle." Here you'll find several pubs, cafes, and bars to while away the evening hours.

For more information on entertainment and nightlife in Graz and Styria, contact local tourist offices, which publish monthly programs of events.

SHOPPING

Graz's **old town** has lot of charming, small boutiques where you can purchase everything from traditional *dirndl* dresses to handcrafted folk art. Venture down some of the narrow, medieval streets heading off the main square for the best buys.

Graz has a wide range of **open air markets** to browse and possibly find the treasure of your trip or a quick bite to eat while on the go. Some good choices are:

- **Farmer's Market**, *Kaiser Josef Platz and Lendplatz*. Open Monday through Saturday from 7 a.m. to 12:30 p.m.
- **Farmer's Market**, *Hauptplatz*. Open Monday through Friday from 6 a.m. to 7 p.m.; Saturday 6 a.m. to 12:30 p.m.
- **Flea Market**, *Karmeilerplatz*. The third Saturday of the month from 6 a.m. to 1 p.m.

If you head into the Styrian countryside, you can find a cornucopia of **wines** to purchase. Vineyards dot the countryside, and most vintners will be more than happy to have you buy a few bottles.

Styria is also known for its **glass**. If you are looking for the best quality, head to the source in **Barnbach**, where you can watch master glass blowers at their craft before purchasing their wares.

SPORTS & RECREATION

Alpine Garden

Enjoy the beauty of the native flora and fauna with a stroll through this Alpine Garden. Contact **Alpengarten Rannach**, *Rannach 15, A-8046 Graz. Tel. 316-69-30-31.* Open April through September daily from 8 a.m. to 6 p.m.; October through March daily from 8 a.m. to 3 p.m.

Water Sports

If you're visiting Styria during the summer months, there are a variety of water sports to keep you busy. If you want to tan without worrying about tan lines, head to the **Schwarzl Lesure Center's nudist beach**. For those who prefer to keep their suits on, there are also beaches for you. The center, near **Graz Thalerhof**, features swimming, pedal boats, and waterskiing.

For the swingers among you, you can find palm trees in Styria's version of the "Copacabana" near **Karlsdorf**. Here you'll find a variety of water sports to entertain you and a nightclub for after-hours fun. The main attraction in the **Piberstein leisure center** is a huge slide. Swimming and sunning are also popular along the lakefront.

To get to Schwarzl or the Copacabana, take the B67 heading south of Graz. To get to Piberstein, take the A2 to Mooskirchen and then the B70 to Piberstein.

TAKING THE CURE

Austrians are firm believers in "taking the cure." In fact, the Austrian national health insurance will pay for cures when prescribed by a doctor. Styria has a wealth of spas where you can soak, smooth, and relax your way to better health.

From Graz, head east along the A2 to Bad Waltersdorf. The city has thermal baths whose hot mineral water is believed to help cure both body and mind. If you get tired of all that water, there is a tennis center located near the baths. Traveling south from Bad Waltersdorf, you'll reach Loipersdorf, where you'll find a water wonderland with steam baths, jacuzzis, a water slide, and whirlpools, not to mention massage facilities, a golf course, and sun bathing.

Hot Springs can also be found in nearby Bad Radkersburg. The old town center is remarkably well-kept despite having withstood invasions by Hungarians, Turks, and the Red Army. If you want to take the cure, there are several spas and beauty farms to take advantage of these fountains of youth. But be forewarned, beauty doesn't come cheap. You're going to have to dig deep into your pockets for your rest and relaxation. Contact Tourist Information, Hauptplatz 1, Bad Radkersburg. Tel. 3476-2545; fax 3476-2509-38.

DAY TRIPS & EXCURSIONS

If you have an extra day or two to stay in Styria, take advantage of one of the many scenic drives only a short distance from Graz. Depending on your interests, you can follow the history of the local iron industry, drink some wine, heal your health with an apple or two, visit an open air museum, tour a medieval castle, or just take in the inviting Styrian countryside.

Apple Road

The Styrian **apple road** meanders through the hillsides between **Puch** and **Weiz**. From Graz, drive along the A2 towards Gleisdorf and then follow the signs towards Puch. Apples, juice, cider and apple schnapps are all produced here. You can sample the best of the bunch from local orchards and then take a bottle of cider or schnapps with you as a memento.

Austrian Open Air Museum

The **Austrian Open Air Museum**, just north of Graz, *(A-8114 Stubing. Tel. 3124-537-00; fax 3124-537-00-18)*, will charm both children and adults. The museum, operated by a scientific foundation, has more than 80 examples of Austrian rural architecture on 50 hectares. You can also see a charcoal burner's hut, a sawmill, a hammer smithy, mills, an old-fashioned grocery and an old school. Craftsmen demonstrate the ancient arts and traditional techniques of cutting wood, pottery, spinning, weaving, lace making and bread baking and will often let you try your hand at their crafts. Plan to spend two or three hours at the museum if you want to see everything.

To get to the museum from Graz, take the A9 towards Salzburg and exit at Stubing. Open 9 a.m. to 5 p.m.; closed Monday.

Herberstein Castle

The **Herberstein Castle**, *8222 St. Johann bei Herberstein. Tel. 3176-8825; fax 3176-8775-20*, once served as a fortress, but now houses a **museum** with a fine collection of antique weapons, minerals, and porcelain. The **zoo** here also has more than 120 animal species on display. To get to the castle from Graz, take the A2 towards Gleisdorf. Then head north along the B54 in the direction of Hartberg. Turn left at Hirnsdorf and follow the signs towards Herberstein. Open April through October 10 a.m. to 4 p.m. Admission for adults is 95 schillings; children, 55 schillings.

While here, head northeast towards **Stubenberg**. The **Schielleiten castle** is two miles east of Stubenberg. The Baroque castle today houses a sports college. Balloon championships are also held here annually. If you're in the mood for some rest and relaxation, head to the **Stubenberg am See**. There are a variety of water sports at the reservoir including, swimming, pedal boats, fishing, or skating during the winter months.

Iron Road

If you want to head off the beaten track, take a ride down the ancient **Iron Road**, lined with countless relics of centuries of ore mining and iron production. The Iron Road runs approximately 40 miles between **Leoben** and **Hammerhaus**. The heart of the Iron region is the **Erzberg**, literally Ore Mountain, which towers 5,000 feet high. The town of **Eisenerz**, at the foot of the mountain, dates back to the 15th and 16th centuries. The town also boast's the country's only completely preserved fortified church.

If you travel down to the nearby market town of **Vordenberg**, you will see several restored early industrial plants. You can tour, for example, a charcoal furnace facility from the early 19th century.

Lurgrotte

Located in the Tannenbenstock, the **Lurgrotte**, *Tel. 3127-8319 or 3125-2218*, is the largest dripstone cave in Austria. Guides will take you on a tour showing and explaining the origin of the stalagmite, stalactites, and the **Pool of the Water Nymphs**. To get to the Lurgrotte from Graz, take the B67 heading north. Admission is 50 schillings for adults and 30 schillings for children. Open mid-April through October 10 a.m. to 4 p.m.; tours held at 11 a.m., 2 p.m. and 4 p.m.; November through mid-April open weekends and by prior arrangement; tours at 11 a.m. and 2 p.m.

Murau

Nestled between the **Niedern Tauern**, the **Frauen Alps**, and the **Seetal Alps**, the town of **Murau** has managed to preserve its medieval character. The town's **castle** was built by Ulrich von Liechtstein in 1232 but was rebuilt in 1643. **St. Mathew's Church** still retains its Gothic character despite renovations during the 17th century. You can also take a ride on the **Murau-Tramsweg steam train** for a picturesque view of the Mur Valley.

Murau is on Route 96 east of Graz. For more information, contact the **Murau Tourist Office**, *A-8850 Murau. Tel. 3532-2720; fax 3532-223122.*

Piber

Piber is the home of the famous **Lippizaner stallions**, the oldest line of thoroughbreds in Europe. In 1850, Archduke Karl founded a stud farm in Lipizza near Triest, breeding horses that had descended from Spanish and Neapolitan stock. The horses were then used by the Spanish Riding School in Vienna.

After the disintegration of the empire, the Lippizaners took up residence in Piber in 1920. The town has a long history of horse breeding, dating back to the 16th century. Lippizaner foals can range in color from black to yellow, but change to gray from the age of three to seven years. Their coats eventually evolve into their famous white hue at the age of ten after repeated sheddings.

You can visit the stud farm from Easter to the end of October. One-hour tours are offered at 9:00 a.m., 10:15 a.m., 2 p.m. and 3:15 p.m. You must call or write to reserve a space on the tour: **Bundesgestut Piber**, *A-8580 Koflach. Tel. 3144-3323.*

To get to Piber from Graz, take the A2 west towards Liebach, then follow the Schilcher wine road until you reach the B70 which will take you to Piber. On your way back to Graz, stop off at **Barnbach** (on the B70), where you can see glass blowers hard at work on their craft, the same techniques used for 200 years. The glass blowers will explain how the glass is produced, how molds are made, how glass is colored, and other technical points. Afterwards, you can stop by the local **glass museum** where more artwork in on display, including pieces from 200 AD. Exhibition information is also in English. Contact the **Stolzle Glass Center**, *Hochtregisterstrasse, A-8572, Barnbach. Tel. 3142-62-141-49.* Open Monday through Friday, 10 a.m. to 6 p.m.; Saturdays 9 a.m. to 4 p.m.; June through August, also open Sundays 10 a.m. to 4 p.m.; 50-minute guided tours are available Monday through Friday at 10 a.m., 11:00 a.m., noon, 2:00 p.m., 3:00 p.m. and 4 p.m. and by prior arrangement.

When you reach Lieboch, take the B76 to the **Stainz Castle**. When Archduke Johann became mayor in 1850, he had the former Augustine convent revamped for his personal residence. The structure was originally Gothic but was transformed into the Baroque style during the 17th century.

During your visit, take a ride on the **Stainzer bottle train**, which runs between **Stainz** and **Preding-Wieslsdorf**. The train, inaugurated in 1892, gets its name from the urine bottles that visitors brought with them to have analyzed by the local doctor. Today, you won't find urine bottles, but wine sold on the train and live music played. This is an especially nice visit to make if you are traveling with children, but adults will be equally enthralled. Contact the **Stainz Tourist Office**, *A-8510 Stainz. Tel. 3463-4950 or 4518; fax 3463-4445.*

Riegersburg

Perched atop a craggy summit 150 meters up, the **Rieger Fortress** was built in 1690 and has eleven bastions and six gates to protect itself from marauding invaders. The Rieger fortress is part of the "empire fence" and was considered the strongest fortress in the chain. The fortress is remarkably well-preserved. Today you can see the hall where knights once congregated and the *Iron Virgin*.

To reach the fortress from Graz, take the A2 to Ilz and then turn south towards Riegersburg. If you continue south, you will see the **Kornberg fortress**, which was built as early as the 13th century. The castle has a beautiful Renaissance court. For the athletes among you, this trip is also easily done by bicycle. Take the train to Feldbach and you can cycle from there. More details and schedules can be obtained from the **Feldbach Tourist Office**, *A-8330 Feldbach. 3152-3079; fax 3152-5804.*

Schloss Eggenberg

Located outside of the Graz's city center, the **Schloss Eggenberg**, *Eggenberger Allee 90, A-8020 Graz. Tel. 316-58-32-64-33 or 55*, is definitely worth a detour if you have the time. Deer, sheep, and peacocks wander lazily around the castle grounds. The medieval castle was renovated in 1625 for the Governor of Inner Austria, Johann Ulrich von Egenberg.

Pietro de Pomis, the Italian architect who designed Ferdinand II's Mausoleum in Graz, was entrusted with the refurbishment. Open April 1 to Oct. 31. Guided tours for 10 a.m., 11 a.m., noon, 2 p.m., 3 p.m. and 4 p.m.

Stift Rein

The **Stift Rein convent** was once the site of a Cistercian abbey dating back to 1129. The convent was transformed into the Baroque style, especially the Roman basilica church. The Stift Rein's frescoes, episcopal rooms, and library are also worth a look. The convent is located off the A9, 15 kilometers northwest of Graz.

Stift Seckau

The **Seckau basilica** was originally constructed in the 12th century in the slightly severe German Romanesque style. In the choir room is a moving crucifixion scene created in the early 13th century. To get to the Stift Seckau from Graz, take the A9 towards Salzburg. At St. Michael, take the S36 via Kobenz to the Stift Seckau.

Styria's Wine Road

One of the primary joys of visiting Styria is experiencing glassfuls of the excellent wine grown in its fertile soil. Stop by one of the many **Buschenschenken**, local vintners who sell their wine and fresh produce to travelers. You can also purchase a few bottles to take back with you for a souvenir of your trip.

Start off your visit at the **Gamlitz Castle**, which has a museum describing the one thousand year history of wine growing in the region. Traveling by car from Graz, take the A9, in the direction of Slovenia, to **Voggau**. Then drive south along the Styrian wine road where you will see signs to the castle. From there drive north in the direction of Leibnitz to the **Seggau Castle**. The majestic castle has a Baroque chapel, gallery, and the largest bell in Styria. But save the best for last – a visit to the castle's 300-year-old wine cellar. As you might imagine, the castle has an excellent selection of the province's light, sweet wines.

After you finish your visit to the castle, drive west along the **Sausal wine road**. The sloping hills of the Sausal mountains between **Lassnitz** and **Sulm** are perfect for wine growing. Several vineyards are open to the public for sampling the best bottles. Farm fresh food is usually sold on the premises if you want to enjoy a leisurely lunch or hardy snack. Here, too, is the **wine museum** in **Kitzeck** where you can find out the secrets of the region's wine production and visit local wine cellars. To get back to Graz, drive east until you hit the A9.

PRACTICAL INFORMATION

Babysitting

If you need a babysitter, you can call the **Austrian Hochschulerschaft**, *Tel. 316-321-490-0.*

Camping

For information on camping in Styria, contact **Central**, *Graz Strassgang, Martinhofstrasse 3. Tel. 316-832578.*

Credit Cards

If your credit cards are lost or stolen, you can call the following numbers 24 hours a day to make a report. The numbers are located in Vienna, so first dial area code *0222.*
• **American Express**, *Tel. 51-29-714*
• **Diners**, *Tel. 50-1-35*
• **Mastercard**, *Tel. 71-7-01-0*
• **Visa**, *Tel. 53-4-87-77*

Emergency Phone Numbers
• **Ambulance**, *Tel. 144*
• **Police**, *Tel. 133*
• **Fire Department**, *Tel. 122*

English Language Bookstore

Most newspaper kiosks in Graz sell a selection of English language newspapers and some magazines. Some sure bets include:
• **Kienreich**, *Sackstrasse 6, A-8010 Graz*
• **Moser**, *Herrengasse 23, A-8010 Graz*
• **Buchhandlung**, *Main Train Station, A-8010 Graz*

Many bookstores, too, have a selection of English and American classics and best sellers. **American Discount**, *Jakominstrasse 12, A-8010 Graz. Tel. 316-83-23-24*, sells comics, magazines, and books from Britain and the U.S.

Exchanging Money

Most banks are open Monday through Friday from 8 a.m. to noon and 2 p.m. to 4 p.m. Otherwise, you can exchange money at the following locations:
• **Wechselstube**, *Main Train Station, A-8010 Graz.* Open Monday through Friday 7:30 a.m. to 1:30 p.m. and 2 p.m. to 6:30 p.m.; Saturdays 7:30 a.m. to 1:30 p.m.
• **Postamt**, *Main Train Station, A-8010 Graz.* Open daily 24-hours a day.
• **Hauptpostamt**, *Neutorgasse 46, A-8010.* Open daily 24-hours a day.

Guided Tours

Guided tours of Graz's old town meet in front of the **Graz-Styria Tourist Information office**, *Herrengasse 16, A-8010 Graz. Tel. 316-83-52-41-11 or 12*. During April through October, tours are run daily at 2:30 p.m. From November to March, tours are available Saturdays at 2:30 p.m.

Guided tours of the **Schlossberg** are also possible from Palm Sunday to mid-October daily from 8 a.m. to 5 p.m. on the hour. Tours start at the **Bell Tower**. For more information, *call 316-83-17-87*. If you're looking for a private guide to show you the sites in Graz or in Styria, contact the **Fremdenfuhrerclub** for Graz and Steiermark, *Tel. 316-586720*.

Lost & Found

• **Fundamt**, *Grabenstrasse 56, A-8010 Graz. Tel. 316-888-2390; fax 316-888-2391*
• **Fundamt**, *Hauptplatz 14, A-8010 Graz. Tel. 316-887-408 or 468*

Luggage

You can check your luggage at the following locations:
• **Main Train Station**, *A-8010 Graz. Tel. 316-9848-1227*. Open daily from 6 a.m. to 7 p.m.
• **Jakominplatz**, *GVB Information, A-8010 Graz*. Open Monday through Friday from 9:30 a.m. to 6:30 p.m.; Saturday from 9 a.m. to 1 p.m.

Medical Treatment

If you need first aid assistance, *call 141* Monday through Thursday from 7 p.m. to 7 a.m. and weekends. For ambulance service, *call 144*.

Pharmacies

Pharmacies in Styria are open in general Monday through Friday from 8 a.m. to noon and 2:30 p.m. to 6 p.m.; Saturdays from 8 a.m. to noon. To find an open pharmacy at other times, check the nearest pharmacy window and you'll find posted the name, address, and number of the nearest open pharmacy.

For assistance, *call 1550*.

Tipping

A service charge is added to your hotel and restaurant bill. However, if you are pleased with the service, it is customary to tip an additional 5 to 10 percent of the check. Taxi drivers and hair dressers also are generally tipped the same amount.

Weather

For the latest weather information, *call 1566*.

21. BURGENLAND

INTRODUCTION

Burgenland is Austria's easternmost province, formed after World War I from land that had previously belonged to Hungary. After World War II ended, the province was occupied by the Russians for a decade. Burgenland still retains its Eastern European flavor, and you'll notice its Hungarian roots from the region's cuisine to its architecture. Burgenland is 1,530 square miles with a population of 271,818 citizens.

Burgenland is predominantly agricultural, with a variety of crops, fruit, and vegetables grown here. The region, which adjoins Styria and Lower Austria, is also known for its **wine production**, so make sure to savor a glass or two on your trip here. There are several "wine roads" to explore in Burgenland. Since the region has not really been discovered by many tourists, you'll find lower prices and a number of less touristy vineyards.

Dating back to the 16th century, the province's vineyards stretch across some 21,000 hectares. Approximately 38 percent of Austria's wines are produced here by about 14,000 growers. The gentle, warm climate and excellent soil provide banner harvests of grapes, from the dry white wines produced around the **Neusiedler See** to the rare dessert wine *Trockenbeerenauslese* and the award winning red wines grown in **Blaufrankischland**.

The provincial capital is tiny **Eisenstadt**, with only 12,500 inhabitants. Located on the southern slopes of the **Leitha Mountains**, the composer **Joseph Haydn** lived and worked here. Music fans should plan a stop to his burial place at the city's **Bergkirche**, or mountain church. The composer **Franz Liszt** was also born in Burgenland, in the town of Raiding.

Probably the most famous natural attraction in Burgenland is **Lake Neusiedl**, which draws visitors around the country during the summer months. In July and August, operettas are performed on the lake stage in **Morbisch**.

ORIENTATION

If you're staying in Vienna, Eisenstadt and Burgenland in general are easy day trip destinations from the capital. There are no direct train lines from Eisenstadt to Vienna, so you're better off driving. Skip this province if you'll be in Austria during the winter months, however. Burgenland's tourist attractions close up shop during the winter months.

BURGENLAND TOURIST OFFICES

If you're planning an excursion to Burgenland, make sure to contact the local tourist offices, who can provide you with information from visiting a local vintner's keller to castle visits.

• Eisenstadt Tourist Office, Franz Schubert Platz 1, A-7000 Eisenstadt. 2682-673-90; fax 2682-673-91

• Burgenland Tourist Office, Schloss Esterhazy, A-7000 Eisenstadt. 2682-63384; fax 2682-63384-20

EISENSTADT

Eisenstadt became the capital of the Burgenland province in 1925, and today is the smallest regional capital in Austria with only 12,500 citizens. The city is famous as the home of composer Joseph Haydn and for its delicious wine grown in the surrounding hills.

The first mention of the town is from a document published in 1118. Eisenstadt became a trading center in 1388, and the ruling Kaniszai family later took control of the city and built a wall around the perimeters to fortify the town. In 1648, **Nikolaus Esterhazy**, a member of the Hungarian noble family, was given the town's medieval castle as a mortgage payment.

Eisenstadt rose to prominence in the 17th century with the growth of a bourgeoisie class. The homes they built with their new wealth are still evident on **Hauptstrasse** and around the rest of the city's pedestrian zone.

ARRIVALS & DEPARTURES

By Air

There are no airports in Burgenland; the closest airport is in Vienna.

By Bus

Buses traveling from Vienna to Eisenstadt leave every 20 minutes from the **City Air Terminal** at the Vienna Hilton.

By Car

Traveling from Vienna, take Route 10 east and head south on Route 304 to reach Eisenstadt.

By Train

If you're traveling to Eisenstadt, you'll have to change trains in Neusiedl am See. You won't have long to wait, since the trains to Eisenstadt are timed to leave shortly after the ones arriving from Vienna. For **train information**, *call 1717.*

GETTING AROUND EISENSTADT

By Car

You won't have any traffic tie-ups in Burgenland, and parking is not a hassle, which is a refreshing change if you're coming from Vienna. If you have car problems, you can contact the local auto clubs for assistance.

• **Autofahrer-Clubs**, *Auster Strasse 126, A-7000 Eisenstadt. Tel. 23*

• **OAMTC**, *Mattersburger Strasse West 34, A-7000 Eisenstadt. Tel. 120*

To rent a car, **Eurodollar** has a local branch at *Ruster Strasse 114, A-7000 Eisenstadt. Tel. 2682-631880.*

By Public Transportation

Eisenstadt is small enough that you'll be able to see the major sights on foot. If you're interested in heading off the beaten track, **Bundesbus** service will take you into the surrounding region. Schedules are posted at the Domplatz.

By Taxi

To order a taxi in Eisenstadt, *call 2682-65010, 65002 or 65198.*

WHERE TO STAY

Large, modern hotels are something of a rarity in this small province. But you'll be able to find comfortable, charming inns and guest houses in Eisenstadt and the surrounding countryside.

Many hotels feature excellent restaurants. As mentioned below in the *Where to Eat* section, most of the better restaurants are attached to hotels, inns, and guesthouses, and they are reviewed as part of each hotel below. Those restaurants independent of hotels are reviewed separately in *Where to Eat.*

The first hotels listed are in **Eisenstadt**, and remaining hotels are listed by town.

Eisenstadt

GASTHOF OHR, *Ruster Strasse 51, A-7000 Eisenstadt. Tel. 2682-62-4-60; fax 2682-64-4-81. Doubles start at 425 schillings per person. All credit cards accepted.*

The Ohr family runs this 26-room hotel in downtown Eisenstadt. Rooms are comfortable but basic. Guest parking is available in front of the guest house, and pets are welcome. Traditional Austrian dishes are prepared in the guest house's restaurant, where more low calorie options can also be ordered.

HOTEL BURGENLAND, *Franz Schubert Platz 1, A-7000 Eisenstadt. Tel. 2682-696; fax 2682-65531. Doubles start at 1390 schillings. All credit cards accepted.*

The 176-bed Hotel Burgenland is a modern establishment, but lacks charm. The staff is also somewhat cool and impersonal. All rooms have cable television and minibars. There's a bar, cafe, and restaurant, featuring the standard Austrian specialties. Guests are free to use the hotel's swimming pool and sauna. Parking is also available for guests.

WIRSTHAUS ZUM EDER, *Hauptstrasse 25, A-7000 Eisenstadt. Tel. 2682-63102. Doubles start at 590 schillings; half-board is available for an additional 120 schillings. All credit cards accepted.*

The 25-bed Wirsthaus Zum Eder is located in the heart of Eisenstadt's pedestrian district. The hotel has a playground for children, and pets are welcome. Rooms are simple but comfortable. The hotel restaurant serves Austrian specialties and regional cuisine with a distinctive Hungarian touch. A guest garden is available during warmer weather.

Bad Tatzmannsdorf
STEIGENBERGER AVANCE, *Am Golfplatz 4, A-7431 Bad Tatzmannsdorf. Telephone and fax 3353-8855-0. Doubles start at 940 schillings per person. All credit rooms accepted.*

Guests are pampered at the Steigenberger Avance. Rooms are light and airy and filled with modern, light-wood furniture. For those who want to keep fit, both indoor and outdoor swimming is available. Golfing, biking, tennis, and exercise facilities are also possibilities. The hotel has supervision for children and you can bring along your pets. An excellent restaurant is also available on the premises.

Bernstein
HOTEL BURG BERNSTEIN, *A-7434 Bernstein. Tel. 3354-6382; fax 3354-6520. Doubles start from 630 schillings per person. All credit cards accepted.*

The Hotel Burg Bernstein is ideal for those who would like to go back to a time when medieval lords and ladies populated the planet. Rooms at the hotel are equipped with fireplaces fed from the hallway so as not to disturb guests. Filled with antiques, the rooms are well appointed and cozy.

Local legend purports that the castle is haunted by Count Johann-Ivan, who died here in 1279. He was called "Red Ivan" because of his bright red hair. His laughter is still supposedly heard ringing through the castle. Guests dine in the impressive former knight's hall and eat by candlelight in the evenings just as they did in days of yore.

Heiligenkreuz

GASTHOF GIBISER, *A-7561 Heiligenkreuz. Tel. 3325-4216-0; fax 3325-42-46-44. Doubles start at 350 schillings per person. All credit cards accepted.*

The Gasthof Gibiser is like no guest house you've ever seen. The thatched roofed structures look like old-time rural accommodations. But don't worry, all 12 rooms have modern amenities. There is a restaurant on-site with dietetic options available. Swimming and cycling are also possible.

Rust

SPORTHOTEL DRESCHER, *Morbischer Strasse 1-3, A-7071 Rust. Tel. 2685-6418 or 6419; fax 2685-6478. Doubles start at 650 schillings per person. All credit cards accepted.*

The 94-bed Sporthotel Drescher knows how to pamper their guests with style. The staff is courteous and friendly, and rooms are large and comfortably furnished. The hotel also has a swimming pool, fitness room, sauna and solarium at your disposal.

Visitors can also enjoy regional specialties in the hotel restaurant, or enjoy a glass or two of the local wine in the house bar.

St. Georgen

INN "ZUM ATTILABRUNNEN," *Brunnengasse 1, St. Georgen. Tel. 2682-62429; fax 2682-62429. Doubles start at 660 schillings; halfboard available for an additional 120 schillings. All credit cards accepted.*

The Wimmer family runs this 36 bed inn, which offers reductions for children. Children under age six can stay free with their parents. There also is a playground for children and a guest garden where you can lounge at the end of a long day. Some rooms have balconies, and all are equipped with cable television. Parking is also available.

WHERE TO EAT

Burgenland's native cuisine borrows heavily from Hungary and Bohemia. **Pannonian** cuisine incorporates farm fresh fruits and vegetables, fish and poultry with a good dose of spicy flavors. You'll often find a shaker filled with paprika on your table to sprinkle on your food if it's not hot enough for you. White beans are a specialty of the region and you can find them in everything from soups to strudels or even sweetened in pies.

Milk-fed roast pork is served on special occasions with the skin crunchy and succulent. Recipes for roast goose and chicken liver dishes have been handed down through the Jewish community and are often featured on regional menus. Dumplings, stuffed with cabbage or cream, are a delicious complement. Wash your meal down with one of the fine wines available throughout the region.

In addition to the hotel restaurants given above in *Where to Stay*, here are some of the better restaurants in Burgenland:

SCHLOSSTAVERNE, *Esterhazyplatz 5, A-7000 Eisenstadt. Tel. 2682-63102. Moderate. Closed Mondays. No credit cards accepted. Closed Mondays.*

If you need a break after finishing your tour of the Esterhazy Palace, head across the street to the Schlosstaverne. The restaurant features typical Viennese and Hungarian favorites like goulash and *schnitzel*. Regional wines are also featured. The food is served in a friendly, although somewhat kitschy, atmosphere and caters to the tourist trade.

HADYNBRAU, *Pfarrgasse 22, A-7000 Eisenstadt. Tel. 2682-61561-17. Moderate. Open 11 a.m. to 11 p.m. All credit cards accepted.*

The Hadynbrau restaurant is a good place to kick back and enjoy a beer or two. During warm weather, the Hadynbrau has a large guest garden with outdoor seating. The restaurant serves family-style stick-to-your-ribs cuisine, and has a wide selection of beer and wine to wash it down.

GRAPE GUIDE

If your knowledge of wine is only as extensive as "white" or "red," the following list may help you decide which regional wine is the right one to suit your taste.

Blaufrankisch *is a dry red wine cultivated near Lake Neusiedl.*

Gruner Veltliner *is a fruity wine with a spicy aftertaste.*

Muller-Thurgau *wine can vary from flowery to full-bodied to light depending on its maturity.*

Muskat-Ottonel *is a full-bodied wine with a bouquet of muscat.*

Neuburger *is a mildly spicy wine.*

Rheinriesling *is a slightly acidic wine.*

Traminer *is a golden wine with a spicy aroma.*

Weissburgunder *is a delicate wine with a burgundy bouquet.*

Welschriesling *is an aromatic wine with a fresh flavor.*

SCHLOSSKELLEREI HALBTURN, *Postfach 13, A-7131 Halbturn. Tel. 2172-8685; fax 2172-859-43. Open Easter through October, 10 a.m. to 10 p.m. All credit cards accepted.*

You'll feel like a member of royalty on your trip to the Schlosskellerei Halbturn. The huge castle, graced at one time by Emperor Ferdinand I and Empress Maria Theresa, is surrounded by vineyards and is an elegant venue from which to sample the wines grown here. If the weather is warm, you can take your glass outside to the manicured garden. Concerts are also held at the castle.

KLOSTER AM SPITZ, *Waldsiedlung 2, A-7083 Purbach. Tel. 2683-5519 or 5526; fax 2683-5519-20. Moderate. Open April through mid-December. All credit cards accepted.*

Bottles of Chardonnay, Sauvignon Blanc, and Merlot can be sampled and purchased at this former monastery now dedicated to wine production and degustation. Delicious dishes from Burgenland are prepared in the restaurant. You can spend the night here as well after enjoying the wine.

WEINAKADEMIE BURGENLAND, *Haupstrasse 31, A-7071 Rust. Tel. 2685-453; fax 2685-6431. Open July through September daily from 2 p.m. to 6 p.m.; October through June, Saturdays and Sundays, 2 p.m. to 6 p.m. All credit cards accepted.*

Go to the source to find out everything you want to know about Burgenland's wine roads. The Weinakademie Burgenland can answer your questions about the production of wine in the region. And after brushing up on your wine history, do a little research of your own with a glass or two of the excellent vintages available here. Bottles are available for purchase to take home as a souvenir of your trip.

GASTHAUS BURGTAVERN, *Burg Lockenhaus, A-7442 Lockenhaus. Tel. 2616-2321; fax 2616-2095. Moderate. No credit cards accepted.*

This guest house is located in the Lockenhaus castle. Plates of goulash and other provincial specialties are served the friendly staff. International dishes are featured on the menu, as well. A wide selection of local wine and beer are on the wine list to wash down your meal.

SEEING THE SIGHTS IN EISENSTADT

Start your tour of the capital at the **Esterhazy Palace**, *Schlosspark; Tel. 2682-618-66-0,* which is still owned by the family. Tours of the castle are available hourly. Concerts by costumed musicians are played in the Haydn Room. (See *Nightlife & Entertainment* section below).

The castle gardens make a good place for a picnic or a stroll through the tree-lined park. The castle is open daily from 8:30 a.m. to 5 p.m. Admission is 60 schillings for adults and 40 schillings for seniors, children and students.

If you continue up the hill past the castle along the Untersbergstrasse, you'll run into to the **Federal Museum of Burgenland**, *Museumgasse 5, Tel. 2682-62652*. The museum has displays on the region's history dating back to the time of the Romans. The museum is open Tuesday through Sunday from 9 a.m. to noon and 1 p.m. to 5 p.m. Admission is 30 schillings for adults and 15 schillings for seniors, students and children.

Just up the hill is the **Austrian Jewish Museum**, *Untersbergstrasse, Tel. 2682-65145*. The museum chronicles the rich history of the Jewish population in Eisenstadt and the rest of the country, decimated during World War II. The museum is open June through October, Tuesday through Sunday, from 10 a.m. to 5 p.m. Admission is 30 schillings for adults and 20 schillings for children.

At the top of the hill on the Esterhazystrasse is the **Bergkirche**, *Kalvarienbergplatz, Tel. 2682-62638*, where **Haydn's tomb** is located. The Baroque church recreates the stations of the cross with lifesize figures carved by Franciscan monks. Admission to Haydn's tomb is 20 schillings for adults and 10 schillings for seniors, students and children.

Music lovers should then head back into town, past the castle, to Haydngasse. The **Haydn Museum**, *Haydngasse 21*, is housed in the musician's former residence where he lived from 1766-1778. The well-preserved house gives a real sense of what the musician's life was like with various musical memorabilia on display. The museum is open from Easter through October, 9 a.m. to noon and 1 p.m. to 5 p.m. Admission is 20 schillings for adults and 10 schillings for seniors, students, and children.

NIGHTLIFE & ENTERTAINMENT

Eisenstadt celebrates the music of longtime resident **Joseph Haydn** with a **music festival** each September. Haydn concerts are also held in the Esterhazy Palace from May through October. The Saturday concerts begin in May, June, September and October at 7:30 p.m. In July and August, the concerts are on Thursdays at 8 p.m. Tickets cost from 150 to 250 schillings. Other Haydn performances are also held at the castle.

The **Lockenhaus Chamber Music Festival** takes place in July and August. For information, contact **Office of the Burgenland Haydn Festivals**, *Esterhazy Palace, A-7000 Eisenstadt. Tel. 2682-618-66-0*. If you'd like to try the best Burgenland wines, make sure to attend **The Festival of 1,000 Wines** at the Esterhazy Palace in Eisenstadt during the last week of August. The festival is held in the **Orangerie** in the castle park.

During the summer, **Lake Neusiedl** hosts operettas performed on a stage set up on the lake at **Morbisch**. For star gazers, the **Burgenland Regional Observatory** is open from 8 p.m. to 9 p.m. and by arrangement. *The observatory is located at Dr. Karl Renner Strasse 1, A-7000 Eisenstadt. 2682-647-13.*

SHOPPING

There is a weekly market in Eisenstadt on **Main Street**, Tuesdays and Fridays, 6 a.m. to noon, if you want to stock up on picnic supplies or other goodies. For wine lovers, many of the local vineyards have bottles of their best vintages available for purchase.

RATING THE VINTAGES

If you're buying wine as an investment or if you just want to decide which wines are the best, Burgenland vintners have rated the wine vintages as follows:

1950: good	1969: excellent
1951: good	1970: moderate
1952: good	1971: very good
1953: very good	1972: moderate
1954: good	1973: excellent
1955: good	1974: good
1956: very good	1975: good
1957: good	1976: good
1958: very good	1977: good
1959: very good	1978: moderate
1960: good	1979: very good
1961: very good	1980: good
1962: very good	1981: very good
1963: very good	1982: good
1964: very good	1983: excellent
1965: poor	1984: moderate
1966: good	1985: very good
1967: very good	1986: excellent
1968: good	1987: good

SPORTS & RECREATION

Biking

Burgenland has more than 500 kilometers of posted cycling paths, and many local inns have facilities catering to bikers' needs. If you need to rent a bike, you can get go to the **railway station** *in Eisenstadt, Tel. 2682-626-37,* or try **Intersport Zink**, *Hauptstrasse 45, A-7000 Eisenstadt. 2682-641-55.*

The regional tourist information also has biking information, including maps, routes and attractions in the province for cyclists. Contact the **Burgenland Tourist Office**, *Schloss Esterhazy, A-7000 Eisenstadt. Tel. 2682-63384; fax 2682-63384-20.*

Golf
Golfers can tee off at the **Golf Club Donnerskirchen**, *Am Golfplatz,* *Tel. 2683-8110.* The club is about 14 kilometers outside of Eisenstandt.

Horseback Riding
For horseback riding, try the **Riding School Haidehof**, *Siegendorfer Strasse, A-7000 Eisenstadt. Tel. 663-919-82-06.*

Ice Skating
You can skate at the **Allsportzentrum Eisenstadt**, *Bad Kissingen Platz 1, A-7000 Eisenstadt. Tel. 2682-676-00.* Open from November through February.

Sport Shooting
The federal rifle range is located behind the **Fire Brigade School** in Eisenstadt. *For additional information, contact Werfelgasse 1, A-7000 Eisenstadt. Tel. 2682-52282.*

Swimming
• **Sport Centre Eisenstadt**, with indoor baths, *Bad Kissingen-Platz 1, A-7000 Eisenstadt. Tel. 2682-676-00.* Open Tuesdays, Thursdays and Fridays 2 p.m. and 8 p.m.; Wednesday 2 p.m. and 5 p.m.; Saturday 10 a.m. to 9 p.m.; Sunday and holidays 10 a.m. to 8 p.m.; closed Mondays and July 1 through August 15. Saunas, steam baths and massage are available Tuesdays, Wednesdays and Thursdays from 2 p.m. to 10 p.m.; Fridays, Saturdays, Sundays and holidays from 10 a.m. to 10 p.m.
• **Stadtisches Parkbad**, outdoor swimming pool *in the Schlosspark, A-7000 Eisenstadt. 2682-621-82.* Open May through September, 9 a.m. to 7 p.m.

Tennis
• **ASKO**, *Industriestrasse, A-7000 Eisenstadt. Tel. 2682-608-201 or 271.* The three outdoor courts can be rented for 100 schillings per hour.
• **Leisure and Sport Facilities**, *Kasernenstrasse 9, A-7000 Eisenstadt. Tel. 2682-635920.* Four indoor and three outdoor courts are available for 100 schillings per hour. The facility is only open to members during July and August.
• **UTC Eisenstadt**, *Schlosspark-Orangerie, A-7000 Eisenstadt. Tel. 2682-62396.* Open 7 a.m. to 3 p.m. Six outdoor sand courts are available for 100 schillings per hour.
• **UTC St. Georgen**, *Am Platz 4, A-7000 Eisenstadt. Tel. 2682-68410.* Three outdoor sand courts can be rented for 100 schillings per hour.

DAY TRIPS FROM EISENSTADT
Kleinhoflein & St. Georgen

If you want to sample some of the delicious wines available in Burgenland but don't want to stray too far off the beaten track, tours are available in **Kleinhoflein**, just west of Eisenstadt. The area came under the sovereignty of Eisenstadt during the Middle Ages and later became the property of the Esterhazy family during the 17th century.

Today, the Eisenstadt tourist office organizes tours of the vineyards and a wine tasting at two taverns in Kleinhoflein. The price per person to sample four wines and pastries is 95 schillings; a glass of wine and a sandwich costs 25 schillings. After your tour, you can have a meal at a local *Heuriger* (wine bar). You can choose from braised beef, roast pork, pot-roast with caraway seed, Bratwurst, blood sausage, sauerkraut and potato salad. The price is 90 schillings per person; with wine, 180 schillings. To reserve a spot, call the tourist information office in Eisenstadt, *Tel. 2682-673-90*. Every year during the first week of July, there is a **Winegrowers' Festival** in Kleinhoflein with the best of the province's new wines.

St. Georgen, just east of Eisenstadt, boasts several cozy taverns where you can sample the local vino. Many farms still retain their rustic character from the 17th and 18th centuries. The Romans once occupied this area and you can still see the inscription "Marcus Atilius" dating from the first century on the stone of Attila in front of the former village fountain.

WINE HARVESTS

Different harvesting techniques change the character of a wine. If you're interested in investing in a few bottles of Burgenland's harvest, here's a list to help you narrow your choices.

Ausbruch *is made from overripe dried grapes and then mixed with must, or the juice of grapes that have not yet fermented into wine.*

Auslese *is wine made from grapes that have been picked over to remove all unripe, blemished or diseased grapes.*

Beerenauslese *is wine made from overripe grapes.*

Eiswein *is wine made from grapes that have frozen and then pressed.*

Spatlese *is wine produced from very ripe grapes picked after the main harvest period.*

Trockenbeerenauslese *is wine made from grapes that have been dried like raisins.*

Neusiedler See-Seewinkel National Park

More than a quarter of Burgenland has been made into a nature preserve, which stretches across the frontier into Hungary. The **Neudsiedler saltwater lake**, occupying 320 kilometers of land, is home to more than 300 plant and animal species, many of which can only be found here. The shallow lake is surrounded by reeds, and is hot and sunny during the summer months.

The Neusiedler See is just 15 kilometers from Eisenstadt, and is one of the country's top resort lakes. Sailors, swimmers, and sun worshippers flock to the banks of the lake during high season. The town of **Podersdorf** is probably the most famous tourist resort on the lake. Admission to the park is 100 schillings for adults and 40 schillings for children. For more information on the park, contact the **Nationalpark Neusiedler See-Seewinkel**, *Ober Hauptstrasse 2-4, A-7142 Illmitz. Tel. 2175-3442; fax 2175-3442-4.*

If you're planning on staying in the area, try the **Sporthotel Drescher** in the town of Rust (see *Where to Stay* above for full information). Otherwise, For more information on accommodations, contact the **Neusiedl am See Tourist Office**, *Tel. 2167-2229.*

Wine Road

Driving through the countryside will give you a real feel for how Burgenland's rich wine harvest is produced. Cottages, wine taverns, and guest houses along the way promise good food and wine to satisfy the most discerning palate. Start your trip on the **Neusiedlersee wine road** in the nearby town of **Jois** located north of the lake. Traveling southwest towards **Winden am See**, you can stop off to see Burgenland's oldest wine press used formerly at an estate operated by the Romans. Continuing south, you'll run into **Breitenbrun**, which is known for its interesting defense tower and bathing facilities.

A bit farther south is the town of **Purbach am See**. According to legend, a Turkish soldier enjoyed the wine here so much that he missed the departure of his unit and hid himself in a chimney. A statue in the town commemorates the event.

Continuing along the lake you'll run into **Rust**, renowned for the storks that make their homes here building their nests in precarious places. The nests, topping roofs, chimneys and other lofty points, have become a symbol of the region. With less than 2,000 inhabitants, Rust is more a village than a town. Another claim to fame is the wine produced here. Just down the coast is **Morbisch**, where operettas are held on the lakeside theater during the summer months. Delicious *Welschriesling* and *Muskat-Ottonel* vintages are also available for tasting and purchasing. The route continues over the hills behind Rust through **St. Margarethen** with its Roman quarry. Continue through **Trausdorf**, **Schutzen**, and **St. George** until you reach the provincial capital of Eisenstadt.

PRACTICAL INFORMATION
Banking & Exchanging Money
You can exchange money at most banks, which are open Monday through Friday from 8 a.m. to noon and 2 p.m. to 4 p.m.

Credit Cards
If your credit cards are lost or stolen, you can call the following numbers 24-hours a day to make a report. You must first dial 0222 in Burgenland.
- **American Express**, *Tel. 51-29-714.*
- **Diners**, *Tel. 50-1-35.*
- **Mastercard**, *Tel. 71-7-01-0.*
- **Visa**, *Tel. 53-4-87-77.*

Guided Tours
There are several guided tours of Eisenstadt available through the tourist office. All tours start outside the Esterhazy Castle. A guided walking tour of the **old town**, taking approximately two and a half hours, costs 500 schillings. The tour includes the Franciscan monastery, the Haydn museum and the castle. Other tour topics include *On the Trail of Joseph Haydn, On the Trail of the Esterhazy Princes, On the Music Trail, Judaism in Burgenland and Eisenstadt,* and *A Walk through the Castle Gardens.*

You can also arrange your own itinerary if you desire. Contact the **Eisenstadt Tourist Office**, *Franz Schubert Platz 1, A-7000 Eisenstadt. Tel. 2682-67-390; fax 2682-67-391.*

Emergency Phone Numbers
- **Police**: *133.*
- **Ambulance**: *144.*
- **Fire Department**: *122.*

Parking
Parking is available in downtown Eisenstadt. Parking costs 5 schillings per half hour with a maximum of two hours parking available. Parking must be paid for from Monday through Friday 7 a.m. to 6 p.m.; Saturdays, 7 a.m. to noon.

Pharmacies
Pharmacies in Burgenland are open, in general, Monday through Friday from 8 a.m. to noon and 2:30 p.m. to 6 p.m.; Saturdays from 8 a.m. to noon. To find an open pharmacy at other times, check the nearest pharmacy window where the name, address and number of the nearest open pharmacy will be posted. In an emergency, *call 1550.*

Post Office

The main post office is located on *Ignaz Semmelweis Gasse 7, A-7000 Eisenstadt. Tel. 2682-62271*. The post office is open Monday through Friday from 7 a.m. to 7 p.m.; Saturdays from 7 a.m. to 4 p.m.; Sundays and holidays from 8 a.m. to 10 a.m.

Tipping

A service charge is added to your hotel and restaurant bill. However, if you are pleased with the service, it is customary to tip an additional 5 to 10 percent of the check. Taxi drivers and hair dressers also are generally tipped the same amount.

Weather

For the latest weather information, *call 1566*.

INDEX

FROM THE PUBLISHER

Our goal is to provide you with a guide book second to none. Please bear in mind, however, that things change: phone numbers, admission price, addresses, etc. Should you come across any new information, we'd appreciate hearing from you. No item is too small for us, so if you have a great recommendation, find an error, see that some place has gone out of business, or just plain disagree with our recommendations, write to:

Angela Walker
c/o Open Road Publishing
P.O. Box 20226
Columbus Circle Station, New York, NY 10023

TRAVEL NOTES

TRAVEL NOTES

TRAVEL NOTES

TRAVEL NOTES

OPEN ROAD PUBLISHING
Your Passport to Great Travel!

Going abroad? Our books have been praised by **Travel & Leisure, Booklist, US News & World Report, Endless Vacation, American Bookseller,** *and many other magazines and newspapers!*

Don't leave home without an Open Road travel guide to one of these great destinations:

France Guide, $16.95
Italy Guide, $17.95
Paris Guide, $12.95
Portugal Guide, $16.95
Spain Guide, $17.95
London Guide, $13.95
Holland Guide, $14.95
Austria Guide, $15.95
Israel Guide, $16.95

Central America Guide, $17.95
Costa Rica Guide, $16.95
Belize Guide, $14.95
Honduras & Bay Islands Guide, $14.95
Guatemala Guide, $16.95
Southern Mexico & Yucatan Guide, $14.95
Bermuda Guide, $14.95
Hong Kong & Macau Guide, $13.95
China Guide, $18.95

<u>Forthcoming foreign guides in 1996 and 1997</u>: Greece, Turkey, Ireland, Czech & Slovak Republics, India, Vietnam, Japan, Mexico, Kenya, Bahamas.

In addition to Las Vegas Guide, check out Open Road's American Vacationland travel series:

Disney World & Orlando Theme Parks, $13.95
America's Most Charming Towns & Villages, $16.95
Florida Golf Guide, $16.95

<u>Forthcoming US guides in 1996 and 1997</u>: Colorado, San Francisco, California Wine Country, Alaska, and more!

PLEASE USE ORDER FORM ON THE NEXT PAGE

ORDER FORM

Name and Address: _____

_____

_____

_____ Zip Code: _____

Quantity	Title	Price

Total Before Shipping _____

Shipping/Handling _____

TOTAL _____

Orders must include price of book <u>plus</u> shipping and handling. For shipping and handling, please add $3.00 for the first book, and $1.00 for each book thereafter.

Ask about our discounts for special order bulk purchases.

ORDER FROM: **OPEN ROAD PUBLISHING**
P.O. Box 20226, Columbus Circle Station, New York, NY 10023